CAUGHT IN THE REVOLUTION

Also by Helen Rappaport

No Place for Ladies
Joseph Stalin
An Encyclopedia of Women Social Reformers
Queen Victoria
The Last Days of the Romanovs
Conspirator
Beautiful for Ever
A Magnificent Obsession
The Romanov Sisters

WITH WILLIAM HORWOOD
Dark Hearts of Chicago

WITH ROGER WATSON
Capturing the Light

HELEN RAPPAPORT

CAUGHT IN THE REVOLUTION

Petrograd, Russia, 1917— A World on the Edge

St. Martin's Press
New York

www.stmartins.com

Library of Congress Cataloging-in-Publication Data

Names: Rappaport, Helen, author.
Title: Caught in the revolution : Petrograd, Russia, 1917—a world on the edge / Helen Rappaport.
Description: First U.S. edition. | New York : St. Martin's Press, 2017. | Includes bibliographical references and index.
Identifiers: LCCN 2016043110| ISBN 9781250056641 (hardcover) | ISBN 9781466860452 (e-book)
Subjects: LCSH: Saint Petersburg (Russia)—History—Revolution, 1917–1921—Social aspects. | Saint Petersburg (Russia)—History—Revolution, 1917–1921—Personal narratives. | Soviet Union—History—Revolution, 1917–1921—Social aspects. | Soviet Union—History—Revolution, 1917–1921—Personal narratives. | Saint Petersburg (Russia)—History, Military—20th century. | Visitors, Foreign—Russia (Federation)—Saint Petersburg—Biography. | Saint Petersburg (Russia)—Biography. | War and society—Russia (Federation)—Saint Petersburg—History—20th century. | Saint Petersburg (Russia)—Social conditions—20th century. | BISAC: HISTORY / Europe / Russia & the Former Soviet Union. | BIOGRAPHY & AUTOBIOGRAPHY / Historical.
Classification: LCC DK265.8.L4 R37 2017 | DDC 355.00947/210904—dc23
LC record available at https://lccn.loc.gov/2016043110

First published in Great Britain by Hutchinson, a Penguin Random House company

First U.S. Edition: February 2017

10 9 8 7 6 5 4 3 2 1

For Caroline Michel

Contents

List of Illustrations

9 Julia Cantacuzène-Speransky, granddaughter of US President Ulysses S. Grant, American wife of a Russian prince, and subsequently a memoirist of the Russian Revolution. (Courtesy of Ulysses Grant Dietz Collection)

10 The intrepid war photographer and cinematographer Donald C. Thompson. (Author's collection)

11 James Negley Farson, American journalist and adventurer. (Alamy)

12 Arthur Ransome, correspondent for the *Daily News* at the time of the Revolution. (Courtesy of the Arthur Ransome Trust. Reproduced with the permission of Special Collections, Leeds University Library.)

13 Journalist Florence Harper, pictured while working as a nurse at an American Field Hospital in Ukraine during 1917. (Author's collection)

14 A bread line in Petrograd in 1917 (© SPUTNIK/Alamy)

15 Nursing sisters and a wounded young soldier at the Anglo Russian Hospital (Library and Archives Canada)

16 The International Women's Day parade in Petrograd, 23 February 1917 that sparked a wave of popular protest at bread shortages. (Everett Collection Historical/Alamy)

17 Donald C Thompson's picture shows how the February Revolution claimed fatal casualties faster than the morgues could cope with. (© akg-images/Alamy)

18 Revolutionary barricades on Liteiny Prospekt, March 1917 (Alamy)

19 Cossack troops on patrol in Petrograd. (Slava Katamidze Collection/Getty Images)

20 'Shoot the Pharaos on their roofs…': a propaganda postcard urging popular resistance to the police (known derisively as 'pharaohs' or *faraony*) who would snipe at revolutionaries from rooftops. (akg-images)

21 The toppling of imperial monuments, February 27 1917. (akg-images)

22 Shop-front Imperial emblems thrown onto the ice under a bridge across the Fontanka Canal (© Look and Learn / Bridgeman Images)

39 Feminist journalist Louise Bryant, who travelled to Russia with Reed, her husband (Evening Standard/Getty Images)

40 People run for cover during a gun battle on Nevsky Prospect in October 1917 (Hulton Archive/Getty Images)

41 A room in the Tsar's Winter Palace, ransacked by the Bolsheviks after they took the Palace with little or no resistance. (Slava Katamidze Collection/Getty Images)

Glossary of Eyewitnesses

Anet, Claude (pseudonym of Jean Schopfer) (1868–1931). Swiss-born French tennis champion, antiquities collector, journalist and writer reporting for *Le Petit Parisien*.

Arbenina, Stella (Baroness Meyendorff; née Whishaw) (1885–1976). British actress from a long-standing family in the Anglo-Russian colony in St Petersburg; she married Russian aristocrat Baron Meyendorff. Arrested after the revolution; released in 1918, she settled in Estonia.

Armour, Norman (1887–1982). American career diplomat; Second Secretary at US embassy in Petrograd 1916–18. Returned to Russia not long after he left, to rescue stranded Princess Mariya Kudasheva, whom he married in 1919. Later served as diplomat in Paris, Haiti, Canada, Chile, Argentina and Spain.

Azabal, Lilie Bouton de Fernandez *see* Countess Nostitz

Beatty, Bessie (1886–1947). American journalist, worked in California for the *San Francisco Bulletin* before travelling to Russia. Continued in journalism after the revolution; during the 1940s based in New York City, became a popular radio broadcaster.

Berlin, Isaiah (1909–97). Russian-born British scholar and historian of ideas; grew up in Riga and St Petersburg; his family moved to Great Britain in 1921.

Bowerman, Elsie (1889–1973). English suffragette; orderly with a Russian hospital unit of the Scottish Women's Hospitals; later the first woman barrister at the Old Bailey.

Bruce, Henry James (1880–1951). Head of the British Chancery in Petrograd; in 1915 he had married the Russian prima ballerina Tamara Karsavina.

Bryant, Louise (1885–1936). American journalist and socialist from the Greenwich Village set; travelled to Petrograd with her husband, *John Reed*, in 1917; married again after Reed's death in 1920 and lived in Paris.

Buchanan, Meriel (1886–1959). Daughter of British ambassador *Sir George Buchanan*; volunteer nurse at British Colony Hospital in Petrograd run by her mother, *Lady Georgina Buchanan*, during World War I. After leaving Russia wrote numerous books and articles about her time there.

Bury, George (1865–1958). Canadian shipper and Vice President of the Canadian Pacific Railway; in Russia during World War I to report on the railway system for the British government. Knighted in 1917.

(Lady) Buchanan, Georgina (1863–1922). Scion of the influential Bathurst family, wife of British ambassador in Petrograd, *Sir George Buchanan*, and mother of *Meriel Buchanan*; active in relief work in Petrograd during World War I and patron of British Colony Hospital.

(Sir) Buchanan, George (1854–1924). Distinguished British diplomat and son of an ambassador. Served in many locations, beginning with Berlin in 1901; British ambassador to Russia from 1910.

Cantacuzène-Speransky, Princess (1876–1975). Born Julia Dent Grant, American socialite, granddaughter of President Ulysses S. Grant. Fled to USA after the revolution and was doyenne of White Russian community in Washington; divorced her Russian husband in 1934.

Chadbourn, Philip (who wrote his account of Petrograd under the pseudonym of Paul Wharton) (1889–1970). American relief worker in France and Belgium during World War I; sent to Petrograd to inspect and report on camps for internees in Russia.

Chambrun, Charles de (1875–1952). French diplomat and writer; First Secretary at Petrograd embassy from 1914.

Chandler Whipple, George (1866–1924). American engineer and sanitation expert who travelled to Petrograd with the American Red Cross Mission as Deputy Commissioner for Russia.

Clare, (Rev.) Joseph (1885–?). English Congregational preacher and bachelor of divinity; pastor of the American Church in Petrograd from 1913. Settled in Illinois after he left Russia and took US citizenship.

Cotton, Dorothy (1886–1977). Montreal-trained nursing sister with the Canadian Expeditionary Force, who served at the Anglo-Russian Hospital November 1915–June 1916 and January–August 1917.

Crosley, Pauline (1867–1955). wife of US Naval attaché, Captain Walter Selwyn Crosley; in Petrograd March 1917–March 1918, the Crosleys had a hair-raising escape out of Russia during the Civil War.

Dearing, Fred (1879–1963). American diplomat, worked at Peking legation 1908–9; in Russia in 1916–17 oversaw the transition from ambassador George F. Marye to *David R. Francis*.

Dorr, Rheta Childe (1868–1948). American journalist, feminist and political activist; friend of *Emmeline Pankhurst*. Went to Petrograd as correspondent of the *New York Evening Mail*, and published one of the earliest American accounts of the July Days. A motor accident after her return to the USA seriously impaired her professional life thereafter.

Dosch-Fleurot, Arno (1879–1951). American journalist; remained in Europe as foreign correspondent after 1917 and became special correspondent for International News Service in Berlin. As an outspoken critic of Nazis, was arrested and interned; in 1941 settled in Spain.

Farson, Negley (1890–1960). Born in New York, he settled in the UK. In Petrograd during World War I, as agent for an Anglo-American export business trying to secure orders for motorbikes from the Russian government. Later turned to travel writing and journalism; sometime foreign correspondent of *Chicago Daily News*.

Francis, David R. (1850–1927). US ambassador to Russia 1916–18; formerly mayor of St Louis (1885) and governor of Missouri (1889–93).

Fuller, John Louis (1894–1962). Indianapolis businessman and insurance executive; trainee with National City Bank in Petrograd 1917–18. Colleague of *Leighton Rogers, Fred Sikes* and *Chester Swinnerton*.

Garstin, Denis (1890–1918). English cavalry captain seconded as intelligence officer in the British Propaganda Unit in Petrograd; killed during the Allied Intervention at Arkhangelsk.

Gibson, William J. (dates unknown) Born in Canada, he grew up in St Petersburg and served in the Russian army in 1914; newspaper correspondent in Petrograd 1917; left Russia in 1918.

Grant, Julia *see* Princess Cantacuzène-Speransky

Grant, Lilias (1878–1975). Hospital orderly from Inverness, serving with the Scottish Women's Hospitals on the Eastern Front; visited Petrograd with her fellow orderly *Ethel Moir.*

(Lady) Grey, Sybil (1882–1966). British VAD, who assisted *Lady Muriel Paget* in the running of the Anglo-Russian Hospital; daughter of former Governor-General of Canada and cousin to British Foreign Secretary, Sir Edward Grey.

Hall, Bert (1885–1948). American combat aviator who flew with the French Lafayette Escadrille prior to US entry into World War I.

Harper, Florence (1886–?). Canadian staff reporter for *Leslie's Weekly*, who worked in tandem with war photographer *Donald Thompson* in Petrograd.

Harper, Samuel (1882–1943). American Slavicist; made numerous trips to Russia with official delegations as interpreter and guide, including the 1917 Root Mission to Petrograd. An unofficial adviser to *David R. Francis.*

Heald, Edward (1885–1967). Member of International Committee of the YMCA, sent to Russia to monitor the treatment of German and Austrian POWs. In Petrograd 1916–19.

Hegan, Edith (1881–1973). Canadian nurse from St John, New Brunswick, who served with Canadian Army Medical Corps in France before being posted to the Anglo-Russian Hospital in May 1916.

Houghteling, James (1883–1962). Chicago-born diplomat and newspaperman; special attaché at US Petrograd embassy; Vice President of *Chicago Daily News* 1926–31, later became a commissioner for US Bureau of Immigration & Naturalization.

Jefferson, Geoffrey (1886–1961). English surgeon at the Anglo-Russian Hospital; when it closed he transferred to the Royal Army Medical Corps on the Western Front. In later life he became an eminent neurosurgeon and FRCS.

Jones, James Stinton (1884–1979). South African-born mechanical engineer; worked in Russia 1905–17 for Westinghouse on the electrification of the Petrograd tramways; also oversaw installation of generator at Alexander Palace at Tsarskoe Selo.

Jordan, Phil(ip) (1868–1941). Black valet, cook and chauffeur from Jefferson City, Missouri, in service to *David R. Francis* and his family from 1889; accompanied Francis to Russia in 1916.

Judson, William J. (1865–1923). US army engineer; military attaché at Petrograd embassy June 1917–January 1918, responsible for security of US citizens in Russia.

Kenney, Jessie (1887–1985). Yorkshire-born cotton mill worker who joined the suffragette movement; worked closely with *Emmeline Pankhurst Muriel (1876–1938)* in the WSPU. After 1920 gave up political campaigning; later pursued a writing career, but remained unpublished.

Knox, General (Major-General Sir Alfred Knox) (1870–1964). British army officer; military attaché in Petrograd from 1911, observer on the Eastern Front; in 1924 became a Tory MP.

Lampson, Oliver Locker (1880–1954). British MP; in 1914 appointed a commander in the Royal Naval Air Service's Armoured Car Division, which was sent to assist the Russian army on the Eastern Front; returned to UK to continue serving as an MP after the war.

Lindley, Francis (1872–1950). Counsellor at the British embassy 1915–17; consul-general in Petrograd 1919; later served as British ambassador to Japan (1931–4).

Lockhart, Robert Bruce (1887–1970). British diplomat and spy, vice consul at Moscow 1914–17, but made frequent visits to Petrograd. Acting British consul-general after February Revolution; left Russia before the October Revolution, but was back in Moscow in January 1918.

Lombard, (Rev.) Bousfield Swan (1866–1951). English chaplain attached to the British embassy and the English Church in Petrograd from 1908, much respected in the British colony. Arrested and interned by Bolsheviks in 1918.

Long, Robert Crozier (1872–1938). Anglo-Irish journalist and author; Petrograd correspondent for Associated Press. From 1923 to his death, Berlin correspondent for *New York Times*.

Marcosson, Isaac (1876–1961). American journalist and writer from Kentucky; reported from Petrograd for the *Saturday Evening Post*.

Maugham, Somerset (1874–1965). English novelist and short-story writer; sometime spy with the British Secret Intelligence Service during World War I. These experiences formed the basis for his *Ashenden* collection of short stories published in 1928.

Moir, Ethel (1884–1973). Nursing orderly with the Scottish Women's Hospitals on the Eastern Front; in Petrograd with fellow nurse *Lilias Grant*.

Naudeau, Ludovic (1872–1949). French war correspondent for *Le Temps*; arrested by the Bolsheviks in 1918, he spent five months in prison in Moscow.

Néry, Amélie de (dates unknown). French essayist and journalist, active 1900s–20s, who wrote under the pseudonym Marylie Markovitch.

Nostitz, Countess (Lilie Bouton de Fernandez Azabal) (1875–1967). French-American adventuress and socialite from Iowa; originally a repertory company actress in New York, as Madeleine Bouton. Fled to Biarritz after the revolution; after Nostitz's death there in 1926 she married a third time and settled in Spain.

Noulens, Joseph (1864–1944). French government minister sent to replace ambassador *Maurice Paléologue*. In Petrograd from July 1917. Back in France, he remained an anti-Bolshevik campaigner, as leader of the Society of French Interests in Russia.

Oudendijk, Willem (later William Oudendyk) (1874–1953). Distinguished Dutch diplomat, in service 1874–1931 in China, Persia and Russia. Ambassador to Petrograd 1917–18. Awarded an honorary knighthood (KCMG) for his efforts on behalf of British subjects stranded in Russia after the revolution.

(Lady) Paget, Muriel (1876–1938). British philanthropist; set up soup kitchen for the poor in Southwark 1905; engaged in medical relief work in Russia during World War I. With *Sybil Grey* founded the Anglo-Russian Hospital in Petrograd.

Paléologue, Maurice (1859–1944). French career diplomat, contemporary of *Sir George Buchanan*. French ambassador to Petrograd 1914–17; elected to the Académie française in 1928.

Pankhurst, Emmeline (1858–1928). English suffragette leader, founder of the Women's Social and Political Union (WSPU) in 1903; lifelong political activist and campaigner for women's rights.

Patouillet, Louise (?–?). Nothing is known of the life of this French resident, in Petrograd from 1912, beyond the fact that she was married to Dr Jules Patouillet, director of the French Institute in Petrograd, but she left an extremely valuable diary of her time in the city, now in the Hoover Institute at Stanford University in California.

Pax, Paulette (stage name of Paulette Ménard) (1887–1942). Born in Russia, Pax returned there in December 1916 as a member of the resident French troupe at the Mikhailovsky Theatre. She left Russia in September 1918, and in 1929 became co-director of the Théâtre de l'Oeuvre in Paris.

Poole, Ernest (1880–1950). American novelist, sent to report on the Russian Revolution for the *New Republic* and *Saturday Evening Post*; Pulitzer Prize Winner in 1918.

Ransome, Arthur (1884–1967). British journalist, correspondent of the *Daily News*. Briefly returned to Russia in 1919 for *Manchester Guardian*. Later a successful novelist, famous for his children's series *Swallows and Amazons*.

Reed, John (1887–1920). American rebel, writer and poet, famous among the bohemian set of Greenwich Village for his social campaigning and outspoken left-wing views. Arrived in Petrograd September 1917 with his wife *Louise Bryant*.

Rhys Williams, Albert (1883–1962). American Congregational minister, labour organiser and ardent communist. Close friend of *John Reed*.

Robien, Louis de (1888–1958). French count, military attaché at French embassy in Petrograd from 1914 to November 1918.

Rogers, Leighton (1893–1962). Clerk with National City Bank of New York's Petrograd branch 1916–18; volunteered for military intelligence 1918. On his return to USA worked in aeronautics for US Department of Commerce. Friend and colleague of *Fred Sikes* and *Chester Swinnerton*.

Seymour, Dorothy (1882–1953). English Voluntary Aid Detachment nurse (VAD) at the Anglo-Russian Hospital; daughter of a general, granddaughter of an admiral, she had a position at court as a Woman of the Bedchamber to Princess Christian.

Sikes, Fred (1893–1958). Princeton graduate who worked at the Petrograd branch of the National City Bank of New York 1916–18; retired as Assistant Vice President of the bank in New York. Colleague of *Leighton Rogers* and *Chester Swinnerton*.

Stebbing, Edward (1872–1960). English professor of forestry; sent on assignment to Russia during World War I to investigate wood supplies for British army trenches and light railways.

Stoker, Enid (1893–1961). English VAD at the Anglo-Russian Hospital; met *Negley Farson* while in Petrograd and married him in London in 1920. Their son was the writer and broadcaster Daniel Farson.

Stopford, Bertie (Albert) (1860–1939). English art dealer, specialist on Fabergé, socialite and friend of Prince Felix Yusupov.

Swinnerton, Chester (1894–1960). Massachusetts-born Harvard graduate; trainee clerk with the National City Bank's Petrograd branch. Worked for the bank for many years in South America after he left Russia. Friend and colleague of *Leighton Rogers* and *Fred Sikes*.

Thompson, Donald (1885–1947). American war photographer and cinematographer from Kansas, in Petrograd January–July 1917.

Walpole, Hugh (1884–1941). New Zealand-born journalist and novelist; Red Cross worker in Russia when war broke out.

Returned to Petrograd as head of the Anglo-Russian Propaganda Bureau 1916–17 with *Harold Williams* and *Denis Garstin*.

Wightman, Orrin Sage (1873–1965). American doctor, served in US Army Medical Corps during World War I; in 1917 a member of American Red Cross medical mission to Russia.

Williams, Harold (1876–1928). New Zealand-born journalist, linguist and ardent Russophile. Petrograd correspondent for the *Daily Chronicle* and official at the Anglo-Russian Propaganda Bureau with *Hugh Walpole* and *Denis Garstin*. Fiercely anti-Bolshevik, he fled Petrograd with his Russian wife and became foreign editor of *The Times*.

Wilton, Robert (1868–1925). British journalist; European correspondent of *New York Herald* 1889–1903, then *Times* Special Correspondent in Petrograd. Returned to journalism in Paris after leaving Russia.

Winship, North (1885–1968). American diplomat; consul-general in Petrograd and many consulate posts thereafter; retired as US ambassador to South Africa 1949.

Woodhouse, Arthur (1867–1961). English diplomat; British consul at Petrograd 1907–18.

Woodhouse, Ella (1896–1969). Daughter of British consul in Petrograd, *Arthur Woodhouse*.

Wright, J. [Joshua] Butler (1877–1939). American diplomat; replaced *Fred Dearing* as counsellor at the US embassy in Petrograd October 1916. Later served as an ambassador in Hungary, Uruguay, Czechoslovakia and Cuba.

Author's Note

In Russia in 1917 the old-style Julian calendar, running thirteen days behind the Western Gregorian calendar, was still in use, a fact that creates endless confusion and frustration for historian and reader alike. Many of the foreign eyewitnesses resident in Petrograd* found it confusing, too, and although living for some time in Russia, chose to ignore the Julian calendar, dating their diaries and letters home to the UK, USA and elsewhere by the Gregorian one. Some occasionally noted both dates, but most did not; others, like Jessie Kenney, struggled to maintain both dates in their diaries – and ended up in a total muddle.

In order to spare the reader considerable pain on this score, and because this book tells the story of the February and October Revolutions in Russia as they happened, by the Russian calendar (and not as March/November, by the Western calendar), all dates of letters, diaries and reports quoted in the text that were written in Russia at the time events were taking place, have been converted to the Russian old-style (OS) calendar, in order to fit the chronology of the book. The original Gregorian (NS) dates are clear to see in the original sources referred to in the notes, though

---

* St Petersburg had been renamed Petrograd on the outbreak of war with Germany in 1914.

in some cases, to avoid confusion, especially where an event occurred outside Russia, both dates are given.

Many of the eyewitnesses used widely diverging spelling styles for Russian names and places. In addition, Philip Jordan had his own extremely idiosyncratic style of punctuation, capitalisation and spelling, which has been deliberately preserved in order to convey the immediacy and excitement of his narrative. In order to spare the reader the endless repetition of [*sic*], these spellings, and any other spelling oddities in eyewitness accounts, have been retained as given, and explained where necessary.

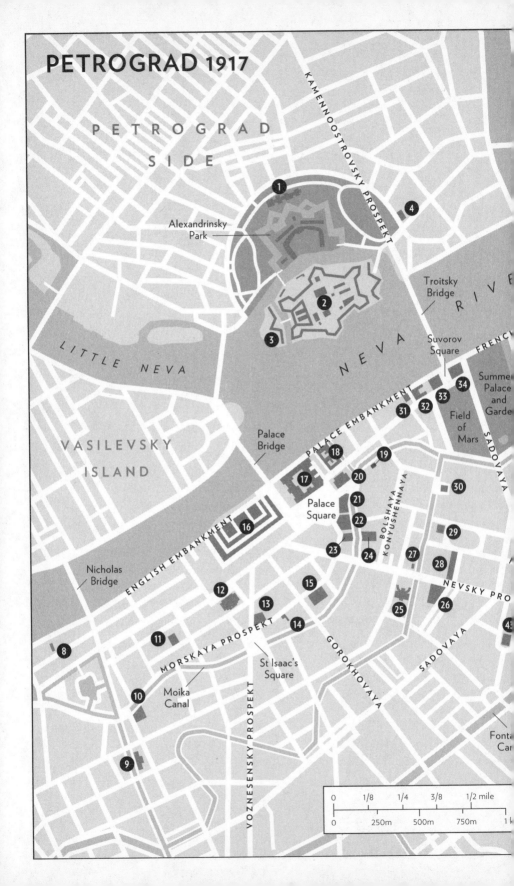

PETROGRAD 1917

PETROGRAD SIDE

Alexandrinsky Park

KAMENNOOSTROVSKY PROSPEKT

Troitsky Bridge

Suvorov Square

NEVA RIVER

FRENCH

Summer Palace and Garde

Field of Mars

SADOVAYA

LITTLE NEVA

VASILEVSKY ISLAND

Palace Bridge

PALACE EMBANKMENT

Palace Square

BOLSHAYA KONYUSHENNAYA

Nicholas Bridge

ENGLISH EMBANKMENT

NEVSKY PRO

MORSKAYA PROSPEKT

St Isaac's Square

Moika Canal

GOROKHOVAYA

SADOVAYA

VOZNESENSKY PROSPEKT

Fonta Car

| 0 | 1/8 | 1/4 | 3/8 | 1/2 mile |
| 0 | 250m | 500m | 750m | 1 k |

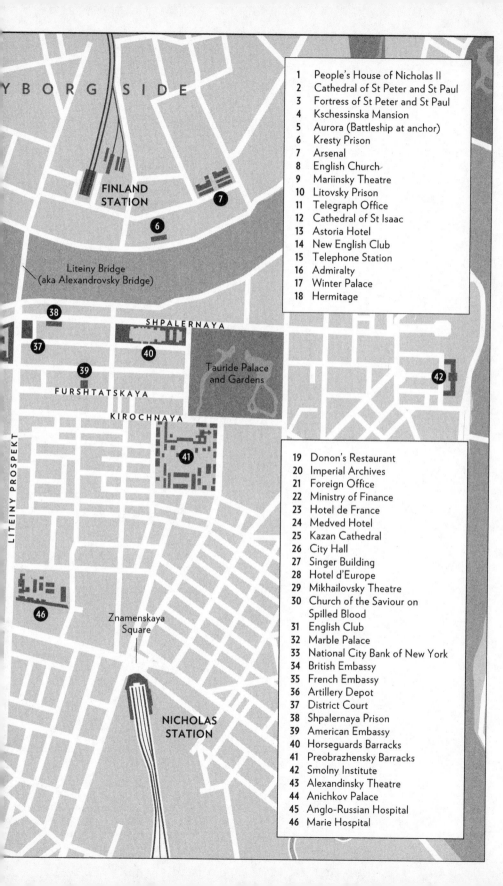

YBORG SIDE

FINLAND STATION

Liteiny Bridge
(aka Alexandrovsky Bridge)

SHPALERNAYA

Tauride Palace
and Gardens

FURSHTATSKAYA

KIROCHNAYA

LITEINY PROSPEKT

Znamenskaya
Square

NICHOLAS
STATION

1 People's House of Nicholas II
2 Cathedral of St Peter and St Paul
3 Fortress of St Peter and St Paul
4 Kschessinska Mansion
5 Aurora (Battleship at anchor)
6 Kresty Prison
7 Arsenal
8 English Church
9 Mariinsky Theatre
10 Litovsky Prison
11 Telegraph Office
12 Cathedral of St Isaac
13 Astoria Hotel
14 New English Club
15 Telephone Station
16 Admiralty
17 Winter Palace
18 Hermitage

19 Donon's Restaurant
20 Imperial Archives
21 Foreign Office
22 Ministry of Finance
23 Hotel de France
24 Medved Hotel
25 Kazan Cathedral
26 City Hall
27 Singer Building
28 Hotel d'Europe
29 Mikhailovsky Theatre
30 Church of the Saviour on
   Spilled Blood
31 English Club
32 Marble Palace
33 National City Bank of New York
34 British Embassy
35 French Embassy
36 Artillery Depot
37 District Court
38 Shpalernaya Prison
39 American Embassy
40 Horseguards Barracks
41 Preobrazhensky Barracks
42 Smolny Institute
43 Alexandinsky Theatre
44 Anichkov Palace
45 Anglo-Russian Hospital
46 Marie Hospital

CAUGHT IN THE REVOLUTION

PROLOGUE

'The Air is Thick with Talk of Catastrophe'

Petrograd was a brooding, beleaguered city that last desperate winter before the revolution broke; a snowbound city of ice-locked canals and looming squares. Its fine wide streets and elegant palaces of pink granite and coloured stucco fronted by rows of airy columns and arches no longer exuded a sense of imperial grandeur but, rather, a sense of decay. Everywhere you went amid the forbidding architecture of this 'city for giants' you could hear the 'swish of the wind, and the tinkling of many, many bells of all sizes and tones', rounded off by the 'compelling boom of the great bell of St Isaac which comes from nowhere and envelops everything'.[1] In the grip of winter, with its broad vistas laid open to the arctic cold blowing in across the Gulf of Finland, Russia's capital had always assumed a chilly, haunting beauty on the grand scale that was peculiarly its own. But now, three years into the war, it was overflowing with thousands of refugees – Poles, Latvians, Lithuanians and Jews – who had fled the fighting on the Eastern Front. The capital was subdued and discouraged, and a 'malign, disturbing atmosphere' hung over it.[2] The winter of 1916–17 was also marked by a new and ominous fixture on the landscape: the long silent queues of downcast women huddling in the cold, waiting interminably for bread, milk, meat – whatever they could lay their hands on. Petrograd was weary of war. Petrograd was hungry.

Such had become the daily grinding hardship for the majority of the Russian population at large; and yet, despite the visible and crippling wartime shortages and the anguish of deprivation etched on the faces of its inhabitants, the city sheltered a large and diverse foreign community who were still thriving. The city might be Russian, but big international industry was still humming across the River Neva in the working-class districts of Vasilievsky Island, the Vyborg Side and beyond – where the great cotton and paper mills, shipyards, timber yards, sawmills and steelworks were still being run largely by British owners and managers,* many of whom had lived in Russia for decades. The vast red-brick Thornton's woollen mill – one of the biggest in Russia, founded in the 1880s – employed three thousand workers and was owned by three brothers from Yorkshire. Then there was the Nevsky Thread Manufacturing Company (established by Coats of Paisley, Scotland); the Neva Stearin Soap and Candle Works, run by William Miller & Co. of Leith, who also owned a brewery in the city; and Egerton Hubbard & Co.'s cotton mills and printing works.

A host of specialist stores in the city catered to the needs of such privileged expatriates, along with the wealthy Russian aristocracy. Even in 1916 you could still window-shop in front of the big shining plate-glass windows of the French and English luxury stores along the Nevsky Prospekt: Petrograd's equivalent of Bond Street. Here the French dressmakers, tailors and glovers – such as Brisac, couturier to the Empress, and Brocard the French perfumier, who also supplied the imperial family – continued to enjoy the patronage of the rich. At the English Shop (better known by its French rendering as the 'Magasin Anglais') you could buy the best Harris tweeds and English soap and enjoy the store's 'demure English provincialism', fancying yourself 'in the High Street in Chester, or Leicester, or Truro, or Canterbury'.[3] Druce's imported British goods and Maples furniture from the Tottenham Court Road; Watkins & Co., the English bookseller, was patronised by many in the British colony; other foreign

---

* Germans, too, but they had all left with the outbreak of war in 1914.

expatriates could catch up with the news back home by stopping off at Wolff's bookshop, which sold magazines and newspapers in seven different languages. Everywhere, still, in Petrograd, 'there was not a single shop of importance but displayed boldly lettered notices: "English spoken", "*Ici on parle Francais*" [and, until the outbreak of war], "*Man spricht Deutsch*"'.[4] French was still the lingua franca of the Russian aristocracy and bureaucracy, the *Journal de St-Pétersbourg* being the semi-official organ of the Russian Foreign Office and much in demand during wartime, with so many French diplomats and military attachés in the city. But English had even greater exclusivity, as the language of the 'higher circles of the Court' and the imperial family.[5]

By the autumn of 1916 the diplomatic community in wartime Petrograd was dominated by the Allied embassies of Britain, France and Italy, and the still-neutral USA – the large diplomatic contingent of Germany and Austria-Hungary having departed in 1914. Expatriate life in the city had always traditionally devolved to the dominating presence of the British colony of some two thousand or so nationals, its embassy and its gossipy focal point, the Anglican Church on the English Embankment, popularly known as the 'English Church'. Recalling his years in Petrograd, the church's resident priest, Rev. Bousfield Swan Lombard (who also served as chaplain to the British embassy from 1908), spoke of a community that was 'hospitable beyond all expectation', but whose outlook on life he had found disturbingly 'ultra-conservative'. 'So far from being broad and unfettered', the colony was 'narrowed by convention to such an extent that it took me quite a long time to realize that such conventionality was possible'. It was a highly insular community that had remained mistrustful of change or innovation. 'Any new suggestion was met, not by "it is impracticable, or unworkable",' wrote Lombard, 'but by either "it has never been the custom here" or it is "quite out of the question".'[6] He admitted regretfully that he was 'amazed at the narrowness and small-mindedness of the British colony; it resembled a little gossipy English village, or perhaps better still, a Cathedral close'.[7]

Life in this socially incestuous Barchester-like enclave was largely reduced to 'small coteries of intimate friends', as antiques dealer and socialite Bertie Stopford remembered.[8] Many doggedly clung to their English ways, to the extent of refusing to learn or speak Russian, and sent their children back to boarding school in England; most of the rest insisted on English or Scottish governesses and tutors, or else, failing that, French ones. For their social life the British colony tended to prefer their own parties, concerts and theatricals, though they all loved the Russian ballet. They baffled the Russians with their passion for sport, and ran their own cricket, football, tennis, yachting and rowing clubs; they even had a club for racing pigeons. They played golf together at Murino – a course they had constructed ten miles north-east of Petrograd, 'in a stubborn attempt to let nothing stand in their way of expressing themselves'.[9]*

The closed, clannish society of the British colony extended also to its New English Club at number 36 Bolshaya Morskaya. Although a few British diplomats were allowed honorary membership of the ultra-elitist Imperial Yacht Club immediately opposite – patronised by the aristocracy and senior members of the court and imperial civil service – it was the New English Club that was the exclusive preserve of the colony, frequented by 'practically all the clubbable Britons' in the city, its chief function being to promote the interests of British business under the chairmanship of the resident ambassador.[10] It allowed only a handful of chosen Americans to be members. Negley Farson, an American entrepreneur who had been in Petrograd for some time grappling with venal officialdom in his attempts to sell motorcycles to the Imperial Russian Army, abhorred this narrow world. The British expats 'lived like feudal lords … in baronial fashion, with their *abonnement* [subscription] at the Ballet, their belligerent private coachmen, their New English Club on the

---

* According to Negley Farson, the British embassy had their own golf balls sent out from England in the embassy despatch bags, as 'golf balls were as valuable as hawk's eggs in war-time'.

Morskayia, their golf club, their tennis club, their "English Magazine" [the Magasin Anglais]', which was the 'only place in Russia where one could get good shoes or leather goods', and their 'hordes of servants'. He resented the social cachet they enjoyed, which opened doors far more easily than those he was banging on, notably at the Russian War Ministry. 'An Englishman, any Englishman in Tsarist Russia, was automatically a Milord – and treated as such,' he noted.[11]

In Petrograd during the war years there was certainly no 'Milord' more to the manner born than the British ambassador, Sir George Buchanan, who oversaw the diplomatic mission and the British Chancery at its prime position at number 4 Palace Embankment, located a short walk from the Winter Palace and facing the River Neva. The embassy occupied a section of a grand mansion rented from the Saltykov family, who retained rooms at the back of the house facing the Field of Mars – the large military parade ground located not far from the Winter Palace. Arriving in St Petersburg in 1910 from an ambassadorship in Sofia, Bulgaria,* Buchanan and his wife Lady Georgina had inherited the existing furnishings of reproduction Louis XVI furniture and de rigueur crystal chandeliers and red brocade hangings of any embassy, but had augmented them with their own collection of fine furniture, books and paintings collected during their long diplomatic life in Europe. This personal touch, as their daughter Meriel recalled, gave the rooms 'a more homelike appearance, so that sometimes with the curtains drawn, one could almost imagine oneself in some old London square'.[12]

Sir George had in fact been contemplating removing the embassy to better premises for some time, only for the outbreak of war in 1914 to put paid to such ambitions. Although it might have looked grand on the surface, the embassy had several shortcomings. Its sewerage system was antediluvian and the building

---

* Buchanan had previously served in Vienna under his father, as well as in Rome, Tokyo, Berne, Darmstadt, Berlin and The Hague.

was in need of considerable restoration and redecoration. It required a substantial staff to maintain its baroque state rooms, its Chancery offices, located on the first floor, and – two flights of circular stairs above – the ballroom and large dining room that were used for bigger official functions. An all-essential English butler, William, was supported by a host of footmen, housemaids and an Italian chef, as well as numberless Russians employed to do menial household tasks and run the kitchens.[13] The Buchanans had brought a motor car with them, and their own English chauffeur, but also maintained carriages and sledges and a Russian coachman to drive them.

Occupying centre stage not just at his own embassy, but as the acknowledged dean of the diplomatic community in Petrograd, Sir George Buchanan was highly regarded by Russians and foreigners alike and inspired the greatest loyalty – if not hero worship – in those who worked for him. He was that archetypal gentleman-diplomat: an austere, monocled Old Etonian, the son of Sir Andrew Buchanan (himself a diplomat who had also served at the embassy in St Petersburg), and a man of honour in the old-fashioned sense of the word. Tall, slim and urbane, Buchanan was a classical scholar and a good linguist (though he spoke no Russian), who was widely read but who secretly loved detective novels and enjoyed nothing better than an undemanding game of bridge. His 'imperturbable serenity' and formality could at times be misinterpreted as excessively austere, and some of his staff found his 'baffling simplicity' and slightly effete absent-mindedness disconcerting. 'He was as gentle at bridge as in all else, but dreamily unaware of whether he was playing bridge or Happy Families,' recalled one of his staff.[14]

But there was no doubting Buchanan's modesty and – when the time came – his courage, or his unswerving loyalty towards those in his employ. It was abundantly clear to all who worked with him in those last dying days of imperial Russia that Sir George was by now a sick man, whose ill health, eroded by his unstinting dedication to duty and an increased workload during the war, had been made worse by his anxieties about the

precarious position of the Tsar and the growing threat of revolution.* Although Sir George occasionally managed a fishing trip
to Finland or a game of golf at Murino, by the end of 1916 he
seemed, to British diplomat Robert Bruce Lockhart, 'a frail-
looking man with a tired, sad expression'. But he had become
a familiar and respected figure on the streets of the capital, and
'when he took his daily walk to the Russian Foreign Office, his
hat cocked on one side, his tall, lean figure slightly drooping
under his many cares, every Englishman felt that here as much
as the diplomatic precincts of the Embassy itself was a piece of
the soil of England'.[15]

If at times Sir George might be seen to be fading, his formidable wife made up for his flagging energies. Lady Georgina, née
Bathurst, was herself 'of the purest purple'. 'As every Britisher
knows,' quipped Negley Farson, 'there exist only three families:
"The Holy Family, the Royal Family – and the Bathursts".'[16] Lady
Georgina was an imposing woman, whose 'heart was in proportion to her bulk', and her prodigious energies were matched by
her decided and well-voiced opinions. She was 'indiscreet and
quick to take offence: a generous friend but a dangerous enemy',
as some of her female associates in the British colony came to
discover, and she 'sat on a dozen committees and quarrelled with
the lot'. She ran the domestic life of the embassy 'like clockwork'
and 'never fail[ed] in that passion for punctuality which in the
Ambassador amounted almost to a mania'.[17] Since 1914, Lady
Georgina had also risen to the challenge of war work, comman-
deering the embassy ballroom and filling it with long tables loaded
with cotton wool, lint and materials for her twice-weekly sewing
parties. Here ladies of the British colony came to 'roll bandages,
to make pneumonia-jackets, all kinds of first-aid dressings, pyjamas,
dressing jackets, and dressing gowns' – some for the wounded at
the front, the rest for use in the British Colony Hospital for

---

* The climate in St Petersburg never suited Sir George and his health suf-
fered, so much so that when Sir Edward Grey discovered how often Sir
George was ill, he offered him the post of ambassador to Vienna – but
Sir George opted to stay in Petrograd.

Wounded Russian Soldiers. Located in a wing of the large Pokrovsky Hospital on Vasilievsky Island, the hospital had become Lady Buchanan's personal fiefdom after she had set it up on the outbreak of war; her daughter Meriel also worked there as a volunteer nurse.[18]

After Russia had entered the war in 1914, the old established expatriate community in Petrograd was augmented by the arrival of a newer, brasher breed of Americans: engineers and entrepreneurs dealing in war materiel, manufactured goods and munitions. American staff at International Harvester (the farm-machinery manufacturer), Westinghouse (for several years involved in the electrification of Petrograd's trams) and the Singer Sewing Machine Company (which had brought the first machines to Russia in 1865) now rubbed shoulders on the streets of the city with fellow countrymen sent from New York to run the Petrograd branches of the National City Bank and the New York Life Insurance Company, not to mention with American YMCA workers who had set up the Russian equivalent – the Mayak (Lighthouse) – there in 1900. In April 1916 the Petrograd diplomatic community had found itself welcoming a new American ambassador, after the incumbent George Marye had unexpectedly resigned – supposedly due to ill health. The gossip suggested, however, that he had been quietly pushed by the State Department, which had thought him too pro-Russian at a time when the USA was still neutral in the war.

Marye's successor was the most unlikely of candidates. A genial Democrat from Kentucky, David Rowland Francis was a self-made millionaire who had made his money in St Louis from grain-dealing and investments in railway companies. He had served as governor of Missouri (1889–93) and had lobbied for St Louis to stage the highly successful Louisiana Purchase Exposition of 1904 – better known as the St Louis World's Fair – as well as the summer Olympics later that same year. His ambassadorial experience was, however, nil, although in 1914 he had been offered and had declined an ambassadorship in Buenos Aires. Nevertheless, the choice of Francis for Petrograd seemed logical: he was a man of proven business acumen, whose primary role would be to renegotiate the US trade treaty with Russia that had been broken off in December 1912 in response to the tsarist government's anti-Semitic policies. Russia, as Francis well knew, was eager to buy US grain, cotton and armaments.

On 21 April (NS; 8 OS) 1916 Francis had sailed from Hoboken in New Jersey on the Swedish steamship *Oscar II* with his private secretary, Arthur Dailey, and his devoted black valet-cum-chauffeur, Philip Jordan. His wife Jane stayed at home in St Louis in the care of the couple's six sons, due to her poor health and her dread of facing the legendarily freezing Russian winters; Francis had not insisted on her accompanying him, knowing full well that his wife 'would not like it' in Petrograd.[19] In her absence, and reticent about embracing the social life of the city (like his counterpart Buchanan, he spoke no Russian), Francis relied very heavily on the protective 'Phil', as he liked to call him: a man he respected as 'loyal, honest and efficient and intelligent withal'.[20]

Jordan, whose African American origins are unclear, was a small, wiry man who had grown up in Hog Alley – a squalid slum district of Jefferson, Missouri, notorious (much like New York's Bowery) as a haunt of thieves, prostitutes and drunks. His early life had been spent as a hard drinker and gang member, regularly caught up in street fights. Later he worked on the riverboats along the Missouri, before, in 1889 – and now ostensibly a reformed character – he had been recommended to Francis, the newly elected governor of Missouri. After a brief period working for the subsequent governor, Jordan returned to the Francis family's grand mansion in St Louis's prosperous West End in 1902, serving as valet or, as Americans then termed it, 'body servant'. Here he had seen four US presidents – Cleveland, Roosevelt, Taft and Wilson – come and go as visitors, and had been taught to read and write by Mrs Francis, who was considerably more forgiving than her husband of Jordan's occasional lapses into heavy drinking, and to whom Jordan became devoted.[21]

The culture shock awaiting Francis and Jordan – freshly arrived from the balmy American South to cold, wartime Petrograd – was enormous. During their crossing Francis's Russian interpreter, a young Slavist named Samuel Harper, had done his best to give the inexperienced ambassador 'a crash course on what he might expect in Russia'. Harper came to the conclusion, on hearing Francis in conversation with some American businessmen heading to Petrograd on the same ship, that he was a 'very blunt, outpoken American, who believed in speaking his mind regardless of the rules of diplomacy'.[22] The contrast with the buttoned-up and immaculately schooled Sir George Buchanan could not have been clearer; the two ambassadors were to have little in common.

Upon arriving in the Stockholm Express at Petrograd's Finland Station on 15 April, Francis had headed for the US embassy, only too painfully aware of what awaited him: 'I had never been in Russia before. I had never been an Ambassador before. My knowledge of Russia up to the time of my appointment had been that of the average intelligent American citizen – unhappily slight and vague.'[23] Such disarming candour made it inevitable that his peers in the diplomatic community would view him disparagingly. As Robert Bruce Lockhart put it, 'Old Francis [did] not know a Left Social Revolutionary from a potato' but, to his credit, 'he was as simple and as fearless as a child'. Francis's kind-hearted, tolerant and well-meaning manner was not, however, admired by some of his more experienced embassy staff, to whom he seemed a 'hick' from St Louis with no understanding of Russian politics. Lacking the public-school background and years of assiduous honing in the arts of continental diplomacy that had come so naturally to his colleague Buchanan, Francis seemed ingenuous, to say the least. Arthur Bullard, an unofficial US envoy to Russia, thought him 'an old fool'; and 'a stuffed shirt, a dumb head' was the opinion of Dr Orrin Sage Wightman, who arrived in the city later with a US Red Cross Commission.[24] But to the Russians, who saw in America the prospect of lucrative and much-needed commercial relations, the new ambassador was 'easily the most popular diplomat in Petrograd'.[25] Francis, moreover, was socially engaging in a way that his British counterpart was not. He made no bones about his enjoyment of the finest Kentucky bourbon and fat cigars; he chewed plugs of tobacco and was able to 'ring' the spittoon at a distance of several feet. Unlike the dithering Buchanan at his games of bridge, Francis's amiable simplicity did not extend to cards; he was 'no child at poker', as Lockhart learned to his cost. Whenever he joined the US ambassador for a game, Francis always cleaned him out.[26]

In the summer of 1916 Francis and chauffeur Phil were delighted to finally take delivery of the ambassador's Model T Ford, specially shipped over from Missouri. They took great pride in riding around in it with 'a three-foot Stars and Stripes wired to the radiator cap', which made people wonder 'whether the breeze of the car's motion wave[d] the flag or the flag waving ma[de] the Ford go'.[27] The US embassy was very well positioned at 34 Furshtatskaya, in a well-to-do district in the centre of the city populated by Russian civil servants and other foreign diplomats. It was also a short walk from the Duma, the tsarist State Assembly housed at the Tauride Palace on Shpalernaya, and beyond it the Smolny Institute, which would become the focus of Bolshevik activities during the October Revolution. Like the British embassy, it was rented from a Russian aristocrat – Count Mikhail Grabbe – and suffered from similar limitations. It was, recalled special attaché James Houghteling, 'a disappointing two-story affair without dignity of façade, squeezed into the middle of a block with a big apartment building on one side and another modest residence on the other'.[28] Its interior was in need of decoration and was poorly furnished, so much so that Francis thought it looked like a 'warehouse'.[29] He soon started looking for better premises but, much like Buchanan, was thwarted in his attempts to find anything that suited while there was a war on.

Francis's office – from the balcony of which he could stand and observe the street below – was located on the second floor, along with a bedroom and sitting room. But the rooms were very cramped. The embassy was understaffed and in disarray; far worse, as far as Francis was concerned, the coffee was 'not very good', either.[30] He liked to entertain and to dine out with fellow Americans, as he missed his large family back in St Louis. US businessmen – especially executives of the National City Bank that had recently set up in Petrograd – were often invited to join him for meals. He also struck up a friendship with the American socialite Julia Grant, a granddaughter of Ulysses S. Grant who had married into the Russian aristocracy as Princess Cantacuzène-Speransky (though her friends in the US colony somewhat crassly called her 'Princess Mike') and who had a suite at the Hotel d'Europe.* The Princess lavishly entertained Francis, as did other wealthy aristocrats, either in their Petrograd town houses or in private rooms at their favourite hotels.

From the outset, Phil Jordan had a strong sense of responsibility for 'The Governor', as everyone had customarily addressed Francis since his years in the post in Missouri. He acted as the ambassador's minder whenever Francis ventured forth on the streets of Petrograd, and together they proceeded to muddle through the difficulties of becoming acquainted with all things Russian, notably its cuisine. As Francis told his son Perry: 'Phil and I are still trying to get along with the Russian cook whom he is having great difficulty in instructing how to prepare a meal in the American way, as she does not understand a word of English, and he can't speak a word of Russian.'[31] Help was soon at hand in the guise of an acquaintance Francis had made on the ship to Russia: Madame Matilda de Cram, a Russian returning to Petrograd, who lived nearby and became a regular visitor at the embassy, volunteering also to teach Francis French and Jordan Russian. Francis's friendship with Madame de Cram, which included taking her to the races on his day off, was conducted much to the consternation of his staff and of Allied counter-intelligence, who

---

* Julia Grant and her prince had enjoyed a swish high-society wedding at one of the Astor mansions on Newport Rhode Island in 1899, in the presence of the glitterati of the East Coast, who had lavished the couple with gifts of diamonds, Sèvres porcelain, monogrammed silver and Lalique glass. Grant was one of several American 'buccaneers' who married into the Russian aristocracy and were doyennes of the Petrograd social set before the revolution.

had her marked as a German spy, out to seduce the gullible new ambassador.³²*

Nevertheless, thanks to Madame de Cram, the resourceful Jordan soon had adequate Russian to go shopping unaided, claiming that 'I'm making out pretty well since I learned the language.' So resourceful was he that Jordan was soon finding kitchen utensils and furnishings for the embassy, including a decent-sized dining table that could seat twenty.³³ Having found their feet, Francis dispensed with the Russian cook and thereafter Jordan prepared his breakfast, until they managed to engage a 'negro cook who is very black, a West India negro named Green'. Since his arrival, Jordan had been greatly struck by how 'few negroes' there were in Petrograd, and 'none like our negroes'.³⁴ Francis noticed, too, explaining to his wife that Phil, who was 'relatively pale skinned' and was 'almost white enough to pass for a white man', did not go out on the streets with the Trinidadian cook because he was 'so black'.³⁵ Jordan and Green seemed to spend most of their time 'scheming to get food', and somehow or other conjured dishes for the ambassador's table despite the extreme shortages, for, armed with his pidgin Russian, Jordan turned out to be 'fearless about roaming the streets and haggled at the markets, mixing in with the multicultural, polyglot crowd'.³⁶† There was no doubting how much Francis missed his American luxuries: he waited months for the case of hams and bacon that he had ordered from New York to get to Russia, and even longer for two cases of Scotch whisky shipped from London that still hadn't arrived, come October.³⁷

The resourceful Phil Jordan had rapidly become 'invaluable' in all matters relating to the day-to-day running of the embassy.³⁸

---

* With no solid evidence to substantiate such allegations, and suggestions that his marriage was not happy, it seems more likely that the lonely Francis, who liked a pretty face, simply enjoyed Madame de Cram's female friendship and company.

† More significantly, with Francis's assistance, Jordan was one of only two Americans granted permission by the Petrograd Chief of Police to take photographs in the city.

As embassy official Fred Dearing noted in his diary: 'One sees in the instant that Phil is somebody. No one could be less obtrusive, but definitely somebody.'[39] He was close at hand to assist Francis when, to celebrate the Fourth of July, Francis had bravely mounted a successful reception for over one hundred guests. 'I engaged a first class orchestra of nine pieces,' he told Jane, and 'thanks to Phil we had a delicious punch in addition to the tea served from the samovar which we had recently bought. We had caviar sandwiches, tomato sandwiches, and what appeared to be unknown to the Russians, we had delicious ices.'[40] The members of Petrograd's American colony had greatly welcomed such a party and its culinary treats, but getting himself known on the snobbish Russian and diplomatic social circuit was quite another matter for the new ambassador. Francis admitted to Jane in July that 'I have made comparatively few social acquaintances among the Russians.'[41] He eschewed the genteel tea and cocktail parties of the British embassy and the incestuous chit-chat of the continental diplomatic corps, preferring a good game of poker. They in turn were somewhat disdainful of his diplomatic dinners. Sir George Buchanan, a man tainted by the social snobbery and racial prejudice of his generation and class, dreaded invitations from Francis. If asked to dine at the American embassy, Buchanan would lament, 'Ah, we're going to have a bad supper ... cooked by a Negro.'[42] And on most such occasions there was no orchestra, merely the loyal Phil, who as general factotum wound up the gramophone behind a screen, in between serving the guests.[43]

If the truth be told, neither Francis nor Buchanan particularly enjoyed the social round of Petrograd society. It was their flamboyant French counterpart, Maurice Paléologue, who was the most accomplished socialite in the diplomatic corps and who also 'held the best dinner parties for the smartest and most frivolous set'.[44] Indeed, the suave and gossipy Paléologue seemed to spend more time socialising than on diplomatic business. He was regularly seen at the ballet and opera – both of which were enjoying their heyday during the war. When not there, he seemed to be 'forever in the grand ducal drawing rooms gossiping with the Princesses', or dining out with the Petrograd glitterati.[45]

For members of the diplomatic community like Paléologue, as well as other foreign nationals in the city, war till now had not been so hard to bear. The hottest ticket in town was still a night at the ballet at the Mariinsky Theatre. All Petrograd society – Russian and expatriate – went to see and be seen at its Wednesday evening and Sunday afternoon performances, and all still dressed up for the occasion. Most seats were sold by private subscription and well in advance; people would pay up to 100 rubles to obtain one of the few made available for sale. Even at this time of food queues, you could still see crowds standing in line for tickets for the ballet. Ambassador Francis rated the autumn season at the Mariinsky the 'best in the world'; together with most of the diplomatic community, he had sat 'spellbound' through a three-hour performance of *Don Quixote* starring prima ballerina Tamara Karsavina.[46] The two other major Petrograd theatres were still flourishing: the Alexandrinsky, for straight theatre, and the Mikhailovsky, with its resident French troupe, which was the centre for French culture among the Russian intelligentsia and was where they all went to practise their French.

Petrograd, for all its privations and its growing atmosphere of social disaffection, still provided 'the perfect life of dissipation' for those unrepentant sybarites craving excitement and self-indulgence.[47] Nicholas II might have introduced a ban on vodka sales in 1914 to control the legendary drunkenness of Russia's largely peasant, conscript army, but if you had the right money you could still be served fine wines, champagne, whisky and other hard liquor in the *cabinets privés* of the best restaurants and hotels in the city.[48]* In former years the Hotel de France and Hotel d'Angleterre had enjoyed the patronage of the French and English colonies, but during the war it was the Astoria that gained pre-cedence. It had been built in 1912 on the eastern side of St Isaac's

---

* Ordinary Russians could only get alcohol on the black market, or on a doctor's prescription.

Square at the corner of Bolshaya Morskaya and Voznesenskaya, to cater to tourists coming to St Petersburg for the 1913 Romanov Tercentenary; and it was named by its Swedish architect, Fredrik Lidvall, in honour of the renowned New York hoteliers, the Astor brothers.

Such had been its popularity with British visitors that the Astoria had set up a bureau to deal specifically with their needs and boasted a 'gigantic map of the London tube system and a large library of English books from Chaucer to D. H. Lawrence'.[49] With 'ten elevators, an electric light system for calling servants, city telephone lines, an automated vacuuming system, steam-driven central heating, as well as 350 rooms soundproofed with cork insulation', the hotel also had a grand restaurant that catered for up to two hundred people, a Winter Garden atrium and Art Nouveau banqueting hall.[50] Its French restaurant had become a place of welcome retreat for war-weary Russian officers home from the front, as well as for Allied attachés, embassy officials and expatriates – a magnet, too, for discreet high-class prostitutes. Although its rival, the Hotel d'Europe, which also offered a roof garden and luxurious glass-domed restaurant, was a favourite haunt of Ambassador Francis, most new foreign arrivals in the city headed for the Astoria. Such, however, had been the influx of visiting military men that by the end of 1916 the hotel had lost much of its pre-war glamour, so much so that Italian-born restaurant manager Joseph Vecchi felt it had become 'a kind of glorified barracks'.[51]

Vecchi rued the severe shortages that prevented him from providing the kind of grand dinners that even a year ago he had still been able to conjure up for private parties. For food supplies to Petrograd had, by the end of 1916, shrunk to about one-third of what was needed. A severe lack of manpower on the land had affected output, with so many peasants conscripted into the army; but many of the shortages were artificial, caused by profiteering and the breakdown in the national railway system. At depots and supply centres in the food-producing south, flour and other food supplies lay stranded and rotting, for lack of rolling stock to bring them by rail to Russia's hungry cities in the north. There was still plenty of food available out in the provinces, as many foreign visitors testified, and hard-pressed housewives often made gruelling journeys out of the city in attempts to buy butter, eggs, meat and fish from the local peasantry. By now stories were rife in Petrograd about the deliberate stockpiling of flour, meat and sugar by speculators in order to push the prices ever higher. Even the moneyed classes could no longer obtain white bread, but they could certainly still lay their hands on fine food when they wanted to have a party, as National City Bank employee Leighton Rogers noted with amazement, when invited that winter to the house of a Russian acquaintance for 'just a little family affair':

> The huge buffet in a reception room looked as though a food warehouse had burst open – pickled fish, sardines, anchovies, smelts, herrings, smoked eel, smoked salmon; bowls of caviar, entire hams, tongue, sausage, chicken, paté-de-fois-gras; red cheese, yellow cheese, white cheese, blue cheese; innumerable salads; basket of celery, pickles and olives; sauces – pink, yellow, lavender. All this and much more was piled in three great tiers, with an immobile cascade of fruits in the centre, and flanked by rows of vodka and kummel carafes.[52]

It turned out that this bacchanalian feast was merely the *zakuski*, or hors d'oeuvres, preceding a full sit-down dinner of salmon, roast venison and pheasant, followed by ice-cream bombe and yet more fruit and cheeses, served with wines from claret to burgundy and champagne. At the end of the dinner, as a special treat, Rogers's Russian host had produced the ultimate treat for his American guests: 'two packets of Beeman's Pepsin chewing gum'.[53]

Beyond the doors of this and other comfortable private mansions 'Russia lay like a prostrate Mars, starving to death,' wrote Negley Farson, who till now had led an unrepentant sybaritic life in the clubs and restaurants of the city.[54] But even he had become disenchanted with staying up all night on binges with his expatriate friends and cronies, enjoying champagne and crayfish in the company of prostitutes in the *cabinets privés* at the Villa Rodé – a restaurant near the Stroganovsky Bridge that was patronised by Grigory Rasputin, the Tsar's and Tsaritsa's controversial spiritual guru and adviser. All the fashionable restaurants were feeling the pinch – including Contant's, haunt of the Dutch ambassador Willem Oudendijk (later known as William Oudendyk); and the Café Donon, a favourite of US embassy official J. Butler Wright. The old expatriate life at the New English Club had also 'dwindled to nothing': 'Its beefsteak dinners had vanished forever' by the end of 1916, as Farson recalled.[55]

Most basic foodstuffs, like milk and potatoes, had quadrupled in price since the outbreak of war; other crucial commodities such as bread, cheese, butter, meat and fish were as much as five times more expensive. Ella Woodhouse, daughter of the British consul, recalled that 'we had to keep a maid, whose only job was to stand in queues for milk, for bread, or whatever else there was to be had'.[56] As winter set in, the queues got ever longer and more resentful, with 'more and more talk of inefficiency and corruption in high places'. Official wastage and mismanagement of food and fuel supplies (with only wood and no coal available) were on a colossal scale; corruption among Russian officials was rife. Petrograd felt like a city under siege: no one had the appetite for self-indulgence any longer. 'The Roman Holiday atmosphere of the Hotel Astoria was gone. Fear had now taken its place.'[57] In his daily walks along the Embankment, Sir George Buchanan was appalled by the long queues for food. 'When the hard winter weather sets in these lines will become inflammable material,' he wrote in November 1916. At the US embassy, Fred Dearing had much the same sense of foreboding: 'The air is thick with talk of catastrophe,' he wrote in his journal.[58]

For those in big business – the textile mills, copper factories, munitions works – the profits continued to mount, while for their workers the spectre of famine seemed ever more present. 'An air of deep despondency already by then hung over the capital,' recalled Willem Oudendijk. 'It was clear that the war put too heavy a strain on the country's economic life … Cabs had practically disappeared and tram-cars rumbled along, packed to overflowing.' The muddy streets were shabby and the shops depleted. The Russians to whom he spoke put it all down to the rottenness of the bureaucratic system:

> Conversations were carried on mostly in whispers as if one was afraid of being overheard, although there was nobody near, and the conviction was expressed that things could not go on as they were, that a storm was approaching, although nobody seemed to have a fixed idea whence it would come nor how much damage it would cause.[59]

'Everyone from Grand Dukes to one's sleigh driver all thunder against the regime,' observed Denis Garstin of the British Propaganda Bureau in Petrograd.[60] From the grandest mansion to the shivering bread queues, one topic of conversation prevailed: the Empress's relationship with Grigory Rasputin. Against all the objections of the imperial family, Nicholas and Alexandra had stubbornly refused to remove him from his favoured position, and had made matters worse by appointing a series of increasingly reactionary ministers. With Nicholas away at army HQ, Alexandra was left alone, alienated from the Russian court and most of her relatives, and relying ever more heavily on their 'friend'. In her intense isolation she took nobody's advice seriously, except Rasputin's. Repeated warnings were sent to Nicholas of the escalating danger to the throne; his uncle, Grand Duke Nikolay Nikolaevich, begged him to stop his wife from bringing the monarchy into further disrepute by meddling in the affairs of government. 'You stand on the eve of an era of new troubles,' he warned. Sir George Buchanan was of the same mind: 'If the emperor continues to uphold his present reactionary advisers, a revolution is, I fear, inevitable.'[61]

In this atmosphere of 'strained suspense', people were talking openly about the need for a palace coup and for the Empress to be shut up, out of harm's way, in a nunnery.[62] Unrestrained innuendo and gossip about 'The Dark Powers' that she and Rasputin represented were the sole topic of conversation in the exclusive clubs, where 'Grand Dukes played *quinze* and talked of "saving" Russia.'[63] The assassination of Rasputin seemed the only solution – the panacea that would avert crisis and save the monarchy from the brink of disaster.

On the night of 16–17 December 1916 Rasputin went missing. Over at the Mariinsky Theatre, French ambassador Paléologue had been enjoying Smirnova dancing the lead role in *Sleeping Beauty* that night, and recalled that her 'leaps, pirouettes and "arabesques" were not more fantastic than the stories which passed from lip to lip' about plots to remove the Empress and her 'friend' from power. 'We're back in the days of the Borgias, Ambassador,' confided an Italian diplomat.[64] When Rasputin's body was fished out of the river a few days later, Alexandra was ruthless in her response, confining Rasputin's hot-headed young murderers, Prince Felix Yusupov to his estate in the country, and Grand Duke Dmitri Pavlovich to house arrest, while the Russian public celebrated their act of 'heroism'.

A powerful, fatalistic atmosphere had descended over the city by the end of the year. 'The approaching cataclysm was already in every mind, and on everybody's lips,' recalled Robert Bruce Lockhart.[65] The sense of doom was made worse by the blackout of the streets at night, 'for fear of the Zeppelins', the darkness broken only by searchlights fanning the sky for them. Russia could not hold out much longer against Germany on the Eastern Front. Fourteen million men had been mobilised since 1914 and losses so far amounted to more than seven million killed, wounded or captured. Yet still the demand for conscripts was insatiable; all over the city – on the Field of Mars, Palace Square and the embankments along the Neva – one could see the constant drilling of column upon column of soldiers and field artillery. Ordinary Russians looked on with increasing indifference; 'the desperate and embittering old problems of how to get enough to eat reabsorbed their attention'.[66]

For Leighton Rogers, Petrograd in winter was 'the weather waste heap of the world'; he had hardly seen the sun since his arrival in October and, when it did emerge, it was gone by 3.00 p.m. 'We seem to be away up on top of the world shrouded in white mists which swallow its brilliance.'[67] As flurries of snow and intense cold set in, everyone wondered how much longer the current explosive situation would prevail, how long it would be before 'the lines of shivering women, their feet numb and frozen, their trembling fingers clutching their shawls tighter round their heads' might vent their anger and storm the food shops.[68] Everywhere you went there were groups of them:

shuffling, pushing, jostling each other; eager, trembling hands outstretched for their basin of soup, querulous voices asking for just a little more, begging for a bottle of milk to take home to a dying baby, telling long, rambling, pitiful stories of want and misery and cold.[69]

Wilfully blind to the gathering resentment on the streets, the demi-monde indulged in a last gasp of spending as Christmas approached, partying in the theatres and cabarets and nightclubs of the city:

Through the revolving-doors of the Hotel Astoria passed the same endless procession of women in furs and jewels and men in glittering uniforms. Across the bridges limousines passed to and fro and *troikas* made music in the streets – the music of sleigh bells and steel runners on the snow ... As ever, the streets were thronged, the tram-cars crowded to suffocation, the restaurants doing a roaring trade. And everywhere people talked, as they only talk in Russia, the land of endless talk.[70]

Out across the Neva the squalid, barrack-block tenements of the industrial quarter of the Vyborg Side had seen a major strike by 20,000 metal and armaments workers on 17 October. Ground down by war, disease, unsanitary living conditions, low wages and hunger, they were demanding improved pay and conditions ever more vociferously. 'Every unusual noise, even the unexpected sound of a factory whistle, was enough to bring them into the streets. The tension was becoming painful. Everyone, consciously or unconsciously, was waiting for something to happen.' In the workers' quarters, revolutionary talk 'ran like fire through stubble' and revolutionary agitators were there to further fan the flames of dissent.[71] After a second major strike on 26 October, thousands of workers were locked out. By the 29th, forty-eight factories were in lockdown and 57,000 workers on strike. Fierce clashes with the police continued until these workers were reinstated.[72]

To many in the diplomatic community, the collapse of Russia seemed imminent and British subjects were already being urged to go home. But although Sir George Buchanan was emphatically predicting revolution, David Francis was of the opinion that this would not happen 'before the war ends' or, more likely, 'soon thereafter'.[73] He and his staff celebrated Christmas US-style (on what was 12 December, on the Russian calendar) with 'turkey and plum pudding'.[74] Sir George, meanwhile, had more serious things on his mind. Deciding to make one final attempt to warn the Tsar of the danger of imminent revolution, he set off for the Alexander Palace, fifteen miles south of the city at Tsarskoe Selo. 'If the Emperor received him sitting down,' he told Robert Bruce Lockhart before he left, 'all would be well.'[75] When Buchanan arrived on 30 December, the Tsar received him standing. Nevertheless, Buchanan tried hard to persuade him of the seriousness of rising discontent in the city, and urged him to do his utmost to restore confidence in the throne by making social and political concessions before it was too late: 'it rested with him either to lead Russia to victory and a permanent peace or to revolution and disaster,' Sir George later wrote. But Nicholas dismissed his concerns and said he was exaggerating.[76] Half an hour later a gloomy Buchanan left. He had said his piece and was relieved to 'have got it off his mind'.[77] But his advice had fallen on deaf ears, as he had anticipated. Nicholas had further alienated public opinion recently by appointing the arch-reactionary Alexander Protopopov as Minister of the Interior – a man bent on preserving the autocracy at any cost, and a known associate of Rasputin – an act that, moreover, prompted other ministers to resign en masse in protest.

As New Year 1917 arrived, over at the US embassy Phil Jordan had somehow managed to get hold of contraband Russian champagne for a party. The rugs were rolled back and there was dancing into the early hours.[78] French ambassador Paléologue saw the old year out at a party at the home of Prince Gavriil Konstantinovich, where everyone talked of the conspiracies against the throne and 'all this with the servants moving about, harlots looking on and listening, gypsies singing and the whole company bathed in the aroma of Moet and Chandon *brut imperial* which flowed in streams!'[79]

At the Astoria Hotel the band played 'It's a Long Way to Tipperary' during dinner, as an English nurse looked forward to leaving the city, after witnessing the misery of Polish refugees at the British colony's soup kitchen:

And here we are in the Astoria Hotel, and there is one pane of glass between us and the weather; one pane of glass between us and the peasants of Poland; one pane of glass dividing us from poverty, and keeping us in the horrid atmosphere of this place, with its evil women and its squeaky band![80]

With even the tsarist secret police now predicting the 'wildest excesses of a hunger riot', the smashing of that one fragile pane of glass seemed inevitable.[81]

PART 1

THE FEBRUARY REVOLUTION

1

'Women are Beginning to Rebel at Standing in Bread Lines'

In November 1916, Arno Dosch-Fleurot,* a seasoned journalist working for a popular US daily – the New York *World* – had arrived in Petrograd fresh from a gruelling stint covering the Battle of Verdun. A Harvard-trained lawyer, from a prestigious Portland family, he had turned to journalism and had been covering the war since August 1914, when his editor in New York offered what seemed to him the dream ticket: 'Suggest you might like to go to Russia.'[1] But getting there wasn't easy in war-torn Europe; Fleurot had had to cross the Channel to England to pick up a boat from Newcastle to Bergen. This had been followed by a long rail journey through Norway, Sweden and north to the Finnish checkpoint at Torneo, where he had grown frazzled, arguing with customs officials about 'letting [his] typewriter though without paying duty'. As he boarded the train for Petrograd's Finland Station, the customs officer had attempted to defuse his enthusiasm: 'I know how your papers like sensations,' he said, 'but you won't find any in Russia, I am afraid.' Fleurot

---

* Dosch-Fleurot was the son of a German immigrant to Oregon. He had adopted his French mother's surname, Fleurot, during the war to avoid difficulties when reporting on the Western Front.

was expecting his assignment to last twelve weeks or so; in the end he would spend more than two years in Russia.[2]

Although he had wired ahead and booked a room at the Hotel de France, on arrival he found that it was full. They offered him the billiard-table to sleep on. It was, he recalled, very hard, 'and more conducive to reflection than sleep'.[3] He was excited to be in Russia after two years on the Western Front, but this was virgin territory for him and he was full of all the classic preconceptions:

> I checked up on my notions about Russia and found I had a sordid one from reading Dostoievsky's *Crime and Punishment*, a tragic one from seeing Tolstoy's *Resurrection*, a terrible one from reading George Kennon's *Darkest Siberia*.* I recalled for the first time in years, stories a nurse of Finnish origin used to tell us children about cruel czars poisoned by apples, of *boyards* who threw serfs to wolves ... I had a jumble of Nihilists with bombs, corrupt functionaries, Red Sundays, cruel Cossacks.[4]

Acknowledging how 'very little' he and his fellow Americans knew or understood about the Russian situation, Fleurot was soon given a briefing on what to expect by Ludovic Naudeau, correspondent for *Le Temps*, whose despatches from the Russian front had impressed him greatly. Naudeau had taken Fleurot to Contant's swanky restaurant for smoked salmon and caviar, where he warned him that 'Russia hits all writing men the same way':

> You fall under a spell. You realize you are in another world, and you feel you must not only understand it: you must get it down on paper ... you will not know enough about Russia to explain anything until you have been here so long you are half-Russian yourself, and then you won't be able

---

* Kennon (1845–1924) was a notable American traveller and explorer who had written numerous exposés of the Russian penal system in Siberia.

to tell anybody anything at all about it ... You will find yourself tempted to compare Russia with other countries. Don't.[5]

Fleurot and Naudeau were by no means the only foreign journalists in Petrograd just before the revolution broke. The reports of Reuters correspondent Guy Beringer, as well as those of Walter Whiffen and Roger Lewis of Associated Press, were being syndicated in the West, and there was an established coterie of other, mainly British reporters in the city: Hamilton Fyfe for the *Daily Mail*, Harold Williams, a New Zealander writing for the *Daily Chronicle*,[*] Arthur Ransome of the *Daily News* and *Observer*, and Robert Wilton of *The Times*, all of whom were filing regular reports, though generally without bylines.[†] Fleurot was soon joined by fellow Americans Florence Harper – the first American female journalist in Petrograd – and her sidekick, photographer Donald Thompson, both of whom worked for the illustrated magazine *Leslie's Weekly*.

The unsinkable Thompson, from Topeka, Kansas, was a scrawny but feisty five feet four inches, familiar for his signature jodhpurs and flat cap, the Colt in his waistband and the camera he carried with him everywhere. He had tried eight times to get to the Western Front as a war photographer – each time being turned back by the military authorities, his film or cameras confiscated. He finally made it, filming at Mons, Verdun and the Somme, among many locations on the front line, and smuggling his film back to London or New York. He had headed to Russia in December 1916 with Harper, having been tipped off that 'they expect trouble here', and with an additional commission to shoot footage for Paramount.[6]

---

[*] Williams's reports were also syndicated to the *Daily Telegraph* and *New York Times*.
[†] Many of the reports were simply credited as being 'by our Petrograd correspondent' – or something similar – and it is difficult applying credit where due to some of the front-line reporting by British and American journalists during the revolution.

Like many Americans in Russia for the first time, Thompson, Harper and Fleurot, as well as others who followed, had 'come breezing into Petrograd with that all-conquering, all-knowing American optimism'. But 'gradually the weather, the melancholy of the Russians, the seriousness of everything under the sun, would dampen their mood'.[7] To get to Petrograd, Harper and Thompson had taken the alternative route into Russia then available: a boat across the Pacific to Japan and thence to Manchuria, where they picked up the Trans-Siberian railroad. They arrived complete with Thompson's bulky cameras and tripod and Harper's extensive and mostly unsuitable wardrobe, Thompson having noted with amusement that 'Florence Harper, on account of her extra baggage, had to buy six extra railroad tickets'.[8] Arriving in Petrograd at 1.00 a.m. on 13 February 1917, they headed to that beacon for all foreign visitors – the Astoria Hotel – only to be told there were no beds. After much wheedling, Harper was given 'a cubbyhole so small that there wasn't even room for my hand luggage'.[9] Thompson, however, was obliged to spend his first night wandering the freezing-cold streets in a blizzard until he was able to find a cheap third-class hotel.

The difficulties of finding accommodation in the city were now extreme. US special attaché James Houghteling had noted that 'Every hotel is jammed and no house or apartment for rent stays on the market for twenty-four hours. Guests sleep in the private dining rooms and the corridors of the hotels, and one can never get a bath before nine A.M. or after nine P.M. because some unfortunate is bedded down in every bath-room.' Arriving in January, he had noted that his own hotel smelt 'like a third-class boarding house in Chicago'.[10]

Much of the desperate shortage of rooms in the capital was a consequence of Germany having issued a threat in mid-January that its submarines would torpedo even neutral ships on sight; no passenger or cargo boats were running from the main terminals into Russia from Norway and Sweden, leaving many foreign nationals and travellers trapped in Petrograd. 'There are hundreds of people waiting here to get away, and hundreds more in Sweden and Norway,' wrote Scottish nurse Ethel Moir.[11] Arriving in Petrograd in January, she and fellow nurse Lilias Grant had found themselves dumped out of the train from the Romanian front, into a 'great steep bank of snow', after which they had struggled with their kit bags to find *droshkies*,* and had then only secured one night in a hotel, sleeping on the floor.[12] After a fruitless search the following day, they appealed to Rev. Lombard at the English Church, who managed to get them rooms at the colony's British Nursing Home. It had been such a pleasure for them, after the rigours of the field hospitals, to spend the evening with Lombard, revelling in 'a real English fire, comfy armchairs, hot buttered toast'. These were 'such unheard-of luxuries', as too was the experience of sleeping 'in real beds and between sheets' again. But they were anxious about getting home: 'It's easier to get into Russia than to get out of it!' wrote Moir. 'And from what we hear, it will become yet more difficult – there are rumours of a *revolution* on all sides – one hears it everywhere.'[13]

While waiting to leave the city and get back to the UK, Moir and Grant visited Lady Georgina Buchanan and her daughter Meriel and learned something of the tireless relief work being undertaken in Petrograd by the members of the British colony, particularly with the thousands of refugees fleeing the fighting in their eastern homelands. They were pouring into the Warsaw Station after days crowded into freight cars, and from there were sent to filthy temporary wooden barracks nearby. These were little more than sheds filled with triple or quadruple rows of bunks, housing two to three hundred people each. Other refugees sought shelter in the draughty open hangar that was the station itself – sleeping on the cold stone floors or climbing into empty trucks and freight cars. Some were housed in damp, windowless cellars. Disease was rife, particularly outbreaks of measles and scarlatina; everywhere one looked, the refugees 'lay all day long with expressionless, bulging eyes, half stupefied in the stifling stench of the place.'[14]

---

* A *droshky* was a two-wheeled horse-drawn carriage for hire, the Russian equivalent of a hansom cab or taxi.

The sight of so many pitiful children with insufficient clothing and often no shoes, their bodies and hair crawling with lice, had galvanised a surge of expatriate philanthropic work. Twice a day the lines of refugees formed at the door of the feeding station set up for them, shivering in their rags and waiting for the brass token that entitled them to a piece of black bread and a bowl of English porridge, 'doled out to them by the bustling ladies of the British Colony' and led from the front – as always – by the redoubtable Lady Buchanan.[15] Donations of clothes and shoes for the refugees were sorted at the British embassy by more groups of lady volunteers, whom she had also commandeered; the room used for the purpose, as her daughter Meriel recalled, 'resembled nothing more than an old rag-market'.[16] Not content with her work at the embassy and at the refugee feeding station, Lady Buchanan was also patron of a maternity hospital for Polish refugees in Petrograd, which had been opened by the Millicent Fawcett Medical Unit in Russia, with substantial help from the Tatiana Refugee Committee, named for the Tsar's second daughter, who was its honorary head.

As self-appointed *grande dame* of the colony's war work, Lady Buchanan had therefore been somewhat put out when her domain was invaded by a rival, in the guise of the small, frail but feisty Lady Muriel Paget. A passionate philanthropist, who had spent nine years running soup kitchens for the poor in deprived parts of London, Lady Muriel was, like the ambassador's wife, from the upper echelons of the aristocracy: a daughter of the Earl of Winchilsea and married to a baronet.[17] Having heard of the appalling casualty rates suffered by the Russian army on the eastern front, Lady Muriel had lobbied a distinguished committee of supporters in the UK, including Alexandra the Queen Mother, for an Anglo-Russian Hospital Unit to be set up in Russia under the auspices of the Red Cross.[18] As its chief organiser, she headed the hospital's team of surgeons, physicians, orderlies and twenty trained[*]

---

[*] The trained nurses were Red Cross sisters, principally from St Thomas's and St Bart's, London.

and ten volunteer (VAD) nurses; she also had plans for three field hospitals to be established in Russia. Funded by donations from the British public, the hospital had beds for 180 wounded Russian soldiers, or two hundred if the staff pushed the beds closer together. It had been fortunate to secure for its premises Grand Duke Dmitri Pavlovich's neo-baroque palace, loaned for the duration of the war thanks to some persuasion by Sir George Buchanan.

Located at number 41 Nevsky, on the corner of the Anichkov Bridge opposite the Dowager Empress's palace on the Fontanka River, the palace was a handsome, dark-pink stuccoed building with cream pilasters and surrounds, but its suitability as a hospital left much to be desired.* Its drainage was primitive and the plumbing non-existent.[19] Running water, baths and lavatories had to be installed as a matter of urgency, while the lofty, gilded concert hall and two interconnecting large reception rooms were turned into hospital wards. An operating theatre, X-ray department, laboratory and sterilising rooms were created in other partitioned rooms. All the palace's lovely parquet floors were covered in linoleum and the tapestries and damask-silk wall hangings, as well as plasterwork cherub carvings, were masked with plywood.

Lady Buchanan's modest British Colony Hospital on Vasilievsky Island, with its forty-two beds for soldiers and eight for officers, was inevitably eclipsed by the grander and better-funded new Anglo-Russian Hospital, which proudly raised the Union flag above its front door.[20] On 18 January 1916 it had been officially opened by the Dowager Empress and the Tsar's two eldest daughters, Olga and Tatiana, with various other grand duchesses and dukes as well as the Buchanans in attendance. Lady Buchanan

---

* Built in the eighteenth century as the Beloselsky-Belozersky Palace, it was reconstructed in the nineteenth and in 1883 was bought by Grand Duke Sergey and his wife Ella, sister of the Empress. After the Grand Duke was assassinated in 1905, his wife took the veil and gifted the palace to Dmitri Pavlovich, who retained his own private apartments there on the ground floor. It was here that he and Felix Yusupov took refuge, hysterical and covered in blood, after they had murdered Rasputin.

had posed for the obligatory group photograph swathed in large hat and furs, but did not disguise her resentment: 'I have nothing to do with the Anglo Russian Hospital,' she would complain to her sister-in-law, 'as Lady Muriel Paget has carefully kept me out of it.'[21] It was just as well, for all Lady Georgina's time was already consumed by her own relief work, which even extended to the mounting of a benefit performance in February of *Lady Hunt-worth's Experiment*, by Mrs Waller's Company, a London-based troupe that had been touring Europe – all proceeds going to the purchase of 'warm clothing for the Russian soldiers'.[22]

Lady Georgina was ubiquitous that winter: not just at the embassy workroom and the refugee feeding station, but sorting hospital stores at a Red Cross depot and helping escaped Russian prisoners of war as they arrived back home. 'I have given shirts, socks, tobacco etc to nearly 3000 besides giving them all clothes for their wives and children. They write me such letters of gratitude,' she wrote in a letter home. But by the beginning of 1917 she was complaining of never having 'a moment to sit down, and as for reading a book or any such luxuries one never can indulge in even thinking of the like'. Her hospital was full. No bed was empty for more than a day; 'in fact they telephone every day to ask if we can't possibly take in more ... everything is beginning to run short'.[23] The Anglo-Russian Hospital was also besieged. Since opening, it had been rapidly filled to overflowing with serious cases, many of them with terrible septic wounds. In the main these were the result of gas gangrene, the scourge – so surgeon Geoffrey Jefferson observed – of the Russian front. The smell from the suppurating wounds was terrible, for many of the wounded had taken four or five days to be brought to Petrograd from the front. But it was far too cold to throw open the windows for more than a few minutes at a time to clear the air.[24]

Dorothy Seymour, a VAD who had recently transferred to the Anglo-Russian Hospital from nursing on the Western Front, had found her arrival in Petrograd rather disconcerting. The city was 'very smelly, very large and very unwarlike, much more so than London'.[25] The war may have seemed a long way away, but not, however, the heightened sense of social tension that she encountered: 'politics are thrilling out here but it's difficult to get a grasp of them at all, it's such a glorious muddle,' she wrote to her mother. But they were lucky: 'being Red Cross we are very well fed'; they even had the luxury of having their 'hot water bottles filled at night and hot water in the mornings'.[26] As the daughter of a general and granddaughter of an Admiral of the Fleet, and holding an honorary position at court as a Woman of the Bedchamber to Princess Christian,* Dorothy was extremely well connected. But she failed to be impressed by the ambassadress: 'Lady G.B. is very sniffy about who she invites and has a deadly household, so nobody takes much notice of her,' she told her mother. Apparently the snobbish Lady Buchanan 'drew the line at VADs' when inviting people to tea, so Seymour cultivated her own contacts on the Petrograd social circuit, going to the ballet, to the opera to see Chaliapin sing *Boris Godunov* and dining out almost every night with British naval and military attachés – noting with surprise that in wartime Petrograd 'no man changes for dinner'. She counted herself lucky that her work in the bandaging room at the ARH was 'light'. It was difficult enough coping with learning Russian, but for many of the VADs – missing their English Cross & Blackwell jam and having to share cramped, inadequate quarters or spend hours making up bandages at the Winter Palace hospital, instead of nursing – Petrograd was a challenge.[27]

Seymour's eighteen-year-old fellow VAD, Enid Stoker,† was not having an easy time of it. She was shocked by the level of suffering endured by the wounded – shocked in equal measure to her admiration of their stoicism *in extremis* and their simple peasant faith, expressed in frequent prayers before the icons that hung in the corners of their wards. They sang a lot and played the balalaika and had a childlike gratitude that touched her, but

---

* Queen Victoria's daughter, Princess Helena, was married to Prince Christian of Schleswig-Holstein.
† Enid was a niece of Bram Stoker, author of the Gothic novel *Dracula*.

some of their stories were heartbreaking.[28] She remembered one young soldier, Vasili, from Siberia who had had both legs amputated. One day he was lying on the top of his bed with his stumps on a pillow, 'when an old peasant came into the ward. He had travelled, goodness knows how, nearly a thousand miles to see his son,' as Stoker recalled. But as soon as he saw him, he began to shout, 'the tears pouring down his cheeks'. Stoker was dismayed to be told by their interpreter that the old man was cursing the boy:

> Why hadn't he *died*? Then they would have got a small pension for him – now look at him, a hopeless burden. How could he work on the farm now? Just another useless mouth to feed and they were nearly starving already.[29]

In Russia there were by now more than 20,000 repatriated soldiers who had lost either arms or legs. Dorothy Seymour rather enjoyed her work taking men such as these – 'the cripples' – out for drives in *droshkies* around snow-covered Petrograd and treating them to tea.[30] Some of them had never left their villages till they were conscripted, and after months on end in the hospital had not yet had sight of the capital. It was better than sitting rolling bandages all day. Much to Lady Buchanan's chagrin, Seymour – thanks to her position at the British court, with the Tsaritsa's aunt, Princess Helena – was delighted to receive a personal invitation to visit her at Tsarskoe Selo. How could she resist the opportunity to see a woman who was 'busy making history that will count large in the future'?[31] The words were rather more prophetic than Seymour could have imagined.

By January 1917 the Petrograd winter was wearing down everyone at the hospital. Lady Paget's deputy, Lady Sybil Grey*

---

* A 'very charming and sensible woman, worth 17 Lady Muriels', in the view of ARH surgeon Geoffrey Jefferson. 'They are all very fed up with Lady M here, as she has such silly ideas and is always wanting some fresh scheme.' The triumvirate of Grey, Paget and Lady Georgina Buchanan would prove to be volatile, with one nurse describing them as 'formidable, brave, dutiful and decidedly rivalrous'.

(another well-connected aristocrat who was the daughter of a former Governor-General of Canada), was finding the cold hard to endure.[32] 'The sun doesn't shine like in Canada,' she wrote in her diary. 'If people like us rarely get our rooms above 50° what must it be for the poor?' Yet the city could still look spectacular: St Isaac's Cathedral, which could be seen from the hospital, 'lately completely covered with snow is quite beautiful, pillars and all looking like white alabaster, bronze statues against the white, the whole surmounted by a golden dome. The two lovely slender graceful gold spires take every glimpse of sunshine one ever gets.'[33] For all the privations, Grey – like other nurses at the ARH – acknowledged that there was something exhilarating about the place: 'I wouldn't be out of Russia for anything now.' She was certain that the recent murder of Rasputin had been the prelude to something far more dramatic. 'It is curious isn't it that things of immense moment and importance can only be accomplished by intrigue and murder,' she wrote home, referring to the killing of Rasputin by close members of the royal family, Prince Felix Yusupov and Grand Duke Dmitri Pavlovich. 'Can you imagine Tecks, Connaughts etc.* doing the like in England?'[34]

While Seymour was keen to stay and watch events unfold, elsewhere in Petrograd there were British nationals, such as nurses Grant and Moir, who were desperate to get home. British consul Arthur Woodhouse, based in offices on Teatralnaya Ploshchad near the Mariinsky Theatre, had been busy since the outbreak of the war helping repatriate British subjects stranded all over Russia – from the Baltic to the Urals. 'There was a stream of people wanting to go home, which was to turn into a flood, with the refugees from territories overrun by the Germans,' recalled his daughter Ella, noting that many of them were 'those who had lost their jobs in the general upheaval, like the hundreds of governesses who had been employed by wealthy families all over the country … After years abroad, these pathetic women were returning to the old country, many of them with no real homes

---

* These were aristocratic families closely linked to the British royals.

to go back to.' It was a sad sight; 'such numbers of them came in tears that we named them the H.H.H. class (helpless, hopeless, hystericals)'.[35]

Embassy business struggled on, in the face of this mounting workload and predictions of imminent social breakdown. The first day of the Russian New Year, a day of intense cold, had been marked by a glittering reception for eighty members of the diplomatic corps in the ballroom of the Catherine Palace at Tsarskoe Selo. While US ambassador Francis – along with his nine members of staff – had eschewed the formal diplomatic paraphernalia of knee breeches, buckled shoes and plumed hats, choosing to wear a dress coat and wing collar, the rest of the diplomatic community travelled out in full rig, on the 'sumptuous' special train provided.[36] From there they processed in sleighs laden with fur rugs through the swirling snow, past the frosted trees of the park, to the ringing of sleigh bells. All it needed was 'some baying wolves' to make it the classic Russian scenario, thought American diplomat Norman Armour.[37] 'There this enchanted wonderland lay before our eyes,' wrote French diplomat Charles de Chambrun: 'The ornate façade of the palace stood waiting for its guests, illuminated by a thousand lights and surrounded by a semi-circle of whiteness.' Still, he wondered – as did many of his fellow diplomats – 'after all that had already happened, and all that people were saying, and all that was still brewing, how were we going to find the master of all this magnificence?'[38]

'After shedding countless wraps' the assembled diplomats waited until the double doors to the red and gilded reception hall were thrown open by two tall Ethiopian guards in turbans and they were 'ushered into the most imposing room that I had ever seen, lined with endless gold mirrors and countless electric lights,' recalled J. Butler Wright. They were then arranged in groups in order of precedence, behind their 'dean', Sir George Buchanan, and his staff, when Nicholas II, simply dressed in a grey Cossack *cherkeska*, entered the room to greet them. During the course of the two-hour reception he conversed charmingly, with his usual smiles and handshakes, and in perfect English or French. 'He asked me how long I had been here, how I liked it, whether the cold was too severe and promised beautiful weather in the summer,' recalled Wright.[39] Nicholas was a master of such empty pleasantries, but he became visibly uncomfortable when Sir George Buchanan seized the opportunity to impress upon him 'the necessity for a strong offensive on the Eastern Front to relieve pressure on the Western'. Norman Armour thought this inappropriate of the British ambassador on such a purely social occasion: 'I watched as the Emperor twisted his astrakhan cap, displaying increased irritation as Buchanan talked on.'[40]

Otherwise, the Tsar's responses in conversation were mundane, his eyes kindly but vacant. In the opinion of Charles de Chambrun, it was clear that he was 'not taking much interest in the replies'.[41] Ambassador Francis, seduced by the Tsar's superficial charm, failed to notice his air of exhaustion: 'We were all impressed with the cordiality of His Majesty's manner, by his poise and his apparent excellent physical condition, as well as by the promptness of his utterances,' he noted in his diary. To his mind, the Tsar 'gave appearance of having supreme confidence in himself', so much so that he was happy to go off 'for a smoke' with US naval attaché Newton McCully and talk about 'the fall of Porfirio Diaz* in Mexico' – rather than the state of Russia.[42] But Wright, like his companion Armour, had thought Nicholas 'seemed very nervous and his hands fidgeted continually'. French ambassador Paléologue concurred: Nicholas's 'pale thin face' had 'betrayed the nature of his secret thoughts'.[43]

All in all, it was an impressive gathering, of which much was made retrospectively by memoirists, Francis included, as marking 'the glitter and pomp of a dying era'.[44] 'Little did any of us realize that we were witnessing the last public appearance of the last ruler of the mighty Romanoff dynasty,' he later wrote in his memoirs; the Tsar had seemed to have no idea that 'he was standing on a volcano'.[45] Chambrun's overall impression was that

---

* The Mexican president, ousted in a coup in 1911, who had died in exile in 1915.

Nicholas had looked 'more like an automaton needing winding up than an autocrat fit to crush all resistance'.[46] A wider air of exhaustion and foreboding had been detected, too, by Ambassador Paléologue: 'among the whole of the Tsar's brilliant and glittering suite, there was not a face which did not express anxiety'. After enjoying the sherry and sandwiches and tipping the staff 'liberally', the diplomatic corps headed back to Petrograd.[47] A few hours later Wright was drinking vodka and gorging himself on caviar and *zakuski* at Armour's flat on the Liteiny, to celebrate the New Year. In the days that followed, Wright enjoyed trips to the opera to see Tchaikovsky's *Evgeniy Onegin*, the ballet with Meriel Buchanan at a packed Mariinsky Theatre, bridge at Princess Chavchavadze's ('a rather brilliant gathering'), dinner at the Café de Paris and skating at an exclusive private club, where being a member of the diplomatic corps 'was always and everywhere an Open Sesame'.[48] If the Tsar was standing on the edge of the volcano, then so too were most of the diplomatic community, along with the blinkered sybarites of Russian high society.

Eight days after the Tsar's reception an Allied delegation of high-ranking British, French and Italian officials led by Lord Milner – an eminent member of David Lloyd George's War Cabinet – arrived in the city for a major conference aimed at consolidating continuing cooperation with Russia and keeping her in the war. Although the expatriate community looked forward to the inevitable junketing that such a visit would generate, it came at a time of serious industrial unrest. For on the very day the mission arrived in the capital, 150,000 workers went on strike and marched in commemoration of the massacre of peaceful protesters, killed that same day, twelve years previously. Bloody Sunday 1905 was an ever-present memory for the oppressed working classes of Petrograd, as tension continued to build in the city.

Tsarist officialdom, however, was preoccupied with the more immediate crisis in Petrograd's desperate accommodation shortage, which the arrival of the mission had provoked. Guests on the ground floor of the already overcrowded Hotel d'Europe had their rooms commandeered for the duration, but found there was '*nowhere* to go and no rooms to be had at any price'.[49] A last-ditch orgy of official parties beckoned over the next three weeks, prompting a brief lifting of spirits in the weary capital. 'For a short time one could almost have imagined oneself back in pre-war St Petersburg,' recalled Meriel Buchanan, who made the most of the glittering social whirl:

> A sudden gaiety swept over the town. Court carriages with beautifully groomed horses and the crimson and gold of the Imperial liveries passed up and down the streets. An endless stream of motors stood at all hours of the day before the Hotel d'Europe, where the Missions had been lodged. Dinners and dances took place every night; the big royal box at the ballet was filled with French, English and Italian uniforms.[50]

Nicholas II once again put on his gracious public face for a gala dinner at Tsarskoe Selo, with Sir George Buchanan sitting at his right hand. The gathered delegates joined in the charade of sharing 'meaningless remarks about the Alliance, war and victory'. Nicholas was, as always, 'vague' in conversation and, after a succession of dutiful and dull exchanges, withdrew with a smile.[51] The reclusive Empress had, as usual, been absent. It was left to the leading ladies of the Petrograd aristocracy, in the guise of Grand Duchess Vladimir and Countess Nostitz (an American adventuress who had married into the aristocracy)*, to organise some of the other lavish entertainments laid on for the mission, with Nostitz claiming that she had been chosen to host the reception on 6 February at her home because 'the Empress was

---

* Her real name was Lillie (Madeleine) Bouton. Daughter of a grain elevator worker from Iowa and sometime actress in American repertory theatre and on the Continent, she had charmed the extremely wealthy Count Grigory Nostitz, a military attaché at the Russian embassy in Paris, into marrying her; he was the second of three aristocratic husbands.

too ill to receive at the Palace'. It would leave an abiding impression on her:

> The night of that last splendid reception is stamped forever on my memory. I have only to close my eyes to see again our rose and gilt salon with its magnificent old family portraits, its exquisite tapestries, crowded with that brilliant assembly of guests. All the Court, the cream of Petrograd society, three hundred of its greatest names, all the Diplomatic Corps and their wives, the members of the Delegation – Lord Milner, one of England's foremost Ministers, Lord Brooke, Sir Henry Wilson, Lord Clive, Lord Revelstoke, Sir George Clerk, General de Castelnau, France's hero, Sociologue, the Italian delegate, Gaston Doumergue, they were all there that night.[52]

When the visit came to an end, few felt it had achieved anything of political significance. Robert Bruce Lockhart had been far from impressed with the 'interminable round of festivity', later observing that 'rarely in the history of great wars can so many important ministers and generals have left their respective countries on so useless an errand'. Ambassador Paléologue felt likewise: the conference had dragged on for three weeks 'to no purpose', and 'no practical result ha[d] emerged from all the diplomatic verbiage'. What point was there, he asked, in the Allies sending Russia huge consignments of materiel – 'guns, machine-guns, shells and aeroplanes' – when she had 'neither the means of getting them to the front nor the will to take advantage of them?'[53]

Lord Milner had also confided that he thought the trip a waste of time, having realised 'the inefficiency of the Russians' at getting anything done, and had decided that Russia was doomed – at home, and at the front. It was, however, 'the general consensus of informed opinion, both Allied and Russian', that 'there will be no revolution until after the war'.[54] Maurice Paléologue, though, saw it differently. As the French delegates prepared to return home, he gave them a message to take to the President in Paris: 'A revolution crisis is at hand in Russia ... Every day the Russian nation is more indifferent towards the war and the spirit of anarchy is spreading among all classes and even in the army.' The October strikes in the Vyborg Side had, in Paléologue's view, been 'very significant'; for when violence had broken out between strikers and the police, the 181st Regiment – called on to assist the police – had actually turned on them. A division of Cossacks had had to be 'hastily called in to bring the mutineers to their senses'. If there were to be an uprising, Paléologue warned, 'the authorities cannot count on the army'. And he went even further: the Allies must also quietly prepare for the likely 'defection of our ally' – out of the war and, with it, its role in the defence of the Eastern Front.[55] Sir George Buchanan was now so consumed by a mounting sense of imminent disaster that he reported to the British Foreign Office in London that 'Russia will not, in my opinion, be able to face a fourth winter campaign if the present situation is indefinitely prolonged.' Trouble, 'if it comes, will be due to economic rather than political causes'. And it would begin 'not with the workmen in the factories, but with the crowds waiting in the cold and the snow outside the provision shops'.[56]

By February the daily consignment of flour to Petrograd had dropped to just twenty-one wagonloads, instead of the normal 120 needed. What white bread there was 'had become greyer and greyer until it was uneatable', due to excessive adulteration. Official mismanagement, corruption and wastage of supplies were prodigious, made worse by a crippled rail network that was unable to transport food efficiently from the provinces – where it was still plentiful – to the cities that most needed it. People were incensed to discover that, due to the hikes in the price of oats and hay, much of the black bread – the staple diet of the poor – was being fed to the capital's 80,000 horses to keep them alive: 'every horse was eating up the black bread allowance of ten men'.[57] Sugar was now so scarce that many of the *patisseries* and confectionary shops had had to close. Word spread like wildfire about food going to waste, of 'millions of pounds of cheap Siberian beef' being left to rot in railway sidings:

Few of the munition-workers, whose wives or children spent more than half their time in the queue before a bread-shop, had not heard of the 'fish graveyards' of Astrakhan, where thousands of tons of the spoiled harvest of the Caspian were buried; and all classes had heard of the 'saccharine rivers' which travellers had seen flowing from leaky sugar warehouses in the great beet-growing districts of South Russia and Podolia.[58]

'While we put jam in our tea and work-people drank it unsweetened,' wrote US official Philip Chadbourn, inspecting internment camps for Germans in Russia, 'everyone knew that the country was full of grain, and that the provincial towns were full of flour'.[59] On 19 January an official announcement of imminent bread rationing – as little as one pound per person a day – sparked panic buying. People were now standing so long in line at the bakers' shops that they were suffering from hypothermia. If they were lucky enough to get any, they would hurry off, 'hugging close to themselves the warm piece of bread they had bought, in a vain attempt to receive from it a little heat'.[60]

Even the foreigners were suffering, albeit relatively speaking. 'We are so short of everything here now, that ham or bacon is more acceptable than a bouquet of orchids,' complained J. Butler Wright at the US embassy, adding that 'whisky is in the same category'. He was overjoyed when a courier arrived from Washington with twenty-seven pouches of mail, as well as 'bacon, Listerine, whiskey, dioxygen,* marmalade, papers, etc etc'.[61] Trying to keep warm in his hotel room, photographer Donald Thompson could still get coffee, 'but it's coffee only in name and the bread is not bread at all'. He was, he admitted, 'beginning to feel the pangs of hunger – even in the Astoria Hotel'.[62]

Hunger was made worse by the continuing sub-zero temperatures affecting the supply of fuel to the city by rail. Rowing boats on the Neva were chopped up for firewood, and even more

---

* Dioxygen was apparently used as a tooth-whitener at this time.

desperate measures were resorted to: 'at dead of night' people slunk into the nearest cemetery 'to fill whole sacks with the wooden crosses from the graves of poor folk' and take them home for their fires.[63]

Once more there was a wave of strikes. This time, the tsarist police were taking no chances. On Minister of the Interior Protopopov's orders, machine guns were being secretly mounted on the roofs of all the city's major buildings, particularly around the main thoroughfare, the Nevsky. J. Butler Wright noted the darkening mood on 9 February:

The Cossacks are again patrolling the city on account of threatened strikes – for the *women* are beginning to rebel at standing in bread lines from 5.00 A.M. for shops that open at 10:00 A.M., and that in weather twenty-five degrees below zero.[64]

He had it on reliable information that 'the day set for the opening of the Duma will be the day for a socialist outbreak'. In anticipation of this, 14,000 Cossacks had been brought in to Petrograd to bolster army reserves.[65]* They were patrolling the streets of Petrograd on 14 February when the Duma reopened after its Christmas recess, but the predicted trouble never came. Proceedings at a densely crowded Tauride Palace were carried off in an atmosphere of despondency rather than confrontation. Thinking the crisis over for now and that it was safe to 'take a short holiday', an exhausted Sir George Buchanan and his wife set off for a much-needed ten-day rest at the dacha of a friend in the British colony located on the little island of Varpasaari in Finland.[66]

---

* Most of the army units now in Petrograd were reservists, the cream of the regular army having gone to the front, leaving largely inexperienced conscripts in the city, some of whom were industrial strikers, forced into the army as punishment.

2

'No Place for an Innocent Boy from Kansas'

On Saturday 18 February 1917 a dispute over the sacking of workers at the vast Putilov munitions works on the south side of the city sparked a walk-out in the gun-carriage shop. Soon the rest of the workforce followed and the management enforced a lockout. Tens of thousands of laid-off workers were milling on the streets, and the pitiful queues at the bakers' shops were getting ever longer. Beyond their hotel windows, Florence Harper and Donald Thompson could see the people lining up overnight, and they went out onto the bitterly cold streets, looking for a story. Billboards everywhere were pasted over with proclamations from the military police 'imploring the people not to make any demonstrations or cause disorders that might halt the manufacture of munitions or paralyze the industries of the city'.[1] Thompson recalled how the people 'tore them down the minute they were posted and spat on them'. Some of the shops on Bolshaya Morskaya near their hotel were already boarding up their windows. The two Americans knew that trouble was coming. 'In fact, I was so sure of it,' Florence Harper later wrote, 'that I wandered around the town, up and down the Nevsky, watching and waiting for it as I would for a circus parade.' Thompson was delighted. He had brought his favourite Graflex cameras made by the Eastman Company of New York and had police permits to 'photograph any place in Petrograd'. 'If there's a revolution coming … I am in luck,' he crowed.[2]

Political agitators – Socialist Revolutionaries, Bolsheviks, Mensheviks, anarchists – were now out in force among the striking Putilov workers and in other factories across the river in the Vyborg and Petrograd Sides, all of them 'preaching a general strike as a protest against the government, food-shortage and war'.[3] Over dinner with Maurice Paléologue, Grand Duchess Vladimir had told him that she expected 'the most dire catastrophes', if Nicholas continued to resist the need for political change. 'If salvation does not come from above,' she warned, 'there will be revolution from below.'[4]

Paléologue had lately been reading the *Philosophical Letters* of Petr Chaadaev, the Russian philosopher exiled to Siberia in 1836 for his supposedly seditious writings. Chaadaev had observed that 'The Russians are one of those nations which seem to exist only to give humanity terrible lessons.' Paléologue felt that the country was once again living out that prediction. The brief 'stimulant' of the Allied mission had already evaporated. 'The artillery, war-factory and supply and transport departments have fallen back into their old casual and leisurely ways,' he noted despairingly. The mission's attempts to galvanise the Russian war effort had been met with the 'same dead weight of inactivity and indifference, as before'.[5] The only thing that cheered him was the prospect of music and dancing at a 'large and glittering party' to be held at Princess Radziwill's on the coming Sunday, the 26th. But he had to admit it was 'a curious time to arrange a party', and a dangerous time, too, for the Emperor to have left the capital and gone back to army HQ five hundred miles away – under the false reassurance, from his Minister of the Interior, Protopopov, that the situation was under control.[6]

For fully three weeks the average daily temperature had been -13.44 degrees Centigrade and there had been heavy falls of snow.[7]* Walking on the Liteiny Prospekt on the morning of 22 February, Paléologue was struck by 'the sinister expression on

---

* Sources conflict on the correct temperature, with many giving it as much lower than it really was. See endnote.

the faces of the poor folk' who had been standing wearily all night waiting for bread. The public mood was shifting from stoicism to anger; many women were spending forty hours or more a week like this and, in indignation, some of them had thrown stones at the bakers' windows that day. Others had joined in and some looting had taken place. Cossack patrols were out in force, 'an evident intimation to the city to keep quiet', and there were also a lot more soldiers on the streets. 'The age of the new recruits', as J. Butler Wright noted, was 'younger than ever before'.[8]

Donald Thompson left the Astoria that morning to buy a new pair for boots for his Russian interpreter, Boris – a young wounded soldier, now out of hospital, whom he had requested be assigned to him, as Boris spoke very good English. One of the bakeries near the Astoria was under police guard, after the queues had smashed its windows to try and get at the bread. A besieged milk shop nearby had just put out a sign saying, 'No more milk'. 'If you could see these bread lines and see the looks upon the faces of these people as you pass,' he wrote to his wife, 'you would hardly believe that this is the Twentieth Century.'[9] He was ashamed, he told her, to have to walk past such people while wearing his 'heavy fur coat', while they stood in the cold 'almost in rags'. Groups of striking workers from across the river had made their way into the city, prompting some of the shopkeepers on the Nevsky to close their premises. People on the streets were 'nervous, jumpy, starting at shadows, waiting for they knew not what'.[10]

Although the temperature was still -9 degrees, Thursday 23rd dawned gloriously sunny. When he went out that morning Thompson noticed that 'dozens of machine-guns' had been mounted on the tops of buildings overnight. Boris, who had been out on a night-time recce on Thompson's behalf, had come back assuring him that 'we are going to have a revolution in Russia'.[11] Thompson went to the telegraph office to send his wife a message, but the woman on duty told him not to waste his money – 'nothing was allowed to go out'. Later, with Florence Harper, he was walking near the British embassy and saw a crowd of women gathering at the Field of Mars, the big parade ground located behind it; soon these women were joined by a group of work-men, and then 'almost as if by magic hundreds and hundreds of students came into view'.[12]

It was International Women's Day, an important date in the socialist calendar, established in 1910 by the German Social Demo-crat Clara Zetkin to promote equal rights for women, and the embattled working women of Petrograd intended that their voices should be heard. Hundreds of them – peasants, factory workers, students, nurses, teachers, wives whose husbands were at the front, and even a few ladies from the upper classes – came out onto the streets. Although some carried banners with traditional suf-frage slogans, such as 'Hail, women fighters for freedom' and 'A place for women in the Constituent Assembly', others bore impro-vised placards referring to the food crisis: 'Increase rations for soldiers' families', or even more openly revolutionary calls for an end to the war – and the monarchy. But food was, fundamentally, what they all called out for that day: 'There is no bread,' they shouted as they marched, 'our husbands have no work.'[13]

As columns of women converged on Nevsky and Liteiny Prospekts, more militant female textile workers at five of the major manufacturers on the Vyborg Side had gone on strike that morning. They had then descended on the major metalworks and munitions factories – shouting, banging on doors and pelting the windows with snowballs – to get the men, including those at the crucially important state Arsenal, to come out in sympathy.* By midday 50,000 workers across the river had walked out. Some of them went straight home, but others marched to the Liteiny Bridge to cross over to the Nevsky Prospekt and swell the ranks of the Women's Day marchers, only to encounter police cordons on the bridge barring their way. The more determined among them had scrambled down onto the frozen river and made their way across the ice instead; others managed to get through the

---

* The munitions workers were well paid and, as they were key workers, they were also receiving larger bread rations, so they were therefore more reluctant to come out on strike.

police block at the Troitsky Bridge from the Petrograd Side, only to be forced back by police when they crossed the Neva.

On the Field of Mars, Harper and Thompson watched as several men and women were raised up on the shoulders of others, shouting, 'Let's stop talking and act.' A few of the women began singing the Marseillaise. 'It was a queer Russian version that one couldn't quite recognize at first,' recalled Harper. 'I have heard the "Marseillaise" sung many times, but that day for the first time I heard it sung as it should be.' This was because, she asserted, 'the people there were of the same classes and were singing it for the same reason as the French who first sang it over a hundred years ago.'[14] As the crowd moved off, heading for the Nevsky, 'a tram came swinging round the corner'. They forced it to stop, took the control handle and 'threw it away in a snowbank'. The same happened to a second, third and fourth tram, 'until the blocked cars extended all the way along the Sadovaya to the Nevsky Prospekt'.[15] One tram full of wounded soldiers in the care of nurses even joined in, as the crowd, now numbering about five hundred, surged forward, still singing the Marseillaise, the women holding boldly to the centre of the Nevsky as the men took to the pavements.

Thompson and Harper found themselves carried along with the tide. Every policeman they passed tried to stop the marchers, but the women just kept on forging ahead, shouting, laughing and singing.[16] Walking at the head of the column, Thompson saw a man next to him tie a red flag onto a cane and start waving it in the air. He decided that such a conspicuous position at the head of the marchers was 'no place for an innocent boy from Kansas'.[17] 'Bullets had a way of hitting innocent bystanders,' he told Harper, 'so let's beat it, while the going is good.'

That day, in response to increasing tension in the city, the commandant of the Petrograd garrison, General Sergey Khabalov, had had posters pasted on walls at every street corner, reassuring the public that 'There should be no shortage in bread for sale': if stocks were low in some bakeries, this was because people were buying more than they needed and hoarding it. 'There is sufficient rye flour in Petrograd,' the proclamation insisted. 'The delivery of this flour continues without interruption.'[18] It was clear that the government had run out of excuses for the bread crisis – lack of fuel, heavy snow, rolling stock commandeered for military purposes, shortage of labour – and the people would not be fobbed off any longer. Hunger was rife, fierce and implacable in half a million empty bellies across the working-class factory districts. *Times* correspondent Robert Wilton was appalled at official dilatoriness in dealing with the shortages: 'Here was a patent confession of laxity. Whom was it expected to satisfy? The Socialists who had already made up their minds for revolution, or the dissatisfied "man in the street" who did not want revolution, but pined for relief from an incapable Government?'[19] An urgent conference of ministers was being held at the Duma that day, the people were told, to settle the food crisis and organise the revictualling of Petrograd. But by now the crowds were convinced that the bakers were deliberately withholding bread from them.

As the day went on, the ranks of women marchers in and around the Nevsky swelled to around 90,000. 'The singing by this time had become a deep roar,' recalled Thompson, 'terrifying, but at the same time fascinating.' There was 'fearful excitement everywhere'.[20] Once more the Cossacks 'appeared as if by magic', as J. Butler Wright observed, their long lances glancing in the sunshine. Thompson watched them time and again attempt to scatter the columns of marching women by charging them at a gallop, brandishing their *nagaikas* (short whips), but the women merely regrouped, cheering the Cossacks wildly each time they charged.[21] When one woman stumbled and fell in front of them, they jumped their horses right over her. People were surprised: these Cossacks weren't the 'fierce guardsmen of Tsardom whom the crowds had seen at work in 1905', when hundreds of protesters had been killed in the Bloody Sunday protest. This time they were quite 'amiable', playful even; they seemed eager to capitulate to the mood of the people, and took their hats off and 'waved them to the crowd' as they moved them on.[22] It turned out that many of the Cossacks were reserves, their reticence about driving the people back compounded by the difficulty some of them had in handling their horses, which were unused to crowds.[23] So long as they only asked for bread, the Cossacks told the marchers, they would not be on the receiving end of gunfire. There were, inevitably, many agents provocateurs in their midst, eager to turn the protest into a violent one, but for the most part the crowd remained 'good tempered', as Arthur Ransome noted in that day's despatch to the *Daily News*. He hoped there would be no serious conflict. 'The general character of excitement,' he concluded was, for now, 'vague and artificial' and without political focus.[24]

And so it went on, until six in the evening. As the mob surged to the constant drumbeat calls for *khleb* (bread), the Cossacks charged and scattered people in all directions, 'but there was no real trouble'. The police had rounded up anyone who had attempted to stop and give speeches, but protesters had otherwise walked the streets with their red flags all day long and, much to Thompson's surprise, had not been fired on. But he knew this was not the end of it: 'I smell trouble,' he wrote to his wife that evening, 'and thank God I am here to get the photographs of it.'[25]

It was left to the tsarist police to finally disperse the crowds, who had largely gone home by 7.00 p.m. as the cold of evening drew in. But public antipathy and violence towards the police was growing, in particular towards the special mounted police on their black stallions, whom people despised as *faraony*, 'pharaohs' – that is, tyrants (an allusion to the 'tall shaving-brush busbies of black horsehair' that they wore). 'Their appearance wiped the smile away,' noticed Arno Dosch-Fleurot, 'and when they began really roughing the crowd with their sabres drawn', he heard 'the first murmuring of the snarl which only an infuriated mob can produce'.[26]

Across the river, in the industrial quarters, acts of sporadic violence had erupted throughout the day. On the Petrograd Side at Filippov's large bakery – a Moscow franchise that supplied many of the bakers in the city daily by rail – the *babushki* in the bread line had finally lost patience after standing in the cold for hours, only to be told there would be no bread that day.[27] They had broken in the front door and raided the place; it was later said that they had 'found quantities of black bread in the rear storerooms'. Grocery stores nearby had had their windows smashed, too; in another bakery that was stormed, the *babushki* who had led the assault found white bread rolls 'meant for the restaurants'. After breaking the bakery's windows, they took the rolls and sold them off for a quarter of the price to those desperate for bread.[28]

That evening Harper and Thompson ventured across the Troitsky Bridge to find out what was going on in the industrial districts. They found the street in some places 'jammed with excited men and women' and stayed until 11.00 p.m., when Thompson noticed that rather too many people were eyeing Harper's expensive seal coat. Boris, their translator, advised a speedy exit; he'd overheard some of the women say that 'she ought to have her face cut to pieces'. 'Look how she is dressed! Yes, she gets bread but we get nothing.'[29] The women clearly had mistaken Harper for a rich Russian. Hurrying back to the Astoria at midnight, the two journalists were stopped several times by police and had their papers checked. They couldn't help noticing that a 'great many troops were patrolling the city' – for that day a disorganised and elemental force had finally been let loose on Petrograd. The flame of revolution had been lit among the hungry marchers on the Nevsky and the strikers across the river. Throughout the night strike-committees in the Petrograd and Vyborg Sides were plotting to seize the moment. Revolution – 'so long talked of, dreaded, fought against, planned for, longed for, died for' – had come at last, 'like a thief in the night, none expecting it, none recognizing it'.[30]

Overnight the levels of disquiet in Petrograd rose considerably, as rumours spread about the introduction of a 'bread ticket system'. Resentment was further fuelled by the fact that the bread was being released for sale at times when people were at work and could not go out to queue to buy it. On Friday 24 February things took an inevitable, violent turn: more bakers' shops were attacked and destroyed, and as Arthur Ransome reported to the *Daily News*, such was the desperation for food now that people even 'seized bread from those who had succeeded in buying it'.[31]

It was another bright and sunny morning, and a five-degree rise in the temperature to -4.5 degrees had encouraged huge crowds to come out of doors and gather again on the Nevsky.[32] Anticipating an escalation in protests, General Khabalov had posted further proclamations overnight announcing that 'all gatherings on the streets are absolutely forbidden' and warning that he had commanded his troops 'to use their arms freely and to stop at nothing in maintaining order'.[33] An American working at the consulate in the Singer Building heard people talking of seeing 'armoured street cars mounted with searchlights' patrolling the city for several nights now, with 'many machine guns sticking out of the portholes'. 'All the police stations are full of machine guns, with soldiers dressed as policemen to handle them,' he was told. 'Rot,' said someone else, 'the soldier-boys won't shoot at their own people.'[34]

The seething sense of resentment made itself felt especially on the few overcrowded trams that were still running. Many were already out of commission and stood idle and empty, with 'no one to repair them and no new ones'; others had been derailed and even overturned by the crowds.[35] Everyone on the streets that morning seemed 'sure now of having a spectacle', as Arno Dosch-Fleurot noted. He was out among them near the Kazan Cathedral. Green student caps were conspicuous everywhere, and one of the students told him that 'the universities had gone on strike in sympathy with the bread demonstration'.[36] The shops were open, however, and the city still had 'a certain effervescence', with most people on foot and less willing to move on, when ordered by the police, than they had been the previous day.[37]

People were crossing the Neva all morning from the Vyborg and Petrograd Sides, where a succession of excited factory meetings had been held. Most of the workers there had gone on strike and had been urged to arm themselves with 'bolts, screws, rocks', even lumps of ice, and go out and 'start smashing the first shops you find'.[38] En route to the Liteiny Bridge, strikers had once more targeted the bakeries; scuffles had broken out, followed by looting. The route across the bridge was again blocked by soldiers and Cossacks, though the latter refused to charge the strikers when ordered to do so. Once again the strikers resorted to the ice – around five thousand of them – to cross to the city centre.[39] From the windows of their Chancellery, French diplomats Louis de Robien and Charles de Chambrun saw them making their way over the Neva 'like a chain of black ants' 'in Indian file', as they weaved in and out of 'conglomerated blocks of ice and thick snow'. The Cossacks on the other side watched them, galloping up and down the embankment, 'very picturesque on their little horses' and brandishing lances and carbines; but they did not venture on to the ice to stop the strikers.[40]

By midday there were about 36,800 people marching on the streets of central Petrograd.[41] The trams had come to a standstill and, with the roads impassable, the *izvozchiki* (*droshky* drivers) had given up and taken their horses home. The crowds continued to push and shove their way forward, squeezing past and even under the bellies of the Cossacks' horses when they tried to bar their way. French resident Amélie de Néry sensed a difference between these protesters and the 'elated and mystical' ones of 1905, whose marching had had the air of a religious ceremonial. These 1917 crowds were realists, she noted. 'Two years of war had hardened them far more than a century of tranquillity and peace could have done.'[42] As they progressed, the crowds were 'met by a good deal of bullying and harrying by police and troops' – again without the use of lethal weapons.'[43] The Cossack squadrons caracoling over the snow on their wiry little horses continued to surprise with their restraint, even as more and more red flags appeared among the columns of marchers. Whenever they halted, 'the men and women gathered about them and invited them to join them'. 'You're ours,' they shouted at them, as the Cossacks smiled and parted to let them through. 'You are not going to fire on us, Brothers! We only want bread!' *Times* reporter Robert Wilton heard them say to the armed troops they encountered. 'No, we are hungry like yourselves,' replied the Cossacks.[44]

Bert Hall, a US aviator attached to the Russian Air Service, was in Petrograd that day and, like Thompson and Harper, his first experience of Russia was proving a baptism of fire. He wrote in his diary of 'endless mobs of people marching along singing wild songs, throwing bricks into street cars'. He saw workmen carrying placards not just calling for bread, but saying 'Give us land!' and 'Save our souls!', and at the end of one procession 'a little girl carrying a tiny banner' on which was written 'Feed your children!' It was, he recalled, 'the most pathetic thing I ever saw in my life'. Why didn't the Russians just 'go ahead and have a revolution and get it over?' he said to his Russian companion. Ah, but 'God still loves the Tsar,' he was told; 'it would be a misfortune to revolt against a ruler who stood in well with God'. Hall was outraged:

> The common people are hungry; they have been hungry too for a long while. Christ, why doesn't the Tsar do something about it! What a chance for some wise American organizer! Think of it! All of Russia might go to pot for the want of a little wise management.[45]

As the crowds moved up and down the Nevsky all day, people living along it threw open their windows to watch and cheer. The British and Canadian staff at the Anglo-Russian Hospital, as well as their patients, had a ringside view of events from the second-floor windows of their wards. The nurses had been given orders on the 22nd 'to remain indoors and not to go out on the streets, except to the hospital and back'.[46] The ARH had been 'full of soldiers ready for any emergency' – thirty men from the Semenovsky Guards regiment had been deployed there to guard them, with three on the front door with fixed bayonets. The staff had been told to prepare to evacuate the premises at very short notice. But this rapidly proved impossible, because of the surge of people coming down the Nevsky.[47] 'They just hurled past,' recalled Canadian nurse Dorothy Cotton, 'and the Cossacks riding in the opposite direction to them rode right into them and scattered them.' A few stray casualties were brought to the hospital for treatment – shot by policemen disguised as soldiers, so it was claimed.[48]

Florence Harper and Donald Thompson had been out on the streets since early that morning, 'trail[ing] the mobs', though for most of the time they were 'pushed up and down the Nevsky' willy-nilly, running, sliding in the snow and often hugging the sides of buildings so as not to get trampled.[49] They ended up being virtually carried down to the Kazan Cathedral, a traditional rallying point, where many of the columns of demonstrators had already gathered in the square that fronted it. Some knelt down, bared their heads and prayed, and others gathered in small groups around speakers.[50] The reticence of the Cossacks to break up the crowds persisted, so much so that 'the Prefect of Police' – so Lady Sybil Grey was told – had driven up to the cathedral in his motor car and had 'ordered the officer commanding a patrol of Cossacks to charge the people with drawn swords'. The officer had refused: 'Sir, I cannot give such an order, for the people are only asking for bread.' On hearing this, the crowd had cheered loudly 'and were cheered in return by the Cossacks'.[51] Thompson and Harper noted this response, too. There was no violence, 'it was a very good-natured mob'. Except in one respect: they had seen a secret policeman 'trying to take a picture' of someone addressing the crowd. He was quickly spotted and set upon, his camera smashed; they would have killed him, had he not been rescued by a mounted *faraon*. Thompson had been taking photographs himself, 'using my small camera', but was 'careful not to attract attention'. He had noticed how 'ugly' some of the police were getting and that many of them were dressed as soldiers or Cossacks.[52]

At four in the afternoon Harper and Thompson nearly got themselves trampled outside the Anglo-Russian Hospital on their way back up the Nevsky. The Cossacks had come riding down, 'laughing and chaffing with the mob' and giving them 'a poke with their lances' if they did not move fast enough. They were riding abreast in tight formation, such that the two journalists couldn't squeeze by and had to rush into the storm-door of the hospital, but Harper had still received 'a most awful jab with the butt of a lance' as a Cossack rode past. He was just a boy of about eighteen, she noticed; he told her to move on, but she refused and so he jabbed her again. 'That was enough,' she recalled; she 'flew across the bridge and back down the Nevsky', with Thompson in tow.[53]

By 8.00 p.m. on Friday most of the demonstrators in central Petrograd had gone home, vowing to return the following morning. This second day of mass demonstrations had seen more workers out on strike than at any other time during the war; and their activity was now becoming violent, turning in particular on the police and mounted *faraony*. In response, General Khabalov had ensured that many more machine-gun placements were set up in the attics of mansions, hotels, shops, clock and bell towers up and down the Nevsky, and on the roofs of railway stations. He also had infantry and machine gunners in reserve and a huge stockpile of rifles, revolvers and ammunition, which, although designated for the front, had been retained for use in Petrograd, should the need arise, and 'stored in the various police stations'.[54]

The foreign news correspondents in Petrograd caught up in these events, and now realising their growing significance, were all frustratingly hampered by one thing: they could not get the truth of the situation out to their papers in the UK, the US and elsewhere, because of the strict tsarist censorship being applied to all telegraph messages sent from the city. Arno Dosch-Fleurot had written a daily cable about the 'bread-riots' and had 'gone with it to the young officer in charge of the censorship'. And every day the response had been the same: the man had 'offered me tea but no hope of getting the news out'. When he finally wrote a positive piece 'about the enthusiasm of the populace for the Cossacks', his despatch was allowed through.[55] For some time Robert Wilton of *The Times* had been having similar difficulties, reduced to making only vague allusions to the growing discontent in the capital, 'owing to the disorganization of the food supplies'. Today, Friday, he had written a despatch about the 'prolonged debates' going on in the Duma on how to combat the food crisis, confirming that meanwhile the behaviour of the demonstrators had on the whole been 'devoid of a seditious or vindictive character'. 'Bread supplies assured,' he telegraphed, quoting General Khabalov – a positive spin on an escalating situation, written in order to get his report past the censors.[56] The word 'revolution' was not mentioned.*

Throughout the night of the 24th there were occasional volleys of firing; and yet, astonishingly, the social life of the city continued. The Alexandrinsky Theatre was packed that evening for a performance of Gogol's *The Government Inspector.* Indeed, the audience had been 'in a lively humour at this satire on the political weaknesses of the mid-nineteenth century'. Few seemed willing to believe that a 'greater drama was at that moment unfolding in real life throughout the capital'.[57] Leighton Rogers and several colleagues from the National City Bank had headed out for supper at the Café de la Grave, located in the basement of a building on the Nevsky. En route they had their first experience of the Cossacks, a troop of whom came hurtling at them, 'galloping at full tilt down the sidewalk ... shouting like mad, carbines bouncing on their backs, sabres flopping at the horses' sides, and mean looking steel lances flourishing'. Rogers and his party took one look and ran for their lives. After dining they headed home in the dark; the atmosphere of the city was 'like a taut wire'. Troops of mounted Cossacks were still out in force, lined up all the way down the Nevsky, 'compelling pedestrians to walk up the middle of the street between a double row of horses and steel points'. 'It was hardly a pleasant sensation,' Rogers recalled. 'All the way I could feel myself wriggling on one of

---

* Nor was it till after the Tsar's abdication on 3 March, when the tsarist censorship collapsed and proper reporting could begin, meaning that the earliest reports out of Russia were not published in the West until around 16 March (NS).

59

those lances like a worm on a hook.' 'I'll never fish with live bait again,' he resolved.[58]

In search of a story, Arno Dosch-Fleurot had made 'a long tour' that afternoon through the Vyborg Side and had found it 'thickly policed by infantrymen'. There were a few trams still running, 'but otherwise the district was ominously silent'. The only people on the streets had been those in the familiar bread lines and groups of workers on corners, whose 'silent gravity' struck Fleurot as 'something to reckon with'. Thompson noticed them too when, after dinner at Donon's, he ventured into the outlying areas until 3.00 a.m.[59] Over at the French embassy, First Secretary Charles de Chambrun wrote to his wife, pondering the news he had just heard that a general strike had been declared for the following day. More marches, more protests were coming. But what could a mob 'without alcohol, without a leader and without a clear objective achieve?' he wondered. As night fell, Petrograd waited expectantly.[60]

3

'Like a Bank Holiday with Thunder in the Air'

'Oh this interminable Russian winter with its white roofs for so many long months and its slippery roads,' French resident Louise Patouillet wrote ruefully in her diary, by now long accustomed to the kind of low grey sky that greeted the city with a new fall of snow on Saturday 25 February.[1] Leighton Rogers, in contrast, struck an excited note in his own journal: 'What a day! The general strike is on, all right, and trouble has begun.' That morning, on their way to the bank, he and his colleagues had 'found the streets thick with police, both a-foot and mounted; no factories working, and the Nevsky a long line of closed shops, with here and there a boarded up door or window.' He had heard rumours that the first person had been killed the previous night when trying to break into a bread shop; the people on the streets seemed on the lookout for excitement, 'like a crowd at a great country fair', but Rogers 'hated to think of what one shot would do.'[2]

Had he known the extent to which the strikers were now arming themselves for an inevitable street fight with the police, Rogers might have been even more alarmed. Across the city, embassies and legations were being warned by telephone not to allow their staff to go out. Yet that day the somewhat foolhardy Rogers had set off from the National City Bank with 'nine million roubles worth of short term Treasury Notes' to get them 'stowed away' in a safe-deposit vault at the Volga-Kama Bank ahead of Sunday closing. He put the notes – the equivalent of $3 million – in his jacket pocket and headed off from the bank, which was housed in the former Turkish embassy on Palace Embankment. But the streets were so choked with crowds that he had been forced to go the long way round. Outside the Mikhailovsky Theatre he stopped for a while to study the poster for the latest French season; the next thing he knew, a colleague from the bank came running after him shouting, 'Where the hell have you been?? … We've been phoning all over the city for you!' When they had called the Volga-Kama Bank they had discovered Rogers hadn't yet arrived; they were worried that something had happened to him, for they had been tipped off 'that a revolution ha[d] started'.[3]

Violent protest was certainly the intention of the workers over in the factory districts that morning, as they gathered for a huge march on the city. This time they had ensured that they wore plenty of padding under their thick coats, in order to ward off blows from the lead-tipped *nagaiki* used by the *faraony*. Some even crafted metal plates to wear under their hats, to protect them from blows, and filled their pockets with whatever metal projectiles and weapons they could lay hands on in their factories.[4] At noon the crowds began their descent on the Nevsky, but the *faraony* were ready for them at the Liteiny Bridge. As the crowd surged forward to try and cross it, the *faraony* charged them; but though the crowd parted to let them through, it quickly closed once again in a pincer movement around the commanding officer, pulling him from his horse. Someone grabbed the officer's revolver and shot him dead, while another beat at him in a rage with a piece of wood.[5] It was the first defining act of violence against the police that day.

On the south side of Petrograd the powerful Putilov workforce had joined the strike and, as the day went on, the strike spread inexorably across the city, bringing out everyone, from shop workers to waitresses, to cooks and maids and cab drivers; key workers in the supply of the city's electricity, gas and water and the tram drivers were also out in force. A few bread shops had been open, but by early afternoon were forced to close, and striking postal workers and printers had ensured that there were no mail deliveries and no newspapers. The strikers' numbers were swelled by at least 15,000 striking students, as fifteen different columns of marchers converged on the Nevsky. But no one knows exactly how many strikers surged through the streets of Petrograd that day – official figures vary from 240,000 to 305,000.[6]

The impromptu bread protests of two days ago had now expanded into a political movement, coloured by more and more acts of violence and looting. On the Liteiny, Amélie de Néry saw a young boy who had helped to loot a small Jewish shop stand there offering six dozen stolen mother-of-pearl buttons for a ruble. An insignificant act of theft, perhaps, but for de Néry it signalled a worrying change in public attitudes brought on by the protests – a lack of distinction between 'yours' and 'mine'. Perhaps tomorrow, she wondered, 'a more serious collapse in moral values would be unleashed'.[7] For the time being, though, there was still no outward sign of a systematic organised revolt; the movement remained inchoate, leaderless. 'Is it a riot? Is it a revolution?' asked Claude Anet, Petrograd correspondent of *Le Petit Parisien*, who – like the other foreign journalists in town – had had no luck in telegraphing the news back to his paper in Paris.[8]

Bitter cold prevailed once more, but with all the trams stopped and many shops closed there was little traffic on the streets, enabling the crowds to mill on the Nevsky, 'eddying up and down in anxious curiosity' and gathering in knots on street corners. Leighton Rogers recalled a 'curious, smiling, determined crowd', but he also sensed something else: that it was 'dangerous'.[9] Troops were out in force at the natural gathering points at major intersections along the two-mile stretch of the Nevsky, from the Winter Palace at its northern end, down past the Kazan Cathedral to Znamensky Square and, on its south side, the Nicholas Station. Like the Cossacks, the troops seemed unwilling to exert force, and the crowds appeared hopeful that they had won them over.

But everything changed in the afternoon when the troops and *faraony* were ordered to clear the crowds. The whole of the Nevsky was one seething mass of people as the police pushed at them, striking with sabres, while the Cossacks charged and swashbuckled. Inevitably people fell and in the melee were trampled by horses or by each other, as the crowd swelled and surged, all the way down to the popular meeting point at Znamensky Square. Here Donald Thompson had seen police mounting a machine gun on the balcony of a house at eleven that morning; a confrontation was clearly brewing.[10] After lunch he and Harper had walked back down there to observe the enormous gathering of workers, strikers, students and even some middle-class and professional people pressing together in front of the ugly equestrian statue of Alexander III. Many had taken their hats off and were shouting, 'Give us bread and we will go back and work.' As elsewhere, the troops hung back, and the Cossacks seemed to be taking an interest in the speeches. The women in the crowd were as bold as the previous day, approaching them and placing 'coaxing hands' on their rifles. 'Put them down!' they pleaded. 'Think of your own mothers and sweethearts and wives!' Others fell on their knees: 'We are your sisters, workers like yourselves. Do you mean to bayonet us?'[11]

One speaker after another leaped up on the statue's plinth to harangue the crowd, which became uglier as time went on. Around 2.00 p.m. Thompson saw a well-dressed man in furs enter the square in a sleigh, shouting at the crowd to let him through, only to be 'dragged out of his sleigh and beaten'. Thompson saw him run to take refuge in an abandoned tram nearby – but a group of workers followed him and one of them, armed with a 'small iron bar', proceeded in an outburst of rage to beat the man's head 'to a pulp'. This 'seemed to give the mob a taste for blood', for as they surged forward some of them started smashing the windows of those shops not already protected with iron shutters. Some of these protesters, however, were actually police in disguise. Thompson recognised one of them: a member of the tsarist secret police, the Okhrana, who lived at his hotel, now dressed as a workman and pushing soldiers off the pavement as though he were 'an anarchist of the worst type'. Boris, his interpreter, assured him this was so: the Okhrana were known to be 'mingling with the mob' and trying to incite them into attacking the soldiers'.[12]

By late afternoon Harper – having already walked the best part of ten miles around the city that day – announced that she was exhausted and was going back to the hotel. Thompson, however, persuaded her to stay a little longer. They hung back in a side street and watched. Every now and again the Cossacks galloped through the square to clear the crowds, but it was futile: 'they would re-form again, like water after the passage of a boat'.[13] Harper and Thompson were both watching – she back in the direction of the Nevsky, he in the square – when at about 4.00 p.m. Thompson heard a loud explosion. Someone had thrown a grenade or bomb from the roof of the Nicholas Station; Thompson saw the crowd instinctively raise their hands in the air, indicating that they were unarmed. Shortly afterwards another explosion followed as the Cossacks struggled to control the crowd.

Then Harper saw them – a platoon of *faraony* came galloping into the square, 'slashing at every side with their sabers', until suddenly a Cossack leaped forward and ran the officer leading the *faraony* through with his lance* and he fell dead from his horse. After this 'the Cossacks yelled and charged the *faraony*, hacking and swinging with their whips' until they 'broke and fled' in terror.[14] 'You should have seen the crowd,' wrote another American eyewitness: 'People kissed and hugged the Cossacks, climbing up on the horses to reach them. Others kissed and embraced the horses, the Cossacks' boots, stirrups, saddles. They were given cigarettes, money, cigar cases, gloves, anything, everything.' Thompson's interpreter, Boris, seemed greatly moved by this moment. The 'day of days' had come, he told Thompson:

---

* Accounts vary considerably – some say one of the Cossacks fired, but Thompson, who was at the scene, is very clear that it was a sabre blow.

'The Cossacks are with the People.' It was the 'first time in the history of Russia that a Cossack had disobeyed orders'.[15]

According to Harper, about five hundred or so of the mob then detached themselves and started back up the Nevsky 'carrying a red flag that was bigger than anything we had seen'.[16] She and Thompson trailed them back up the street, during which time the crowd was charged three times by the police and they 'had to turn and run'. Harper was terrified that she might be tripped by the running crowd and get trampled underfoot, but it was the sabres of the police that scared her most. She decided to head back to the Astoria, but as she and Thompson were approaching the Singer Building, they decided they might first take refuge for a while in the US consulate there. A block before, they could see that a crowd had gathered round the window of Pekar's *patisserie* – a franchise at the Hotel d'Europe boasting a window of luxury cakes and confectionery (which even Leighton Rogers thought 'a rash display for these hard times'). The crowd were eyeing the food 'they couldn't have', when suddenly a workman smashed the plate-glass window and grabbed a box of biscuits.[17] The noise drew even more people, closely followed by the police, who opened fire.

Arthur Reinke, an American telephone engineer with Westinghouse, which had offices in the Singer Building, had watched from his balcony in horror as the *faraony* had ridden into the crowd that had gathered, 'beating the people down with their *nagaikas*', and at how, in response, 'the people had roared and hooted and threw stones and bottles at the police'. He had wanted to get back to the Hotel d'Europe where he was staying, but the mob outside Pekar's 'simply filled the Nevsky from edge to edge … tearing down the street towards me, while bayonets were blinking in the distance and bullets flying'. Taking a deep breath, he made a run for it and reckoned, in so doing, that he 'establish[ed] the engineering department's record for the hundred-yard dash, making that hotel corner before the mob cut me off' – only to find the hotel doors bolted. After he had pounded with sufficient force, a porter finally let him in.[18] Claude Anet had had the same problem when he got caught in the mob at the Europe: he had found 'all the doors, carriage-entrances' and other means of escape nearby firmly closed, 'as though by a miracle'. With great difficulty he had made his way against the current of people to the safety of a house near the Anichkov Bridge.[19]

Boris had not been surprised at the attack on Pekar's: the café, he told Thompson, was rumoured to be 'full of German agents and food controllers who met there and decided each day what they would charge for food', which is why the mob had wreaked vengeance upon it.[20] The place was completely wrecked and five people sitting inside had been killed, as well as the workman who had broken the window. The bodies of the dead were quickly carried off; the shop window was boarded up and the 'clotted snow' carefully swept away, but the story spread down the Nevsky like 'quicksilver' until it reached the Nicholas Station, where the police had again used a concealed machine gun to disperse the angry crowd.[21]

The disturbances outside Pekar's had taken place only a short distance from the Anglo-Russian Hospital, from where the nurses had seen the mob coming down the Nevsky from the Singer Building. The nurses had all been snatching time whenever they could that day to watch the crowds and help deal with some of the wounded who were carried in from the street. Canadian VAD Edith Hegan was struck by the strangeness of the situation: usually at the front their first sight of the wounded had been after the battles, when they were brought to the field hospitals, but here in Petrograd 'we have only to look from our second-story window to see riots continually in progress and wounded and dying falling everywhere as the police charge the streets from time to time'. She and three of her compatriots went down to the Anichkov Bridge that afternoon to take a closer look, but were severely reprimanded for doing so. Returning to their window seats, they could hear the 'click of the machine guns which the police had hidden in the houses'.[22] Their Russian patients begged them to come away from the windows, as bullets were already hitting the hospital.

Disturbances continued up and down the Nevsky until early evening. At around 6.00 p.m. Arno Dosch-Fleurot had been out near the Singer Building with a British military adviser, when they had both had to dive for cover as a squad of *faraony*, their sabres drawn, came charging round the corner into the Nevsky on the pavement, striking at the mob with the edge of their blades in an attempt to drive them off the street.[23] But all their efforts failed: there were now two or three thousand people on the Nevsky – a 'running mob' – and Fleurot saw the *faraony* bayonet several demonstrators. From the window of his room in the Hotel d'Europe as he dressed for a concert, British socialite Bertie Stopford* had seen 'all the well-dressed Nevski crowd running for their lives down the Michail Street [Mikhailovskaya], and a stampede of motor-cars and sledges – to escape from the machine-guns which never stopped firing'.[24] He saw 'a well-dressed lady run over by an automobile, a sledge turn over and the driver thrown into the air and killed. The poorer-looking people crouched against the walls; many others, principally men, lay flat in the snow. Lots of children were trampled on, and people knocked down by the sledges or by the rush of the crowd.'

Thompson, Harper and Boris, too, were still out on the streets and constantly having to dive for cover.[25] Boris was sure that some of the rounds the troops had fired had been blanks or that they had fired into the air – otherwise there would have been far more people killed. It was the police manning machine guns on the roofs of buildings who had done most of the killing.[26] The demonstrators had responded with every kind of weapon they could lay their hands on: revolvers, home-made bombs or missiles – bottles, rocks, metal, even lumps of snow. Some had hand-grenades that had found their way back from the Eastern

---

* Stopford's credentials remain mysterious. He went to Petrograd in August 1916, ostensibly to sell a wireless installation for aeroplanes to the Russian government, but soon ingratiated himself into the top drawer of the Russian aristocracy and the Petrograd social circuit, from which position he passed on insider information to Sir George Buchanan.

Front. And all day long they had continued to urge the troops to come over to their side.[27]

At Russian-army HQ (Stavka) at Mogilev nearly five hundred miles away, Nicholas II had received news of the violent turn of events in Petrograd, although Protopopov had failed to transmit the true gravity of the situation to him. Thinking firmer measures by police and troops were all that were needed, Nicholas had therefore not seen the necessity of returning to Petrograd, instead telegraphing Khabalov and ordering him to 'quell by tomorrow the disturbances in the capital which are inexcusable in view of the difficulties of the war with Germany and Austria'. His wife had written, dismissing the day's events as no more than the workers blowing off steam, 'a hooligan movement', 'young boys and girls running about and screaming that they have no bread, only to excite'. Had it been very cold, she felt, 'they would probably stay indoors'.[28] Besides, Alexandra had far more serious things to think about: three of her five children, Alexey, Tatiana and Olga, were down with the measles.

Seeking some light relief from the day's traumatic events, Florence Harper and Donald Thompson went that evening to the Mikhailovsky premiere of a French farce, *L'Idée de Françoise*, accompanied by the US vice consul. Thompson found it a bore and left early with Boris, to walk the streets of the factory districts, where he 'found things more exciting'.[29] French embassy attaché Louis de Robien was also at the premiere, but the imperial boxes were empty and the grand dukes absent. One of the company, actress Paulette Pax,* had found the whole performance unnerving – particularly the audience, with its 'profusion of jewels and sumptuous outfits' – bearing in mind what had been going on outside all day. She felt that none of them had taken much notice of the play: their minds were elsewhere, their applause half-hearted. 'What we were doing was ridiculous,'

---

* In Paris in 1912 Pax had briefly been mistress to the British secret agent Sidney Reilly.

she wrote in her diary, 'performing a comedy at such a time made no sense.'[30]

Arthur Ransome had not, however, considered the situation so serious when he wrote his despatch that night, noting how most of the crowd ('including many women') had been out simply to watch other people make trouble. The 'general feeling' had been one of 'rather precarious excitement like a bank holiday with thunder in the air', he suggested, emphasising the 'extremely good relations between crowd and Cossacks'. The objective of the disturbances had been 'vague'. Arthur Reinke thought much the same: that night he had found the highways jammed with people who, in the face of extreme provocation by the police, had remained 'merely curious'.[31] But the imposition of a curfew saw them all hurrying to their homes by 11.00 p.m., leaving 'long rows of ugly-looking Cossacks on their ponies drawn at intervals across the street' and large splotches of blood visible on the white snow, bearing 'mute witness' to what had happened that day.[32] J. Butler Wright never forgot 'the pervading smell' on the Nevsky late that afternoon; it came from 'the disinfectants and first-aid remedies administered to those who had been shot down'.[33]

Out on the Petrograd Side, a restless Donald Thompson was still in search of a story with Boris at 2.00 a.m., when he finally came face-to-face with the first hideous manifestation of mob violence. Marching towards them came a rowdy group of about sixty people, 'who had taken two heads and jammed them on poles and were carrying them down the middle of the street'. They were the heads of policemen, so Boris said. Thompson had seen enough red for one day: red flags, red blotches on the snow; and now severed heads. They saw more bodies on their way back to the Astoria, and Thompson later discovered that 'a great many policemen were killed or seriously wounded' by mobs in the Vyborg and Petrograd Sides.[34] All through Saturday night there was a great deal of screaming and yelling and incessant firing in those districts, as the violent scenario continued to unravel. For Philip Chadbourn, that day had been a point of significant and perhaps optimistic transition – 'the blank between the

70

reels' – separating 'the black misery and injustice of the first reel' and the 'red revolt and bright heroics of the second'.[35]

There was an ominous stillness in the city on the beautiful, cloudless sunny Sunday morning that followed; but overnight General Khabalov had resolved that draconian measures would have to be taken to keep the situation under control. New placards posted across the city announced that all workers would have to return to work by Tuesday 28th or those who had applied for deferments of their military service would be sent straight to the front. All street gatherings of more than three people were forbidden. At a meeting of the Council of Ministers that had gone on from midnight till 5.00 a.m., Khabalov had given assurances that 30,000 soldiers, backed up by artillery and armoured cars, would be on the streets, with orders to take decisive action against the demonstrators.[36]

Overnight the drawbridges across the Neva had all been raised and the remaining fixed bridges were heavily guarded by armoured cars and machine guns. Though the crowds took to the ice once more, there were now so many that it took a long time for them to cross. There were fewer Cossacks about that morning, but a lot more police on patrol, and troops were manning all the bridges intersecting the Nevsky with the Ekaterininsky Canal and the Moika and Fontanka Rivers, and also on guard outside the railway stations. By late morning many of these positions were being reinforced with machine-gun posts. The Red Cross was in evidence, too, positioning horse-drawn ambulances in side streets in anticipation of the inevitable resumption of violence.[37] This time Khabalov was taking no chances and had ensured that most of the troops on the Nevsky were training detachments from the guards regiments, brought in from the military academies. They were all heavily armed with rifles and bayonets – the authorities assuming that, as NCOs, these men would be less reluctant to shoot, if ordered to do so.[38]

It seemed as though the whole city was out of doors that morning, and on foot – for there were no trams or cabs. People seemed determined to get to church as usual or simply enjoy the fine weather for a promenade along the Nevsky. Couples were pushing their babies in prams, just like any ordinary Sunday; children were skating on the ice rink in the Admiralty Gardens. It seemed to Donald Thompson, as he left the Astoria with Florence Harper, 'that all the children in Petrograd were out'.[39]

Most of the shops and cafés facing the Nevsky were closed, however, and a lot of them had their shutters down or had been hastily boarded up.[40] The city seemed 'violated', thought Louise Patouillet, who was unnerved by the changes that the disturbances had already wrought. Overnight, and despite the families out walking in such a seemingly carefree manner, the atmosphere had crystallised into something darker, edgier. Revolution was 'in the air you breathed', noted an English visitor. What organisation there was remained impromptu, of a 'hand-to-mouth character'.[41] The Russian government had warned foreign nationals not to go out, but Thompson and Harper were unable to resist the temptation to mingle with the crowds on the Nevsky once more with Boris, although, as Harper recalled, 'neither of us liked the look of the situation'. People were desperate for news, and groups formed round anyone who had any to tell.[42] The one predominating topic of conversation – aside from debate about how many had already been killed or injured, heard time and time again by foreign eyewitnesses during the revolution – was that much of the firing on civilians had been done by *faraony* disguised as soldiers or even as Cossacks. People were sure of this because the *faraony* rode 'large, fine animals', and the Cossacks' horses were 'very small and shaggy and generally unkempt looking'. They could tell the difference.[43]

By midday the approaches to the Nevsky had become blocked with dense crowds flooding in from all sides of the city and attempting to converge there. Thompson and Harper headed for the Medved ('The Bear') – a popular French restaurant on Bolshaya Konyushennaya near the Singer Building – for a midday lunch before the restaurant's limited supply of bread ran out. Thompson was well prepared for possible action and had his 'gyroscopic camera' concealed in a bag so that he could take photographs.[44] After leaving the restaurant and walking back down to the Nevsky they could see a mob, waving red flags and singing the Marseillaise, gathering lower down near the Anichkov Bridge. 'Those poor devils are going to get it,' Thompson warned, and as they turned to take shelter they heard a roar and saw 'fifty mounted police dressed as soldiers' charge the mob and drive them down the side street.

But no sooner had this crowd been moved on than another one gathered on the bridge. A student clambered up on one of the equestrian statues and started waving a red flag and making a speech; Thompson stopped to get a picture and watched as the mob moved off and straight into the 'snarl of a deadly machine gun and the spit of rifles'. He had seen the police pulling a machine gun into the middle of the tram-tracks. 'Volley after volley rang out,' recalled Harper. 'The dead were thick; the wounded were screaming as they were trampled down.' Soon everyone was prostrate, hugging the pavement or lying in the snow – Thompson and Harper included. It felt as though 'hell itself had broken loose on the Nevsky', for they were under fire 'from every point', bar the shops behind them. Bullets were also coming at them from machine guns on the roofs of buildings and 'sweeping all around'.[45]

Thompson managed to take a few photographs before he and Harper got up and made a run for it. They smashed their way through the window of a glove shop to take cover, closely followed by about ten or fifteen others, many of them bleeding. Right in front of their eyes they had seen a little girl hit in the throat by gunfire, and a well-dressed woman standing near them had collapsed with a scream as her knee was shattered by a bullet. After crawling back out into the street, Thompson and Harper were once more thrown to the ground by rifle fire coming from the police on the Anichkov Bridge. All around people lay dead and dying in the snow – Thompson counted twelve dead soldiers, Harper noted far more women and children than men: thirty dead in all. The two reporters lay there in the snow for more than an hour, numb with cold, but too frightened to move. Harper 'had a vague idea that I was freezing to death'; she wanted to cry. And then the ambulances appeared and started collecting the dead and wounded and they decided this was fortuitous: they could pretend they were wounded and be picked up and taken to safety.[46]

The nurses at the Anglo-Russian Hospital had also seen the fighting in which Thompson and Harper had been caught up, a short distance from the Anichkov Bridge. VAD Dorothy Cotton had been reliably informed that there would be a renewal of disturbances by 3.00 p.m. and, just as predicted, at around 2.45 they were all watching from the windows when a company of Pavlovsky guards, lined up at the major junction of Sadovaya with the Nevsky (just west of the Anichkov Bridge), were ordered to clear the street. Lady Sybil Grey had seen how they 'lay down in the snow and fired a volley into the people', who all fell onto their faces.[47] Then a machine gun opened fire from a rooftop and 'swept the street in every direction', as people tried to crawl away on their stomachs. Others 'rushed where they could. They darted into side streets, pressed against the walls of houses, hid prone behind heaps of snow or behind streetcar posts.' It had all been 'a case of quite unnecessary provocation on the part of the police', she recalled.

Many people had taken refuge in the doorway of the hospital, noticed Edith Hegan.[48] She could not help being impressed by the Cossacks, galloping up and down the Nevsky like 'a tawny streak' trying to clear the crowds. She saw one of them charge at a man who seemed to be leading the crowd, and how he 'described an arc in the air with his sword. I saw the sword descend, and while I held my breath in horror it neatly sliced off the top of the man's hat.' The man had not seemed to be 'in the least frightened' and had 'walked calmly on, while the crowd cheered them both impartially'. Not so long ago, she added, 'that Cossack would have sliced off the man's head'.[49]

When things quietened down, people rushed to help the wounded. Philip Chadbourn saw 'two young workmen in high boots and black reefers' who were 'lying on their backs, with blood running from their mouths'. 'As I stood over them and looked into their unseeing eyes, a woman stooped, peered into their faces, shuddered and said, "What a shame! Boys, only boys!"[50] Nearby, 'six men wearing green students' caps' passed, who were 'bearing over their heads in the street a corpse on a sign-board'. Others stopped a passing limousine; they made the two occupants get out, placed wounded civilians inside and ordered the chauffeur to take them to the hospital. Chadbourn saw the same thing happen 'with two private sleighs'. Elsewhere, the wounded and dead were carried away by the crowd; others were left lying in huddles until horse-drawn and motor ambulances came along and picked them up.

With its 180 beds full of wounded from the front, the ARH could offer little other than first aid to a dozen or so victims who were brought in rapidly, many of them dying almost as soon as they arrived, as Edith Hegan recalled.[51] She and her fellow nurses did what they could for the wounded, 'but at night the authorities took them away, except two or three who were too near death to be moved'. Eighteen more wounded were carried into the city Duma a short way down the Nevsky from the ARH, which students had helped turn into a makeshift Red Cross station. All afternoon Lady Sybil Grey saw the motor ambulances pass by unceasingly up and down the street. In a single hospital three hundred wounded were taken in. There were another sixty at the Mariinsky Hospital on the Liteiny and more than one hundred at the Obukhov Hospital on the Fontanka.[52]

In the early evening the 'most sanguinary episode in the Revolution', as Robert Wilton later described it, had occurred at Znamensky Square, where a dense mass of people from the Nevsky had converged with another crowd coming up Ligovskaya, the major thoroughfare to the south of the square.[53] 'Local police leaders on horseback rode among the crowd ordering them home,' recalled Dr Joseph Clare, pastor of the American Church,[*] who witnessed the scene. 'The people knew the soldiers

---

[*] The Congregational Church in Petrograd had become known as the 'American Church' because the previous American ambassador and many of his suite had worshipped there.

were on their side and refused to move.' Lined up in front of a hotel facing the square were men from the 1st and 2nd training detachments of the Volynsky Regiment. When their commander ordered them to disperse the crowd, the soldiers begged the crowds to move on, so they would not have to use their weapons, but the people refused to budge. Angrily the officer had one of the reluctant soldiers arrested for insubordination and again ordered his men to fire. 'They shot in the air, and the officer got mad, making each individual fire into the mob,' recalled Clare. Finally he raised his own pistol and started firing into the crowd. Then 'suddenly came the rat-tat-tat of a machine-gun. The people could hardly believe their ears, but there was no doubting the evidence of eyes as they saw people falling.'[54] Robert Wilton saw it, too: the Maxim gun placed on the roof of a nearby building – probably the one Donald Thompson had seen the previous day – had opened fire on the crowd. But this time something extraordinary happened: the troop of Cossacks positioned in the square had turned and fired at the gunners on the house tops. 'It was a veritable pandemonium,' Wilton recalled, as 'with a great howl of rage' the crowd scattered behind buildings and into courtyards, from where some of them began firing at the military and police. Forty or so were killed and hundreds wounded.[55]

The 'fratricidal roar' of fighting continued to echo across the Nevsky until dark, with small, independent groups of people constantly looking for trouble, some of them armed; the mob was 'on the *qui vive* with excitement', Philip Chadbourn recalled, but with the city such a sprawl and the streets so wide, incidents often took place disconnected from each other and it took time before word was transmitted in respect of what was going on where.[56] As one American noticed, it was the 'queerest sensation' that day 'to find it so quiet in certain sections, and the next minute to round a corner and find an ambulance picking up the dead and wounded'.[57] Arthur Ransome had telegraphed that he had 'scuttled' round a street corner to get out of the way of machine-gun fire, only to find 'four men peacefully scraping ice from pavements with hoes'.[58] The truth was that, with so much random firing, no one knew who was friend or foe and it was a difficult and dangerous news story for any journalist to follow.

Exhausted though she was, Florence Harper's professional instincts had kept her out until early evening: 'It was too exciting in the streets.' Back at the Astoria, she had overheard a fat Chicago shoe salesman bewailing the fact that he would never 'have his wild tales of running six blocks from the mobs and the fighting' believed, when he 'sat over a stein of beer, surrounded by a few congenial souls in his favourite café in Chicago'. 'They will just call me a liar!' he wailed. He found himself stranded at the Astoria, it being too dangerous to go back to his hotel at the Nicholas Station, and he would spend the next three days there repeating his tale of miraculous survival. 'I hope his friends in Chicago did believe him,' Harper later wrote, because – like herself and Thompson and many other foreign observers that day – 'he was there and in it all.'[59]

None of them, however, knew exactly how many had been killed on Sunday: Robert Wilton thought two hundred at least; others, like Harper and Thompson, had noted the dead and wounded at particular points of conflict – some the victims of machine guns and crossfire in and around the Nevsky and Znamensky Square, others ridden down by the *faraony* or killed from falling under the horses of the Cossacks. But the casualties had been carried off in all directions: to hospitals, to temporary dressing points, to the morgues or simply back home by friends and relatives. Nobody was counting. However many died, the evidence of the day's violence was everywhere to be seen, as Robert Wilton noted: 'I saw hundreds of empty cartridge cases littering the snow, which was deluged in blood.'[60]

After dark, when the crowds had cleared from the Nevsky, the soldiers involved in the shootings at Znamensky Square and on the Nevsky had returned to their barracks, angry and upset that they had been forced to fire on the crowds. Robert Wilton had walked to the British embassy to call on a shocked Sir George

Buchanan, who had just managed to get the last train back to Petrograd from his brief holiday in Finland, to find himself in the midst of a revolution. 'I was walking through the Summer Garden when the bullets began to whiz over my head,' Wilton remembered.[61] One hundred of the Pavlovsky guards in their nearby barracks on the Field of Mars, hearing how earlier in the day members of the 4th Company had been ordered to open fire on crowds near the junction of the Sadovaya and the Nevsky, had decided to take action. The police, they were convinced, had been 'provoking bloodshed'.[62] These men had set out for the Nevsky with a few rifles and ammunition, intent on dissuading their comrades from shooting on demonstrators, when they were confronted by mounted *faraony*. Firing broke out, but the soldiers had soon run out of ammunition and were forced back to their barracks, where they gave themselves up. The nineteen ringleaders were arrested and were incarcerated in the Peter and Paul Fortress; the rest were confined to barracks. There was an immediate clampdown on news of the mutiny, but soon word was out.[63]

That evening, actress Paulette Pax headed back to the Mikhailovsky Theatre, wondering if the scheduled performance of *L'Idée de Françoise* would go ahead. When she arrived she found her fellow actors all extremely upset and full of stories of the day's atrocities. They had no stomach for farce that evening, and the auditorium was practically empty. But the rule was that a performance would only be cancelled if the audience numbered fewer than seven. Pax groaned when the box office rose above that low bar; but, to their credit, the actors took to the stage and performed the play 'as though to a full house'.[64]

Two members of that small audience were British embassy official Hugh Walpole and Arno Dosch-Fleurot, who thoroughly enjoyed themselves. Stella Arbenina, an Englishwoman married to Baron Meyendorff, was there, too. Everything had been 'perfectly quiet' on the streets when she had arrived, and she had sent her coachman and horses home, not wanting to keep them waiting in the cold for two hours. On entering the theatre, she had been dismayed to find that although the French plays usually filled the auditorium to capacity, there were only about fifty people present and all of them 'looking as out of place and apologetic as ourselves'. Quite the worst moment, though, came during the interval, when any Russian officers present in the audience were obliged, by tradition, to stand and face the imperial box, an 'act of empty homage' to an absent tsar.[65]

At the Mariinsky Theatre – a venue usually filled to bursting – a performance of the ballet *La Source* had also played to a half-empty auditorium. Down on the Fontanka, the much-anticipated party at Princess Radziwill's palace went ahead as planned, although the carriages bringing guests had been refused entry to the Nevsky and had had to go the long way round. Charles de Chambrun and Claude Anet were there and noted how preoccupied the guests were, though everybody 'tr[ied] to dance in spite of it'. Anet watched as Grand Duke Boris Vladimirovich took to the dance floor; was he witnessing this scion of the Russian aristocracy dancing 'his last tango', he wondered? Bertie Stopford was also present, soaking up one last gasp of old-style imperial decadence; he stuck it out till 4.00 a.m., when Prince Radziwill sent him home to his hotel in his own car, as 'occasional bullets still whistled up and down'.[66]

Maurice Paléologue was exhausted, having spent the whole day 'literally besieged by anxious members of the French colony' wanting to get out of Petrograd. He went out to dinner with a friend that evening rather than attend the Radziwill party. But on his way home he passed the palace and saw a long line of cars and carriages waiting outside. The party was still in full swing, but he was not tempted to join it. As he noted in his diary that night, Sénac de Meilhan, historian of the French Revolution, had written that there had also been 'plenty of gaiety in Paris on the night of the 5th October, 1789!'[67]

As late-night partygoers made their way home there was a terrible eeriness about the city. Stella Arbenina had noticed it after leaving the Mikhailovsky Theatre. Normally the square outside would be full of activity – coaches, sledges and motor cars waiting to take theatregoers home, and a 'gay crowd of people wrapped in furs'. But that night the square had been 'completely empty'; there was not a taxi or sledge to be had, and she had been obliged to walk home in the moonlight and the intense cold. 'Every now and then we heard a distant shot far away, but the streets we walked through were completely deserted.' The silence was ominous and made the 'creaking of the snow under our feet seem disproportionately loud'. Petrograd seemed like a dead city.

Claude Anet noticed the same false air of 'tranquillity'. Petrograd was 'deserted, lugubrious, hardly lighted at all'. Cordons of troops were still out, guarding the Nevsky at barricades at every intersection. Here and there groups of Cossacks could be seen patrolling in the snow, enveloped by white steam rising from their horses' backs. It was like passing through one great military camp, recalled Anet.[68] Norman Armour, who had stayed late at the Radziwill party, noticed it too as he walked back to his apartment overlooking the Neva: 'I felt I might have been back in the days of the Crimean War,' he recalled. It was bitterly cold and 'the sentries in the streets had built fires and had stacked their guns near them, just as you see in old paintings in the Hermitage'.[69] The only illumination came from the powerful beam of a searchlight mounted on the spire of the Admiralty tower, raking up and down the deserted Nevsky, which 'stretched ahead a broad streak of ghastly white' under its glare.[70]

Over at the state Duma in the Tauride Palace, frantic meetings had been taking place all day. Frustrated at the continuing lack of a response from the Tsar, Duma president Mikhail Rodzianko had seized the initiative and telegraphed him at Stavka about the gravity of the situation, warning that anarchy reigned in the capital, that food, fuel and transport supplies were in chaos and – in an attempt to galvanise him – asserting that the government was 'paralyzed'. It was perhaps an overstatement and it ran counter to General Khabalov's messages to Nicholas, which had sought to assure the Tsar that everything was under control. Rodzianko was insistent, however, that in order to defuse the dangerous situation it was essential that a new government in which the people had confidence be formed immediately. Fearful of a coup within the Duma, Prime Minister Golitsyn had stepped in and pre-empted Rodzianko by proroguing it, instead of the Duma waiting for Nicholas's reply. (Nicholas, as it turned out, had decided no answer was necessary.) Rodzianko was outraged: the Duma was the constituted authority of Russia, he insisted; its prorogation was a violation of Russian law. He urged his colleagues to rally round and defend it, and a temporary committee was hurriedly organised.[71]

Revolution had now been articulated politically: in the seat of government, by some of the guards regiments, and by the once fiercely loyal Cossacks. The workers, outraged at the indiscriminate firing on the crowds that weekend, had formed their own militias and spent that Sunday night plotting not only to continue the strike and demonstrations, but also to seize weapons and turn the protest movement into nothing less than an armed uprising. 'Since one o'clock today it has been a bloody Sunday for Russia,' Donald Thompson wrote to his wife when he was finally back at the Astoria that evening. He had been out walking the freezing cold streets till 3.30 a.m., flashing his US passport to get through the barricades and returning at regular intervals to warm up, before he finally sat down. Wherever he had gone that evening he had encountered 'ugly looking mobs'. He had heard the rumours of mutiny among some of the troops. 'If this spreads to other regiments, Russia will be a republic in a few more hours,' he told her.[72] Everything now depended on how the disaffected troops – in particular the Pavlovsky, Volynsky and Preobrazhensky Regiments – would respond on Monday. 'I wish you would send me some sugar,' he added. 'I also need some quinine and aspirin tablets.' He wasn't feeling well. But, as things turned out, he wouldn't have a chance to write again for the next three days.

4

'A Revolution Carried
on by Chance'

All through Sunday, Leighton Rogers and his colleagues
from the National City Bank had been stranded at their
office on Palace Embankment, it being too dangerous
for them to leave the building and go back to their various lodg-
ings. They had sat there all afternoon and evening, 'listening to
the crackling rifles, the ripping machine-guns, and wondering
what it all meant.' To them 'it sounded worse than it really was',
Rogers concluded; but they took no risks and kept the lights off.
When it got so dark that they couldn't see, they had to stop
reading and writing letters, by which time it had all got too
much for Chester Swinnerton. Known to his colleagues as the
'Count', for the flamboyant twirly moustache that matched his
bravado, Harvard graduate Swinnerton got to his feet and proclaimed with a theatrical gesture that they were 'a great bunch
of Americans' and shouldn't be afraid of a 'little shooting'. 'What's
the use of sitting here all night?' he asked, 'a bullet can come
through the window and pick you off as well as it can in the
street. I'm not going to stay; I'm going to walk home, the firing
be damned, and sleep in a good bed. Good night.'[1]

With that, Swinnerton donned his hat, coat and galoshes and
slammed the door. He hadn't gone far when he encountered a
'little insignificant cuss', holding in his hand 'a pistol big enough
for a real man. It wasn't one of our nice little snub nose revolvers, but a real pistol, and in his hands it didn't appeal to me in

the least'. Realising he had encountered the new revolutionary everyman, of whom there were many now prowling the streets with weapons they hardly knew how to handle – and seeing a mob of fifty more or so in the distance, firing at random – Swinnerton decided to 'beat it back to the bank'. His colleagues heard a burst of rifle and machine-gun fire as Swinnerton came rushing back in through the door. 'Well, I guess I won't go home after all,' he said sheepishly. 'It's cold there and warm here.'[2]

That night, after sharing out the few cigars and cigarettes they had left, they all bedded down as best they could under their heavy greatcoats. The incongruity of their sumptuous situation – sleeping on ornate gold couches under cut-glass chandeliers, in what had been the former Turkish embassy's big Moorish reception room – was hardly conducive to a restful night.[3*] They would spend the whole of Monday there, too, living on black bread, cabbage soup and tea. Occasionally one or other of them would dash outside to see 'if there was anything to be seen' and, upon discovering that indeed there was – far too much for comfort, in fact – would dash back in again.[4]

During the weekend's disturbances US ambassador David Francis had wisely taken note of official advice and stayed indoors. At his request, the embassy had been provided with an eighteen-man guard of soldiers, but he had been apprehensive that their 'fidelity' was of an 'uncertain quality'.[5] He was worried, too, about the risks being taken by his staff, some of whom had been hovering outside on the pavement rubber-necking what was going on. He ordered them to come inside and lock the gates.[6] It was just as well, for events on what would become known as 'Red Monday' crowded thick and fast, in such a dislocated and unpredictable fashion that there was great danger of being caught in the crossfire.

---

* The former Turkish embassy had been housed, till the outbreak of war in 1914, in the Kantemirovsky Palace at number 8 Palace Embankment; the building was subsequently leased by the NCB for its Petrograd offices. The huge high-ceilinged rooms on the second floor were converted to bank facilities, fitted out with desks, typewriters and adding machines.

It had been a huge shock to Meriel Buchanan, arriving back in Petrograd at eight o'clock that morning from a visit to friends in the country, to find there were no trams and no *droshkies* at the station to transport her and her luggage to the British embassy. She was forcibly struck by how Petrograd had been dramatically – irretrievably – transformed in her absence: 'In the bleak, gray light of that early morning the town looked inexpressibly desolate and deserted, the bare, ugly street leading up from the station, with the dirty stucco houses on either side, seemed, after the snow-white peace of the country, somehow the very acme of dreariness.'[7] But that wasn't all: there was an air of dread and suspense about the city that made her anxious parents glad to have her back. She spent most of that morning shut up and 'forbidden to go out ... sitting on the big staircase of the Embassy gleaning what information [she] could from the various people who came and went'.

By 11.00 a.m. it was clear that the capital was in the thick of a revolution, for by then disturbances had assumed 'formidable proportions', shifting away from the Nevsky and focusing on the northern end of the Liteiny, around the District Court – one and a half blocks away from the US embassy on Furshtatskaya, and closer as well to the British embassy on the Palace Embankment.[8] Although David Francis would be at his desk all day Monday, trying to make sense of the turbulent events of the last few days in a long despatch to Washington – and hampered by the loss of the phone line, which had been vandalised – Sir George Buchanan had insisted at 11.30 a.m. on taking his usual morning drive with his French colleague Paléologue to the Russian Foreign Ministry.[9] Both men had been extremely blunt with the Minister of Foreign Affairs, Nikolay Pokrovsky, as Buchanan reported later in a ciphered telegram to London. It was an 'act of madness to prorogue the Duma at a moment like the present', Buchanan had told him, for doing so would make it impossible to contain the revolt. Pokrovsky's assurance that a 'military dictator' would be appointed, and troops sent by Nicholas from the front to 'quell the mutiny', only alarmed the two ambassadors further. Yet again, they wearily concluded, Nicholas had failed to choose the path of conciliation and political concession. Such draconian, repressive policies – of which the reactionary Proto-popov was the chief architect – would do nothing, Buchanan argued, but inflame the situation and bring Russia 'face to face with revolution' at what was now a decisive stage in the war.[10] Paléologue shared Buchanan's gloom, reflecting on his own coun-try's turbulent history: 'In 1789, 1830 and 1848, three French dynasties were overthrown because they were *too late* in realizing the significance and strength of the movement against them.'[11]

Events had, in fact, taken a decisive turn in the early hours of Monday 27 February when the army, as many had predicted, began mutinying. At 3.00 a.m. in his room at the Hotel de France, Arno Dosch-Fleurot had heard 'lively rifle fire' nearby. He got dressed to go and investigate, but the roads were closed and he couldn't get through. He could tell, however, that the firing was coming from the Volynsky Regiment's barracks near the junction of the Moika River and Ekaterininsky Canal. Overnight, and following the example of the Pavlovskys, some of the Volynskys, who had been ordered to fire on the crowds on Sunday, had decided to mutiny.[12] When the soldiers lined up for duty, some of them turned on their commanding officer and shot him dead. They were unable, however, to persuade the rest of the regiment to join them, and so they headed off to incite other regiments, picking up a rabble of civilian supporters along the way. Maurice Paléologue had been dressing when, at around 8.30, he had heard a 'prolonged din' coming from the direction of the Liteiny Bridge. He saw a regiment of men approaching a disorderly mob of people crossing from the Vyborg Side and anticipated a 'violent collision', but instead 'the two bodies coalesced'. 'The army was fraternizing with revolt.'[13] Already a point had been reached that morning from which there would be no turning back.

The coming together of troops and revolutionists gathered rapid speed as the Volynsky mutineers headed to the depot bat-talion of the Preobrazhensky and Lithuanian Regiments, as well as the 6th Engineer Battalion – all located close to their own barracks, and most of whom soon joined them, the last-named even bringing their marching band. By the end of the day the commanders of a battalion of the Preobrazhensky and a battalion of the Volynsky had been killed by their men, as well as numerous other officers. The desertion of the Preobrazhenskys from their barracks near the Winter Palace was particularly damaging, for they were the finest of the old guards regiments, legendary as the 'chief pride and protection of the Russian monarchy' and, like the Cossacks, they had until now been a bulwark of imperial authority.[14] Donald Thompson had got caught up among the triumphant mutinying troops as he crossed the Field of Mars on his way to the US embassy that morning: 'Soldiers were firing volleys into the air with their rifles ... Instead of treating me as an enemy, several of them threw their arms about me and kissed me.' He had his camera and started taking photographs; they were all eager to pose for him, and nobody took any notice when he stopped to photograph the corpses of 'twenty-two officers who had been killed' in the mutiny earlier that morning.[15]*

In those first few hours most of the rebellious soldiers appeared disorientated and numbed by the momentous decision they had made, and for some time they had no sense of where to go and what to do, other than incite other regiments to join them. One group forced their way past a training detachment of the Moskovsky Regiment guarding the Liteiny Bridge and marched to the Moskovsky's barracks on Sampsonievksy on the Vyborg Side. Here, a portion of the regiment was eventually persuaded to join them in the afternoon, accompanied by motor lorries full to the brim with looted rifles; meanwhile the better-disciplined Bicycle Battalion, the only armed unit in the city, resisted all inducements to join in.[16] Elsewhere, such was the euphoria among the rebellious troops that many simply walked around shouting, cheering

---

* Here, as in other instances where Thompson refers to specific photographs that he took at the time, the negatives – or even prints of them – do not seem to have survived. Nor were they included in Thompson's book of photographs of Russia in 1917, *Blood-Stained Russia*.

and arguing among themselves 'like schoolboys broken out of school'. For a while leadership, as such, of the mobs of soldiers and civilians devolved to acts of spontaneous bravado or rabble-rousing on street corners. But one objective was clear: the mutineers had to arm themselves.

With that in mind, at around 10.00 a.m. a group descended on the Old Arsenal at the top of the Liteiny at the junction of Shpalernaya, which housed both the Artillery Department and a small-arms factory. This group smashed in the gates and killed the elderly colonel in charge.[17] British military attaché Major-General Sir Alfred Knox had been in the building, conferring with Russian colleagues, when he had seen 'a great disorderly mass of soldiery, stretching right across the wide street and both pavements'. They had no officer in charge, but were led instead by 'a diminutive but immensely dignified student'.[18] Knox and his colleagues crowded round the windows to watch what would happen. There was an 'uncanny silence'; then the sound of the windows and door on the ground floor being smashed in. As firing broke out, the crowd surged through, killing and wounding several of those on duty. In a mad frenzy rifles, revolvers, swords, daggers, ammunition and machine guns – whatever came to hand – were eagerly looted by soldiers and civilians alike. Looking over the banisters, Knox could see them snatching the swords of Artillery Department officers as they left the building, while 'a few hooligans were going through the pockets of coats left in the vestibule'. They even broke the glass of display cases to remove rifles – even though these were 'specimens of the armament of other nations that were without ammunition and would be of no use to them'.[19]

Outside on the Liteiny, by around 11.00 a.m. others had turned their attention to the hated bastions of tsarism – the nearby District Court and Palace of Justice, together with an adjoining remand prison. The prison was quickly burst open; its mainly criminal inmates awaiting trial were set free and handed weapons as they left, and the prison was set on fire. The District Court was torched, too, thus destroying all the criminal records contained within – a symbolic act that was also clearly to the advantage of all those freed convicts.[20] The ensuing conflagration, however, not only destroyed police records, but also valuable historical archives dating back to the reign of Catherine the Great; and when the fire-engine crews arrived, the mob prevented them from tackling the blaze. French newspaperman Claude Anet saw how 'an elderly man, fastidiously dressed, was wringing his hands' at the sight of the building now 'vomiting flames'. 'Don't you realize that all the Court records, archives of value beyond price, are perishing in the flames?' he cried, to which a rough voice from the crowd answered him: 'Don't worry! We shall be able to divide your houses and land among the people without the help of any of your precious archives!' – a response that was greeted with 'a roar of delight'.[21]

Over at the US embassy, where he was meeting Ambassador Francis (who seemed to him 'very cool and collected'), Donald Thompson had got word that it was all happening down on the Liteiny. He hurried there with Boris and Florence Harper, to find 'a mob of about a million people, it seemed to me; and this mob was out for blood', armed 'with every weapon you can think of'.[22] He started taking surreptitious photographs with his small camera, nervous of being mistaken for a police spy, and noticed an English photographer for the *Daily Mirror** and Claude Anet doing likewise. Anet had run back to his hotel room to get his camera and had been taking photographs from behind a car on the Liteiny, when he was spotted and quickly found himself pinned against a wall by three bayonets. As the soldiers harangued him, a young female student had joined them and 'began to denounce me fiercely'. He told them he was a Frenchman, a journalist. Did they want to see his papers? 'Take the films,' he said to them 'and leave me the camera. I am your ally.' Things were getting extremely ugly when someone sprang forward, snatched the camera from Anet's hands and made off with it. He was dismayed at having lost 'a valuable Goerz lens'.[23]

---

* Probably George Mewes, one of the *Mirror*'s first war photographers and the only official British photographer assigned to the Russian army at the front.

Thompson did not fare well, either. He found himself virtually transfixed by the vortex of violence on the Liteiny, with people all around him running about screaming, 'Kill the police!' – when suddenly he himself was arrested and hauled off to the police station. He showed them his US press pass, but he and Boris were locked in a suffocating small cell with about twenty others, the sound of rifle- and machine-gun fire all around, shouts and screams and the 'smashing of doors and the crashing of glass' – 'a roar such as I never heard before in my life,' he recalled. And there they languished while Boris tried to convince the police that the 'Amerikansky' was genuine. It wasn't long before the mob broke into the police station, smashed the lock to his cell and the next thing he and Boris knew, 'people were throwing their arms around Boris and me and kissing us, saying that we were free'. In the front office, as he made his way out, he 'found a sight beyond description': 'Women were down on their knees hacking the bodies of the police to pieces.' He saw one woman 'trying to tear somebody's face with her bare fingers'.[24]

The Liteiny was by now a scene of 'indescribable confusion', ablaze from the fires at the District Court and Palace of Justice, the air thick with the crackle of random shooting. An abandoned, overturned tram was being used as a platform from which a succession of speakers attempted to harangue the mob, but Louis de Robien recalled how it was 'impossible to make head or tail of the disorderly ebb and flow of all these panic-stricken people running in every direction'.[25] After the stampede on the New Arsenal, three field guns – which no one knew how to operate – had been dragged out from the gun factory, along with trench mortars and a considerable stock of ammunition, and placed at a hastily made barricade of piles of crates, carts, tables and office furniture in front of the District Court, which commanded the whole length of the Liteiny down to the Nevsky. This was backed up by machine guns on the brow of the Liteiny Bridge behind them, in case any loyal tsarist troops should arrive from the northern side.[26] When a group of still-loyal Semenovskys did arrive, there was a pitched battle between them and a company of Volynsky mutineers – watched by groups of civilians huddled into side passages and doorways, many of them women and children tempted out by the 'spirit of curiosity', and who then took enormous risks, 'walking out calmly under a lively fire to drag back the wounded'.[27] James Houghteling saw the wounded being carried off as fast as they fell, leaving behind 'long trails of fresh blood' in the snow. He was astonished to see how, in between bouts of fighting, civilians scuttled back and forth across the Liteiny, intent on carrying on shopping as normal, even lining up outside the bakeries and dispersing only when they heard machine-gun fire. To many of the bewildered civilian population, the events swirling around them were unreal, 'as though they were watching some melodrama in one of their cinematographs'.[28]

Such was the abandon with which weapons looted from army barracks, the arsenal, prisons and police stations were handed out to all and sundry that crowds of civilians, workers and soldiers were soon parading round gleefully, brandishing them and firing off at random, as British mechanical engineer James Stinton Jones encountered:

> Here would be a hooligan with an officer's sword fastened over his overcoat, a rifle in one hand and a revolver in the other; there a small boy with a large butcher's knife on his shoulder. Close by a workman would be seen awkwardly holding an officer's sword in one hand and a bayonet in the other. One man had two revolvers, another a rifle in one hand and a tram-line cleaner in the other. A student with two rifles and a belt of machine-gun bullets round his waist was walking beside another with a bayonet tied to the end of a stick. A drunken soldier had only the barrel of a rifle remaining, the stock having been broken off in forcing an entry into some shop.[29]

Arthur Reinke of Westinghouse was alarmed by how freely weapons and ammunition were given to children: 'It was an interesting ... sight to see a young Russian boy of fifteen clumsily handling a gun and trying to fit a cartridge in place. Children walked about with huge cavalry sabers. Self-appointed student guards often were seen armed with Turkish sabers or Japanese swords with wonderfully carved handles.' 'Even street urchins seemed to have picked up revolvers, and were blazing away at stray pigeons,' noted another.[30]

There was no safe haven for any officers seen walking the streets that day who did not immediately surrender their weapons, when challenged. Even women were on the attack; nurse Edith Hegan saw 'one fierce officer, covered with decorations and looking very much annoyed, try to saunter down the Nevsky, pursued by a crowd of women who stripped him of his arms. His sword fell to a gray-haired woman who shrieked apparently uncomplimentary Russian epithets at him as she contemptuously bent the sword over her knee, broke it in two, and lightly tossed it into the canal.'[31]

By midday the rabble of weapon-toting civilians in and around the Liteiny had been joined by 25,000 soldiers from the Volynsky, Preobrazhensky, Litovsky, Keksgolmsky and Sapper Regiments. Arno Dosch-Fleurot recalled the dense crowd jamming the street for a quarter of a mile, 'carried on by its own faith in itself'.[32] Everywhere, amidst the mighty roar of revolutionary excitement, the singing and cheering and shouting, the fighting colour of scarlet was in evidence – in crude revolutionary banners, in rosettes and armbands and in red ribbons tied to the barrels of rifles.

Events gained even greater momentum when the revolution went mobile. The major Military Garage in Petrograd was broken into and all the motor cars and some armoured trucks were taken.[33] Private garages of the wealthy everywhere across the city were forced open, and their motor cars and swanky limousines summarily confiscated. These vehicles were promptly draped in red banners and driven madly up and down the Liteiny and elsewhere – often by inexperienced drivers who were delirious with the thrill of speed – crammed with soldiers with bayoneted rifles thrust out of the windows. Some cars had machine guns poking out of their smashed rear windows; armed rebels even lay along the car bonnets; but the most familiar form of revolutionary joyriding – and one vividly remembered by many eyewitnesses – was that of men riding shotgun, lying along the wide running boards of motor cars, their rifles at the ready. They would become the poster-boys of the revolution as, in the hours to come, these armoured motor cars and trucks played an important role in disseminating news of events. 'Thunder[ing] back and forth through doubtful streets ... they carried conviction of force.' It was the presence of these cars and trucks that accounted for the rapid control of the city,' in the opinion of American journalist Isaac Marcosson, covering events for *Everybody's Magazine*. 'It could not have been done afoot.'[34]

The liberation of prisoners from the remand prison next to the District Court was but one of many assaults on the city's jails that day. The prisons were, along with the police, the primary targets of popular fury against the old regime. At around midday Major-General Knox had seen 'a stream of troops ... crossing the bridge to liberate the prisoners in the Krestovsky prison'.[35] Known as The Kresty (meaning 'crosses', from its layout), this prison of solitary confinement and its adjoining women's prison had been built in 1893 on the northern bank of the Neva near the Finland Station to accommodate up to one thousand prisoners, but by 1917 was overcrowded, with more than double that number. It took surprisingly little effort for a small mob of fewer than one hundred to force its way in, shooting the commandant and liberating the inmates – political and criminal alike.

William J. Gibson, a Canadian who lived on the Vyborg Side, saw the first to be released: 'Two men and a woman ... walking towards me dazedly and holding hands as if blind. They wore coarse prison clothes, and the tears streamed down their cheeks. Although not old, all three were practically white-haired. They were political prisoners, and had been in close solitary confinement since 1905.'[36] The trauma of such sudden and unexpected release, when all hope had long gone, was clear to see in the faces of many other 'pale and trembling' politicals, as they emerged from their long incarceration 'looking very ill'. Having been confined in windowless cells, they were blinded by the daylight. Others were so weak they had to be carried outside, where they 'grovelled on the ground and kissed the feet of their comrades who had liberated them'. A few were so overwhelmed that they simply sat down in the snow and wept. Perhaps the most emotive release came at the transportation prison behind the Nicholas Station on Znamensky Square, where, during tsarist rule, every Wednesday morning those condemned to Siberian exile – including the novelist Fyodor Dostoievsky in 1849 – were despatched by rail, chained together by the wrist in groups of 100–150.[37]

At the Krestovsky, as at the District Court, all the prison records were removed and burned in a huge bonfire in the prison yard and the building then set on fire. At the House of Preliminary Detention on Shpalernaya, 958 prisoners were set free; others from the Litovsky prison near the Mariinsky Theatre were liberated the following day. All of the political prisoners were cheered; those who had been imprisoned for a criminal offence in some cases 'were thrashed and told they would forfeit their lives if they were caught again'.[38] There were, however, some prisoners who could not be reached, as Bousfield Swan Lombard noted, 'because in many cases the inmates of prisons were locked in underground cells and in the confusion the keys were lost'; with the prisons then being set on fire, 'most of them were roasted alive before it was possible to liberate them'. Those who did emerge had 'hardly anything on, in the way of clothes'. The crowd took pity on these 'wrecks of humanity' and they were 'accommodated with the most amazing assortment of garments. Little men were dressed up in very long trousers and an enormous man might be seen struggling into a coat and waistcoat much too small.'[39]

Throughout that terrifying day in Petrograd many observers became alarmed by the increasing anarchy and violence of the mob. It might later be asserted – indeed, it became one of the abiding myths of events in February– that this was a 'benign revolution',* but that was not the impression of the many foreign nationals who witnessed it. 'It was like watching some savage beast that had broken out of its cage,' recalled Negley Farson; there would be a price to pay for the release of the more hardened criminals, bestialised by brutal prison conditions, who proceeded to incite the crowds to violence, arson and mass looting, creating an extremely volatile atmosphere.[40] As of that Monday, it became dangerous for any foreign national to venture onto the street without wearing some token of sympathy with the revolution – a red ribbon or armband of some kind; James Stinton Jones took the precaution of wearing a small Union Jack in his buttonhole; another English couple sewed them to their coat sleeves.

Stinton Jones also wisely tuned into the mood of whichever crowd he found himself in: 'As I roamed about I would find myself in one mob shouting: "Long Live the Czar", and then in another mob shouting: "Long Live the Revolution." Whichever one I happened to be in I shouted with them.'[41] Walking to the Duma, Isaac Marcosson encountered 'trucks bristling with guns'. Despite the fact that he had deliberately put on an English trenchcoat and cap, 'the number of young boys with revolvers who looked me over made me feel it was a very easy time in which to be killed'. He was quite sure that 'my continued existence depended on the sanity of any one of thirty or forty very excited men and boys on each truck'.[42] Soon permits would be required for everything. 'I was given a sheaf of papers all covered with stamps and signatures,' recalled one British officer, 'permission to wear a sword – permission to carry a revolver and an identity card which said that I was heart and soul in favour of the new regime!'[43]

As Donald Thompson had already learned that morning, foreigners were constantly being stopped and challenged on the

---

* The term was probably first coined in Hamilton Fyfe's report from Petrograd in the *Daily Mail* for 16 March 1917 (NS), which talked of it being a 'benign revolution' that would rid Russia of the 'pro-German and reactionary elements'.

streets for being policemen or spies, and some were killed if they could not produce proof of identity quickly enough. 'Walking from my house to the Embassy was no joke,' recalled British embassy official Francis Lindley:

Seething crowds of youths brandishing knives and swords and letting off pistols in the air were not made more pleasant by the fact that I could talk very little of their language. Had one of them said I was a German, I should have been done for before I could explain. For it was rather surprising that in the first days of the Revolution anti-German feeling was vocal and several of my patriotic friends with German names were murdered.[44]

That day 'anybody could have a gun for the asking', and with so many untrained and inexperienced people now in possession of them and not 'hav[ing] a care as to which way the gun was pointing when they tried it out for the first time', such indiscriminate firing inevitably led to many innocent bystanders being killed and wounded.[45] Some accidents were the result of sheer bravado: drunks and hooligans firing at random, others showing off to their girlfriends about how to load and fire their weapons. 'Little boys also delighted in picking up dropped cartridges and throwing them into the fires which were burning outside the police-stations,' recalled James Stinton Jones, the resulting explosions causing mayhem and injury. He witnessed one particularly chilling incident involving a boy of about twelve, who was brandishing an automatic pistol while warming himself by a brazier with a group of soldiers:

Suddenly he pulled the trigger and one of the soldiers fell dead. This so alarmed the boy, who had no idea of the mechanism of the deadly weapon he held, that he kept the trigger pulled back and the automatic pistol proceeded to empty itself. It contained seven bullets, and it was not until they were all discharged that the boy released his hold of the trigger. The result was that three soldiers were killed and four seriously injured.[46]

At 1.00 p.m. on Monday, nurse Dorothy Seymour noted in her diary that the men of the Semenovsky Regiment guarding the Anglo-Russian Hospital had 'opened the door and walked out to join the revolutionists without a word to us'.[47] Fighting had been going on all day around the hospital, recalled Edith Hegan, 'machine guns very busy' from nearby rooftops and 'all kinds of unexpected places', the bullets 'throwing up a little shower of snow as they hit the pavement'. Bousfield Swan Lombard, who had made his way to the ARH to see how the staff were doing, found when he got there that 'all the windows were shattered'. He was 'most impressed and very proud to find the British nurses at their posts'. They had ensured that their patients were safely lying under their beds, 'and there they stood, each by her bed, calmly accepting the broken windows and the howling mob outside as an everyday occurrence'.[48]

All day long, people had flocked into the hospital from the street, trying to escape the shooting, and a steady stream of mixed casualties of soldiers and civilians was taken in. Although Dorothy Seymour and four other nurses did manage to get back to the nurses' home on Vladimirsky 'under rather heavy fire from police in windows above armed with revolvers', it was decided that no other nurses should risk it, and the rest had to bed down in the hospital. 'Some slept in the bandage-rooms on tables and stretchers', but they could only snatch brief periods of sleep, as 'many wounded were constantly being brought in'.[49] On several occasions that evening an angry crowd had burst into the hospital and demanded the building be searched for 'hidden police and machine guns' – but the hospital commandant, General Laiming, had assured them this was not so, inviting them to inspect the roof and reminding them that the palace's owner, Grand Duke Dmitri Pavlovich, had been exiled for the murder of Rasputin (and was thus on their side).[50] As they left, the crowd demanded

that the hospital hang a Red Cross flag from its window confirming its neutrality. Lady Sybil Grey hurriedly organised this:
'we made them out of old sheets and a Father Christmas coat,
and also put a lantern with a red cross on it outside the door'.[51]
No sooner had they done this than the flags were pulled down
and used to drape commandeered motor cars. Many of the nurses
sat up by the windows, not wanting to 'miss anything'. Those
who had made it back to their dormitory – two blocks down
the Nevsky on Vladimirsky, through what Dorothy Seymour
described as a 'shilling shocker' night – were too anxious to sleep
and 'spent half the night standing at the window', listening to
the 'terrible agitation' on the street outside.[52]

On Monday morning French actress Paulette Pax had, much to
her amazement, received a call from a friend in the city asking
if there would be a performance at the Mikhailovsky Theatre
that night; and, if so, could she get tickets? This had come just
as Pax had been listening to the sound of the mob and gunfire
in the streets near her apartment in the centre of Petrograd.
Becoming increasingly fearful of looters, she had rushed to hide
away her most precious possessions, with the help of her two
Russian maids, had battened all the shutters and done her best
to protect the doors and windows against possible attack with
mattresses and piles of cushions, before taking refuge, terrified,
in the kitchen. Outside in the courtyard she could hear a crowd
approaching, shouting and jeering, and she prepared herself for
the worst. But it was not her apartment they were heading for:
the mob had come in search of two *faraony* up on the roof of
her apartment building, who had been targeting the crowds below
with a machine gun; and who were quickly overcome and dragged
away.[53]

This incident was symptomatic of the manhunt now in progress.
A long-overdue day of reckoning had arrived, as popular hatred
was visited, with a savage vengeance, on the police. Their presence on the streets had almost totally evaporated and they were
now being systematically 'dug out like rats' from their vantage

points and hiding places.[54] Many had gone into hiding in private houses or had disguised themselves. Mutinying soldiers were particularly enraged to discover that some police had been instructed to wear the uniforms of familiar regiments in order to convince the people that the army was loyal to the old government.[55] All over the city, police stations and the homes of police and judges were attacked and sacked and their possessions thrown from the windows: 'underclothes, ladies' bonnets, chairs, books, flower-pots, pictures, and then all the records, white and yellow and pink paper, all fluttering in the sun like so many butterflies'.[56] Other policemen barricaded themselves into their stations with supplies of food and ammunition, and held out until overcome by their attackers; a few were still manning machine guns on rooftops and in church belfries (which they knew the pious would be loath to attack). When the police were cornered, the mob were merciless: every building connected with them was attacked and sacked, in particular the large block of buildings at number 16 Fontanka, which housed the headquarters of the Okhrana – the tsarist secret police – 'an object of almost fanatical hatred', for its accumulation of information on not just political but even religious dissidents. Here, 'every document, book and scrap of paper' that could be found was brought outside and ceremonially piled onto huge bonfires in the streets.[57] In all, around twelve police stations were set on fire that day – on the Petrograd and Vyborg Sides as well as in central Petrograd; the wisps of blackened pages bearing mug-shots, fingerprints and surveillance records, which had been the bedrock of official oppression for so long, now piles of ash settling in the snow or scattering in the wind.[58]

During the February Revolution there were far too many incidental acts of murder of policemen for any reliable record ever to have been taken of the numbers killed. A very few, when caught by more responsible sections of the mob, were taken to the jails – though the 'crowds would sometimes break through *en route* and strike and kick them to death'.[59] It became a common sight to see policemen being attacked and finished off out of hand – shot, bayoneted, clubbed to death – on the street, their dead bodies left untouched. 'Food for the dogs,' some Russians called it. 'There was no hope for them unless they surrendered,' recalled Dr Joseph Clare, 'and even then not much hope, for I know a place where thirty or forty policemen were pushed through a hole in the ice without as much as a stunning tap on the head – drowned like rats.'[60] Nobody in the city was immune to the experience of such savagery, as Meriel Buchanan recollected of that afternoon, when 'a few English ladies, courageously facing the very real danger of the streets, came to the usual weekly sewing party' at the British embassy. Together they had sat:

in the big red and white ball-room talking in hushed voices, listening to the distant sound of fighting still going on near the Liteynia and comparing notes of what they had seen on their way to the Embassy. One had met a mob of drunken soldiers and workmen who had trussed a policeman up in ropes and were dragging him along the frozen road, another had seen an officer shot down on the doorstep of a house, still another had passed a crowd gathered round a huge bonfire and had been told they were burning a sergeant of the Secret Police.[61]

Such scenes of mindless cruelty left an indelible impression on the seven-year-old mind of the future historian Isaiah Berlin, who vividly remembered a 'horrifying spectacle' when out walking with his parents later that day, as they saw one policeman, 'evidently loyal to the tsarist government, who, it was said, had been sniping at the demonstrators from a rooftop, being dragged by a mob to some awful end: the man looked pale and terrified and was feebly struggling with his captors'. The image, Berlin recalled many years later, had 'remained with me and infected me with a permanent horror of any kind of violence'.[62]

With so much rampant anarchy unleashed on the streets of Petrograd, Duma president Mikhail Rodzianko had sent an urgent telegram to the Tsar that morning, insisting that he return to the city and warning that 'the last hour ha[d] come in which to decide the fate of the country and the dynasty'.[63] Nicholas replied that he was coming back with a reserve of troops to quell the rioting. In the interim the Duma members were at a loss as to how to deal with events that had taken them totally by surprise. With Russia plunged into political uncertainty, the Duma at the Tauride Palace was a magnet for Petrograders all day. Arno Dosch-Fleurot made his way there on foot from the Hotel de France, following the crowds. En route he had noticed the road getting 'thicker and thicker with automobiles and lorries filled with excited unarmed soldiers and serious civilians with rifles'.[64] By about 1.00 p.m. the crowd of thousands massing outside the doors to the Duma was thick with 'green-uniformed and green capped students; many waving red flags and red bunting and listening to revolutionary speeches', all anxious to offer their support to the formation of a new government and seeking instructions on what they should do.[65]

Once the residence of Catherine the Great's lover, Prince Grigory Potemkin, the Tauride Palace – a graceful Palladian building of white colonnades, grand reception rooms and columned galleries – had been home to the Imperial State Duma since 1906. But within hours of events on Monday it had been transformed into a rackety military-camp-cum-political-hustings, where urgent meetings were held to establish a provisional government to take charge of the extremely volatile situation. With difficulty Fleurot had made his way into the building and found it full of troops. 'Everybody seemed to be hungry; bread, dried herrings, and tea' were being endlessly handed around.[66] If anything, 'the mental confusion within was more bewildering than the revolution without', for the whole place seethed with tension and excitement, as regiment after regiment arrived and was 'drawn up in ranks, four deep, down the whole length of the Catherine Hall' – the main lobby and promenade of the Duma – to swear its allegiance to the new government. Rodzianko addressed each of them in turn, urging them to 'remain a disciplined force', to stay faithful to their officers and return quietly to barracks and be ready when called.[67]

At around 2.30 p.m. in the semicircular main hall an enormous, mixed assembly of moderate and liberal members of the Duma met to organise themselves, under Rodzianko's leadership, in hopes that a reformed, constitutional government could yet be salvaged from the wreckage. A twelve-man Provisional Executive Committee was eventually elected that evening to take control of the situation. One of its first acts was to order the arrest of the members of the Council of Ministers – the Upper House of the Duma, and guardians of the old regime – who met at the Mariinsky Palace. Some of them had already tendered their resignations, including the Prime Minister Nikolay Golitsyn; others had gone into hiding, and revolutionary patrols were now searching for them.

Even as the Duma members were establishing their own committee, elsewhere in the Tauride Palace a large group of soldiers and workers intent on nothing less than the declaration of a socialist republic and Russia's withdrawal from the war were meeting with the more moderate Mensheviks and Socialist Revolutionaries (the left-wing Bolshevik presence was yet to make itself felt), with the objective of electing their own Petrograd Soviet of Workers' and Soldiers' Deputies.[68] Its most immediate call, made in a hastily produced leaflet, was not, however, a political one – rather, it was an appeal to citizens to help feed the hungry soldiers who had taken their side, until their revictualling could be properly organised. Petrograders quickly responded, welcoming men into their homes to warm themselves and be fed; restaurants offered free meals; old men were seen in the street 'with large boxes of cigarettes, which they handed out to the soldiers'.[69]*

At about nine o'clock that evening an American resident† went out to have a look at what was going on and encountered 'a

---

* This act of generosity, however, was not always well received, for the troops disliked finely made cigarettes, preferring the very strong, cheap Russian *papirosy* made from vile-smelling *makhorka*.
† Sadly it has not been possible to identify this eyewitness, who published his vivid and valuable account anonymously.

very well dressed intelligent man, running breathlessly up the Kamennoostrovsky Prospekt' on the Petrograd Side, 'stopping a few moments every block to tell the great news: "The Duma has formed a temporary government."' Such an event seemed unimaginable for a country so long under the heel of autocratic rule, he wrote, 'astounding, colossal, not to be grasped at once or even half understood'. Later, at midnight, he went out again and found a 'tremendous mass of people in the square on the Petrograd Side surrounding a truck packed with soldiers from which a 2nd lieutenant was telling the crowd the news: 'Now it's all right,' the American heard him shout, 'there'll be a new government. Do you understand? A new government, and there'll be bread for everybody.' The American was as overwhelmed by this seismic change in Russian political life as were the Russians themselves:

> I don't think any man's mind that night, except the very leaders in the Duma, could stretch fast enough and far enough to do more than struggle with the realization of the simplest and most elementary facts of the revolution – with the plain fact that there actually *was* a revolution.[70]

Throughout the afternoon David Francis had received reports from his staff of the dead and wounded on the Liteiny as clashes there continued; many of the newly armed mob were constantly prowling up and down Furshtatskaya outside the US embassy, some on foot and others in motor cars.[71] One of Francis's officials, returning to his apartment from the embassy that evening, had seen no sign of any remaining loyalty to the old regime, 'but had passed a thousand or more cavalrymen riding quietly toward the Neva and abandoning the streets of the city to the mutineers and revolutionists'. By this time mutiny had spread to the south of the city and the Semenovsky and Izmailovsky Regiments had joined the revolution; by late evening 66,700 men of the imperial army in Petrograd had mutinied. The revolutionaries were now in control of the whole city, except for the Winter Palace, the

Admiralty and the General Staff – still guarded by loyal troops, as were the telephone exchange and the telegraph office.[72]

By nightfall, the first account of the day's events – as published in a crude news-sheet headed *Izvestiya* – had been haphazardly strewn onto the streets from the windows of motor cars. Copies were pounced upon, read and digested, shared and passed around as hungrily as the bread that the people all craved.[73] The whole day had been 'a Revolution carried on by chance', in the opinion of aviator Bert Hall – 'no organization, no particular leader, just a city full of hungry people who have stood enough and are ready to die if necessary before they will put up with any more Tsarism'. Only a week previously Hall had met the Tsar at Pskov and received a decoration for his work with the Russian air service. Today, watching 'that mob of screaming people', he had thought of the 'tired, far-away look in the Tsar's eyes' when he met him. 'He must have known that the dry rot had eaten the heart out of things.'[74]

Later analyses of events in February would often draw comparisons with the French Revolution of 1789 – the storming of the Kresty prison in particular seeming reminiscent of the fall of the Bastille. Returning late to his wife at their apartment on the Petrograd Side, Philip Chadbourn was reminded of Charles Dickens's *A Tale of Two Cities*. The whole of Kamennoostrovsky Prospekt – the main arterial road leading into the Petrograd Side from the Troitsky Bridge – was:

> literally choked with a great surging mass of the revolutionists, who had tramped over here from the fighting zone, to proclaim victory and to draw all lukewarm persons to their flaming cause. It was an earnest, serious crowd, devoid of ranting or vandalism; its temper was that of Russian music – strength with pathos, optimism without joy. Gray army trucks throbbed in the midst of it, loaded with soldiers, women, and boys bearing crimson banners. Bayonets were decked with scraps of red bunting, and bonfires lit up pale faces and eager eyes. Now and again a touring car would thread its

way nervously through the mob, stopping every hundred yards for a student to make a one-minute speech, or continuing to bore its way while Red Cross nurses threw out handfuls of bulletins. The Socialists got out literature so fast that it seemed as if the pent-up energy and stifled utterances of years were behind their presses; strange scraps of paper such as were never seen before in this city floated freely in the air with the headline, 'We asked for bread, you gave us lead.'[75]

Eventually Chadbourn wormed his way through the crowd at the Troitsky Bridge and took in 'the glory of the view that lay before [him]'. 'Over my right shoulder the turrets and castellated walls of Peter and Paul, fortress and prison, threw their grim silhouette against the dying sun, a dynasty gone to rest. To the left the sky was all molten gold and forked with giant tongues of flame; the High Tribunal, Courts of Justice, and jails, instruments of injustice in the Old Order, were making room for the New.' When he and his wife went to bed that night, 'the sky from our windows was still bright from the fire. Rifles snapped fitfully, and the yelling of bands of hooligans reached our ears through double panes.'[76]

Chester Swinnerton and his colleagues also watched the fires across the river on the Petrograd and Vyborg Sides from their vantage point at the bank: 'one great red glare on the horizon with a number of smaller ones, while a continuous intermittent popping of guns could be heard'. It reminded him of the Fourth of July back home; 'people on the street seemed to be in a holiday mood', but it was a 'blessing', he thought, that they had been unable to get hold of much liquor.[77]

Returning to his room at the Astoria Hotel, naval officer Oliver Locker Lampson had no doubts: 'That night Revolution was King, and as no exact news was possible, and the wildest stories were circulated, I opened the double windows of my room and looked out. A rumour as of multitudes cheering arose in one huge roar from the city, and through it came the incessant rattle of shots and the sputtering of maxims. The sky in the east was quite bright and many buildings seemed on fire.'[78]

'Petrograd was flaring like the set-piece of a colossal firework display,' recalled William J. Gibson. But while the night sky was dramatic, and the atmosphere in the city exhilarating, others such as Major-General Knox were already looking beyond the intoxication of the moment: 'The prisons were opened, the workmen were armed, the soldiers were without officers, a *sovyet* [Soviet, a workers' council] was being set up in opposition to the Temporary Committee chosen from the elected representatives of the people.' All this was a matter of serious political concern. To Knox's mind, Petrograd 'was already on the high road to anarchy'.[79]

5

Easy Access to Vodka 'Would Have Precipitated a Reign of Terror'

Heavy firing could still be heard across Petrograd for most of Monday night; by Tuesday 28 February the revolutionaries had commandeered large numbers of machine guns and were using captured armoured cars 'with considerable effect'.[1] The many soldiers now aimlessly roaming the streets unsettled everyone. Meriel Buchanan watched from the British embassy as a group of them crossed the Neva from the Petrograd Side; they seemed already to have 'lost their upright, well-drilled bearing, they looked slovenly and bedraggled, they held themselves badly, slouching along, their collars undone, their caps stuck on at any angle, an odd assortment of weapons tied on to them with bits of rope or string or scarlet tape.' Some, incongruously, had officers' swords buckled round their waists, while others had 'two or three pistols stuck into their pockets or hung round their neck on a bit of string'.[2]

It was no wonder that over on the volatile Petrograd Side from which this rabble had come, Philip Chadbourn had become fearful for the safety of his wife and three-week-old baby son and had gratefully accepted an offer to stay with friends on the French Embankment. But there were no cabs to be had; Esther Chadbourn was still weak, and two friends had to assist her in walking into the city, with her husband leading the way with the baby in his arms. As they emerged into the street, his wife took one look at the crowds and the barricades and field artillery and her nerves totally gave way. 'Each time a shot rang out,' Philip remembered, 'she would call ahead to me, "Don't let them kill my baby, my baby!", while passers-by stopped and stared at her, their eyes full of tears.' Once safely installed in their friends' house, the couple 'watched the progress of the revolution from the front windows' commanding the quayside, as one continual procession of motor cars roared past, loudly tooting their horns. On the streets it was the same jubilant crowds as the previous day, trashing the police stations and 'throwing armfuls of records out of windows onto blazing street bonfires' with a 'righteous zest'.[3]

Stubborn to the last, Sir George Buchanan, impeccable as ever with his 'high straight collar and his high straight face', headed off on foot again that morning to the now effectively defunct Russian Foreign Ministry, intent on paying 'a farewell visit to Monsieur Pokrovsky', who had not yet been arrested.[4] His staff begged him not to go: there was fighting going on between two rival factions of the Pavlovsky Regiment in the Millionnaya, the street immediately behind the British embassy. Lady Georgina found her husband putting on his overcoat in the hall, 'rather like a naughty little boy caught in an act of disobedience'. She remonstrated with him to take the car, but Sir George was insistent: 'I had much rather walk'; and with that he took up his gloves and stick, 'with his fur cap set at the rakish angle he always affected' and, in true British bulldog spirit, headed off. It was only later that his daughter Meriel discovered that as her father had crossed Suvorov Square and headed off down the Millionnaya, 'word had gone round that the British Ambassador was coming down the street, and ... with one accord, the soldiers put down their rifles and stood waiting respectfully till that tall grey-haired figure had passed, when they once more renewed their fusillade at each other with undiminished vigour'.[5]

Chester Swinnerton and his colleagues at the National City Bank had watched in disbelief as Sir George walked past the bank, 'surrounded by an admiring throng of the populace, most of them armed to the teeth, and Sir George bowing and smiling as if he were at a court function'.[6] Buchanan had found Pokrovsky alone at his ministry, without electricity and with no access to the telegraph. Walking back with Maurice Paléologue, who had also arrived, the two ambassadors had been cheered by a group of students on the Palace Embankment. They insisted on giving Paléologue a lift in an armoured car to the French embassy, during which journey he was harangued by a boisterous student: 'Pay your respects to the Russian Revolution! The red flag is Russia's now; do homage to it in the name of France!'[7]

Undeterred by his experience that morning, Sir George ventured forth again in the afternoon with the same unshakeable sangfroid, accompanied by his Head of Chancery, Henry James Bruce, to pay a visit to Russian diplomat Sergey Sazonov* at his hotel on the Nevsky, though he admitted in his later memoirs that 'the rattle of machine guns overhead was not a pleasant accompaniment'. The experience had terrified Bruce, who, on their return to the embassy, reported how the 'Old Man' 'had refused to turn back or take cover, and had remained perfectly calm, laughing and talking as if nothing had happened'.[8]

At the US embassy, David Francis, anxious for the safety of his staff, had ordered the Stars and Stripes to be raised over the building, due to the incessant firing all day and the frequent arrival of mobs asking what the building was and demanding to enter and search it. Other embassies raised their flags too, while down at the US consulate in the Singer Building on the Nevsky, things had become extremely precarious because of sniping from its roof, and the consul, North Winship, had prepared his most valuable archives for immediate evacuation. The consulate, he reported, was under constant threat of attack; indeed, it had 'been under suspicion since the beginning of the war as being German,

---

* Sazonov had been appointed Russian Ambassador to Great Britain early in 1917, but the outbreak of the February Revolution had prevented him from taking up his post.

the masses believing the Singer Company to be a German corporation'. He had repeatedly had to defend the American eagle on the top of the building, which the mob wanted to tear down, thinking it a German eagle.[9]

That day several foreign nationals were caught up in the most dangerous debacle yet, which took place at the Astoria Hotel on St Isaac's Square. For the last six months, since being commandeered 'as a luxurious headquarters for the higher officers', the Astoria, the second-biggest and most modern hotel in Petrograd, had been popularly referred to as the 'Military Hotel'.[10] Every room was crammed with either Allied officers – French, Romanian, Serbian, British and Italian – or Russian officers on leave from the front, many of whom had their wives, mothers and children with them. There were also a few resident foreign journalists, such as the Americans Harper and Thompson.[11]

For days everyone had feared an attack on the hotel. Naval attaché Oliver Locker Lampson had already urged that residents avoid the downstairs hall in case of any stray shots from the street, and ordered that Allied officers occupy the basement. He had heard reports that an agent of Protopopov's had taken refuge in the hotel and that the revolutionaries would 'inevitably come and search for him'. He was well aware, too, of the predicament of the Russian officers: 'If the Government won and got here first they might be shot for not having helped: if the Revolutionaries were successful and reached us, then they would be shot for not joining in.' Eventually it was decided to move all Allied officers upstairs and transfer the Russians below. As anticipated, at around 4.00 a.m. a deputation of soldiers and civilians had arrived, demanding that the Russians billeted there join the revolution. They had been persuaded to disperse on receiving assurance from those officers 'that they were on leave, that the foreign nationals would observe neutrality and that no one would start shooting from the building'.[12]

But four hours later trouble ignited, when a regiment gathered for a parade in St Isaac's Square. At 9.00 a.m. YMCA worker

Edward Heald was heading to his office when, at the corner of Gogol, he saw 'column after column of soldiers, in martial order, greeted with the shouts of the people assembled in the square', red flags flying, a band playing and making 'a brilliant spectacle'. The troops had lined up facing the Astoria Hotel when 'suddenly there was a tremendous volley and the sidewalks and squares were emptied of people in the twinkling of an eye' and Heald hurried to safety.[13] In his nearby office building he watched from the sixth-floor window as some of the soldiers threw themselves down in front of the cathedral, firing at a machine-gun position on the roof of the Astoria. From inside the hotel, Locker Lampson saw the soldiers dive helplessly into the snow for cover, 'first a man here and then one there would stop suddenly and remain, black against the white and stretched out quite flat, until soon the place seemed empty except for these dead bodies'.[14]

According to Donald Thompson, who was in the hotel at the time, some hothead or policeman hidden somewhere on the top floor of the Astoria had opened fire, enraging the crowd outside who had gathered to watch the parade. Woken from an exhausted sleep by the shooting, Thompson had grabbed his camera, broken out a windowpane and begun photographing the mob rushing across the square and stampeding the hotel. During the ensuing fusillade a Russian female guest ran into his room screaming that the police were firing from the roof. He warned her to keep away from the window, but '[i]nstead, she pulled aside the curtain to look out. She was shot through the throat.' Thompson 'carried her back to the bathroom where she died about fifteen minutes later'. He was furious: 'I lost a lot of my film, thanks to this woman's damn foolishness.' Soon afterwards, hearing shots being fired inside the hotel, he hurriedly pinned an American flag to his door and hoped for the best.[15]

Locker Lampson, meanwhile, had identified where he thought the firing was coming from: 'no sound came from the room, except the smack of striking bullets'. He rammed the door in and found two terrified women in their nightdresses – Princess Tumanova and her mother. There was blood everywhere and he got them out of the room to administer first aid.[16] According to Canadian eyewitness George Bury, the revolutionaries had quickly 'brought up a couple of armoured motors with three machine-guns apiece' and had opened 'a furious cannonade upon the position on the roof of the Astoria from where the shots had come', the bullets instead 'ripping into the suite of General Prince Tumanov located just below it'. One of the women had been wounded in the neck and was later taken to the Anglo-Russian Hospital.[17]

By now the hotel had been stormed by 'a howling, raging mob, armed to the teeth', which sacked the ground floor, 'killed some Russian officers, and surged up the staircase, shooting up the lift and in every direction,' as Sybil Grey recalled.[18] Glass was showered everywhere as the hotel's huge plate-glass windows were shattered by gunfire. Florence Harper was terrified as the mob 'spread over the ground floor like rats'. 'Everyone was panic-stricken'; the only ones who kept their heads, as she recalled, were the 'British officers attached to the General Staff'. With smoke pouring out of the elevator-shaft and down the stairway, pandemonium reigned. 'Terrified women were rushing around, some of them fully dressed, some only half dressed, begging to be saved.' 'The coolest woman in the hotel,' she noted, 'was an Englishwoman who was found sitting on her trunk, which was packed, smoking a cigarette … ready for any emergency that might take place.'[19]

Fearful for the safety of the women and children, the British officers 'formed a guard in front of them', calling on the mob to fall back or they 'would protect them to the last man'.[20] Two of them, General Poole and a Lieutenant Urmston who spoke good Russian, tried to hold the rabble back on the stairs and reason with them: 'if they intended to kill everybody in [the hotel] at least they should allow the officers to remove the women and children first'. There was an ominous pause, recalled Harper, after which 'a big, burly soldier reached down in his pocket, pulled out a package of the vilest kind of cigarettes', handed one to General Poole and invited him to share a smoke. The lieutenant lit a match, 'held it to the general's cigarette, then to the soldier's, and then blew it out, explaining to the soldier that it was bad luck to light three cigarettes with one match. That appealed to the soldier, who, like all Russians, was very superstitious'; the gesture seemed to defuse the situation.[21] *Times* correspondent Robert Wilton was convinced that 'the coolness and pluck of the British and French officers alone prevented the wholescale murder of Russian Generals, ladies, and children' at the Astoria that day, and that the 'Allied uniforms inspired sufficient respect to contain the violence'. On seeing the British uniforms in particular, Sybil Grey noticed, some of the crowd even 'took off their hats and said, "English officers! Forgive us, we do not wish to bother you," and passed on in the most courteous manner possible to do more destruction to the hotel and its inmates'.[22]

They remained intent, however, on laying hands on the Russian officers inside. 'What are you going to do with them?' called out the wife of one: 'Shoot some of them outside and arrest the others,' cried their spokesman laconically. 'They asked for it.' Some of the Russian officers resisted, including the old general in charge, and were shot on the spot; others came forward willingly, hands in the air, shouting, 'We're for you', and were allowed to keep their swords and arms. Yet others were dragged to the square outside. James Stinton Jones saw some of them being summarily shot in the courtyard of the empty German embassy on the other side of St Isaac's Square.[23]

After wrecking the foyer of the Astoria, the first place the mob headed for was the kitchen: 'it was quite a sight to see a soldier with a huge officer's sword cutting up a tub of butter and passing it out to the people,' recalled the intrepid Chester Swinnerton, who could not resist leaving the safety of the bank to investigate. In the downstairs hall Leighton Rogers, who joined him, saw 'a crowd of soldiers were stuffing themselves' with 'such food as they had never tasted before and shouting the Marseillaise ... to the accompaniment of a piano'.[24] Foreign residents were fearful for their personal possessions as the intruders, 'scenting loot in the carpeted corridors and luxurious flats of the hotel', mounted the stairs.[25] One of the looters assured a British journalist who begged them not to loot their rooms, 'You come up and show us which are the foreigners' rooms and we won't go in.'[26] When a soldier arrived at the room of another lady resident, she 'came to him with her hands full of money'. 'What's this for?' he asked. 'We're on quite a different job here.'[27]

While there may have been a degree of honour among these thieves, 'the hotel was at their mercy' and it was decided that 'the spectacle of a wounded woman might avoid trouble'. And so, as Locker Lampson recalled, 'they laid the wounded Princess Toumanov on a mattress in the passage and surrounded her with pillows covered in blood'. Soon the crowd 'came on in yelling parties, gesticulating and arguing, and reached the fourth floor to demand all our arms. The moment they saw the princess they calmed although one drunken civilian let his rifle off over her head.' The British officers gave up their revolvers and swords and showed the revolutionaries where the telephones were, 'which were all destroyed'. Once again the situation was contained and, although some small articles of value were taken from the rooms of residents, 'on the whole the search was orderly'.[28]

Once the brief pitched battle on the ground floor of the hotel was over, every stick of furniture and every chandelier had been smashed and the Russian officers hauled off, the mob's remaining objective was to seek out any alcohol. Having anticipated this, several British officers had gone down to the Astoria's famous wine cellars to destroy the wine and spirits before the looters got to it. Although some bottles had already been eagerly carried away, the officers, led by Captain Scale and 'with the help of students and some soldiers intelligent enough to realize the disastrous consequences' if the mob got its hands on the alcohol, set about 'smash[ing] bottles until their arms were so weary they could not lift them', as Florence Harper witnessed. 'They staved in all the casks of cognac and whiskey until they were literally knee deep in everything from champagne to vodka.'[29]

Outside on the square, the crowd knocked the necks off those bottles that they had managed to loot with the butt-ends of their rifles and began drinking the contents, as a constant flow of people continued 'rushing in and out through the slippery blood-stained doors carrying great piles of paper and records' to throw on a bonfire in the square.[30] Some of the revolutionaries had attempted to remonstrate with their comrades at the sight of large piles of broken bottles and had grabbed what they could and poured it away, urging them not to 'spoil our fight for freedom by drinking and looting'.[31] This spirit of revolutionary purity continued to prevail when later that afternoon Florence Harper saw a man flourishing a bottle of wine outside the Astoria. As he raised it to his mouth, 'a student came along, snatched it out of his hands, broke it, and said, "Don't drink! If you do, all our work will be undone."' Such admonitions had little effect, however. James Stinton Jones witnessed the inventive ways used by some soldiers to carry away what they did not drink on the spot, outside the Astoria: they 'poured wine into their top-boots and then wandered away to consume more elsewhere'.[32] Everyone agreed it was a mercy that the mob had not been able to lay hands on more from the hotel cellars. 'This was one time when prohibition was a blessing to Russia,' wrote Edward Heald – the Astoria's copious supply being, of course, for the benefit of guests only. Heald, like many other eyewitnesses, was convinced that 'if vodka could have been found in plenty, the revolution could easily have had a terrible ending'. His compatriot James Hough-teling agreed: easy access to vodka 'unquestionably would have precipitated a reign of terror reminiscent of the French Revolution'.[33]

Back inside the wrecked foyer of the Astoria, in sight of the potted palms still standing, incongruously, in their brass pots, 'the revolving doors were spinning round in a pool of blood'. The great plate-glass windows were 'jaggedly shattered and gaping', causing the expensive curtains to make 'a torn and draggled track in the snow outside'. 'The furniture was grotesquely dismembered and upset, papers, books and even stationery were strewn half-burnt everywhere.' The hotel tea room and the big restaurant were also a scene of utter devastation. 'Bodies were littered about, and the wounded crying piteously.'[34] James Houghteling went with an American colleague to inspect the damage and was bemused to discover 'in one room where the furniture was a pile of kindling wood and even the electric brackets had been torn away … large framed photographs of the Tsar, the Tsarina and the Tsarevich hanging on the walls perfectly undisturbed'.[35]

Upstairs, residents remained cowering and hungry all day in their barricaded rooms, until eventually the women and children were allowed to be taken away to safety in convoys of military and embassy cars. Some of them took refuge in the Italian embassy across St Isaac's Square, others at the Hotel d'Angleterre next door. Florence Harper tried to get something to eat at the Angleterre, but found its dining room packed with people – Romanians, Russians, Serbs, French, English, Japanese – 'every allied nation, every neutral nation' – all 'scrambling and fighting for food'. She went back to the Astoria to try her luck there, but found the same scene: hundreds of people waiting to get cabbage soup and some kind of game, which she labelled 'roast crow'. It was unsafe to eat any vegetables, even when there were any, because of the danger of dysentery, so she stuck to tinned sardines and Dutch cheese. 'Someone had found some ship's biscuits', which they shared, and had 'bribed the waiter for some cocoa'.[36]

Later that evening any Allied officers who wished to leave the hotel were allowed to do so and were cheered by the lingering crowd as they departed. But many decided to stay – 'not from choice, but from necessity, because all the Petrograd hotels were full'. Such in fact was the accommodation crisis that by nightfall some of the British officers came back: 'I might just as well be blown up as freeze to death,' one of them told Harper, for rumours had persisted all day that the Astoria would be destroyed – 'they were going to blow it up with dynamite'.[37]

For hours after the attack on the Astoria 'drunken soldiers littered the sidewalks'. Amid the huge piles of broken glass, furniture and books from the hotel, women 'went around gathering bits of broken plates, or anything they could lay their hands on'. 'The souvenir hunters were busy,' noted Florence Harper, but through it all 'the mob was the best natured mob I have ever seen'. However, for 'days and days afterward there was a reek of wine' in the locality of the hotel that she found 'sickening', and broken glass underfoot everywhere in the square. This, plus the burnt-out remains of the bonfires, transformed the once-beautiful St Isaac's Square into 'a desolate sight'.[38] Shutters replaced the broken windows of the Astoria and, for its embattled guests, making do in rooms now riddled with bullets, there was no electric lighting and no heating, either. 'It was rather like inhabiting a monastery in the war zone,' recalled British intelligence officer Denis Garstin.[39]

Looting had in fact been in evidence all over the city that Tuesday, much of it the work of many of the eight thousand criminals liberated from the city's jails. English governess Louisette Andrews recalled seeing people – predominantly soldiers and sailors – running down the streets with strings of looted sausages draped around their necks, or clutching legs of lamb and armfuls of fur coats. But the most sought-after looted items, she recalled, were expensive watches: 'they were the one thing the mob all went for', and soon there was 'not a watch to be had in any jewellers' shop' in Petrograd.[40]

Burglary, sexual assault, mugging and acts of drunken violence were all on the increase. As nurse Edith Hegan wrote in her diary: 'It seems to have been a terrible mistake to turn loose the convicted prisoners, for they have gone quite mad with blood lust and are leading the mob into all sorts of depredations.' There was, she noted with alarm, a 'deadly fixedness of purpose in the crowd to-day, as if it had crystallized its own desires'.[41] What she and other foreigners witnessed was the ugly face of *stikhiya* – the elemental spontaneity of anarchy in its most destructive, primeval form. An impulse long latent beneath the surface of civilised Russian society, *stikhiya* had from time to time found its explosive expression among the peasantry as a 'primitive force of the oppressed classes, to which any political articulation remained alien'; and now, in Petrograd, it was being unleashed on its age-old class enemies.[42]

This raggle-taggle army bent on retribution continued to patrol the streets, armed with every kind of imaginable weapon. There was still a great deal of random firing – into the air 'or as best amuses them … shooting at every thing and every body'.[43] And all this despite printed leaflets being distributed, exhorting people not to fire guns 'promiscuously' and to save their ammunition – 'for the time is coming when it will be needed'.[44] Self-appointed bands of vigilantes, some of them released criminals disguised as soldiers, now instituted random and often violent house-to-house searches: not just for police still evading capture, but also for any hidden supplies, especially of weapons, alcohol and food. Homes abandoned by their terrified owners – particularly members of the aristocracy – were a prime target, the mob helping themselves, with aimless compulsion, to the finest but most useless furniture and furnishings, china and glass. Nervous citizens barricaded themselves in their homes; any refusal to admit search teams led to doors being battered down and occupants who resisted being ruthlessly shot: young and old, women and children.

General Count Gustave Stackelberg – a Russian-Estonian nobleman and former counsellor to Nicholas II – was shot and killed in front of his wife when his home on Millionnaya was stormed, but not before he had put up fierce resistance and killed several of his assailants with his revolver. Leighton Rogers and his colleagues at the National City Bank had seen Stackelberg (as they later discovered) come running outside onto the Palace Embankment, firing several shots before cowering behind a lamp post. He didn't last long: 'a bullet cleaned the top of his head right off,' recalled Swinnerton.[45] Yet in the midst of this, as Swinnerton noticed, 'about a hundred yards away a soldier and his sweetheart were sitting on the parapet and chinning [chattering] away as if they hadn't a care in the world'. Stackelberg's body was left there in the middle of road, where it was trampled by passing mounted patrols. When Swinnerton and his colleagues returned home from work that night, it had been stripped of most of its uniform – 'for souvenirs', Rogers supposed. It was later tossed into the Neva, or rather onto it, for it landed on the river's frozen surface and was left to languish there.[46]

With such rampant hatred of the old order being demonstrated on the streets, it was inevitable that some members of the Russian aristocracy would appeal to Sir George Buchanan and other ambassadors for sanctuary. This put Sir George in a difficult position, as he could only extend his protection to those who were British subjects.* When their home was looted and destroyed by the mob, the daughters of Count Vladimir Freedericksz, minister of the Imperial Court who was away with the Tsar at Stavka, had begged the British embassy to take them and their sick mother in. They were refused, supposedly due to 'the social vanity' of Lady Buchanan, who had complained, 'I don't know why I should take in the Countess Fredericks when she never once asked me to her house or to her box at the Opera.'[47]† In contrast, Ambassador Francis had sent out his Second Secretary Norman Armour 'to brave the bullets', specifically to invite the US national Countess Nostitz, who lived three blocks away, to 'take up quarters at the Embassy that [she] might be under the protection of the American flag'. Nostitz was touched by his offer, but preferred to remain with her Russian husband and trust to her luck.[48]

Although entry into private homes by revolutionists was frequently violent and terrifying, it occasionally resulted in a more

---

* Such as Victoria Melita, Grand Duchess Kirill – known as 'Ducky' in the royal family – who was a daughter of Queen Victoria's son, Prince Alfred.

† In the end, Rev. Bousfield Swan Lombard at the British Chaplaincy gave refuge to Countess Freedericksz and her two daughters, under the alias of 'Mrs Wilson', Buchanan telling him, 'you must do it off your own bat' and that he could not officially sanction it. The women were taken into the British Colony's Nursing Home. The countess was sworn to secrecy and certain preconditions by Bousfield Lombard, but she and her daughters soon broke all the rules and had to be moved.

conciliatory turn of events, as Ella Woodhouse, daughter of the British consul, remembered of the moment when a group came to their apartment, demanding admission to search:

> Father invited them into the dining room, where we were having tea by the light of one or two candles, the electricity was off. They all sat down. I do not remember whether they were actually offered tea, but I retain the picture of the tense circle, round the long table in the dark room, lit only by flickering candles, the boys sitting awkwardly as father began explaining very politely, that they were welcome to search the place, but that they would then be violating diplomatic immunity, which he was sure they must know was a serious offence in a civilized country. This approach led to a general discussion on the aims of the Great Revolution. Gradually they relaxed and all joined in. The discussion continued for quite a long time. Then, with expressions of mutual goodwill, they went away.[49]

But there was no such *politesse* for wine and provision shop owners. J. Butler Wright reported that they were 'either forced to open their establishments, or the shops themselves were broken into', although there was some attempt to keep control of the situation and 'ensure that goods were distributed fairly and shop owners paid'. James Houghteling was delighted to learn that his cook had 'bought from soldiers at ridiculously low prices all sorts of supplies, bolts of cloth, flour etc., which were taken from government stores that had been refusing them to the people for months'.[50] Some of the premises that were searched revealed surprises: a cache of thousands of rifles and ammunition was found in a store in a butcher's shop, probably hidden there by the police. When the crowd broke into the house of one police officer, 'they found a whole shop-full of everything, flour (of which we have been able to get none), cognac, herrings,' reported his English neighbour.[51] A dyer's and cleaner's that had been boarded up for months contained piles of hams, long thought unobtainable. Endless hoards of flour and sugar (which the government had claimed were exhausted, but had been stockpiled for bribery) were unearthed, 'for the most part in the private residences of police officers' – so many, in fact, that this reinforced the widespread public conviction that the police had been 'systematically using their opportunities to corner food-supplies in their districts'. Arthur Ransome reported that 'some policemen had even been keeping live hens in their room'.[52]

The relentless search for policemen continued throughout Tuesday. In a last-ditch attempt to evade capture, some of them adopted an unconvincing disguise as women, as James Stinton Jones related. The bigger men 'hardly did justice to the fair sex' and their identity was 'invariably betrayed by their general bearing and size'. He noticed one of them – 'a man, standing fully six feet, and broad-shouldered, and his general bearing and walk was certainly anything but feminine'. He was quickly spotted by the crowd, who 'stopped him and took off his hat, which came away with a long wig and the thick veil, leaving a very coarse-featured masculine face with a heavy moustache. He immediately fell on his knees and begged for mercy, but the crowd dispatched him without further ado.' Down near the canal Amélie de Néry saw twelve bodies of policemen that had been stripped naked and left lying there.[53] Not long afterwards she came upon another sinister sight:

a flat sledge on which a naked body had been thrown and covered with a white sheet, the legs hanging over the sides a little and the naked feet dragging along in the snow. A bulge in the sheet covering the chest suggested its head had been cut off. Patches of blood spattered this miserable bundle. It was probably the mortal remains of some policeman or other being taken off to a mortuary somewhere.[54]

James Stinton Jones saw the 'horrible appearance of the snow' after a policeman had literally been torn 'limb from limb' on the street by an enraged mob. He also was told of some police officers caught in their homes being tied to their divans or sofas, 'covered with kerosene and then set alight'. Dorothy Seymour heard tell of a local police chief being tied up and thrown on the bonfire outside his police station. Leighton Rogers was shocked to discover that a policeman who had shot a soldier on the corner outside their apartment 'was promptly bayoneted and beheaded, much to the horror of our little servant girl who chanced to be passing'. Once discovered, individual policemen manning guns on rooftops could never hold out for long, and 'with an exultant shout, one by one, forced to the edge at bayonet point, they crashed to the street below to be spit upon and reviled by the gathering crowd'.[55]

6

'Good to be Alive These Marvelous Days'

Reporting on events to the Foreign Office at the end of March 1917, Hugh Walpole concluded that 'On the whole, it may be truthfully said that, so far as Petrograd was concerned, by the Tuesday evening the revolution was over.'[1] The tsarist government was finished; the Arsenal – last rallying point of the old regime – had finally surrendered at 4.00 p.m. when the rebels had threatened to turn the guns of the Peter and Paul Fortress onto it. The whole of the army in Petrograd had now thrown in its lot with the revolutionaries, including the elite naval unit – the Guard Equipage commanded by Grand Duke Kirill – the Cadet Corps and 350 officers of the General Staff College; finally even the garrison that had guarded the imperial family at Tsarskoe Selo had joined them.[2]

But 'grave anxiety' remained among the diplomatic community as to the future, with the struggle between the new Soviet and the Executive Committee of the Duma intensifying. 'So successful, in fact, had everything been, so far beyond men's wildest hopes,' Walpole noted, 'that no one could believe that a sharp reverse was not in store.' Quite simply, 'it was all too good to be true'. *Times* correspondent Robert Wilton had been convinced from the start that 'the institution of the Soviet was tantamount to preparing beforehand the overthrow of any Coalition Government', and he could see the 'utter hopelessness' of the efforts of the moderates in the Duma to institute some form of democratic government.[3]

Foreign observers all wanted to see how this new power struggle would pan out, and many made their way to the Tauride
Palace on Tuesday 28 February to watch history in the making.
Troops had been arriving there all day from outlying areas to
pledge their allegiance to the revolution, accompanied by endless
deputations of workers and civilians. The Shpalernaya was 'a wild
concourse of disorganized troops and populace, all happy and
good-natured,' recalled James Houghteling, 'a kaleidoscope of
soldiers, armed and unarmed, civilians, mounted Cossacks, automobiles full of red-cross nurses and of uniformed students, and
trucks packed tight with humanity and bristling with bayonets
and red flags'. Amélie de Néry was caught up in the crowd, too:
'the Christlike heads with fair or auburn beards of *muzhiks*, clean-
shaven faces of soldiers, grimy lambskin coats, fur dresscoats,
long-haired hats or student caps – all undulating, swelling or
pitching like a sea!' Amidst these dense crowds were 'motor-lorries
loaded with as many as thirty excited soldiers, motor-cars, bat-
teries of guns, on which children were disporting themselves,
patrols of cavalry'.[4] Some students were there on horseback; the
people called them the 'black hussars'. Yet more lorries full of
joyriding soldiers were arriving every minute and 'unloading great
trucks of provisions into the main entrance of the Tauride Palace,
as if the national assembly expected to be besieged'.[5]

For young New Yorker Leighton Rogers, it was 'a spectacle
never to be forgotten': 'a shifting, wavering sea of faces now
parting and billowing up against the walls as a new arrest borne
in an open truck picked its way to the gates, now washing over
the swathe again in eager restlessness. Now silent when some
important personage mounted the gate to give instructions, now
bursting into a mighty roar as some popular hero sifted through
on his way to the halls.'[6] James Houghteling saw some captured
policemen brought in. 'It seemed rather decent to give these
hated enemies even a drumhead court-martial,' he thought. Some
of them were still wearing their black uniforms, a few were disguised as soldiers and others were dressed as *dvorniki* (doormen),
who had a reputation for being police spies. But 'the great bulk

were broad-shouldered thugs only to be identified as policemen out of uniform'. 'Some were heavily bandaged and had to be dragged along,' Houghteling noticed. 'A few fidgeted nervously and hung back, but most were surprisingly stolid.' He expected to hear the inevitable volley of shots, but no, these policemen were not summarily shot, but were apparently taken off to 'some extemporised prison'.[7]

Visitors accessing the Duma were now expected to produce 'curious scraps of various paper which served as passes', as George Bury recalled, and 'which were inspected by volunteer students and schoolboys'. 'Inside the courtyard the masses of soldiery and people were more tightly wedged than ever': it took twenty minutes for him to cross some thirty yards of courtyard and mount the few entrance steps to the Duma portico. There was such a crush at the door that he had difficulty making his way through. By dint of a lot of polite pushing and shoving ('May I pass, allies?', 'Let me through, little brothers'), Bury made his way through to the vast white-pillared Catherine Hall, 'like a cathedral nave a hundred yards in length', which was filled with 'the same mob listening to impassioned speeches delivered from tables and chairs or the steps and balcony leading to the door for the higher tiers of seats in the legislative chamber'. A pitched battle for precedence was taking place; a cacophony of shouting by would-be speakers vying to be heard above the din: 'soldiers, young officers, frenzied political orators, even an occasional deputy were busy tasting the sweets of "freedom of speech" for the first time for a dozen years past'. Bury sensed the release of long-held feelings repressed since the 1905 Revolution: 'a little bit of Hyde Park on a Sunday morning in the forgotten days before the war'.[8]

The beautiful Tauride Palace had by now been transformed into one great warehouse. 'Half the great rotunda, which serves as first antechamber, was filled with machine-guns and belts, ammunition boxes, and the like in great piles as if flung in anyhow, together with hundreds of rolls of soldiers' cloth, and a heap of boots, all in the utmost disorder, balanced on the opposite side by a rampart ten feet high of sacks of flour,' reported George

Bury.[9] The Circular Hall was equally piled high with provisions of all kinds, its fine parquet floor 'strewn with cigarette ends and empty tins and papers and bags and cardboard boxes and even broken bottles'. Hugh Walpole despaired at the 'dirt and desolation' he saw, in the midst of which 'a huge mass of men stirred and coiled and uncoiled like some huge ant-heap', joined by yet more soldiers 'tumbling in like puppies or babies with pieces of red cloth tied to their rifles, some singing, some laughing, some dumb with amazement'.[10]

Within the Tauride Palace the chaotic idealism of the first couple of days of revolution was now giving way to hard bargaining over the form of Russia's future government. The Soviet of Workers' and Soldiers' Deputies had held its first plenary session that day, in an atmosphere that had been a far cry from the bourgeois restraint of the Duma's former occupants. Instead, a motley crowd of vociferous factory workers and peasant soldiers, resembling 'a giant village assembly', had crammed into a densely packed, hot and smelly room, its tables littered with bread and herring, all of the attendees eager for debate.[11] General Knox observed Duma chairman Mikhail Rodzianko in the Catherine Hall urging the mass of soldiers gathered there to 'go back to their barracks and maintain order, as otherwise they would degenerate into a useless mob'. But Knox noted little sign of organisation or of people working. 'Soldiers lounged everywhere'; in one room he saw Duma member, Boris Engelhardt, 'trying to function as Military Commandant', sitting at a table 'on which was a huge loaf of half-gnawed black bread' and trying in vain to 'make himself heard above the noise of a rabble of soldiers, all spitting and smoking and asking questions'.[12]

It was already abundantly clear that any power-sharing between two such diametrically opposed groups as the Executive Committee of the Duma and the new Soviet would be extremely fraught. For the members of the Soviet, the former Duma members of the Executive Committee represented the enemy: the old order of capitalists, the bourgeoisie and the aristocracy. It was clear to George Bury that the Soviet was rapidly becoming 'the real master of the situation'; its members had the rifles and the brute force. But for now it was the old guard of the Duma that possessed 'the self-assurance and the technique of governing', even as a procession of former tsarist ministers arrived under arrest throughout the day.[13]

Come the afternoon, a cowed and cadaverous-looking Boris Stürmer, former President of the Council of State, was brought in, his teeth chattering with fear. Alongside Stürmer was Pitirim, the Metropolitan of Petrograd. Claude Anet saw Stürmer arrive, surrounded by soldiers bristling with revolvers – 'an old man, his cap in his hand, enveloped in a big fur-collared Nicholas cloak reaching to his feet. His face was as white as his long beard; his pale blue eyes were expressionless; he appeared to notice nothing, to have fallen into his second childhood, and advanced, seemingly unconscious of his surroundings, with tottering steps.'[14] Metropolitan Pitirim – a close associate of Rasputin's, who had been found hiding at the Alexander Nevsky Monastery – was still wearing his black gown and gold episcopal cross and seemed 'prey to the most abject fear'. With his mouth half-open and terrified eyes, he looked like a condemned criminal being led to the scaffold.[15] Then former Prime Minister Ivan Goremykin arrived, 'a Carnival figure' with his great flamboyant whiskers, and wearing his tsarist order of St Andrew defiantly pinned to his coat like some kind of protective talisman.[16] Ivan Shcheglovitov, President of the Imperial Council and former Minister of Justice and a bastion of the old reactionary order, was brought in under arrest at 5.00 p.m., his hands bound.

But the man all the revolutionaries had been searching for – the notorious Minister of the Interior, Alexander Protopopov, roundly despised as the Empress's puppet – was not found at his empty apartment, which had earlier been ransacked and relieved of a considerable stash of champagne. Finally, at 11.15 p.m. he shuffled into the Tauride Palace in a shabby fur coat and gave himself up. After two days 'wandering about the streets, seeking refuge with his friends and being refused by all', he capitulated, claiming he 'desired the welfare of [the] country'.[17] Having, so it was said, handed over a large map of Petrograd with all the police hiding places marked on it, he was taken off 'pale and tottering' to a prison cell in the Peter and Paul Fortress, to join many other representatives of the old regime.[18]*

Chaos continued to prevail all Tuesday at the Tauride, which was now 'a complete babel of agitations, ambitions, disputes and alliances', as every kind of committee was created to satisfy the political demands of the many competing factions: 'committees for provisions, committees for passports, committees for journalists, committees for students, committees for women helpers … for social right, for a just Peace, for Women's Suffrage, for Finnish Independence, for literature and the arts, for the better treatment of prostitutes, for education, for the just division of the land'. The atmosphere in the Catherine Hall became increasingly disorderly in the crush, with many delegates standing and craning to see the presidium, where speakers stood on the table to be seen and heard. 'The noise grew more and more deafening, the dust floated in hazy clouds. The men had their kettles and they boiled tea, squatting down there, and the shouting and screaming rose and rose like a flood.'[19] And throughout the palace, in every room and every committee, over and over again, one heard loud and repeated exhortations to the *tovarishchi* – the 'comrades'.[20]

In this new-found atmosphere of hectic but comradely solidarity, where all were basking in a strange and uneasy new equality and accepting orders from no one, frequent attempts were made by Alexander Kerensky, a prominent member of the Provisional Executive Committee, to appeal to the soldiers and workers gathered there to revert to some kind of military discipline. According to Ambassador Paléologue, the Duma members had been 'utterly taken aback by the anarchical behaviour of the army'.[21] 'They never imagined a revolution like this,' he reported, 'they hoped to direct it and keep it within bounds through the

---

* Sybil Grey heard that proof was found in Protopopov's apartment of 'plans to open the wine-shops in order to provide an excuse for firing on the people when they were drunk'.

army', but this was clearly impossible. As Paléologue wrote in his diary that day, 'The troops recognize no leader now and are spreading terror throughout the city.' Reluctant to return to their barracks and to their old commanders, many of them had 'given up their arms to the crowd and were drifting listlessly about the streets watching the progress of the fight'.[22]

By the end of that day there was even less likelihood of the Executive Committee regaining control of the obstreperous remnants of the army; for in a clear bid for primacy, the Petrograd Soviet had issued Order No. 1 tackling some of the soldiers' long-standing grievances against the imperial government. All army titles were now abolished, it announced; no officers were to be saluted, and the rank and file were to be addressed by the formal *vy* and not the informal (and, to them, demeaning) *ty*. From now on, Russia's military would take its orders from a plethora of soldiers' and sailors' committees reporting to the Soviet – not to the Duma.[23]

Intense cold descended during the night of 28 February/1 March, with the temperature plummeting to −26 degrees Centigrade, accompanied by a heavy fall of four to six inches of snow. The following morning a grey and gloomy sky cast a pall over the city as snow fell all day, muffling the sporadic sound of shouts and gunfire. The low temperatures transformed the blackened shells of burnt-out buildings with 'long icicles hanging from the eaves'. Everywhere the smell of burning lingered and 'paper ash still floated in the air'.[24]

Florence Harper and Donald Thompson walked up to the American embassy from the Astoria to survey the scene. 'Except for smashed windows and dead horses lying around the streets, there were no signs of the recent disturbance,' Harper noted.[25] Indeed, anyone who had risen early enough would have been greeted by a 'soft, immaculate whiteness' covering the streets and temporarily concealing the debris, spent bullets and bloodstains of five days of violence. Leighton Rogers also went out to take a look:

Shattered glass is greenish on the snow and where not smashed, windows are pierced with neat holes. Doors are splintered and spotted with lead. Buildings have smallpox – wherever a bullet strikes these brick and stucco structures out comes a chunk as big as a plate. The huge clock on the end of the Singer Building – the only modern office building in Petrograd – though still brightly lighted, stopped running a day or so ago in deference to three punctures in its vitals. Here and there lies a horse or an abandoned motor car put out of commission by flying bullets or a collision.[26]

Overnight, proclamations had been posted exhorting everyone, as 'citizens', to play their part in restoring order. Chester Swinnerton was impressed by the extraordinary sangfroid of Russians as they attempted to get back to normal. He and his bank colleagues 'wandered out to take some pictures'. Up on the Liteiny – the scene of such violence two days before – 'it was just like a Sunday School Picnic'. But they had barely walked a hundred feet along it when there was 'a b-rrrrrrrr – put put put put put – and a machine gun began to rattle from the corner house. We, in company with all those within twenty five yards, ducked into a nearby courtyard.' Their female Russian companions 'had a death grip on my arms', but within a minute were 'peeking out again'. 'You absolutely cannot beat the Russian curiosity,' Swinnerton wrote later, '[they] exhibit the most wonderful nonchalance and casualness. Little children will walk calmly thru the firing, laughing and playing as usual.' He had asked two little boys if it was safe to go on to the Nevsky:

'Yes. Perfectly safe.'
'Aren't they shooting there?'
'Oh yes, some shooting.'
'Anybody being killed?'
'Oh, yes, a few have been killed, but it's perfectly all right there.'[27]

Late in the evening and into the night of 1–2 March, Florence Harper could still hear a machine gun firing from St Isaac's Cathedral. It had been going on for the last couple of days, but that night a group of Cossacks stormed the cathedral and found forty police holed up in the basement. Exhausted from days without sleep and being hunted from one house to another, the police made their last stand. The Cossacks killed them then and there, and found six of their machine guns on the roof along with enough ammunition 'for a month'.[28]

The revolution was now firmly in the hands of the people, and by Thursday order was at last being restored. Students were enrolled into an ad hoc militia to help keep the peace and patrolled the streets wearing special armbands, accompanied by three or four soldiers under their command. The fires were out; some of the worst criminals who had been set free had been recaptured and secured in prison again. The militia had disarmed many gun-toting civilians during the day, by order of the Duma committee. Drunks were being arrested and numerous signs were posted 'asking all the comrades to refrain from liquor'.[29] Officers who had gone over to the revolution were given back their arms and returned to their regiments to restore discipline. Controls were brought in over armed motor vehicles careering dangerously round the streets. Cars were stopped by rows of militia barricading the road and allowed to pass only if they had official documents – otherwise they were summarily confiscated.[30]

People were going back to work, huddled into their greatcoats against the cold. Shops had reopened and housewives were out searching for food, their shopping bags over their arms. Milkmen were out pulling their sledges loaded with large pots of milk. Most important of all, with a resumption of rail deliveries of flour, limited supplies of freshly baked bread were available once more. Telegraph and telephone lines were restored and the post was being delivered. Workers began to clear the snow, and the streets started to take on their old aspect. Even the boats out of Petrograd were back to their old running order. Everything seemed to indicate an unexpectedly rapid return to normality.

Looking back on events of the past five days, David Francis was impressed, informing the US State Department that it had been 'the best managed revolution that has ever taken place, for its magnitude'.[31] English medical orderly Elsie Bowerman, who had been stranded in the city on her way home from the Eastern Front, remarked in her diary that 'Revolutions carried out in such a peaceful manner really deserve to succeed.* Today weapons only seem to be in the hands of responsible people.' 'Politics have begun this morning again,' reported an American resident, 'and we seem to have emerged from a sort of hermetic isolation, when the other side of the river seemed very far away and we only knew of what was happening at the other end of the Petrograd side by hearsay.'[32] Out on the Nevsky, Edward Heald followed a great parade of people with banners, who seemed to him 'joyously, freely, intensely, spiritually happy'. Seeing events unfold in Petrograd at street level, as he had done, had been 'thrilling and indescribable', he wrote in his diary. 'It has been good to be alive these marvellous days.'[33] The air of celebration was bolstered by news from Moscow that the struggle there had been brief and 'an easy victory for the revolutionists'. 'Normal life was scarcely interrupted for more than one day' in Russia's second city, noted one observer, 'and even less in other cities.'[34]

Several, like Elsie Bowerman, glossed over the horrors and looked for the positives: during the revolution, she recalled, foreign nationals such as herself had 'met with the utmost politeness and consideration from everyone'. Oliver Locker Lampson concurred, his view – like Bowerman's – limited by a narrow perspective on the true brutality that had taken place. 'This tremendous change has been wrought without excess, without insult to women, without any cruelty,' he thought. Indeed, he had seen so little of the terrible bloodshed that he professed that 'the crowds are not nearly as noisy as those in an English election'. All in all, it had been 'the Revolution of a noble, generous-hearted people'.[35]

---

* In 1912, then aged twenty-two, Bowerman had been a survivor of the *Titanic* disaster.

Captain Osborn Springfield of the Royal Artillery was of the same mind. His preconception that 'Revolution meant mass executions and thousands of casualties' had received a 'rude shock' in Petrograd. 'It had all seemed so comparatively peaceful. After the first natural excitement – normality had returned so quickly.' 'But were things normal?' he added. Like other foreign observers, he would later find such rose-tinted optimism had been premature. The wishful thinking that this had been a relatively bloodless, peaceful revolution – a revolution filled with hope of a new beginning for Russia – was soon shattered. As Springfield himself soon admitted, 'I was to find that much worse was to come.'[36]

Many of those recording their response to the February Revolution were inevitably drawn to comparisons with Paris 1789. For one American observer the enduring image of 28 February – a day of great transition – had come with 'the only romantic sight' he had seen: of 'a figure straight from the old engravings of the French Revolution' moving against the crowd:

> It was a young girl in a thin, shabby overcoat, with light clipped hair, on which perched a khaki soldier's cap with a big bunch of red ribbon in front. Strapped around her waist was an enormous curved gendarme's sword. She was trotting towards the firing, stopping every few steps to peer ahead, shading her eyes against the setting sun.[37]

Such an image – reminiscent of Marianne, allegorical figure of the French Revolution – was indeed evocative; as, too, for French witness Amélie de Néry, was the use of the word 'citizen'. It was the first time she had heard it on the streets of Petrograd. French ambassador Paléologue, however, thought the spirit of the French and Russian revolutions 'quite dissimilar'. What had happened in Petrograd, he wrote, was 'by its origins, principles and social, rather than political, character' far more reminiscent of revolutionary events in Paris in 1848. The overnight blossoming of such romantic idealism had about it a sense of unreality that was hard for many to absorb, but de Néry best summed it up:

'You had to have lived here, you had to have seen the constraint impinging on all public life, the strict supervision by the police, their lack of goodwill, the spying, the informing and everything feeling false and underhand hanging in the air, slavery masquerading as liberty, in order to understand the joy which radiates in everyone's expression now. At last, this great people can breathe, they have cast off their chains, along with the weight that has been oppressing them for centuries. Everyone is cheerful, smiling.'[38]

Chester Swinnerton had similar sentiments: 'The present movement is the fall of the Bastille. Next should come the march to Versailles.' He hoped 'that is as far as the parallel will continue'.[39] But, as things turned out, Versailles would not come to Petrograd. The last act of old imperial Russia was even now reaching its sad conclusion three hundred miles away from the capital, in a railway siding at Pskov.

7

'People Still Blinking in the Light of the Sudden Deliverance'

On the morning of Wednesday 1 March, Philip Chadbourn visited the 'charred and smoking shell' of the Courts of Justice on the Liteiny and found its courtyard full of people 'delving for souvenirs of that which was already a thing of yesteryear'.[1] The grand staircase had been entirely destroyed, 'only the lower third of a marble empress remained on her pedestal. The blackened torso lay at my feet, the imperial head, orb, scepter, crown, among the debris.' At the end of a long dark corridor he reached one of the inner courts and shuddered when he found himself 'inside this great human cage where everything was steel and stone, clanked, and was cold'. In some of the cells he could see the remains of a final meal of black bread, abandoned 'when the last call to freedom had come'. In the wrecked commandant's office he 'walked off with an oil portrait of the Emperor under [his] arm'. Inside the chapel, its Byzantine fittings were 'in wildest disarray; books, vestments, and robes were strewn about the floor. The marble altar was damaged and the crowd was curiously handling the ceremonial vessels.' Suddenly a young soldier 'snatched up a richly embroidered robe and flung it over his shoulders; next, he put on a long embellished collar; and last of all, he jammed a battered mitre on the side of his head. Then he opened the Testament and began to intone in a comic bass voice.' Chadbourn could not help thinking that, only a week previously, such irreverent behaviour would have been 'unthinkable'. But here was 'a whole world gone topsy turvy': 'the incredible is becoming a common sight, the commonplace has quite disappeared'.[2]

Caught in the middle of it all, foreign residents remained confused and fearful – hiding in their apartments, 'nervous, uneasy, troubled, starting at the least sound,' as Claude Anet reported. 'Whither were we drifting? What would happen on the morrow … Would a government nominated at Petrograd be accepted by Russia? Would it be able to re-establish order?' they asked each other. At the homes of fellow French residents, Anet noted a mounting concern about the situation beyond Russia: 'The great question, the terrible question, was this: "What of the War?"'[3] For the time being the revolution had obliterated all thought of it, in the minds of ordinary Petrograders. They had even forgotten about the Tsar, whose imminent return had been expected for days.

It wasn't until three in the morning of 28 February that Nicholas II had finally left Stavka at Mogilev on the imperial train, only to be turned back six hours from Petrograd, at Bologoe, by striking railway workers who had torn up the railway lines. Instead Nicholas had headed for Pskov, where he arrived early in the morning of 1 March, having telegraphed Rodzianko in Petrograd and reluctantly agreed to political concessions. But it was too late. Rodzianko's response had been blunt: 'It is now time to abdicate.'[4]

A weary and depressed Nicholas, preoccupied with being reunited with his wife and sick children and concerned about the fate of the Russian army at the front, talked things over with General Ruzsky at his HQ at Pskov. Ruzsky also advised abdication. Thereafter Nicholas offered little resistance to further pressure placed on him to capitulate, by special envoys and Duma deputies Alexander Guchkov and Vasily Shulgin after they arrived by train from Petrograd. His act of abdication was, Nicholas asserted, for the sake of the country; in making his decision, he took no account of political demands. His duty, first and foremost, was 'to God and Russia'.[5] But he also took the decision to abdicate on behalf of his haemophiliac son, Alexey, dreading the inevitable separation and exile from him that Alexey's succession under a regency would have prompted. On the afternoon of 2 March the Tsar agreed the draft of his abdication manifesto and signed it shortly before midnight, designating his brother, Grand Duke Mikhail, his successor. Barely a day later Mikhail declined the throne, unless offered to him by a Constituent Assembly elected by all the Russian people. But the creation of such a body was, as Mikhail well knew, still a pipedream.

At 1.00 a.m. on 3 March, Nicholas's train headed back to Mogilev and from there on to Tsarskoe Selo. Notices in the Petrograd papers of 5 March reported that the ex-Tsar had 'gone to take a badly earned holiday in Livadia in the Crimea'. However, on 9 March a pale and exhausted Nicholas, in the uniform of a colonel of the Cossacks of the Guard, finally re-joined his family, who had already been placed under house arrest at the Alexander Palace.[6] While Nicholas had indeed expressed a wish to be allowed to go and live in Crimea, this had been summarily refused. There were hopes that King George and the British government might be prevailed upon to take them in, but tentative discussions soon came to nothing. As Nicholas and his family awaited news of their fate, he was treated like any other Russian and referred to as 'Citizen Romanov' or, as many came to refer to him, just plain 'Nikolay'. As for the Tsaritsa, the newspapers had reverted to her former name, Alix of Hesse.

Maurice Paléologue was shocked at the speed with which the Tsar had capitulated: it had all 'taken place in such casual, commonplace and prosaic fashion, and above all with such indifference and self-effacement on the part of the principal hero,' he thought. 'The Czar of all the Russias has been dethroned as easily as a recalcitrant school-boy is made to stay in after school,' wrote Edith Hegan, on hearing the news. 'The dynasty of the Romanoffs had disappeared in the storm,' observed Claude Anet. 'It had found no one to defend it; it had crumbled away as if all life were extinct in it.' 'Nikolai has abdicated. Everybody is relieved. There will be no Vendée,'* wrote another (American) observer.[7] Most of the Americans in Petrograd were equally enthusiastic, but Donald Thompson couldn't help wishing that if the Tsar had returned to the city sooner, and if he had driven straight away down the Nevsky Prospekt 'and stood up in the back of his automobile with his hat off and talked, as Teddy Roosevelt would have done, he would still be Czar of Russia'. It seemed simple enough to him: give the people bread, and agree to a new government. Thompson felt sorry for the Tsar: 'at heart he was a real Russian and even now I believe if he were asked, he would go to the front and fight for Russia'. As for the 'brilliant future' that everyone tried to convince him was coming, now the Tsar had gone, Thompson didn't think it 'very promising'.[8]

Over at the Tauride Palace, with the grudging agreement of the rival power base of the Petrograd Soviet of Workers' and Soldiers' Deputies, and in a continuing atmosphere of 'fierce excitement', a twelve-man Provisional Government had been formed on the evening of 2 March, drawn from members of the Duma.[9] 'Solidly respectable' and 'eminently bourgeois' in composition, and in contrast to the Soviet, which opposed the war, it confirmed its loyalty to the Allies and its hopes of instituting a constitutional government. Prince Georgiy Lvov, a mild-mannered liberal and landowner, with long years of experience as an administrator in local government, was called in from Moscow and nominated prime minister. He would, however, soon be eclipsed by the more domineering and competing voices of Alexander Kerensky, promoted to Minister of Justice, and the energetic liberal monarchist Pavel Milyukov, as Minister of Foreign Affairs. Taking over as Minister of War was the wealthy merchant and newspaper owner Alexander Guchkov, who had

---

* An allusion to the conservative, royalist counter-revolution staged in the rural western French province of the Vendée in the wake of the French Revolution of 1789.

just played a key role in the Tsar's abdication. Rodzianko, the Duma president, remained in office at the head of a body that continued to function until September, but was now effectively sidelined by the more forceful figures in the new Provisional Government.[10]

All of the members of the Provisional Government, bar the socialist Kerensky, were of the old industrialist or landowning class, a fact to which Kerensky had found it hard to reconcile his political principles. It soon became apparent that because of his leftist leanings, Kerensky was the only member of the new government likely to carry any real weight with the Soviet (of which he was also appointed Vice Chairman of its Executive Committee). Indeed, Kerensky – who had joined the Socialist Revolutionary Party in 1905 and had been elected to the Duma in 1912 – worked hard to keep a foot in both camps.

He cultivated the Soviet's approval through a combination of his personal magnetism and a clever eloquence born of a career as a defence lawyer working with imprisoned political activists. It would, however, take all his considerable skills to handle this increasingly obstructionist and truculent body – the Soviet's rank of deputies having already rapidly swelled to an unmanageable three thousand. Intoxicated with their new-found liberty, the Soviet's politically naive membership of inexperienced workers and soldiers were having radical Marxist theories pressed upon them by militant socialists in their midst, and were absorbing these like blotting paper. Such theories ran counter to the Provisional Government's objective of maintaining a democratic form of government until a Constituent Assembly could be properly elected by the Russian people, by means of a universal, direct and secret ballot.[11] But this would not take place until after the war was over. The prospect of how a largely illiterate peasant population would respond to the previously unimaginable freedom of such a plebiscite was summed up by a comment repeated time and time again, in variant forms, on the streets of Russia: 'A republic! Of course we must have a republic, but we must have a good Czar to look after it.'[12]

It took a raft of major political concessions for the Petrograd Soviet to agree to the creation of the Provisional Government, including an 'immediate amnesty in all political and religious affairs, including those convicted of terroristic attempts, military insurrection, and agrarian crimes ... Liberty of word, press, assembly, unions and strikes ... Abolition of all class, religious and national limitations and the ... substitution of national militia in place of the police, with elected leaders and subject to the local administrations.'[13] As for the thorny but increasingly pressing issue of votes for women, Kerensky told Claude Anet that this, too, would be postponed until after the inauguration of a Constituent Assembly: 'They had neither the time nor the means to organize so vast a change in so limited a period.'[14] For now, Kerensky's first task as Minister of Justice was to oversee the amnesty for all political prisoners, which followed on 6 March; on the 12th the death-penalty was abolished.

Although the Provisional Government had professed itself loyal to Russia's continuing war effort, Allied military attachés in Petrograd were already expressing grave misgivings about the state of the Russian army and its continued participation. Many, like General Knox, were fearful that it was on the brink of capitulation and that the Germans would take Petrograd. Knox had personally considered the Soviet's controversial Order No. 1, instructing soldiers and sailors to obey orders from the Provisional Government only if sanctioned by the Soviet – 'a deathblow to the Russian army'. In Knox's view, the Petrograd garrison had degenerated into an armed mob and there was no enthusiasm for the war in the rank and file. At a meeting at the US embassy a very pessimistic view also prevailed; the revolution, it was agreed, would 'take all the starch out of the troops at the front' and Russia could no longer figure 'as a factor in the war'. Troops at the front were deeply demoralised and deserting in droves. 'If peace does not come soon they will lay down their arms.'[15] Ambassador Paléologue had received assurances from Milyukov that his government intended to continue 'ruthlessly prosecuting the war to victory', but admitted that 'the direction of Russian affairs is now at the mercy of new forces' – which Paléologue put down to 'extremist proletarian doctrine' – of the kind now being propounded by the Soviet.[16]

Russia's effectiveness in the war had been further undermined by violent acts of rebellion in the Baltic fleet at Kronstadt, the naval fortress nineteen miles to the west of Petrograd that protected the city's sea approaches. All sense of discipline in the army seemed to have evaporated. Instead, a new breed of soldier-citizens were gaining ground who considered they had no need to obey orders, having instead, as Arno Dosch-Fleurot put it, merely 'a vast, vague, contagious conception of liberty'.[17] Claude Anet noticed the loss of bearing in the soldiers he saw parading on the streets, 'slouched now in a slovenly and careless manner, in bad order, without keeping the time which had been taught them so carefully'.[18] The punctilious Sir George Buchanan was horrified at the levels of disrespect now being shown by the rank and file on railway trains, where he saw them 'crowd into first class carriages and eat in Restaurant cars while officers wait'. Officers were humiliated at every opportunity: 'I saw venerable generals,' recalled Isaac Marcosson, 'with the wound and service stripes of two wars on their sleeves, hanging by the strap of the tramcars while every seat was occupied by a grinning and sometimes jeering common soldier.'

Such a breakdown in respect was also galling to military men like US aviator Bert Hall. On the afternoon of 3 March he saw an old general in a railway station trying to get something to eat. Some soldiers nearby began hurling offensive remarks at him and, when the general sent for an armed guard to arrest the offending soldiers, the guard turned on him and arrested the general instead. 'They took the old man outside and a crowd gathered around,' recalled Hall. Then someone said, 'What shall we do with him?' 'Let's hang him; he was once on the side of the Tsar!' And they lynched him there and then.' Hall knew him: 'He was a good old man and one of the few artillery experts in all Russia.'[19]

With the Tsar's abdication, a new form of public recreation rapidly took hold across the city: the systematic tearing down and destruction of all imperial insignia and other visible trappings of the old regime.[20] All along the Nevsky and other major thoroughfares gangs of soldiers appeared and began removing the double-headed eagles and Romanov arms from store-fronts that had supplied the Imperial Court, as well as from their favourite clubs and watering holes, such as the Imperial Yacht Club. Nicholas's name, Romanov crests and insignia, photographs and paintings of the imperial family – all were ruthlessly eradicated. There was even talk of melting down Falconet's fine statue of Peter the Great, erected by Catherine the Great in Senate Square. The word 'Imperial' was defaced on signboards and brass plates everywhere it was found. They even tore down the imperial eagle on the front of the Anglo-Russian Hospital: 'Our Palace Eagle met its end, a heap of plaster on the road it had proudly gazed on for many years,' noted Dr Geoffrey Jefferson. The staff were also ordered to take down the Russian flag above the front door: 'this is not the flag of our nation,' they were told.[21]

Ladders were brought from all directions by citizens eager to remove the old imperial blight on the face of the new socialist Russia. When there were no ladders to be had, people shinned up buildings and onto roofs to do the job. Once thrown down into the street, the insignia were stamped on, burned on huge bonfires or simply flung into the canals. A few people – some of them foreign residents – were eager to get their pickings: 'We wanted souvenirs,' wrote James Houghteling, 'but everything we saw was too big.'[22] Unfortunately, in their eagerness to do away with all trace of the Romanovs, the self-appointed iconoclasts roaming the streets in search of targets failed to distinguish between the Russian imperial eagle – symbol of oppression – and the American eagle, symbol of freedom. Several of the latter were destroyed, although the Americans managed to save the huge iron eagle atop the Singer Building on the Nevsky, by 'drap[ing] the proud bird in the Stars and Stripes until only the beak protruded from the red, white, and blue folds'.[23]

One of the most obvious targets for the destruction of emblems of tsarism was the Winter Palace. One fanatic, so Associated Press correspondent Robert Crozier Long heard, had even demanded 'the complete razing of the Winter Palace, declaring that "the debris might be left – a heap of shapeless stones and rotting wood – as a finer monument to the fall of the Romanoffs than the handsomest monument to Liberty reared anywhere else on earth"'.[24] Meanwhile, the red flag had already gone up over the palace itself, replacing the yellow imperial flag, and the Romanov coats of arms and eagles on its historic wrought-iron gates were either removed or covered up with red cloth. Such became the demand for red fabric for this, and for the masses of ribbons, brassards and flags in evidence all over the city, that in the end people resorted to simply cutting the blue and white strips away from the now-rejected Russian national flag and displaying the remaining red strip.[25]

As this frenzy of destruction continued, the imperial insignia and aristocratic coronets were even wrenched off the bonnets of commandeered motor cars, and electric street signs forming the large letter 'N' with a crown were also dismantled and destroyed. It was now considered treasonous to buy or display a portrait of the Tsar. 'Where portraits of the Emperor could not be removed – such as those in the Chamber of the Council of Empire – they were covered with white crepe.'[26] Even at the Academy of Art 'the placards attached to the various paintings stating that they were the gift or loan of members of the royal family had all such references cut out.' Church services, too, felt the immediate impact of the change of regime and became considerably shorter, with all the prayers for the imperial family being removed from the liturgy and replaced with a prayer for the 'Divine Protection of the Fatherland'.[27]

The most potent signifier of change for Meriel Buchanan came at a concert at the Mariinsky Theatre, where she was sad to see that the imperial arms and big golden eagles had been torn down in the auditorium, 'leaving gaping holes'. The handsome imperial blue drop-curtain had also gone – replaced by 'an odd red-and-gold one'.[28] All the old tsarist splendour had vanished: the formerly well-dressed ushers in their gold-braided court uniforms now wore 'plain grey jackets which made them look indescribably shabby and dingy'. The clientele of this new egalitarian theatre was also, for her, decidedly downmarket: 'soldiers in mud-stained khaki lolled everywhere, smoking evil-smelling cigarettes, spitting all over the place and eating the inevitable sunflower seeds out of paper bags'. Elsewhere, a motley crowd of unwashed proletarians sat in their day-clothes – leather jackets replacing the usual evening dress – with their 'muddy boots on the brocade sofas'. For Buchanan, the new socialist 'doctrine of Liberty' was one that 'preached a contempt for beauty'. Even the corps de ballet seemed 'less in harmony, slow to obey the conductor's baton, whispering in corners, slack and inattentive in their movements'. This once-beautiful theatre had been transformed into a meeting place, an office. It was all too much for the European old guard and bluebloods of the foreign diplomatic service, such as the Buchanans. This was no brave new world, but one of 'dilapidation, of demoralization and decay'.[29]

The night of Thursday 2 March saw such an intense blizzard that the following morning it was impossible to go out on the streets. Winter was hanging on with a vengeance, the temperature sticking at freezing. With the snow piling up against shop fronts and buildings to a height of about fifteen to twenty feet, the weather certainly 'cooled revolutionary ardour' and, as David Francis noted, 'had the effect of keeping even the rampant socialists within doors'.[30] It didn't last long: on 5 March newspapers finally reappeared, after a week's silence, and vendors were 'almost overwhelmed by the news-hungry populace' venturing out in the cold to read up on the dramatic events of the last few days. For journalist Arthur Ransome, this was an especially heartening sight: 'their tone and even form are so joyful that it is hard to recognize them. They are so different from the censor-ridden mutes and unhappy things of a week ago. Every paper seems to be executing a war-dance of joy … it is as if all Russia had spat out the gags forced in mouths by the old regime of oppression.'

In addition to the newspapers, 'every conceivable kind of incendiary pamphlet was sold on the sidewalk and without restraint' and walls everywhere were 'literally plastered with proclamations, posters and propaganda bulletins'.[31] Returning to Russia for his second term as Dutch ambassador, Willem Oudendijk* was forcibly struck by the freedom of speech that prevailed. On the train in from Finland he had found himself surrounded by 'revolutionary emigrants' on their way back to Russia, who 'talked and talked without ceasing'. 'Everybody thought himself an apostle of a new salvation,' he noted, 'and propounded his views with great vehemence to anybody who cared to listen.'[32] 'Walking the city one could stop and hear opinions freely expressed on any street corner,' Ambassador Paléologue also noted. Impromptu open-air *meetinki* (the English word was rapidly adopted) could be seen 'in progress everywhere'. Groups of twenty or thirty would spontaneously gather, and then 'one of the company mounts a stone, or a bench, or a heap of snow and talks his head off, gesticulating wildly. The audience gazes fixedly at the orator and listens in a kind of rapt absorption. As soon as he stops another takes his place and immediately gets the same fervent silence and concentrated attention.' Paléologue found it an 'artless and affecting sight', particularly when one remembered 'that the Russian nation ha[d] been waiting centuries for the right of speech'.[33]

James Stinton Jones wondered whether the Russians were ready, or able, to deal with such a sudden abundance of liberty. In his view, they were too new to it 'to understand its uses and to know how to avoid its abuses ... The poorer classes of Russia have never been accustomed to having an opinion of their own ... Now they find themselves a political factor, they are hopelessly at sea, the prey of the last unscrupulous demagogue they have heard.' 'It will take time for Russia to realize what she wants,' he

---

* A long-serving and accomplished diplomat like Buchanan, Oudendijk had served in Persia and China and was a gifted polyglot. He had previously been Dutch Ambassador to Petrograd during 1907–8.

added. 'There is no cohesion, no common ideal to inspire her people. She is conscious of having killed a dragon; that is all.'[34]

Not long after the newspapers began printing again, the trams reappeared; only now they were draped in red flags and banners bearing inscriptions such as 'Long Live the Republic'. James Houghteling saw the first one arrive across the Troitsky Bridge from the Petrograd Side, 'with a band playing and a great red banner spread aloft: "Land and the Will of the People".'[35] Everybody in Petrograd was glad to get mobile again, and the familiar trams seemed the final affirmation that life had returned to normal at last. This had not, however, been achieved without some difficulty: the Petrograd Soviet had been obliged to issue a notice 'drawing attention to the ... removal of the operating-handles from cars at the beginning of the revolution and ask[ing] that any patriot having a handle in his possession return it to the Municipal Office'. Having daily had to walk back and forth on foot following the unravelling story, journalist Claude Anet was relieved – he had been covering twelve to seventeen miles a day. 'If the Revolution continued, I should have the legs of a country postman.'[36]

While most expatriates welcomed with a degree of wry cynicism the gradual and spasmodic restoration of services in the city, there were some who remained incorrigibly, hopelessly optimistic about this wonderful new dawn in Russia. Harold Williams of the *Daily Chronicle*, a committed pacifist and socialist from a Methodist background, shared Arthur Ransome's effusive response to events, talking excitedly of a 'flow of brotherly feeling' in the streets and of how the 'strong sense of common responsibility for order has united all classes in one great army of freedom'. Life in Russia, he insisted, was 'flowing in a healing, purifying torrent. Never was any country in the world so interesting as Russia is now. Old men are saying "Nunc Dimittis",* young men singing in the dawn, and I have met many men and women who seem walking in a hushed sense of benediction.'[37]

---

* A canticle from the Gospel of St Luke, the opening words meaning 'Now let thy servant depart in peace'.

There was so much dramatic change for new arrivals in the city to take in. Anglo-Irish journalist Robert Crozier Long was taken aback, upon arriving on 7 March, by the 'unexampled reversal of ranks and conditions which in a week the Revolution had brought about in the most despotic and class-crystallized country of Europe'.[38] 'I found the capital delirious with freedom,' recalled American journalist Isaac Marcosson, who had previously been covering the Western Front, 'the people still blinking in the light of the sudden deliverance'.[39] For Marcosson, the persisting, unreal state of euphoria at recent events was like 'New York City on the night of a presidential election, but with this difference: the returns were piling in all the time and the whole world seemed to be elected'.

Sooner or later the celebrating had to stop and reality must set in. Petrograders were, however, in a strange state of denial, having assumed that 'the revolution meant a free and continuous meal ticket and a four-hour working day'.[40] Russia had to get back to work, but the new-found equality – a world where everybody called each other *tovarishch* and brotherly love reigned – had, like strong drink, gone to people's heads. Puffed up with impossible expectations, and dreaming irrational dreams of vastly reduced working days and greatly improved salaries, many workers – from the highest-paid munitions worker to the lowliest housemaid – were making impossible demands for 50–100 per cent and even 150 per cent wage increases, alongside a dramatic reduction in their working hours.[41] The Putilov works were still idle, with 35,000 men on the streets, and there was a desperate need for munitions at the front.[42] 'I have been told, difficult as it is to credit it,' remarked visiting English forestry expert, Edward Stebbing:

that a bricklayer earns at the rate of 30,000 roubles a year, a hotel waiter 80 roubles a day, a hotel boy 50 roubles, and so on – such wages as no country in the world could afford to pay, and doing only about four to six hours' work for it, and that work so badly performed as to be absolutely harmful. Witness the state of the rolling stock on the railways and the accidents now so numerous. Factory owners, and in fact employers of labour of all kinds, are at their wits' end to get work carried out and keep their businesses going.[43]

This was confirmed by Negley Farson – at that time engaged to Vera Thornton, daughter of one of the Thornton brothers, who owned the biggest mill in Petrograd and who, like other expat factory owners and managers, were fighting a losing battle to keep their Petrograd plants going. 'The workers were like sheep who had been let out of their pen, and the English managers could not get them back,' wrote Farson. 'They had no idea what freedom meant, but most of them took it as an invitation not to work. There was a daily drama in every mill yard as managers tried to reason with workers demanding ridiculously high wages.'

Donald Thompson and Florence Harper had noted a distinct change in the attitude of the staff at the Astoria. 'The servants are beginning to get stuck up with this new-born freedom,' wrote Thompson; his room servant had told him that from now on he would have to shine his own shoes. 'You have to call them 'comrade' or 'friend', he told his wife – rather than addressing them as *chelovek* ('man'); and, like the rank and file in the army, they insisted on the use of *vy* instead of the informal *ty*.[44] A British resident noticed how every evening his two housemaids would 'spend hours standing at street corners along the Nevski Prospekt, listening to orators preaching about equality and justice'. After one such outing, they returned and told him and his wife that 'they were in future going to the cinema every night' and intended to work no more than 'eight hours a day'.[45] Sometimes such high-handedness backfired. A Russian housemaid working for a prominent American resident 'served notice on her master that she wanted an increase of fifty per cent in wages and an eight-hour day'. 'What do you mean by an eight-hour day?' asked her employer. 'I am only going to work from eight until eight' was the reply. Her demand was 'speedily granted'.[46]

The arbitrary enforcement of equal rights and a share of control also manifested itself in a new form of overbearing management-by-committee, which percolated down into every aspect of Russian society (and which would, in the future Soviet Union, evolve into an art form). One day in early March, Claude Anet wanted to make a telephone call at the Duma:

> Three women guarded the approach to it.
> 'You cannot telephone,' they said.
> 'And why?' I asked.
> 'We are reserving the telephone for public affairs.'
> 'But who are you?'
> 'The Telephone Committee.'
> 'And who appointed you?'
> 'We appointed ourselves.'
> Upon which, putting them gently aside, I passed through and telephoned.[47]

There was also a far more worrying aspect to this unbridled, self-righteous sense of equality – and that came in the summary infliction of rough justice. British lithographer Henry Keeling was alarmed to see how 'In Russia where few expected justice and where the police had such wide powers, the abolition of the death-penalty seemed to mean an end of all the checks on social crimes' – especially theft. People acted as self-appointed vigilantes, defending the good name of revolution by summarily punishing those who committed crimes, as Keeling witnessed soon after the revolution:

> A lady in a crowded tramcar in Petrograd ... cried out suddenly that she had had her purse stolen. She said that it contained fifty roubles and accused a well-dressed young man who happened to be standing behind her of the theft. The latter most earnestly protested his innocence and

declared that rather than be called a thief he would give the woman fifty roubles out of his own pocket. Nothing availed him; perhaps they thought he protested too much. He was taken outside and promptly shot. The body of the poor fellow was searched, but no purse was found. The upholders of the integrity of the Russian Republic returned to the tramcar and told the woman that she had better make a more careful search. She did so and discovered that the missing purse had slipped down through a hole in the pocket into the lining. Nothing could be done for the unfortunate victim of 'justice' so they took the only course which seemed to them to meet the case and leading the woman out, shot her also.[48]

On Saturday 4 March, James Houghteling and some of his colleagues at the US embassy decided the time had come for them to see the new politics in action and headed for the Tauride Palace. They had no difficulty getting in, for they were mistaken for an official US delegation – come, hopefully, to recognise the new government. Ushered through into the anteroom of the Duma president, they were greeted by Guchkov, who was a little crestfallen when they admitted the mistake.[49] It was clear that the Provisional Government was anxious for official validation by foreign powers, and the men went straight to the embassy to tell the ambassador.

Whatever might be the vagaries of the improvised form of government now being enacted at the Tauride Palace, in the greater scheme of things David Francis saw its inception as a golden opportunity. He was determined that republican America should make the grand, defining gesture and 'be the first to recognize Republican Russia'.[50] On the afternoon of 5 March he composed a telegram to Robert Lansing, US Secretary of State: 'This revolution is the practical realization of that principle of government which we have championed and advocated, I mean government by consent of the governed,' he argued. 'Our recognition will have a stupendous moral effect, especially if given first.'[51] What is more, by taking this pre-emptive step – ahead of the Allied governments of France, Britain and Italy – Francis hoped the US would thereby increase its trade with Russia and supplant the influence of the British. Expecting the USA soon to enter the war, he also believed this was in America's interests strategically. Having surprised, if not mortified, his staff by composing his telegram without consulting with any of them, Francis asked Phil Jordan to bring his coat, hat and galoshes and, without more ado, he set off in his sleigh to see Foreign minister Milyukov, who ensured that the telegram was safely transmitted to the USA. Less than two days later Francis received Lansing's approval. He was overjoyed. 'It is a great coup to get in ahead of Russia's allies,' he told James Houghteling, 'and it puts the United States in the position of the new government's best friend.'[52]

To mark the occasion, Francis and his 'entire official staff, ten secretaries of embassy and attachés', drove up the Nevsky on 9 March to the Palace of the Imperial Council at the Mariinsky Palace, with the horses of the ambassadorial sleigh sporting flags stuck in the bridle over their outer ear (Norman Armour said it felt like riding 'in a merry-go-round').[53] Francis was in 'full dress evening clothes like a head waiter' – not having any official diplomatic uniform. The entire Provisional Government was waiting for them, though they had had no time to dress for the occasion. They had 'all come directly from their offices and wore sack-suits [lounge suits]'. James Houghteling thought they 'appeared careworn but much elated at having won a place among the nations after so few days in office'.[54] The brief ceremony that followed was 'impressive', as J. Butler Wright noted in his diary, but it was no 'flummy-doodle'. And it was a feather in the cap for the Americans, whose embassy in the eyes of 'certain of our diplomatic colleagues', as Wright knew, 'did not count for much'.[55]

Two days later, Sir George Buchanan, who had only just recovered from illness, made the same trip to the palace with the ambassadors of France and Italy to pass on their official recognition of the Provisional Government. But unlike the enthusiastic Americans, they were dismayed to be received in 'a room with a dirty floor and broken windows'. Maurice Paléologue was appalled by the changes to the palace: the great marble staircases had not been swept since the revolution, he noted, and there were bullet marks everywhere in the plasterwork. General Knox recorded a 'general atmosphere of depression' among the diplomats gathered there that afternoon, all of them fearful that the revolution would make it harder for the Allies to win the war.[56] Sir George, having no Russian, made a brief speech in fluent French – the former language of diplomacy in imperial Russia – which was 'very severe, but much to the point', in which he 'made an inspiriting appeal for the re-establishment of discipline in the army and the energetic prosecution of the war'.[57] While Milyukov responded with a speech of thanks, Paléologue examined the members of the Provisional Government gathered around him: 'Patriotism, intelligence and honesty could be read on every face; but they seemed utterly worn out with physical fatigue and anxiety. The task they have undertaken is patently beyond their powers. Heaven grant that they do not collapse under it too soon!'

One person alone among them struck Paléologue as 'a man of action' – Alexander Kerensky. But he was an elusive figure who kept himself apart and, when seen, appeared waxen and sickly (he was suffering from TB of the kidneys). Paléologue had no doubt, however, that here was 'the most original figure of the Provisional Government'. Kerensky was a man who seemed 'bound to become its main spring'.[58]

8

The Field of Mars

Although life in Petrograd appeared to be getting back to normal, its population had yet to count the true cost of the revolution – the dead. During the disturbances they had been carried off in haste in all directions and for days now their frozen (and in many cases unidentified) corpses had lingered as mute witnesses, stacked up like so many piles of wood in the city's hospitals and makeshift mortuaries awaiting burial, while distraught relatives were still out searching for them.

Wishing to cover such a powerful human-interest story, Florence Harper sought out the hospitals where the dead had been taken. She went first to the one nearest her hotel, a big city hospital on the Fontanka. Not knowing where to find the mortuary, she followed two weeping women across a courtyard 'to a group of isolated buildings that were nothing but shacks'. From the cross on its door, she assumed this was the place. 'There was a stream of people going into it' and she followed. Inside, 'as high as they could be piled, the chapel was full of coffins, some of them painted white and some of them unpainted pine'. She did not try to count them all: 'It was too harrowing.' But looking through the window of an adjoining shack she saw far worse: 'right against the pane, on the other side, was something that made me jump back'. It was the body of a peasant fully clothed, 'but his whole chest had been torn open'. His hands were raised 'as if he were defending himself' and his corpse was soaked in blood from the neck to the waist. His body had not been washed and was 'lying there as he had been picked up, frozen'.[1]

Luckily the cold had preserved the many un-coffined bodies she saw, but it had also left them in grotesque, contorted positions. Along three sides of the shack, Harper saw piles of rigid, muddy and blood-soaked bodies that had been thrown in 'as they had been picked up', some doubled up, others outstretched – men, women and children. Next to that shack was another, and then another with even more. In a big shed opposite she found another 150 bodies piled up. People were pulling at them, searching for loved ones, trying to identify them. 'One in the uniform of the police was beyond recognition,' she noted, 'he had literally been beaten to a pulp.' Very few of the corpses had any boots on – for these were a valuable commodity in wartime and were the first things to be stolen from the dead. With so many to be buried, coffins were scarce and so, once people identified their dead, they would pin a note on them, giving the name and asking for money to help bury them. People visiting these makeshift morgues would throw a few kopeks on the corpses. It was only later, visiting another hospital morgue where the bodies had been properly washed and laid out like wax figures, that Harper finally took in the grim horror of so many deaths.[2]

A big public funeral for the victims of the revolution – or, rather, those among them whose bodies had not already been taken away and buried separately by relatives – was planned but postponed three times because, with no police force to marshal such a huge occasion, the Provisional Government and the Soviet feared it might spark anti-revolution demonstrations.[3] They expected one million or more people to flood the streets, and that they might provoke a riot, given the 'inflamed state of mind' in which the crowds remained.[4] Eventually a date was set for Thursday 23 March. Some had wanted the dead to be buried in front of the Winter Palace, but instead a site was chosen in the centre of the historic old parade ground known as the Field of Mars, bounded on one side by the massive-columned Pavlovsky Barracks, with the British embassy and the Marble Palace at the top end and the Summer Garden along the other side.[5]

Such had been the intense cold that it had proved impossible to dig the trench required manually, and dynamite had to be used to create a sufficiently large grave in the transverse axis of the parade ground. Claude Anet visited the gravesite as it was being constructed.[6] Opposite stood the trees of the Summer Garden, with their 'black and lank branches'; overhead, a grey sky, full of clouds heavy with rain. In the middle was 'a great yellow stain' – the earth that had been removed for the graves. 'Black and white flags, on the top of masts, were waving in the wind around the grave, some of them festooned with green garlands and flowers. Great red placards with inscriptions decorated the circumference of the reserved space.' At its centre a platform draped in red cloth had been built as a vantage point for the members of the government and distinguished guests to watch the ceremony.[7]

Shortly before the funeral took place there was a sudden spring thaw and the streets of Petrograd became a sea of mud and slush; by the preceding day part of the Nevsky was a 'lake of water'. The 23rd, which had been declared a national holiday – 'the first independence day of Russia' – dawned, bleak and wretched.[8] A damp, icy wind blew, with more snow threatened from the heavy lowering sky, as six separate, slow-moving processions set off from different parts of the city at around 10.00 a.m., eventually to converge at the burial site on the Field of Mars. But such were the huge crowds who had turned out to watch, and the ponderousness of the ceremonial, that the groups of marchers bearing the coffins sometimes had to stop for hours to let other processions move on.[9] Traffic was at a standstill and the whole of the Nevsky was 'jammed with spectators from one end to the other', with a forest of flags and black-and-red banners reading, 'Eternal Memory to Our Fallen Brothers', 'Heroes Who for Freedom Fell', 'Hail to the Democratic Republic'. Everyone marching in the funeral processions had been provided with a special ticket to do so and to admit them to the burial site on the Field of Mars. They were divided into rows eight deep, sixteen abreast, led by students carrying white sticks who raised and lowered them to indicate the need to halt or move forward. 'It was exactly like the order and discipline of troops on the march, and trained soldiers could not have marched better,' noted a French eyewitness.[10] The sense of occasion was intense: a 'soul-stirring emotion seemed to possess these long lines of mourners,' wrote an English resident; the city that day seemed 'transformed into a vast cathedral'.[11]

Hugh Walpole noticed large numbers of peasants in the watching crowds: 'They had stood there, I was told, in pools of frozen water for hours, and were perfectly ready to stand thus for many hours more if they were ordered to do so.' Edward Heald estimated seeing 'a hundred and fifty thousand people at one time on the Nevsky' – and this was 'probably no more than a fifth of the total number of marchers in sight at any one moment'. 'There must have been half a million marchers in line,' he estimated. 'And what an impression it made; faces and forms that showed a lifetime of suffering and for whom a "Free Russia" had real meaning.'[12]

American Frank Golder watched the pall-bearers, wearing red sashes across their shoulders and red armbands, processing down the Nevsky. The coffins of the dead were covered in red cloth and were followed by 'a fairly well trained crowd of singers who sang the funeral service'. Behind them came 'numerous organisations with banners and mottoes, some singing church music, others revolutionary and "svoboda" [freedom] songs'.[13] Many bands accompanied the processions, alternating a long slow rendition of the Marseillaise – now unofficially adopted as a national anthem – with the wearisome monotony of Chopin's Funeral March. Every once in a while, noticed Edward Heald, the mourners 'would break out in church music or a prayer or chant and then the spectators would join in with bowed heads and doffed hats'. But although 'Eternal Memory', the Russian Orthodox prayer for the dead, was on the lips of many that day, no official church presence was allowed to conduct the ceremony. No priests, no incense, no crosses, no obsequies at the graveside and no icons, either – the only other accompaniment to this mournful spectacle were the cannons of the Peter and Paul fortress, which fired a salute for each coffin placed in the grave.[14]

All day long and well into the night the processions continued to file along the main routes of the city, linking arms, 'a mighty wave of humanity – old women, children, laborers, servants, soldiers, sailors, priests, people from every walk of life,' recalled Leighton Rogers. 'So constant was the movement and so solid the ranks that non-marchers found it impossible to cross the Nevsky.'[15] Late that night the grave on the Field of Mars remained illuminated 'under the glare of huge military searchlights whose rays, sweeping over the heads of the marchers, caught on the waving banners as they came into the field, their bearers singing a mournful dirge, quite oblivious of mud and slush, to plod on out of the light and disappear into the darkness'. It was, Rogers wrote, 'something never to be forgotten'.[16] Many of the foreign eyewitnesses concurred on the extraordinary calm and discipline with which the huge crowd had marked the occasion, and without the need for any police presence. One million had 'marched and wept' that day. 'A community, once police-ridden, and still quivering with rage at incessant wrongs, kept the peace almost without sign of authority,' observed Isaac Marcosson.[17] 'The threatened Commune became a Public Confessional of serene sorrow. Petrograd was safe as a Sunday School Convention.'

The whole of the solemn, protracted ceremonial of 23 March had, in essence, been a symbolic gesture. Many of the victims had already been buried elsewhere by their relatives, and the coffins did not, of course, include the bodies of any of the numberless dead policemen; Meriel Buchanan heard that some of them even contained stones.* Bertie Stopford noticed that during the ceremony 'sometimes a simple plank of wood was carried alongside of the coffins to represent another victim who had already been buried'. He had counted around 150, but had heard there were

---

* Louise Patouillet was told that a poor woman concierge who had not had the money to bury her recently deceased husband had been delighted to be offered 100 rubles for his corpse to be elevated to that of hero of the revolution in the procession.

168 in all. Claude Anet was told that the authorities had prepared space for 160 coffins. Charles de Chambrun heard rumours that they had bolstered the number of dead for the procession by adding some Chinese who had died of influenza.[18]

One thing is certain: no one who reported on or witnessed the February Revolution of 1917 came away with an accurate figure for the numbers killed and wounded.[19] The official figures published in *Pravda* at the time, and perpetuated in traditional Soviet historiography, were 1,382 killed and wounded*. Many more estimates were circulated at the time, but they ranged wildly. Claude Anet was reliably informed by someone close to Prince Lvov that the 'total of the victims of the Revolution ... amounted to 7,000 for Petrograd – including all the wounded attended in hospitals and ambulances and the dead. To this must be added 1,000 wounded attended in private houses.' He himself estimated around 1,500 dead.[20] French resident Louise Patouillet heard talk of '7000 killed'; but many of the bodies buried that day had not been those of people who had 'died for liberty', for these victims had already been piously interred 'without fuss' in the city cemeteries, in preference to the 'ostentatious obsequies' of the Field of Mars.[21]

Hugh Walpole reported to the British government a consensus that 'the deaths in all amounted to about 4,000'. Arthur Reinke of Westinghouse wrote that the best estimate he had obtained 'placed the number of killed at 3,000 to 5,000; the number of wounded ran into the ten thousands'. The 'most conservative figure' offered to Isaac Marcosson was five hundred dead civilians – but this was not counting the soldiers and policemen who had died. James Houghteling was told that 'there were probably about 1,000 deaths', but that 'in a city of 2 million inhabitants a thousand single deaths were quite possible in such a revolution'. Florence Harper – who had, with Donald Thompson, been close to a lot of the violence at street

---

* The official figures gave only sixty-one police killed and wounded, an extremely low estimate.

level – reported that the lowest estimate of dead was two thousand; the highest ten thousand; Thompson placed the loss of life at '5,000 or a little more'.[22] In general, the most commonly quoted number of dead was around four thousand, as British eyewitness James Pollock summarised: 'The truth probably lies between four and five thousand killed. In the two days before the revolution broke out, some five hundred were killed in the centre of the city; during the three days of fighting many more, and this takes no account of the casualties beyond the river on the Petrograd and Viborg Sides.' Of one thing Pollock had no doubt: 'the agreeable statements made as to the bloodlessness are much exaggerated'.[23]

For the dead of the February Revolution there would be only a collective, secular memorial. 'Since the archaic age of Saint Olga and Saint Vladimir, and indeed since the Russian people first appeared in the light of history, it is the first time that a great national act has been performed without the help of the church,' Ambassador Paléologue wrote in his diary.[24] He was forcibly struck by the contrast: 'Only a few days ago, all the thousands of soldiers and workmen whom I saw marching past me could not see the smallest ikon in the street without stopping, lifting their caps and crossing themselves fervently.'

It was gone 10.00 p.m. when the last of the parade laid down their coffins that day. With darkness having descended over the vast open grave, the crowds finally began dispersing into the freezing night. The following day workmen began filling the grave with concrete. The Field of Mars took on a 'desolate and sinister' aspect, as Maurice Paléologue pondered the ramifications of this momentous day in Russian history:

As I returned to the Embassy by the solitary paths of the Summer Garden, I reflected that I had perhaps witnessed one of the most considerable events in modern history. For what has been buried in the red coffins is the Byzantine and Muscovite tradition of the Russian people, nay the whole past of orthodox Holy Russia.[25]

What he had witnessed was, in effect, the first major public act of what would become a new, official atheism.[26]* Thursday 23 March 1917 was an enormous religious and cultural watershed, from which Russia would not look back for seventy-three years.

---

* Paleologue noted that the Cossacks had refused to take part in the mass funeral because 'the figure of Christ was not displayed', while others complained that the painting red of the coffins was 'impious'. In order to mollify criticism, the Provisional Government later sent some priests to say prayers over the graves.

9

Bolsheviki! It Sounds 'Like All that the World Fears'

'I say! There's an amazing fellow over there on the other side of the Troitsky Bridge,' an excited English resident told Negley Farson one day in early April:

'He's talking rank anarchy! Immediate peace, no annexations, the Dictatorship of the Proletariat, world revolution! Never heard anything like it in my life! ... Advocates the soldiers coming back from the front and the overthrow of the Provisional Government ... *now*! 'Doesn't he know there's a war on?'[1]

In the weeks following the announcement of a political amnesty on 6 March, thousands of Russian émigrés had begun returning to Petrograd after long years of exile – some from Europe, others from Siberia. In a few cases the government funded their return; others made their way back thanks to popular subscriptions raised to help them. Those from Siberia were arriving daily into the Nicholas Station, from which many of them had initially been transported. On 15 March alone, J. Butler Wright noted that five trainloads had arrived there.[2] But on 3 April (the Russian Orthodox Easter Monday) attention was focused elsewhere – on the Finland Station – where the most important figure in the revolutionary movement in exile was about to make his long-anticipated return.

Rumours had been circulating for days about the return to Petrograd of a leading 'socialist fanatic'; Isaac Marcosson had found excited crowds in the streets near the station and, when he asked what it was all about, he was told: 'Lenin is coming today.'[3] Few among the Russian population at large knew Lenin's name or exactly what he represented, but there was no doubt about the inflammatory message this revolutionary leader brought with him, after sixteen long, hard years of exile in Europe.

His real name was Vladimir Ilyich Ulyanov, the 'Lenin' sobriquet being the last of a string of pseudonyms and aliases that he had adopted during his years of political propagandising from a succession of boltholes across Europe. As a Marxist theorist and head of the Bolshevik faction of the Russian Social Democratic and Labour Party (RSDLP), Lenin had been sowing the seeds of discontent from a distance, via a network of underground activists across Russia, who illegally circulated his seditious political pamphlets, including the now-notorious 'What Is to Be Done?' and his underground newspaper *Iskra* (The Spark), both of which called for a people's revolution led by a dedicated intellectual elite.[4]

The foreign community of Petrograd had had little exposure to Lenin's ideas and was equally uncomprehending of his true political colours as a Bolshevik. Indeed, such was the general confusion about him that he was often described by foreign residents and journalists alike as an 'anarchist', a term they applied willy-nilly to a wide range of political activists.* For Sir George Buchanan, Lenin was but one of yet another 'fresh batch of anarchists from abroad' to have arrived recently in the city. Many suspected an affiliation with the Germans: 'That horrible German agent Lenin' was back in the city, working 'day and night to make trouble', Lady Georgina wrote home, convinced that Lenin brought with him the danger of 'German intrigues'.[5] The Americans weren't sure what to make of him, either: 'An ultra-Socialist named

---

* Before the word 'Bolshevik' gained currency, many foreign observers referred to Lenin as a 'Maximalist', which was in fact a term for a member of the extreme wing of the Socialist Revolutionary Party.

Lenin has been doing a great deal of foolish talking and has advised his hearers to kill all people who have property and refuse to divide,' noted Ambassador Francis, who was already worrying that Kerensky did not have the muscle to deal with him. 'We are living somewhat in suspense,' he added in a letter to his son Perry. 'Lenin's followers are an unknown quantity.'[6]

From the moment he arrived, Lenin was clearly bent on undermining and ousting the Provisional Government. One American who had been on the same train that had brought him into Petrograd from the border at Torneo told YMCA worker Edward Heald that Lenin's first words as he got off the train had been, 'Hail to the Civil War.' 'God knows what a task the Provisional Government has on hand without adding to the trouble that such a firebrand can create,' Heald wrote in his diary.[7] The accusations of being in the pay of the Germans would certainly stick, for ·Lenin's return with a dedicated circle of followers had been facilitated by the Germans on a special 'sealed' train that was allowed through wartime Germany to the coast at Sassnitz, from where the group had crossed by boat to Trelleborg and then travelled by train through Sweden and Finland to Petrograd's Finland Station.[8] With word out about Lenin's imminent arrival on the evening of the 3rd, a considerable crowd of supporters, factory workers and the curious had gathered to meet him. Arno Dosch-Fleurot went along, in the company of 'an old revolutionary pamphlet-writer' who had been filling him in on the role of the absent Lenin in the revolutionary movement for the last sixteen years, and on his long-standing grass-roots support in the Vyborg factory quarter, where he had been a political agitator before his arrest in 1898.

When the passengers descended from the special train, Fleurot had searched for this almost mythical figure – a man not seen in the city since his brief reappearance there in 1905–6, and then only by his closest colleagues in the party. But all Fleurot caught sight of was 'a small man with Asiatic features', who had the 'short, unimpressive figure of a Tartar of the Volga, but with the heavy cheek-bones and more decided slant to the eye common among the Mongols'.[9]

Lenin's personal magnetism was, however, undeniable. The shrill, hectoring voice and those inscrutable Kalmyk eyes clearly stirred the crowd of well-wishers and the official party from the Petrograd Soviet that had greeted him, at a Finland Station festooned with garlands and red banners. Even bigger crowds stood waiting in the darkness outside, with bands playing the Marseillaise and the Internationale, the scene 'stabbed by piercing beams from the search-lights of the armoured cars'.[10] From there, Lenin had been escorted to his new political base in the city – a mansion belonging to Nicholas II's former lover.

Across the Troitsky Bridge opposite the British embassy, and within sight of the blue minarets of the city's only mosque, stood the stylish Style Moderne home of Mathilde Kschessinska, prima ballerina of the Imperial Ballet, for whom the mansion had been specially built in 1904–6. Shortly before the February Revolution, warned that she was in danger, she had abandoned it and fled to France.[11] On 4 April, when she looked out of her window on the other side of the river, Meriel Buchanan saw 'an enormous scarlet flag fluttering above the walls'. The house, she discovered, had 'been taken over by a group of political exiles who had just arrived from Switzerland'. Shortly after his arrival there, Lenin had emerged onto the balcony to address the waiting crowd. Soon he was making 'the most incendiary harangues in public', hurling invective at the Provisional Government while bandying his mantra – 'Peace, Bread, Land' – in his new political organ, the newspaper *Pravda*, which had also established a base at the mansion.[12]

Negley Farson contemplated the short distance from there, back across the Neva, to the British embassy, where 'the best diplomatic corps in Russia was guessing which way the cat was going to jump', now that Lenin had arrived to stir up the hornets' nest of political rivalry. Beyond, on Furshtatskaya, the Americans 'were doing likewise', 'and further on the Italians and the French; and further out the whole world – all guessing'.[13] At first Lenin seemed like any other political fanatic, and there were plenty of them populating the streets of Petrograd, haranguing people from every corner. But Sir George Buchanan was seriously concerned: the Provisional Government needed to act swiftly and stop Lenin 'inciting soldiers to desert, to seize the land, and to murder'. That was the simple, brutal message that Lenin had brought with him, as part of his campaign to bring about what Sir George saw as a 'demoralisation' in government and Russia's exit from the war.[14]

'He is the reddest of the red,' wrote Claude Anet. 'This Lenin is what one calls, in the horrible Socialist jargon, a "Defeatist", that is to say, one of those who prefer defeat to the War.' Negley Farson was not taken in by assertions of the new arrival's mythical 'greatness'. 'He was not "great" to any but a few people at that time. He was just this undersized new agitator in an old double-breasted blue suit, his hands in his pockets, speaking with an entire absence of that hysterical arm-waving that so characterized all his fellow countrymen.'[15] Arthur Ransome thought even less of what he deemed Lenin's risible methods of political agitation from the Kschessinska Mansion: 'his proceedings are so exaggerated that they have the air of being comic opera'.

But his seditious influence was soon felt, as Edward Heald noted, when shortly afterwards he saw a street parade organised by Lenin condemning the war and the government: '*There* is the poison that will destroy the democratic revolution,' he noted presciently.[16] Incitement to violence and anarchy was heard everywhere in the city. 'You want to get rich: there is money in the banks,' Louis de Robien heard Lenin exhorting the mob. 'You want palaces, go where you please … You don't want to walk in the mud: stop those cars! … All this belongs to you – it's your turn – you are the power now.' De Robien encountered the impact of Lenin's rabble-rousing in an enormous women's demonstration on the Nevsky, when he heard them singing 'blood-thirsty lyrics to the tune of a hymn': 'We will pillage! We will cut throats! We will disembowel them!'[17]

With the arrival of Lenin, the world beyond Russia finally began to take notice of this new and threatening breed of *Bolsheviki* – the name had rapidly been gaining currency and it sounded, to journalist William G. Shepherd of *Everybody's*

Magazine, 'like all that the world fears'. '*Bolsheviki!* … Can't you see it in the headlines?' he asked his American readers. 'It will stick. It will crackle in everybody's mouth, ear, and brain. *Bolsheviki!*'[18]

Once Lenin was installed, the Kschessinska Mansion, with its team of bullying, incendiary Bolshevist agitators, became a hive of propagandist activity. 'Hundreds of typewriters and duplicators worked night and day, and before long printing presses were also installed', running off anti-government proclamations by the thousand. Lenin was far too busy with meetings and politicising to take time out to address the huge crowds that now began gathering daily beneath the balcony on Kronversky Prospekt, hoping to 'hear the lion roar'.[19] Unlike the flamboyant orator Leon Trotsky,* who returned from exile in New York the following month, Lenin was not one for the limelight. He 'hid himself and allowed his lieutenants to do the work' and only occasionally deigned to show himself. Nor did he waste time trying to win over those who were hostile to him.[20]

At this time Associated Press correspondent Robert Crozier Long was one of the few to be allowed access to the Kschessinska Mansion – a building now approached with some trepidation by terrified local residents, having a reputation as it did for being stashed with machine guns and home to a bomb-making factory. The interior, in line with the depressing 'democratisation' – or rather degradation – of the Tauride Palace, was a sorry sight:

> In a handsome white vestibule, with marble statues, were dirty, spitting soldiers who lounged over desks collating reports … the fine winter-garden had become headquarters of the propaganda league, and was packed from ceiling to floor with pamphlets; Kshesinskaya's bedroom, of the oriental

---

* Trotsky travelled on the same Norwegian ship – the *Kristianiafjod* – as William G. Shepherd and the celebrated muck-raking journalist Lincoln Steffens, both of whom had been commissioned by *Everybody's Magazine* to go to Petrograd to cover events.

luxury of which Petrograd talked, was littered with copies of the incendiary newspaper *Pravda*; and – worst shame of all – her marble and tile Roman bath, the size of a small room, was half full of cigarette ends, dirty papers and rags.[21]

In this former late-imperial splendour Lenin was gathering around him 'all the hot-heads of the revolution', Maurice Paléologue noted in his diary. In his view, the Bolshevik leader was a combination of 'utopian dreamer and fanatic, prophet and metaphysician, blind to any idea of the impossible or the absurd, a stranger to all feelings of justice or mercy, violent, Machiavellian and crazy with vanity'. Paléologue thought him 'all the more dangerous because he is said to be pure-minded, temperate and ascetic. Such as I see him in my mind's eye, he is a compound of Savanorola and Marat, Blanqui and Bakunin.' Donald Thompson shared this alarmist view of Lenin and saw only one logical solution. 'The best thing for Russia to do,' he wrote to his wife 'is to kill Lenine' or at least 'arrest him and put him in prison'. 'If they don't I expect to write you a letter, some day, that this cur is in control of things here.'

The 'innocent boy' from Kansas had it in one.[22]

In early April the celebration of the Russian Orthodox Easter had, all too briefly, shut out the seditious new language of revolution and brought a transitory return to the old days of imperial Russia, the churches conducting mass with all the usual opulent Orthodox splendour and ceremony. Across the city on the Saturday night the bells had begun ringing at midnight, and churches had been packed for the vigil lasting until till 3.30 a.m. on Easter Sunday. Great torches could be seen burning on the four corners of the roof of St Isaac's Cathedral and the whole city was lit up for miles. Louis de Robien noted how 'the great onion domes of the Church of the Resurrection, all gold in the reflection of the light from the stained-glass windows below, glowed in the sky … All the bells were ringing. The cannon of the Fortress were firing salvos.' For a short while, it seemed as though the events of the last few weeks had been 'like a bad dream'. It was, he wrote, 'the Russia of old, rising again with Christ'.[23]

The worshippers in church seemed as devout as ever; Edward Heald thought there was 'a new spirit abroad of released hope and a touching show of brotherhood'.[24] At the Kazan Cathedral, Maurice Paléologue had seen 'the same scenes as in the days of tsarism, the same majesty and magnificence, the same display of liturgical pomp'. If anything, the levels of piety were even more intense – expressed in a huge wave of emotion when the priest announced '*Khristos Voskres!*' – Christ is Risen![25] The arrival of spring soon afterwards added to this feeling of renewal. With the chestnut trees in bloom, the ice floes on the Neva beginning to break up, the gold cupolas gleaming in the spring sunshine, and people and street traders out enjoying the thaw, there came a resurgence of hope. There also came most welcome news from America.

It took J. Butler Wright and his colleagues at the US embassy two hours working with four code books to decipher the formal statement telegraphed to them from Washington that President Wilson had declared war on Germany on 6 April (24 March OS; the embassy received the news two days later). The embassy staff had been receiving anxious calls meanwhile from reporters, members of the Allied mission and 'news-hungry Americans', before it finally summoned them to the embassy to hear the ambassador formally announce just after midnight that America had entered the war. Everyone in the embassy was enormously relieved; the last few days had been a terrible strain. The response in the Russian press was, as Wright recalled, 'positively inspiring'.[26] Several American naval and military officers based in Petrograd immediately came to the embassy and asked to be allowed to go home and enlist. And there was a ready supply of former Russian officers who had lost their posts – some of whom had been in hiding since the revolution – and who now 'haunted' the office of military attaché William J. Judson, 'wishing to go to America'. 'Theirs was an awful lot,' Judson admitted, for 'if their own men or the Bolsheviks did not end up killing them', and America did not offer sanctuary, 'suicide seem[ed] their only recourse'.[27]

The pressures on the US government and its Petrograd embassy to wave a magic wand over the Russian war effort were, inevitably, enormous: '*all* look to us to lend money, muzzle the socialists, straighten out the Trans-Siberian, and generally "buck up" this government – which is going to be a colossal job,' wrote Wright in his diary.[28] The logistical problems alone were legion, notably on the Trans-Siberian Railway, where a chaotic congestion of cars, rolling stock and food and military supplies stranded at Vladivostok was urgently in need of resolution in order to get the system running. A contingent of American and Canadian railroad men were now en route to Russia, headed by John F. Stevens, one of the builders of the Panama Canal, to attempt to bring order to the chaos.

Other foreign visitors, in the main British and French socialists and labour leaders, had been arriving since mid-March to see the changes that revolution had wrought on Russia. British Labour Party representatives James O'Grady and Will Thorne were among the first. They were 'honest decent working men,' admitted embassy official Francis Lindley, but 'they had nothing in common with the intellectual theorists with whom they argued hour after hour. After one of these bouts they would come into my room and refresh themselves with whisky and soda – giving vent to the most abusive description of their opposite numbers. "A lot of b-dy s-ds my dear chap",' said Thorne, of their revolutionary hosts. Meanwhile the Russian socialist press condemned the British delegates as 'hirelings of an Imperialist Government and not representing Labour at all'.[29]

The most prominent Western socialist – and a member of the French War Cabinet – was Albert Thomas, who arrived on 9 April on the same train as a group of exiles returning from France, England and Switzerland. A large crowd had turned out to greet him, headed by the meticulous Paléologue in ambassador's tailcoat and top hat (eclipsing a rather shabby revolutionary guard of honour). '*Now* we see the revolution in all its grandeur and beauty!' an enthusiastic Thomas exclaimed to Paléologue as he stepped from the train.[30] The jovial Frenchman – more 'commercial traveller' than sophisticated politician, in both appearance and manner – was accommodated at the Hotel d'Europe, where he 'trie[d] in vain to act the fierce socialist by eating his wing of pullet from the end of his knife', while Paléologue rued the fact that he was obliged to entertain him at the French embassy with one of his last good bottles of burgundy. Despite Thomas's open endorsement of the revolution, the Russians remained unimpressed by him; as far as they were concerned, he too was a phoney – a 'Socialist traitor', a 'bourgeois' come to represent 'pro-war capitalism'.[31]

For his own part, Thomas confided to his old friend Julia Grant (now married to a Russian prince and known as Princess Cantacuzène-Speransky) that the Russian socialists were 'not socialists at all, but what we call in France Anarchists and Communards'.[32] But there was also another purpose to his mission, and it was one that Paléologue had been expecting. Thomas brought with him a letter from the French government relieving him of his post as ambassador and recalling him to Paris, because 'your position of favour with the Emperor would make it more difficult for you to carry on your duties under the present government,' Thomas explained.[33] Paléologue took the news with his characteristic equanimity, although he resented it coming from the upstart Thomas. He was profoundly concerned about Russia's continuing participation in the war, convinced that it was essential to bolster support for Milyukov and the moderates in the Provisional Government. Thomas, however, supported Kerensky as the only man 'capable of establishing, with the aid of the *Soviet*, a government worthy of our [i. e. Allied] confidence'. Knowing full well that the Soviet was campaigning for a Russian withdrawal, Paléologue telegraphed Paris warning that it was more than likely that she would soon defect from the war.[34]

Until now, Ambassador Francis and his aide J. Butler Wright had remained relatively optimistic about Russia's post-revolutionary political future, but an incident on the night of 9 April had confirmed how volatile the Petrograd mobs still were. Francis had been entertaining guests that Sunday evening when Phil Jordan hurried in with a message warning that a mob waving black anarchist flags was on its way to attack the 'American imperialists' at the embassy. They had apparently been incited to do so in protest at the recent conviction and sentence to death of the American trade-union organiser and political activist Thomas J. Mooney, after a rigged trial in which he had been accused of involvement in a bomb plot during a San Francisco labour rally.* Preparing for his own dramatic Last Stand, Francis immediately instructed Jordan to load his revolver and bring it to him as he waited for a detachment of government militia to come and defend them. Francis vowed to shoot anyone who tried to get inside his embassy, but as things turned out, the mob never got that far and was dispersed soon after setting off. (Exaggerated stories were later circulated that Francis had single-handedly seen them off, which amused him greatly: 'Everyone seemed to prefer the more sensational story, so I suppose I shall have to resign myself to this heroic role,' he later wrote.) Phil was intensely relieved: the ambassador 'had never fired a gun in his life, so far as I know, and I knew if he fired at that crowd, it would probably be the end of both of us'.[35]

Arno Dosch-Fleurot had seen the mob being incited to storm the US embassy by a political agitator down at the Kazan Cathedral: 'Come with me and we'll take the American Ambassador prisoner until they set Mooney free,' he had shouted. Fleurot had hurried to the embassy, to be met by an excitable Phil Jordan: 'Lord a-lucky,' Phil told him:

> ebery night the ambassador takes a walk with only me, I tol' him he oughtn't t' do it. To-night we had some guests still here when de militia telephone. Jes' think if we'd been a-walkin' and dose fellers wid de black flag had a come along. Ambassador Francis only knows two words in Russian

---

* The sentence was commuted to life imprisonment in 1918.

'*Amerikanski Posol*' (American Ambassador). If dose fellers as'ed him anything he'd a said '*Amerikanski posol*'. Wouldn't they 'a' rubbed their han's an' said, Look wa'at de good Lord has gone an brought us.[36]

Inevitably, in both Francis's subsequent memoirs and other retellings of the incident, Jordan's vivid vernacular was sanitised.* The protest itself turned into a damp squib. Blame for inciting it was soon laid at Lenin's door, but privately it had unnerved Francis and worried embassy officials about the safety of their mission and US nationals in the city in this new escalating climate of anarchy.[37]

On 18 April (OS; 1 May NS) the Petrograd Soviet decided to observe European May Day according to the Western calendar, 'so as to fall in time with the proletariats of all countries and illustrate the international solidarity of the working classes, in spite of the war and the illusions of the bourgeoisie'. If the Field of Mars burials had been the first public act of mourning of the revolution, the 'colossal demonstration' planned for May Day at the same location was to be its first public holiday.[38] Guests at the city's hotels were warned they would have to fend for themselves; staff were taking the day off, and no rooms would be serviced or meals served. All restaurants, businesses, offices and shops would be closed. Nor would there be any trams or *izvozchiki*. 'No one did a thing all day,' Leighton Rogers later recalled, 'except parade and rant.'[39]

From 5.00 a.m. people began congregating in central Petrograd. Donald Thompson, making the best he could of the chaos still prevailing in the Astoria, jumped out of bed in his bullet-riddled room when he heard bands playing outside his window and saw thousands marching past the Astoria towards the Nevsky. All the

---

* In the very different social climate of 1931, long before the days of political correctness, Fleurot had no qualms about representing Jordan's speech as he heard it. For an unedited version of Jordan's letters that retains his idiosyncratic punctuation and spelling, see Mrs Clinton A. Bliss.

bridges were thick with crowds thronging in from the Vyborg and Petrograd Sides carrying red banners. It was sunny, but there was a cold and biting wind and the thawing ice on the Neva had refrozen into great jagged floes. The huge and orderly march-past of celebrants lasted the whole day and was carried off to great theatrical effect – several foreign observers later recalled it as being, for them, the high point of the public celebration of the revolution. For visiting British Labour MP Morgan Philips Price, it seemed like the dawning of the Red Day of Socialism. 'I do not think I ever saw a more impressive spectacle,' he later wrote:

> It was not merely a labour demonstration, although every socialist party and workmen's union in Russia was repre-sented there, from anarcho-syndicalists to the most moderate of the middle-class democrats. It was not merely an inter-national demonstration, although every nationality of what had been the Russian Empire was represented there ... [it was] really a great religious festival, in which the whole human race was invited to commemorate the brotherhood of man.[40]

This vast parade was, he asserted, revolutionary Russia's 'mes-sage to the world', reflected in 'a steady stream of oratory' that 'flowed from hundreds of speaker's booths that covered every available free spot in the parks and squares of the city'.[41] Edward Heald was there to see it; in the square in front of the Astoria they had erected so many platforms for speakers that he and his YMCA colleagues 'could stand in one spot and hear six different orators going at once from as many platforms'. 'Unhesitatingly, soulfully, forcefully, the stream of eloquence flowed hour after hour. As soon as one speaker would tire, after about half an hour, another speaker would be rushed to the platform, hoisted up, and carry on without a second's interruption.' It was the same at the square in front of a Winter Palace decorated with a very long banner proclaiming 'Long Live the *Internationale*', where a seemingly endless succession of speakers – both for and against the government – took it in turns, 'all of them getting rousing cheers'.[42]

Claude Anet was at the Winter Palace as well, covering the story for *Le Petit Parisien*. 'The huge square was like a human ocean in which the swaying of the crowd resembled the motion of waves,' he recalled, with 'thousands of red flags with gold-lettered inscriptions fluttering in the wind'. Everyone seemed tolerant and good-natured. 'I took photographs; I was dressed as a *bourgeois*; obviously I was not one of the people', but the crowd 'stepped back so as not to inconvenience me, and watched me working with interest'. He noticed how carefully and respectfully people listened to the speakers, and how they had an ability to 'endure without end interminable garrulity'.[43] A huge cross-section of Russian workers was present: 'post office and telegraph clerks, students, marines, soldiers, workmen and working women, with bright scarves round their heads ... school-children, urchins of eight to ten years old, girls and boys holding each other by the hand, domestic servants, with a banner proclaiming the emancipation of the waiting-maid, the cook and the footman, waiters from restaurants'.[44] There were dozens of military orchestras, too, playing the obligatory Marseillaise and popular tunes from Russian opera and dance; and banners everywhere calling for 'land, liberty, peace, down with the war'.

Maurice Paléologue had gone to witness the 'splendid spectacle' at the Field of Mars on the eve of his departure from Russia. After three years as French ambassador, it was a time for painful reflection and a deep sense of loss: for him, May Day 1917 marked 'the end of a social order and the collapse of a world'. His years in Russia had left him with little to be optimistic about: the Russian Revolution was 'composed of elements too discordant, illogical, subconscious and ignorant for anyone to judge at the present time what its historical significance may be or its power of self-diffusion'.[45]

Having already had a difficult time of it in Petrograd for the last six months, Leighton Rogers was totally disenchanted. So hungry had he been that day, and so desperate to escape his cold, damp apartment, that he had spent his time wandering round the Hermitage Museum, contemplating Old Master still-lifes of food – 'plucked geese, freshly caught fish, vegetables and fruit' – in preference to admiring the museum's exceptional collection of Rembrandts. Later he had gone in search of supper with a colleague, but everywhere was closed and after several hours they had capitulated and returned to their apartment, where they made do with tea and black bread – 'all there was left in the larder' – and got into bed to keep warm. Rogers had had enough of it: 'Parades, parades, parades. When this is over I shall never want to see another. The streets are blocked with them every afternoon, work seems to have been abandoned and parading adopted as a business.'[46]

Two days after the great wave of optimism of the May Day celebrations the first serious rumblings of conflict in the government broke out, related to the details of Russia's war aims, as laid out in 1914. America's recent entry into the war had indirectly been the cause of what would be a major clash between Milyukov's government and the Soviet. Eager to celebrate the announcement of US entry, Milyukov had given a press interview on the Provisional Government's war aims, in which he had reiterated undertakings made by the tsarist government on the outbreak of war in 1914 to fight for a decisive victory and support post-war annexations by the Allies – notably that of Constantinople by Russia – and the imposition of punitive war reparations on Germany. Milyukov's 'Note', as it became called, had immediately antagonised the pro-peace Petrograd Soviet, which was pushing for Russia's unconditional withdrawal from the war, without strings.

Four days later the government was forced to issue a disclaimer, but it was too late to prevent a surge of violent protest from revolutionaries denouncing Milyukov, insisting that the objectives of the war must hold to democratic ideals, and demanding the abrogation of all treaties with the Allies.[47] Lenin and his followers seized on this conflict of objectives as a trigger for a pitched battle with the Provisional Government, inciting workers and soldiers to protest, in order to compel the government to capitulate or resign. At the Mariinsky Palace on the afternoon of 20 April – where the Provisional Government was in urgent talks with the Executive Committee of the Soviet –25,000 to 30,000 soldiers of the Pavlovsky, 180th, Finnish and Moscow Regiments, as well as some sailors, gathered outside with fixed bayonets, but were eventually persuaded to disperse by General Lavr Kornilov, now commander-in-chief of the Petrograd garrison.[48]

Down on the Nevsky, Donald Thompson saw two mobs – one anarchist, the other pro-Provisional Government – come marching down from the Morskaya and the Sadovaya. 'Someone let fly with a gun and for a few minutes it was simply hell on that corner, with everyone lying down flat on the pavement,' he recalled. Fifteen minutes of pandemonium left six people dead and twelve to fifteen wounded. There was more shooting later, in front of the Kazan Cathedral and near the US consulate, at the Singer Building opposite it. 'A constant uproar prevailed on the Nevsky, till around 10.30 that evening,' Thompson told his wife. 'Thousands were marching for and against the government until finally it reached the point where you didn't know what was what. Boris and I decided to take off our hats and cheer every mob that passed.' But after they got caught up in a group of menacing armed anarchists waving black flags, they ended once again face-down on the pavement, fearing for their lives as firing broke out.[49]

Thompson was anxious to be 'on the ground early' the following morning to catch events as they unfolded. He saw that there were notices up everywhere 'asking the people not to meet on the street any more'.[50] Meetings were now only allowed 'in halls, theatres or public buildings' – a futile attempt to prevent further incitement to trouble. Over the next couple of days random skirmishes and relentless speechifying dominated on the streets of Petrograd. Arno Dosch-Fleurot witnessed a positive 'storm of oratory', as 'people gathered by the tens of thousands to applaud the demands for a peace – without contribution or annexation'. He noted with amusement that this latter phrase had spread like wildfire, with the Russian words *kontributsiya* and *anneksiya* being adopted from English for the purpose (there being no Russian equivalent to express the precise meaning). Unfortunately, some speakers 'believed these words to be the names of towns and proceeded to exhort their listeners 'not to permit Russia to take Constantinople, Annexia or Contributia'. Ella Woodhouse recalled her maid telling her all about it excitedly: 'We want peace. We don't need those two Rumanian towns, Annexiya and Contributsiya. We are sick of war!'[51]

As a result of these violent disturbances, the Provisional Government was compelled to revise its position in a new note to the Allies, opposing any war contributions or annexations as part of a future peace treaty with Germany. All but the Bolshevik members of the Executive Committee of the Soviet accepted this climbdown, and the protesting troops were ordered back to their barracks. The situation had, for now, been defused, but 'the days of Miliukov, Gutchkov and Prince Lvov are numbered,' noted Maurice Paléologue.[52] Prince Lvov looked tired and wan; he was exhausted by overwork and had aged terribly since the revolution, thought diplomat Robert Bruce Lockhart when he arrived from Moscow to visit the prince, noting regretfully that 'he was not the stuff of which revolutionary Prime Ministers are made'. Lockhart sensed the 'same helplessness, the same apprehensions' in other members of the government. The revolution had destroyed all Lvov's old Liberal friends. The only man with any power was Kerensky, because he alone had the support of the Soviets.[53]

'Now you're seeing what we saw in the Seven Days,' one visitor was told by American residents, at the end of what had been 'the most intense and exciting week in the capital since the revolution'.[54] The black flags of the anarchists marching on the Nevsky during the three days of protests had sent chills down Edward Heald's spine; they were out to 'plunge everything into disorder'. Russia, he told J. Butler Wright, was 'on the lid of a powder can'. Negley Farson noted the deep atmosphere of uncertainty.

Everyone was absorbed in the problem of self-preservation, for life in Petrograd 'had become a great gamble'.[55] Out on the Nevsky with US consul North Winship, he had run into a huge parade of chanting people demanding 'Land and Freedom'. But he sensed something new, and deeply sinister, this time:

> A bevy of factory girls marching arm in arm; their shawl-enveloped heads tilted skywards; their placid Slav faces lighted with a look of perfect ecstasy, and they sang as if inspired the Hymn of the Revolution … And then I saw it … a huge black banner, with a white skull and crossbones, which seemed to be grinning over the words: 'Welcome Anarchy!' … There was something loathsome about it, as if it were a flaunting invitation to indulge in all sorts of beastliness.[56]

It was clear that, after the latest debacle, 'Lenin was getting results,' thought Arno Dosch-Fleurot. 'He had hardly been back three weeks and the effect of his activities was to be seen on every side … he supplied a head and a directive to the more violent revolutionists who wanted to seize the power themselves.' Lenin had brought with him the one thing that until now the revolution had lacked: he had 'provided violence with a doctrine'.[57]

Shortly before leaving Petrograd, Maurice Paléologue confided that, in his view, Russia was 'entering upon a very long period of disorder, misery and ruin'. As he set off for the railway station, he pondered the 'final bankruptcy of Russian liberalism, and the approaching triumph of the Soviet. 'Weep, my holy Russia, weep!' he wrote, recalling the words of the village idiot in the opera *Boris Godunov*. 'For thou art entering into darkness.' 'They are recalling Paléologue at the very moment when his "strong manner" could produce results,' wrote his colleague de Robien with considerable regret.[58] As the ambassador's train steamed out of the Finland Station under a great plume of smoke, Charles de Chambrun pondered a great diplomatic era now, with Paléologue's departure, gone for ever:

Farewell, all that panache, the glitter of gold decorations, the wiles of diplomacy, the lavish dishes, the tricolour livery, the powdered footmen and their white stockings! Farewell *belles lettres*, those 'clever' dispatches and pompous, melodious phrases! It's back to simplicity for us! We'll never again see the ambassador's car pulling up outside the residence of the charming Princess Paley, as, in times gone by, people used to see M. de Chateaubriand's coachman dozing on his seat outside Mme Récamier's door. We would never ever forget that we were all there, eyewitnesses to the greatest upheaval in history![59]

Even as Maurice Paléologue was recalled to Paris, Lloyd George's government in London had been debating the future of his equally respected colleague, Sir George Buchanan, and whether he might 'no longer [be] the ideal British representative in Petrograd', despite his equally exemplary track record. For Buchanan, like his French colleague, was now deemed too closely associated with the old tsarist regime to command the respect of the new breed of socialists in government. It was privately agreed that a new envoy should be sent, one more likely to have influence over the 'democratic elements which now predominated in Russia to pursue the war with energy'.[60]

Labour MP and minister Arthur Henderson – a man who shared the socialist sympathies of the Soviet, but who in every other respect had no qualifications whatsoever for the task – was chosen by the British War Cabinet to replace Sir George, who would ostensibly be invited to come home on leave. When officials at the Petrograd embassy's Chancery Office got wind of this they were horrified, and some threatened to resign if it happened. Word reached General Knox, who promptly sent a confidential telegram to Britain warning of the damage Buchanan's recall would cause: 'No British Ambassador at Petrograd has ever to an equal degree enjoyed the confidence of the Russians,' he asserted. Was Sir George to receive the same treatment as the French ambassador – this a man who, like Paléologue, enjoyed the confidence of the moderates?[61]

A despondent Sir George discovered, on Arthur Henderson's arrival on 20 May, that the newcomer had been given full powers to take over the running of the British embassy. Sir George entertained him to a strained dinner, at which Lady Buchanan could barely control her seething resentment. Buchanan himself did rather better at containing 'a certain distaste and fastidious disapprobation', heightened by the fact that Henderson had no French, or any other language in which to converse with the more distinguished polyglot diplomats and politicians seated around the table. Leaving Henderson to it and declining to offer him the comforts of the British embassy, a dignified Sir George went off for a rest in Finland.

Henderson soon discovered the full extent of his own inadequacies, encountering a decided hostility on the part of the embassy staff to his pompous, sententious manner.[62] He was shocked by the anarchy he found in Petrograd and dismayed to find himself victim of the random room-sackings that went on in all Petrograd hotels; 'his dinner jacket and evening trousers had mysteriously disappeared from his room' and nobody had shown the least interest in helping him find them. Forced to admit that he was ill-equipped to deal with the wily Russians, let alone build a dialogue with them, he informed Lloyd George that 'he had come to the conclusion that no good purpose would be served by the removal of a man who understood Russia' as well as Sir George Buchanan.[63] Henderson had shown little real interest, and even less perceptiveness, during his visit, and the Russian socialists who entertained him remained equally unimpressed: 'Your Henderson is bourgeois to his finger-tips,' one of them told an embassy official. 'He is like all the rest of you. He will take his wife to church at eleven o'clock every Sunday morning.'[64]

The day after the departure of Maurice Paléologue another crisis in the government had filled the whole of the diplomatic corps with renewed gloom. On 3 May, Milyukov, Minister of Foreign Affairs, and Guchkov, Minister of War – their positions now untenable, as a result of the 'April Days' protests – had resigned.

Their departure marked an end to any liberal influence in the Provisional Government. The Soviet, with its crucial control of the army, was too powerful to disregard; it was clear that this disjointed and ill-matched dual government of socialist Soviet and bourgeois Provisional Government was not working. The only solution was the formation of a new Coalition Provisional Government on 5 May, once again under the token premiership of Prince Lvov and this time with the inclusion of six social-ists – three of whom, Irakli Tsereteli, Viktor Chernov and Matvey Skobelev, were members of the Petrograd Soviet.[65] Alexander Kerensky – now firmly in the ascendant as Minister of War – was charged with the urgent task of galvanising the Russian offensive on the Eastern Front.

Violence and anarchy, meanwhile, were spreading across the city. 'Anarchy raises her finger higher and higher,' wrote Edward Heald, for it was 'too attractive to the Russian character'.[66] An eight-hour working day was proclaimed in early May but, despite this, production in the factories was in crisis, with dwindling supplies of coal and raw materials forcing many to close. The internal labour situation was made worse by continuing strikes, especially in Russia's crucial coalfields. There was a growing air of public disenchantment as the initial revolutionary euphoria receded; everyone was tired of parades and demonstrations, of talk and endless queues; the streets were 'full of beggars and newsboys and cheap prostitutes'.[67] Pauline Crosley, newly arrived wife of a US naval attaché, was having to employ four maids because of the time they needed to spend standing in line daily 'for bread, meat, fish, milk, butter, eggs, kerosene, candles'. Wood was very hard to get and there were interminable queues also for clothes and cigarettes. "I never imagined I would see so many idle men!' she wrote home at the end of May. 'Thousands of men in uniform doing nothing but sit on benches in the few parks and eat sunflower seeds!' Everywhere she went she heard talk of how Russia could be 'saved'. 'Why don't the Allies save Russia? Why doesn't the United States do something to save Russia?' – she was asked over and over again.[68]

By the end of May there had been many departures and several new arrivals in the expatriate community of Petrograd. James Stinton Jones had been sent back to London, where his account of the February Revolution had been splashed across the pages of the *Daily Mail*, 'with the whole front page covered with my photographs and the reverse side full of the story as I had told it'. In July he published his experiences in book form, as *Russia in Revolution, Being the Experiences of an Englishman in Petrograd during the Upheaval* – one of the first eyewitness accounts by a non-Russian to reach the West.[69] Isaac Marcosson had also left, sailing to Aberdeen and then travelling to London, where he installed himself in the Savoy Hotel to write his *Rebirth of Russia*, published in August. He had not been sorry to see the end of the perennial accommodation problems that he had endured: 'Like most Petrograd hotels during that hectic period,' he later recalled, it had been 'a sort of madhouse sheltering a strange jumble of nationalities, who went elevatorless, sugarless, bathless and almost breadless. The only thing we had in abundance was odour, which is an essential part of Petrograd "atmosphere".' He was glad to enjoy the comforts once more of a real, functioning bathroom.[70]

Several foreign journalists had also left after the excitement of February 1917, because they now found things too quiet in reporting terms. 'Many did not seek to hide their disappointment; they had hoped to find in the Revolution a unique opportunity for obtaining good copy, and instead they were asking themselves every evening how to put together a hundred lines to send to their paper,' recalled one observer:

> In short, the streets, apart from the red flags, the excessive dirt, and the trams laden with soldiers, had their usual aspect. Ministerial crises were neither more nor less frequent than in Paris. The very number of public meetings made them insipid in the end. On the surface Russian life seemed much the same as it had been before the Revolution: the staffs in the ministries were still at their posts, and in this country, free henceforward in a sense that no other country in the

world has ever been, we were reminded by the doorkeepers when we visited the Hermitage Museum that we must remove our hats.[71]

By mid-May – and after almost four years away from home, reporting from Russia and the Eastern Front – Arthur Ransome was weary and desperate to leave. 'There's no getting away from politics and it's my job to watch them as closely as I can and to guess what is happening and what is going to happen,' he wrote to his mother, informing her of his hopes of returning home for a month, 'but ... you can't imagine how sick I am of it all. At the same time things here keep happening so fast that I am equally pulled towards not risking being away ... I daren't leave Petrograd for more than twenty four hours because of the chance of some new political crisis or rather a new manifestation of the almost permanent crisis.' The endless privations endured by many of the foreign correspondents over the last few months had worn them all down, he continued: 'We aren't human beings any more but bits in a machine, and we have to spin round exactly as we must and not occupy ourselves with the landscape for the sake of the rest of the machine.' His colleague Harold Williams of the *Daily Chronicle* had had a nervous breakdown and had gone to the Caucasus for a rest. 'I'd give my eyes ... to get out of Petrograd,' Ransome wrote. 'Petrograd politics with good intervals of the front are all right. But Petrograd undiluted would turn the sanest man crazy.'[72]

On 24 May the intrepid Florence Harper had left her colleague Donald Thompson behind in Petrograd, to volunteer as a nurse with a US flying hospital on the Eastern Front at Dvinsk.* As she left, another took her place as the sole American female reporter in Petrograd. New Yorker Rheta Childe Dorr was a seasoned left-wing journalist, a champion of women's suffrage and labour reform, sent on behalf of New York's *Evening Mail*. Before she left, her managing editor had called her into his office.

---

* Donald Thompson joined her there a couple of weeks later.

'For heaven's sake, Mrs Dorr,' he admonished her, 'don't send us any essays on the Russian soul. Everybody else has done that. Go to Russia and do a job of reporting.'[73] Dorr's determination to do just that would be abundantly demonstrated in the following three months. She would also find herself crossing paths in Petrograd with an old suffragist friend, Emmeline Pankhurst – founder of the Women's Social and Political Union (WSPU) – with whom she had spent time in Paris during the winter of 1912–13 when ghosting Pankhurst's autobiography, *My Own Story*.

With Allied confidence in Russia's war effort crumbling, the indomitable Pankhurst – no longer the bête noire of the British government, having put her suffrage campaign on hold for the duration of the war – had set out for Russia's turbulent capital on her own one-woman mission to galvanise the Russian people. The channel for her pro-war propaganda drive was not, however, the army. It was those the army had left behind: the women of Petrograd.

PART 2

THE JULY DAYS

10

'The Greatest Thing in
History since Joan of Arc'

Emmeline Pankhurst arrived in Petrograd in early June 1917 'with a prayer from the English nation to the Russian nation, that you may continue the war on which depends the face of civilization and freedom'. She truly believed, she insisted, in an address published in *Novoe vremya* (New Times), 'in the kindness of heart and the soul of Russia'.[1] She had travelled with one of her most dedicated associates, Jessie Kenney, a former Lancashire cotton-mill worker who, with her sister Annie, was a staunch WSPU activist. Kenney had been the society's youngest national organiser and, now aged thirty, had become essential support to the tired and frail Pankhurst. It was not a good time for a fifty-nine-year-old woman in Pankhurst's state of health to be in Petrograd, but she was determined, at a critical time in the war, 'to do her darndest for Russia'.[2]

As a lifelong radical and political activist, Pankhurst had always been sympathetic to the revolutionary cause and in the 1890s had entertained prominent Russian political exiles to tea at her Russell Square home in London. On the outbreak of war in 1914 she had immediately abandoned her militant campaigning for votes for women, to support the national war effort, and had been touring Britain rallying women to the cause ever since. She had rejoiced at the overthrow of the old and oppressive tsarist order in February 1917, but by the early summer the Provisional Government in Russia seemed to its Western allies to be increasingly vulnerable. The possibility of Russia pulling out its troops greatly alarmed Pankhurst; it would 'rob the Russian people of the freedom for which they have had their revolution, and would involve them in a far worse slavery than the old,' she asserted. And so she volunteered to go to Russia along with Kenney as 'patriotic British women, loyal to the national and Allied Cause', in order to rally flagging public morale. It was a decision that had greatly dismayed her pacifist daughter Sylvia who, simultaneously, was privately campaigning to see both Britain and Russia out of the war.[3]

Pankhurst's initiative was welcomed with open arms by British Prime Minister David Lloyd George. Although her self-created mission – largely funded by monies raised through the suffragette newspaper *Britannia* – was intended to appeal to all classes, her personal objective was 'to help the women of Russia, to organize them, and to teach them how to use the vote'.[4] She therefore went on the rather grand assumption that Russian working women had no comprehension of the meaning of the vote, or of the power it would invest in them, and she had come 'to give them the benefit of her experience'.* It was, however, Russian women's support for the war that was her immediate concern. They had, after all, played a key role in the February Revolution, their protests about bread shortages triggering the riots; they knew what they wanted 'even better than the men did'.[5]

Prior to their departure, Jessie Kenney had travelled to Paris to consult with Christabel Pankhurst, co-founder with her mother of the WSPU: 'my wardrobe was getting low, and although there would be no time for shopping, it was imperative that I should get the necessary outfit'.[6] She had no suitable clothes for either the hot summer in Russia or the freezing winter, should they stay that long, and so Christabel sorted out

---

* Russian women would have the last laugh in this regard, for they were given the vote immediately after the October Revolution. In Britain only women over thirty were given the vote at war's end in 1918, and all British women over twenty-one did not get the vote until 1928.

some clothes from her own wardrobe to lend Jessie. She also told her to be sure to purchase a 'big solid diary' and keep daily notes. The most important thing she wanted to know was Jessie's opinion of Kerensky, as 'his character might affect the destiny of Russia'. In parting, Christabel also gave Jessie a little bag containing five pounds to keep round her neck: 'money talks, even in Revolutions,' she told her, 'and should anything happen to separate you from Mother, you will get some kind of help.'[7]

Departing by ship from Aberdeen, the two women sailed on the only passenger boat plying regularly between the UK and Norway in wartime – thanks to protection by an Allied convoy. It was crowded with exiles returning to Russia, many of them women and children. From Kristiania they travelled by train into Petrograd on the same train as Lady Muriel Paget and a group of doctors and nurses returning to the Anglo-Russian Hospital. They arrived at 2.30 in the morning to a city that 'seemed wrapped in silence', made magical by 'that mysterious light of the white nights of Russia'.[8] After a few days at the Hotel Angleterre they moved next door to the Astoria, the rooms arranged for them by Czech envoy Thomas Masaryk, who immediately gave them 'two special warnings': one, 'never to go out if there were the slightest chance of getting caught between the opposing mobs', as the women 'had no idea of what the force and violence of a Russian mob could be like'; and the other, to be prepared to go hungry or take the risk of food poisoning – the food in hotels now being 'seriously contaminated'.[9]

Emmeline Pankhurst's host in Russia was a leading feminist and medical practitioner, Anna Shabanova, founder of the Russian Women's Mutual Philanthropic Society – a moderate middle-class organisation that, unlike the WSPU, pursued social reform by strictly legal means.[10] Pankhurst was also assigned three interpreters who went through the Russian papers daily for her. One of them was Edith Kerby, who had been working at the British embassy compiling similar reports on the daily press for the

Anglo-Russian Propaganda Bureau,* and who had asked Sir George Buchanan if she could be released for ten days to be their interpreter. Kerby found the legendary suffragette 'old, quiet and very elegantly dressed, with lace and frills, hats and gloves and a fussy net over her crimped hair etc.' – a whiff of old-style English gentility that seemed incongruous in revolutionary Petrograd.[11]

A few days before Pankhurst's arrival a more prestigious American delegation – the nine-man Root Mission – had reached Petrograd from Vladivostok, on what had till recently been the imperial train, on a goodwill mission for President Wilson. To all intents and purposes, their task was to welcome Russia into the democratic community and gauge her continuing participation in the war, but the mission was conducted 'amid a cloud of uncertainty and speculation', according to Leighton Rogers, who met a few of the mission's 'supernumaries' at the Hotel d'Europe. They didn't have much idea of what they hoped to achieve, he concluded, but – unlike Pankhurst's limited funding – they had 'six hundred thousand dollars to spend and were going to carry out that assignment at least.'[12] Not surprisingly, the leading delegates were accommodated in the luxurious Romanov suites at the Winter Palace and 'fed better than any one in Russia'. They had white bread, and sugar and meat – and, more than that, 'the entire wine cellar of the czar was placed at their disposal'. (Diplomat Norman Armour heard that, after rummaging around in the palace's cellars, their Russian hosts found some rye whisky 'that had been laid in for the visit of General Grant in 1878').[13]†

Despite the lavish hospitality offered to them, by revolutionary Petrograd standards, the members of the Mission had no impact on the ordinary Russian, least of all the unknown Elihu Root,

---

* A library-cum-information-centre on the Fontanka, where people could read the English newspapers; also a front for SIS undercover work in Petrograd.

† The American Civil War general and US President, Ulysses S. Grant, visited Russia during a tour of the Ottoman Empire in 1878. He met Alexander II while in St Petersburg that August.

a Republican, corporate lawyer and former Secretary of State: 'Who is *Gospodin* Root ... was he one of your presidents?' Russians asked Leighton Rogers. 'As far as the Mission represen-ting the real spirit of America goes, it might just as well have come from Abyssinia,' Rogers thought. 'There's just one man in the United States who should have been leading this group, and that's Teddy Roosevelt. He is known and admired over here.'[14] The point of it all escaped Rogers, as it did the newly arrived Californian journalist Bessie Beatty, reporting for the *San Francisco Bulletin*. Root gave press conferences at which she noted the trotting out of 'simple, pat, nut-shell comments'; he had made a couple of speeches in English, which few people had understood, and had shaken the hands of various Russian officials.[15] But the tone of their exchanges had been one of 'cordial reserve', and the feeling remained that Root was a 'capitalist' and 'a hide-bound reactionary' and his mission an opportunistic attempt by a group of US businessmen 'seeking information about Russia to aid in her exploitation'.[16] Root had little grasp of Russia and admitted that it was all cosmetic, a 'grand-stand play'. 'We have here an infant class in the art of being free containing one hundred and seventy million people,' he telegraphed President Wilson, 'and they need to be supplied with kindergarten material.' The Russians, he had concluded, were 'sincere, kindly, good people but confused and dazed'.[17]

While the Root Mission progressed through a succession of hollow diplomatic formalities, it was Emmeline Pankhurst who took centre stage, holding court at the Astoria to a 'representative gathering of the foreign colony of Petrograd as it existed at that time'. She and Kenney were utterly 'tireless' in taking on an exhausting round of receptions, committee meetings and interviews. 'They seemed to me to work day and night,' noted Florence Harper, now back in Petrograd from the flying hospital.[18] Every day was filled with meeting various Russian women activists and reformers, members of the Provisional Government, officials from the Red Cross and YMCA. They also visited the Anglo-Russian Hospital, and Pankhurst gave numerous interviews to

Russian and foreign journalists such as Robert Wilton of *The Times*, as well as catching up with her friend Rheta Childe Dorr, who was also staying at the Astoria. Acting as secretary and amanuensis, Jessie Kenney had a box of visitors' cards that rapidly filled up with invitations to tea with the expatriate social set, so much so that Pankhurst could not cope with the numbers of people wanting to meet her. She and Kenney became increasingly exhausted, finding it difficult to sleep because of the white nights and 'the singing and talking in the streets until the early hours'.[19] They sensed an escalation of political unrest, too: 'one hears rumours and news all through each day of revolutions, strikes and counter strikes taking place so quickly that we never know what will be happening from hour to hour,' Jessie noted in her diary. They feared for the security of the Provisional Government, even though all the Russian women they had met had assured them of their support for it: 'They do not want the Bolsheviks to win, nor anarchy, but want some kind of democratic government,' she added.[20]

Emmeline Pankhurst had been keen to hold a whole series of mass outdoor meetings while in the city, but the Provisional Government was worried that she was too pro-war and that such meetings might be provocative to the Bolsheviks and their supporters. After decades of defying the British government she had no qualms about courting the risk of a hostile Russian reception to what she had to say, but the government flatly refused to grant her permission to address public meetings. This did not prevent her, however, speaking to small groups in private houses and at her hotel, and Kenney at least was allowed to speak to a large outdoor meeting of women factory workers, held 'outside the Anarchist Headquarters under the black flag' on a warm and sunny 18 June, with the assembled women and girls in 'light cotton dresses, and, on their heads, little coloured kerchiefs'.[21] Despite having to speak through an interpreter, Kenney felt she had their 'complete attention' and was 'warmed by the many upturned, smiling faces', as she spoke of the British campaign for female suffrage and her country's support for the Russian government.

1. The Nevsky Prospekt in Petrograd, *c.* 1910.

2. A sewing party at the British Embassy in Petrograd organized by Lady Georgina Buchanan, who stands at the head of the table.

3. Sir George Buchanan,
pictured in 1912.

4. Maurice Paléologue,
the French Ambassador to Russia, *c.* 1914.

5. Sir George Buchanan and family dining with staff at the British Embassy in Petrograd.

6. US Ambassador to the Russian Empire David R. Francis and his valet Phil Jordan, pictured here aboard the Swedish steamship *Oscar II* headed to Oslo from New York.

7. Francis with counsellor J. Butler Wright, being chauffeured in Petrograd by Phil Jordan in the US Embassy's Model T Ford.

8. Leighton Rogers, a young American clerk at the National City Bank of New York in Petrograd.

9. Julia Cantacuzène-Speransky, granddaughter of US President Ulysses S. Grant, American wife of a Russian prince, and subsequently a memoirist of the Russian Revolution.

10. The intrepid war photographer and cinematographer Donald C. Thompson.

11. James Negley Farson, American journalist and adventurer.

12. Arthur Ransome, correspondent for the *Daily News* at the time of the Revolution.

13. Journalist Florence Harper, pictured while working as a nurse at an American Field Hospital in Ukraine during 1917.

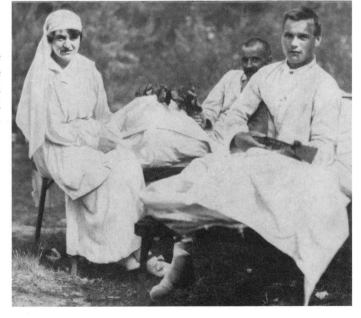

14. A bread line in Petrograd in 1917.

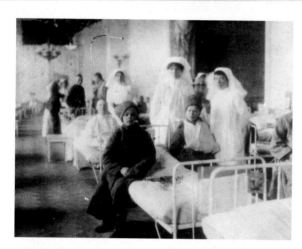

15. Nursing sisters and a wounded young soldier at the Anglo-Russian Hospital.

16 The International Women's Day parade in Petrograd, 23 February 1917, that sparked a wave of popular protest at bread shortages.

17. Donald C. Thompson's picture shows how the February Revolution claimed fatal casualties faster than the morgues could cope with.

18. Revolutionary barricades on Liteiny Prospekt, March 1917.

19. Cossack troops on patrol in Petrograd.

20. 'Shoot the Pharaos on their roofs…': propaganda postcard urging popular resistance to the police (known derisively as 'pharaohs' or *faraony*) who would snipe at revolutionaries from rooftops.

21. The toppling of imperial monuments, 27 February 1917.

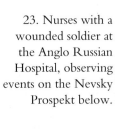

22. Shop-front Imperial emblems thrown onto the ice under a bridge across the Fontanka Canal.

23. Nurses with a wounded soldier at the Anglo Russian Hospital, observing events on the Nevsky Prospekt below.

'How I wished that Mrs Pankhurst and I could have seen more of the people of Russia,' Kenney later wrote, 'for we were getting to love them more and more.'[22]

Of all the women Emmeline Pankhurst and Jessie Kenney hoped to meet in Petrograd, at the head of their list was Maria Bochkareva – commander of the newly formed Women's Death Battalion and probably the most talked-about woman in all Russia. A semi-literate peasant girl from the Volga, Bochkareva had, within the space of barely a year, risen from obscurity to the status of national heroine. Her drunken father had deserted the family when she was young and she was sent out to work as a nursemaid at the age of eight, to help her mother make ends meet. Married at fifteen, she quickly abandoned her brutish husband and followed her lover to Yakutsk in eastern Siberia when he was condemned to exile for robbery. But on the outbreak of war in 1914, and fired with patriotic zeal, she had travelled the three thousand miles to Tomsk, where the commander of the 25th Reserve Battalion was based, and had volunteered for the Russian army. He told her she could only go as a nurse; but Maria Bochkareva wanted to fight. Undeterred, she appealed directly to Nicholas II by telegraph, upon which he agreed to her request, which was ratified by General Brusilov, Commander-in-Chief of the army.[23]

As a fighting soldier, Bochkareva certainly had the right attributes, for she was naturally muscular, stocky and strong. She had had no compunction about cutting off her long brunette plaits on enlisting, and cropped her hair close to her head like any male recruit. Donning her soldier's breeches and high black boots, and after training in marksmanship, she entered service at the front in the 28th Polotsk Infantry. She called herself 'Yashka' and her mannish persona fooled many: 'The strength and breadth, and the deep, full-toned voice of a man, were hers. Passing her on the street, you had to look three times to make sure she was not a man,' recalled Bessie Beatty when she met her in June. 'After the first few days of grumbling protest, her comrades seldom remembered she was a woman.'[24]

During her service at the front in 1915–16 Bochkareva demonstrated great fortitude and courage in battle and was wounded four times, the last time being laid up in hospital for months, and was awarded two grades of the Cross of St George. A devout patriot, she had been an ardent supporter of the revolution when it broke in February, but by the spring of 1917 she was dismayed at how ill-prepared her people had been for freedom. What most alarmed her, however, was the consequent breakdown in discipline and order in the Russian army. By May it had been severely weakened by the war, with more than 5.5 million casualties. Morale was at an all-time low and the rate of desertion alarmingly high. The conscripts at the front didn't want to fight the Germans any more; they just wanted to go home. But Bochkareva wanted to carry on fighting to the bitter end.

To counter this loss of morale, special combat formations – known as 'shock battalions' – had been formed, their objective being to underline the nation's savage determination to die, if necessary, in defence of Russia. It seemed to Bochkareva that the honour and even the very existence of her country were at stake, and she wanted Russia's women to set an example. 'They give men guns to fight death with,' she complained, 'but women simply sit and wait for death.'[25] She insisted that she – and they – would rather die fighting. With this in mind, when Duma president Mikhail Rodzianko visited the front in May, Bochkareva asked him to support her request to Kerensky, as Minister of War, that she be allowed to form a women's 'death battalion' – the first of its kind in the world. 'We will go wherever men refuse to go,' she declared. 'We will fight when they run. The women will lead the men back to the trenches.' Returning to Petrograd, Bochkareva held a mass rally in the plush surroundings of the Mariinsky Palace on 21 May, at which she exhorted:

Men and women-citizens! … Our mother is perishing. Our mother is Russia. I want to help save her. I want women whose hearts are pure crystal, whose souls are pure, whose impulses are lofty. With such women setting an example of self-sacrifice, you men will realize your duty in this grave hour.[26]

Fifteen hundred women answered Bochkareva's call to arms that evening, their numbers bolstered by another five hundred who volunteered after seeing accounts in the newspapers the next day. They were accommodated in four large dormitories at the Kolomensky Women's Institute on Torgovaya, which had been made available especially to Bochkareva as a base.[27] Many were quickly rejected, their numbers being reduced to five hundred mainly eighteen- to twenty-five-year-olds by Bochkareva's strict moral discipline (she abhorred 'loose behaviour', such as flirting with their male instructors); others were let go for failing to take her orders 'in true military spirit'.[28] Some of the more politicised women changed their minds when Bochkareva adamantly refused to allow them to set up Soviet-style soldiers' committees. She was in sole charge, and that was that.

After confiscating all their personal property except their brassieres, Bochkareva marched her chosen recruits off en masse to four barbers' shops to have their heads shaved; a crowd consisting mainly of soldiers waited outside, deriding the women as they emerged bald-headed. The volunteers were then thrown into a rigorous induction course, rising at 5.00 a.m. and spending ten hours a day on rifle practice and training, like any male recruits. Bochkareva oversaw it all closely, barking out orders like any sergeant major and slapping any insubordinate women on the cheek. Soon the battalion was pruned to 250–300, with many leaving voluntarily, unable to tolerate Bochkareva's harsh regime.[29] The only concession was the issue of the cavalry carbine, which was five pounds lighter than the standard-issue infantry rifle.

Those who survived the harsh selection process seemed, to one American reporter who observed them at drill, 'as likely soldiers as any others I had seen ... they took themselves and their work with the utmost seriousness and with the same lack of self-consciousness'.[30] Once they had passed through training, the women donned their standard army-issue uniforms, the only distinguishing marks being special white epaulettes with a red-and-black stripe, and a red-and-black cloth arrowhead sewn to the sleeve – this insignia, also worn by similar male battalions, denoting that they had vowed to fight to the death for Holy Russia and for the Allies.[31]

The Petrograd Women's Death Battalion contained an extraordinary cross-section of women. Some were former Red Cross nurses; the oldest among them was a forty-eight-year-old medical doctor. The rest were a mix of 'stenographers and dressmakers … office girls, servants and factory hands, university students and peasants, and a few who in the days before the war had been merely parasites', as Bessie Beatty noted.[32] As a seasoned reporter currently writing a regular 'Around the World in Wartime' column for her paper, Beatty had arrived in Petrograd not long after Rheta Childe Dorr and, like her, made a beeline for Bochkareva, for the Women's Death Battalion was a great news story and soon featured in the world's press. Both reporters quickly discovered that the women who joined had different, and often dramatic, reasons for doing so.

One such was Bochkareva's twenty-year-old ADC, Mariya Skrydlova. Tall and aristocratic, she was the daughter of an admiral who had distinguished himself in the Russo-Japanese War and was one of six Red Cross nurses who enlisted with the battalion. Convent-educated in Belgium, a talented musician and linguist, Skrydlova was later awarded the Cross of St George for her bravery, but subsequently suffered shell shock and walked with a limp. During the February Revolution, prior to joining the battalion, she had encountered the full force of grass-roots fury against the former aristocracy, when the mob had broken into the naval hospital where she had been nursing and murdered wounded officers in their beds. Other wounded men whom she had sat up nursing through the night, she told Florence Harper, had 'turned on her now that Russia [was] free and cursed her as she never heard a person cursed before in all her life'.[33] After seeing other nurses in the apartment block where she lived murdered, and young girls attacked and raped, she had 'taken off her

Red Cross uniform and vowed that she would not lift a hand while such people were in power'; instead, when she heard of the formation of Bochkareva's battalion, she had gone straight off 'without even putting her hat and coat on, running most of the way' to volunteer. Like her commander, all she wanted to do was to serve Russia.

Despite the obvious dedication of the Women's Death Battalion, not all Russians admired them; out on the streets when they marched along, the women were often greeted by hisses and boos from men. But they gave as good as they got: 'Go back, you dirty cowards. Aren't you ashamed to let women leave their homes and go to the front for holy Russia?' they retorted. Bessie Beatty admired the 'grim confidence' with which they faced the prospect of death under their 'Gospodin Nachalnik' Maria Bochkareva. 'What else is there for us to do?' they told her. 'The soul of the army is sick, and we must heal it.'[34]

During June, Emmeline Pankhurst and Jessie Kenney had regularly visited Bochkareva and her soldiers at their barracks and had had their photographs taken with her. Pankhurst had proudly inspected the women recruits and watched them drilling; she made a point of speaking individually, through her interpreter, to as many of the women as she could. She swelled with pride at the sight of the fearless Maria Bochkareva – 'that wonderful, splendid woman' – at their head. It was, she later said, 'the greatest thing in history since Joan of Arc'. She and Bochkareva, as the commander later related, became 'very much attached to each other' and Pankhurst invited her to dine at the Astoria.[35] In considerable physical decline, after years of repeated hunger strikes and forced-feeding in jail, which had wrecked her digestive system, Pankhurst had a figure that was in stark contrast to the robust frame of her new-found Russian friend, and she seemed prematurely aged. Nevertheless, she stood as erect as she could during inspections of the battalion, immaculate in her white linen suit with black bonnet and matching gloves, raising her right hand in a salute of womanly solidarity – an image captured by Donald Thompson, who took numerous photographs of the battalion that summer after he returned from a visit to the front.[36]*

At a speech that she was allowed to give at a fund-raising concert for the Women's Death Battalion held in Petrograd's Army and Navy Hall on 14 June, Emmeline Pankhurst made the most of the opportunity to praise them: 'I honour these women who are setting such an example to their country. When I looked at their tender bodies I thought how terrible it was they should have to fight, besides bringing children into the world.' 'Men of Russia,' she exhorted, 'must the women fight, and are there men who will stay at home and let them fight alone?'[37]

On 21 June, at a ceremony held in the great square in front of St Isaac's Cathedral and attended by Kerensky, Milyukov and Rodzianko, and other members of the government, Maria Bochkareva proudly received her gold-and-white standard emblazoned 'in black lettering with the words '1st Women's Death Battalion of Maria Bochkareva'. That same day she was promoted to ensign, and General Kornilov presented her with an officer's belt, a gold-handled revolver and a sabre as a token of the nation's appreciation.[38] Rheta Childe Dorr noticed, however, that her women's khaki uniforms were 'rather shabby' and 'about half the girls wore, instead of army boots, the women's shoes in which they had enlisted'. (She later discovered that such was the shortage of army-issue boots that the women got theirs only a day or so before going into action.) Kenney and Pankhurst had also attended and been moved by the sights and sounds of the occasion, in particular the chanting of the priests: 'How Ethel Smyth would love this music!' Pankhurst had exclaimed to Kenney, thinking with fondness of her friend, the suffragist composer.[39]

Two days later, prior to their departure for the front, an open-air *Te Deum* was said for the Women's Death Battalion before an altar erected on the steps of the Kazan Cathedral. Bochkareva and her battalion of women had kept everyone waiting, finally

---

* Many of these photographs were syndicated in the US press and can be seen in Thompson's photographic album *Blood-Stained Russia*.

arriving after 5.00 p.m. 'If they are due to attack, and wait an hour and a half to powder their noses, what will the Germans do to them?' soldiers in the crowd jeered derisively.[40] For the most part, though, the crowd was silent, 'women with tears in their eyes, men who shuffled uneasily in a shamed discomfort' greatly outnumbering the few soldiers, who were 'sullen, churlish, defiant!' Jessie Kenney was there (on behalf of an indisposed Pankhurst), as were Lady Georgina Buchanan and other distinguished residents and visitors, as well as foreign reporters. Florence Harper thought the women of the battalion looked faintly ludicrous in their ill-fitting khaki uniforms and oversized peaked caps, and heard someone describe them as looking like the 'chorus of a third-rate burlesque'.[41] Nevertheless they inspired admiration – and some pity – in most of those gathered there that day, as they proudly stood holding banners proclaiming, 'Death is better than shame' and 'Women, do not give your hands to traitors'.[42]

It was said that thousands of people rushed across the city to pay their respects as the Women's Death Battalion marched away to Petrograd's Warsaw Station after this farewell ceremony, each woman loaded with two hundred rounds of ammunition, the pots and pans on their kitbags making 'quite a racket' as they went, according to Donald Thompson.[43] Many had flowers thrust into their rifle butts by the crowd as they passed. 'Such a number of keen, serious young faces, it made one cry to see them go past … in full soldiers' kit, undaunted by the hardships and weight they had to carry or by all the ridicule they will have to face, ridicule from their countrymen which will probably be harder to face than the German bullets,' wrote a nurse from the Anglo-Russian Hospital. 'There they were going to do a man's job and show the way to the waverers. As we walked with the crowd that accompanied them along the Nevsky, an old general stepped out in front of them and called out, "God bless you! You will all get there, you are not like those others!"'[44]

But pockets of ill feeling towards the women still prevailed. When the battalion marched into Izmailovsky Prospekt the band accompanying them suddenly stopped playing, their way barred by a group of men from the nearby Izmailovsky barracks. Drawing the sabre recently presented to her, Bochkareva stepped forward, ordering the band to strike up again and – head high, with her sabre proudly raised – she led her women on to enthusiastic applause from the crowd, as the soldiers pulled back.[45]

At the station Lenin's Bolshevik supporters did everything they could to foment animosity towards the women as they fought their way through to the train, in which they were given the honour of second-class carriages rather than the uncomfortable third-class ones usually given to troops. Large groups of Russian soldiers stood and hissed and jeered: 'Those women ought not to be allowed to go to war,' reporter William G. Shepherd was told. 'It is a blankety-blank insult to Russia and its men … Everybody knows they are not going to fight. They are only going to the front to insult Russian soldiers and for bad purposes.'[46] Those 'bad purposes' were more clearly articulated by another soldier in the crowd: 'They only enlisted for the purpose of prostitution,' he shouted within earshot of Florence Harper, who had also made her way to the station. She saw how the man's remark provoked a quick response; enraged women in the crowd 'rushed at him, like terriers around a wild animal, scratching his face, hitting him and pulling his hair'. She was afraid the mob was going to beat him to death, and tried to block their path. Militia men fortunately soon arrived and hauled the man off to the police station, the mob trailing after them.[47]

From Petrograd, the Women's Death Battalion's train headed off to the front near Molodechno, where they were assigned to the Tenth Army. On 7 July they went over the top against the Germans, during a five-day battle at Smorgon (in present-day Belarus).[48] By the end of the day fifty of Bochkareva's women were dead or wounded. Shortly afterwards Bochkareva herself was knocked unconscious when a shell exploded near her and she was taken to a field hospital in the rear suffering from shell shock; she landed up in hospital back in Petrograd, promoted to second lieutenant and fiercely proud that not one of her women who went into battle had faltered. Emmeline Pankhurst was pleased and proud to telegraph home to England:

> First Women's Battalion number two hundred and fifty. Took place of retreating troops. In counter attack made one hundred prisoners including two officers. Only five weeks training. Their leader wounded. Have earned undying fame, moral effect great. More women soldiers training, also marines. Pankhurst.[49]

Before leaving for a visit to Moscow, Pankhurst and Kenney had continued to make the rounds of Petersburg society and the émigré community. Pankhurst had met up again with Lady Muriel Paget at the British Russian Luncheon Club – such fashionable watering holes still surviving the depredations of war and rationing. She also met the genial Prime Minister, Prince Lvov, and the now-notorious Felix Yusupov, whom she found altogether charming. Yusupov's 'exquisite courtesy and enunciation of the English language' were greatly to Pankhurst's taste, when he gave her and Kenney a conducted tour of his palace on the Moika, showing them the room where Rasputin was murdered and regaling them with the full grisly details of the story.[50]

Although Pankhurst was not allowed to meet the former Tsar and his wife Alexandra, now under house arrest at the Alexander Palace, she and Kenney did enjoy a private visit to Tsarskoe Selo, where Lenin's erstwhile political colleague and a founder of the RSDLP, Georgiy Plekhanov, was now residing after thirty years in exile in Switzerland. Plekhanov seemed 'pale and sickly', but his manners were faultless when he entertained them to Russian high tea: a bubbling samovar and 'delicious white bread, plenty of butter, and caviar and a few other dainties' – all most welcome to Pankhurst, who was suffering agonies with her stomach. 'What a joy to get some clean, nice, wholesome, digestible food,' she remarked. Plekhanov was extremely courteous; 'there was nothing of the demagogue about him,' thought Kenney, 'and although he had suffered far more greatly for his cause than Lenin, he had none of the latter's hateful bitterness.' He told Pankhurst of his admiration for Bochkareva; and of his concern that Russia be kept from falling into anarchy and remain true to the Allied cause. Kenney never forgot his sad, regretful parting words to them: 'There are two things that people only appreciate when they have lost them,' he told her, 'and these are their health and their country.'[51]

Health was certainly something that Emmeline Pankhurst, like the frail Plekhanov (who died of tuberculosis the following May), had now lost. She was unable to digest the coarse black bread on offer at the hotel, and her Russian admirers – mainly nurses and teachers – took it in turns to queue for precious white bread for her.[52] With the Astoria, like all Petrograd hotels, prey to endless strikes by waiters, chambermaids and cooks (such as that on 30 June), these female volunteers also came and cleaned and serviced her rooms and provided tea and other food. Through all the vagaries of 'life in revolutionary Petrograd, Pankhurst retained her inimitable regal manner, looking, as Florence Harper noted, 'every inch the dowager queen of the militants' at a meeting she held at the Astoria on 'how best to reach the Russian working women and teach them the meaning of politics'.

Harper was no suffragist, although she could not help but admire Mrs Pankhurst's indomitable resolve as well as her undoubtedly good intentions; but her mission, Harper felt sure, was doomed to failure. She had no understanding or experience of the lives and mentality of the Russian working classes, especially the women. 'Here we have suffered for years things that Englishwomen have never even dreamed of,' one of them told Harper. 'What right has Mrs Pankhurst to think she can teach us? We accept and appreciate her sympathy, but that is all. Let her go home and go on with her war work.'[53] Pankhurst's remaining time in Petrograd was, inevitably, largely spent preaching to the converted few rather than rabble-rousing to the masses, as she had hoped.

By the end of June, the summer heat had brought an overwhelming smell of uncleaned sewers to Petrograd, made worse by the malodorous stagnant waters of the canals. A plague of flies descended, bringing dysentery and cholera. Warnings were posted on all public buildings and at consulates and embassies advising people not to eat fresh fruit and vegetables unless thoroughly washed in sterilised water. It was more than Florence Harper could bear, to resist the lure of fresh strawberries; Emmeline Pankhurst and Jessie Kenney were horrified to see her eating them one day, but she stuck to her failsafe of copious doses of castor oil. 'Everyone was suffering from stomach trouble of one kind or another,' she recalled.[54]

Continuing food shortages were making it harder to find anything safe to eat, so she stuck to 'hardtack, caviar, and sardines' – expensive but necessary extravagances if she was to stay well. There was still food to be had in the provinces, and she managed to obtain honey and precious cheese smuggled in by an English friend. But at the Astoria most mornings Harper's requests for bread, milk and butter would all be met by a surly '*Nyet*'. Black coffee was usually the only thing on offer, drunk with a lump of sugar from her precious supply: 'I guarded it jealously, and hid it away carefully, in fact it was the only thing in my room that was always locked up.' A friend arrived one evening with flour, sugar – and bacon, the one thing all Americans craved. 'If he had brought a million rubles, he could not have been more welcome. The excitement of seeing real American bacon,' she recalled, 'was so great that then and there we arranged a luncheon-party simply for the purpose of eating it.'[55]

Dining out had also been greatly restricted by the food shortages; as what little food there was on offer in the restaurants got worse, so the prices rose. Even Donon's – once the haunt of the old imperial elite, and of many in the expatriate community – could offer little more than cabbage soup these days, or 'fish that was generally good, an infinitesimal piece of game or occasionally some meat, a salad of two leaves of lettuce (which no one ate because of fear of dysentery), and a water-ice'. Such a princely meal would set journalists like Harper back nine rubles – the equivalent of $27 at the current government rate. You could still order champagne there, but it would cost you 100 rubles ($300) a bottle.[56]

Everyone to whom Harper spoke was obsessed with food. For the beleaguered foreign residents, missing their favourite delicacies the longer they were stuck in Petrograd, the gift of some culinary treat was a major event. The only real chance of getting something decent to eat came when one of the embassies held a reception or party. During the visit of the Root Mission, Harper noticed how the 'men of the American colony ... would fish shamelessly for invitations to lunch or to dine with friends belonging to the Mission'. 'I do not see what you fellows are grumbling about,' one of its delegates remarked, 'I haven't had such good meals in years.' Florence Harper recalled that the only time she saw good food during her nine months in Russia was when she was invited to a reception at the US embassy on Furshtatskaya, 'when I had real white bread and real ice-cream' – both, no doubt, obtained thanks to the persistence and scheming of the wily Phil Jordan. David Francis certainly did his best to provide rare treats for US nationals, but even he was writing to a diplomatic colleague in July, 'if at any time you can find a man who will bring me fifty pounds of breakfast bacon I would appreciate it'.[57]

One or two small miracles did, however, persist amid all the longing for unobtainable foodstuffs. Each afternoon at the Astoria the pastry chef made French pastry – heaven knows where he got the flour from – and 'each room was allowed two cakes at forty kopeks each'; if Harper bribed the waiter she could usually get more. It was also an open secret among the American colony that if you went to the Café Empire around four in the afternoon, you might be lucky enough to purchase freshly baked white rolls and coffee – with milk. It wasn't a place where respectable women were seen, but Florence Harper went all the same, especially when, as often, she had had nothing to eat since the night before. On one occasion that summer she had gone for thirty hours without food.[58]

Many of the male American expats weren't just missing their favourite food; they also missed their home-grown sports, so much so that the young clerks at the National City Bank asked headquarters in New York to send them out a 'box of baseball equipment'. They staged an impromptu game in the side street between their bank and the Marble Palace, former home of Grand Duke Konstantin. The police soon saw them off, so they set up a pitch at the Field of Mars nearby. 'Our gyrations drew a large crowd of soldiers and civilians,' recalled Leighton Rogers. They 'pressed in so closely upon us that they were in danger of being hit, but they didn't know it until one youngster caught a foul ball right between the eyes'. Rogers was surprised to hear an American-sounding voice call out from the crowd 'Say, where youse guys from?' – it turned out to belong to a Russian who had lived in Boston for five years, where he had become 'an ardent rooter for the Red Sox'.[59]

Officials at the US embassy, however, had little time for recreation. So busy were J. Butler Wright and Ambassador Francis that the only occasion they were able to discuss embassy matters was on the journey out to Murino and back to play the occasional game of golf.[60] The embassy was overburdened with far more work than its staff could handle, as Wright recorded:

Commissioners, visitors, commerce publicity, railroads, extradition, land values, military preparation, naval statistics, finance, passports, prisoners' relief, moving picture propaganda, capacity of printing presses, house furnishing and repairing, lost passports, censorship, mail inspection, wharf and port capacity and dues, relief ships, food supply, strikes, coal mining operations, couriers for mails, ocean cables, etc, etc, etc, make up the daily work of our embassy in these days.[61]

This was not to mention hosting a succession of luncheons, teas and dinners for visiting US officials, who continued to pour into Petrograd after the Stevens Railroad Commission and the Root Mission had distracted them from the realities of a city once more on the edge of a resumption of violence. 'Even the most fanatical optimist could not help acknowledging that the Provisional Government was tottering,' wrote Florence Harper in June. The Bolsheviks, although still in the minority and out-gunned by the Socialist Revolutionaries and Mensheviks, had recently been flexing their muscles at the 1st All Russian Congress of Soviets. During the congress Lenin had launched into a tirade against the war as nothing but 'a continuation of bourgeois politics' with its roots in imperialism.[62] But his attempt to stymie Kerensky's appeal for a mandate to launch a new Russian offensive had failed. In a last-ditch attempt to rally patriotic nationalism, Kerensky had set off on a tour of the south-western front in May, during which he exploited his gift for stump-oratory in numerous hortatory appeals to the troops. On 16 June he ordered a massive Russian artillery barrage of enemy lines and, two days later, a major assault in Galicia. With the so-called 'Kerensky Offensive', the Provisional Government had shot its last bolt.

Meanwhile in the capital there was a resurgence of massive street demonstrations against the war, fomented by Lenin and the Bolsheviks. At the end of June the members of the Root Mission were advised to relocate to Finland for their own safety. 'The Allied colony of Petrograd was disappointed and disgusted,' wrote Florence Harper. 'They knew that if the Mission only waited a little while longer, they would see an exhibition of rioting that would convince its members how weak the Provisional Government actually was.'[63]

11

'What Would the Colony Say
if We Ran Away?'

During the February Revolution, Kronstadt, a grim island fortress and naval base at the mouth of the River Neva nineteen miles from Petrograd, had been the scene of some of the most savage violence when 30,000 sailors had run riot; the admiral and sixty-eight officers – the cream of the Imperial Navy – had been massacred in a brutal orgy of killing, seen as retaliation for the harsh discipline the men had endured under the tsarist system. Since then the area had become a hotbed of revolutionary militancy, stockpiled with weapons seized during the revolution and ripe for Bolshevik exploitation. In defiance of the authority of the Provisional Government, revolutionaries at Kronstadt had seized the ships in dock and the arsenal, and had voted in their own autonomous Bolshevik-dominated Soviet, which had operated as a virtual fiefdom until it finally came under the Petrograd Soviet's control at the end of May.[1] Kronstadt remained a dangerous, volatile place from which the Bolsheviks were planning to draw key support in the coming days; it was also a place that Florence Harper and Donald Thompson wanted to investigate.

At the end of June when they went out to this supposedly forbidding 'fortress', all they saw as they arrived 'was an island of green and white', with the beautiful dome of its cathedral rising above the other buildings. They had been warned that they wouldn't be allowed to land, but 'Thompson just grinned' and marched onshore with his cameras. When stopped and asked why they had come, he explained that he wanted to 'see the men who were making history in Kronstadt'.[2] Together with Harper, he walked along the cobbled streets to the headquarters of the Soviet, where they met 'Tovarishch Parchevsky', the local Bolshevik police commissar. Flattered that Thompson wanted to 'make cinema pictures' of Kronstadt, he placed two cars at their disposal and took them, accompanied by several surly-looking Bolshevik minders, on a guided tour. 'They all looked like cutthroats,' thought Harper. 'They were dirty, unshaven, and most of them were without collars.' A collar, it appeared, was the mark of a bourgeois, 'and in Kronstadt to be a bourgeois was to sign one's death warrant'.[3]*

During the day they spent there, Thompson and Harper's revolutionary minders ensured that they positioned themselves front of camera at every photo-opportunity. 'Each house was pointed out with pride as the scene of another murder,' Harper recalled, as the men told her sickening stories about the 'glorious fight for freedom of the Kronstadt people'.[4] She felt extremely uncomfortable in the company of the *tovarishchi*: 'It isn't pleasant to be an imperialist in a hot-bed of socialism.'

Thompson, however, remained undaunted by the experience, and a couple of days later went out to the Kschessinska Mansion to try and see Lenin. He waited for two hours and, when Lenin finally appeared, asked him to 'pose for a picture'. When Boris the interpreter explained that Thompson was from America, Lenin told him 'he would have nothing to do with me and that we had better leave Petrograd'.[5] There was good reason to heed this warning; Boris had heard talk that the following day – 3 July – there was going to be 'trouble with Lenine and his bunch of cut-throats'. Rumours of a second revolution or coup had been rife ever since the Bolshevik leader's return from exile. 'There is an undercurrent here, plainly evident, but not possible for a

---

* Arthur Ransome wrote similarly of the baiting of the bourgeoisie: 'everyone who wears a collar will be counted an enemy of mankind'.

stranger to trace and impossible to describe, indicating that we may expect an upheaval before very long,' wrote naval attaché's wife Pauline Crosley. 'I know of meetings, drilling, propaganda and accumulation of arms that can only mean one thing. When that thing will happen, no one not in the "meetings" can tell.' But she expected that sooner or later Russians would start killing each other again.[6]

Sure enough, a renewal of violence came in early July when Lenin decided the time was ripe to exploit fatal weaknesses in the Provisional Government. Taking advantage of the recent collapse of the Russian offensive in Galicia, closely followed by catastrophic losses at the front, Lenin and the Bolsheviks set about further undermining public support for the Russian war effort. The offensive was launched on 18 June, with a mass demonstration supposedly calling for public unity: although peaceful, it was deliberately orchestrated into an anti-government protest. With further Bolshevik connivance, other marches and demonstrations that followed rapidly escalated into violence, which the government seemed powerless to control. By the beginning of July its position had been further undermined by the sudden resignation of four Kadet (Constitutional Democrat) ministers on the night of 2/3 July, in protest at the government's capitulation to demands from Menshevik and Socialist Revolutionary ministers for autonomy in Ukraine. This was a concession that the patriotic Kadets would not brook, fearing that it would encourage the separatist instincts of other nationalities and lead to the dismembering of Russia.

Bolsheviks and anarchists seized this undermining of the government's authority by whipping up protests among their supporters in the Petrograd garrison, the navy at Kronstadt and militant workers in the factory districts. Word had also got out among the 10,000 men of the 1st Machine Gun Regiment based on the Vyborg Side that they were to be sent to the front, a move designed to rid the capital of the worst Bolshevik-led troublemakers in the garrison, upon whom Lenin was relying as the muscle of any future coup against the government. After two days of feverish meetings inflamed by speeches from Trotsky and others, the men voted to stage an armed demonstration on the streets of Petrograd, and were joined by others from the garrison, including the Pavlovsky Regiment.[7] But the Bolshevik Central Committee under-estimated how difficult it would be, once stirred, to bring this violent rabble under control. Like dry tinder, the protest quickly broke into crackling flame.

On 2 July, Rheta Childe Dorr had returned to Petrograd after two weeks away at the Eastern Front, to be told that the 'bolsheviki were making trouble again'. The following morn-ing she went out to buy newspapers and was strolling down the Nevsky when she suddenly heard rifle fire and then a machine gun – followed soon afterwards by a cavalcade of motor trucks full of armed men hurtling down the street. Donald Thompson had been out near the junction of the Nevsky and the Fontanka River when he had been caught in crossfire and had thrown himself flat on the ground. He had lain there for some time, along with many other civilians, and had finally made a run for it, fast as 'a Kansas jack-rabbit'.[8] Intermittent firing and an increasing presence of armed men in motor lorries on the streets had followed throughout the day but it wasn't till the evening of the 3rd that the real signs of trouble began.

Meriel Buchanan had been dressing for dinner when she saw several motor lorries and cars full of armed soldiers waving red flags drive past the embassy. After dinner even more vehicles were thundering across the bridge into the city, followed by a huge crowd of Bolshevik-led demonstrators from the factory districts. Sir George and Lady Georgina had planned to take the evening air across the river in their open carriage, but hesitated: 'Some-thing is going to happen,' Sir George warned.[9] Nevertheless, true to their regular English habits, they left, only to be turned back by a jam of vehicles on the Troitsky Bridge. Back on the Embank-ment, they encountered dense crowds of workers on Suvorov

Square opposite the embassy carrying a barrage of banners celebrating anarchy and condemning the war, the bourgeoisie and the upper classes, as more and more vehicles and people continued to cross from the Petrograd Side.

By now the trams had stopped running and all over the city armed soldiers were forcing private motor cars to stop, upon which they 'turned the occupants out and swarmed into their places like so many insects', dragging machine guns inside with them.[10] Diplomats and foreign residents were not immune: Belgian ambassador Conrad de Buisseret's Rolls-Royce was stopped in the street and confiscated by the Bolsheviks, as too was Donald Thompson's hired car (his chauffeur was later killed).[11] Nellie Thornton, wife of one of the mill-owning Thornton brothers, had a far more terrifying experience. She had set off into Petrograd for a trip to the cinema with three little girls, when the Rolls-Royce they were being driven in was cornered by 'six lorries armed with Maxim Guns'. Four men jumped into the car with them and forced their driver to take them to a secluded yard, where they were surrounded by armed men. Nellie thought they were going to be raped or shot; she begged the men not to take the car and make her and the terrified children walk the twelve miles home. Eventually the soldiers allowed them to leave. Why had they done this, Nellie asked them? 'To show you we have the power,' they told her.[12]

That evening the streets of central Petrograd were swarming; many gathered outside the Tauride Palace, where British intelligence officer Denis Garstin, went out among them 'wandering from group to group asking what they really wanted'; but he could get no clear answer from anyone, bar a lot of shouting of slogans. 'No one knew. On the contrary they all wanted to know why they'd been called out with their arms and banners and vague complaints.' Garstin noted anarchist agitators – 'black hatted black-visaged men' – among them, trying to incite people to violence and then disappearing.[13] With 10,000 or more gathered on the Nevsky, firing inevitably broke out, followed by rioting and then looting, in the frenzied search for alcohol that was now gripping the city.[14]* Confusion reigned; the streets were 'all effervescence', crowded with people who had come out to see what was happening, only to find themselves caught up in indiscriminate firing from all sides. 'Everybody was asking everybody else what was going on,' recalled Bertie Stopford. 'A feeling of panic was in the air,' wrote US journalist Ernest Poole of the *New Republic*, who had just arrived, only to be caught up in the thick of what was going on.[15]

At their apartment on Kirochnaya, near the Tauride Palace, US naval attaché Walter Crosley and his wife Pauline had been sitting in their drawing room when the doorbell rang and a messenger arrived, telling them to 'put your most valuable small things in a bag and be ready to leave for the Embassy in five minutes'. When Pauline asked why he told her to look out of the window: 'There they were!!! *Hundreds* of the worst looking armed men I ever expect to see, coming up our street! The rumors were being confirmed and trouble was upon us.' She rushed to pack, as the tramping feet of a mob of 'Anarchists or Leninites' (she wasn't sure what they were) came ever closer – the corner on which their home was located had, she recalled, been 'a very bloody spot' during the February Revolution. As they hurried to leave by the front door, the street outside had become '*filled* with the dangerous looking creatures and we had to face them as we went out'. When the Crosleys reached the US embassy, members of staff were arriving with reports of fighting in many locations; embassy officials estimated that around 70,000 armed workmen and soldiers were 'in charge of the city that night', bolstered by intimidating armed joyriders on trucks and in hijacked private cars.[16]

Lady Muriel Paget of the Anglo-Russian Hospital had been dining at Prince Yusupov's palace on the Moika that evening, when 'suddenly we heard shooting and screaming, and riderless

---

* One French resident heard that tobacconists' shops were a popular target, as too were pharmacies and perfumeries – for their cologne and alcohol, on which the looters got drunk.

horses dashing by'. Some of the bullets had begun hitting the palace, and her host took his guests into the cellar dining room for safety. Someone from the ARH telephoned to warn Lady Muriel not to try to return there, but she insisted. Bertie Stopford, who had been dining with them, volunteered to accompany her, on condition that she 'would remember the rules of Revolution – first, to lie on one's face when shooting was going on, and second, to press against a wall when the mob surged in the streets'.[17] As they ventured cautiously down the side streets, they saw crowds on the Nevsky 'going down into the fire of the soldiers, stepping over the bodies of their dead comrades'. Lady Muriel turned a corner and found herself 'looking into the mouth of a revolver with a fierce Russian behind it. I pushed the revolver away and laughed at the soldier, who let me pass.'

But soon afterwards they got caught up in the mob and were carried along with it for several blocks. They finally got to the hospital at 1.15 a.m., to find that a lot of the wounded from the fighting on the Nevsky had been brought in.[18] On his way back up the Nevsky to his hotel, Stopford saw many more being carried away on stretchers. It was here that Arno Dosch-Fleurot had also found himself trapped in 'the hottest firing that I ever expect to be exposed to' and had flung himself into the gutter to take shelter. He found himself lying alongside a Russian officer. 'I asked what was happening,' he wrote in a despatch to the New York *World* three days later, to which the man replied: 'The Russians, my countrymen, are idiots. This is a white night of madness.'[19]

Such indeed was the madness unleashed that day that by late evening the streets of Petrograd had become 'a complete and unintelligible chaos', in the words of New Zealand journalist Harold Williams. It was hot and muggy even this late, and the crowds wandered 'aimlessly and excitedly' as lorries and motor cars 'buzzed about filled with yelling soldiers'.[20] Crowds of people were still hanging around at the junction of the Liteiny and the Nevsky late into the night. Officials tried to disperse them: 'Go home. Comrades go home. There have already been victims.' But still the crowd lingered. 'It was a strange sight,' wrote Williams, 'this great, silent moving mass in the dusk with the blur of guns, caps and bayonets of the men on lorries and the bent figures of soldiers on artillery horses, all silhouetted against the pale sky.'[21]

Ernest Poole also stayed out till late: 'still the crowds, and still the speeches, still the low incessant roar and the trampling of countless feet'. But there was something different: 'I felt no great mass power here,' he recalled. It wasn't the same atmosphere of excitement and cheering, with people singing and shaking hands, as in the February Revolution, a Russian told him. 'Look at these crowds. They came out only to see what would happen. Now they are through and are going home.'[22] As the Nevsky emptied, all that was left were the ambulances taking away the last of the dead and wounded, and a few soldiers loitering and drinking greedily from the water hydrants, 'while others sat in long lines on the curbs, talking in low voices, most of them smoking cigarettes'.[23]

Tuesday 4 July dawned grey and heavy. As the morning went on, it became suffocatingly hot and oppressive, with people gathering once more for another 'day of waiting'. The air of expectancy on the streets was 'like the first days of the revolution', recalled Louis de Robien.[24] Bessie Beatty also sensed the dramatic change in atmosphere, on her return that morning from a trip to the front, when she emerged from the Nicholas Station 'to find the mercury rising and the Nevsky of the hour strangely different from that with which I had parted'. 'Turning into the Nevsky that morning was like opening a telegram,' she remembered:

> I could never be quite certain what I would find there, but the first glance always told the whole story. Nevsky was the revolutionary thermometer. When the City of Peter pursued the calm and normal way, the wood-paved avenue indicated the fact. When the hectic passions of revolt ran high, the temper of the populace was as plainly registered.[25]

The atmosphere was ominous. There wasn't a tram in sight and hardly any *izvozchiki* and the shutters on the shops were fastened tight; 'in front of the Gostinny Dvor [indoor market] men were out with hammers, nailing boards across the plate glass windows', in which Beatty noticed fresh bullet-holes. There was no mistaking the signs: 'The Bolsheviki were taking possession of the city.'[26] Indeed, the ranks of the Bolshevik-led protesters were dramatically swelled that morning when several thousand 'evil-looking' sailors arrived from Kronstadt on a collection of barges, tugboats and steamers. The presence of the belligerent Kronstadters, armed to the teeth with every weapon they could lay hands on and with their cap ribbons bearing the names of their ships 'turned inside out, so that they [could not] be identified', ensured that that day's street demonstrations became progressively more violent, with machine guns mounted on motor lorries firing indiscriminately into the crowds and people – who 'shrank away' in fear, at the sight of the sailors – rushing aimlessly in all directions.[27]* But the same lack of cohesion and leadership prevailed as the previous day: nobody seemed to know whose side anyone was on, 'least of all the demonstrators themselves', as Harold Williams noted.[28] The violence was confused and elemental, with those among the disorganised mobs who were armed running around firing, often out of sheer fright, and then beating a retreat at the slightest retaliation.

By the afternoon the Liteiny had become 'very agitated', just as it had been 'in the bad days' of February, wrote Louis de Robien, the atmosphere made even worse by the influx of sailors from Kronstadt. 'The road was littered with caps and sticks, lying among the debris of plaster knocked from the walls by the bullets,' he recalled. Everywhere he walked that afternoon he saw groups of 'surly unbuttoned men with their rifles slung across their backs, in their hands, or under their arms as though they were out shooting'. There was no organisation to this rabble; 'they dragged their feet' and were 'all mixed up with the women' and did not want to be regimented or to fight in any disciplined way.

---

* There are no precise figures on how many sailors from Kronstadt headed into Petrograd that day. Some say a couple of thousand, while other sources estimate up to 20,000.

Harold Williams watched an 'endless procession' crossing the Troitsky Bridge. 'I did not notice much enthusiasm,' he recalled. 'Most of the soldiers looked rather tired and bored and none could give any intelligible reason for their demonstration.'[29] As this crowd marched past the British embassy, 'rough looking men came up to the windows with rifles and ordered us to shut the windows,' recalled Lady Georgina Buchanan; they were forced to 'sit in closed rooms, dying of heat' all day, her husband having declined the Provisional Government's offer of a safe refuge.[30] Her daughter Meriel saw 'three thousand of the dreaded Kronstadt sailors' pass by on their way to the Field of Mars and heading for the Nevsky. 'Looking at them, one wondered what the fate of Petrograd would be if these ruffians with their unshaven faces, their slouching walk, their utter brutality were to have the town at their mercy.'[31]

At around two in the afternoon heavy fighting broke out on the Nevsky, when the sailors 'took possession of some machine guns and swept the thoroughfare from end to end, killing and wounding over a hundred civilians and innocent people'. By now the Nevsky was 'black with people, massed across from wall to wall', the low incessant roar of thousands of tramping feet mingling with rifle and machine-gun fire.[32] Bessie Beatty was there, watching in horror and wondering whether this was to be the culmination of the whispered prophecy she had heard over and over again since her arrival: 'The streets of Petrograd will run rivers of blood.'[33] By late afternoon the situation had become extremely dangerous. Up at the American embassy on Furshtatskaya, 'as dangerous a mob as I ever hope to see – composed of half-drunken sailors, mutinous soldiers and armed civilians – paraded through our street, threatening people at the windows, and drinking openly from bottles,' wrote J. Butler Wright in his diary.[34]

Leighton Rogers and his colleague, Princeton graduate Fred Sikes, had been working late at the National City Bank when they had heard thundering horses' hooves outside and had 'got to the balcony just in time to see a troop of some two hundred Cossacks and three light field guns gallop past, officers in the lead shouting and brandishing sabres'.[35] It was a thrilling sight, but they knew that if the government had called in the Cossacks* the trouble was serious. They decided to head for home 'while the going was good'. Dark thunderclouds were gathering overhead and a rainstorm was coming. They were worried about the precious five pounds of sugar they had just managed to obtain through their Russian cook at the bank; it was in a paper bag and would be ruined if it got wet. For safety's sake they decided to head home across the open space of the Field of Mars, 'where we could see what was coming', but they had barely gone fifty yards when they heard the crack of rifles and a 'few bullets went zing-g-g over our heads, then a flock of them ripped the air and spurted dust around us'.

There they were, clutching their precious bag of sugar, and the only possible shelter they could see was 'behind the temporary fence around the huge grave of heroes of the Revolution'. Another volley sent them in a mad dash in that direction, 'with Fred holding the bag of sugar out ahead as though we were trying to catch up with it'. 'Crash! went one of the field guns beyond the Summer Garden, and we landed flat in the dust behind the fence, Fred guarding the sugar like a bag of diamonds.' Eventually they emerged from their place of refuge near the grave as a huge clap of thunder broke overhead and the rain came down. They got home safely with their sugar, noticing how quickly the rain had chased the people from the streets. 'I am wondering if a high pressure hose or two wouldn't be more effective in these street brawls than streams of lead,' pondered Rogers later in his diary.[36]

Over at the British embassy everyone had been at dinner when the doorman had rushed in to tell them that the Cossacks were charging across nearby Suvorov Square on the Palace Embankment. They had all rushed to the big windows in Sir George's study overlooking it, to see a crowd of Kronstadt sailors pouring across the square and along the quay on either side and, 'behind them,

---

* These were eight squadrons of Don Cossacks – the only totally loyal troops on whom the government could still depend.

sweeping in a cloud of dust across the Champ de Mars, came the Cossacks, some of them standing up in their stirrups to fire at the fleeing figures, others brandishing swords, or bending low in the saddles with long lances held at a wicked slant'.[37] As they disappeared from view a sharp volley of firing broke out, followed by the loud report of a field gun, and 'a moment later three or four riderless horses dashed past'. Apparently the troop of Cossacks that Rogers and Sikes had seen riding along the embankment had been ambushed by demonstrators near the Liteiny Bridge and had 'surged into Liteiny Street at the gallop', where it was met by Bolsheviks on a makeshift barricade manned by machine guns, which had cut them to pieces. Bessie Beatty was there and watched in horror as the Cossacks 'wheeled their horses about and fled but not before half a dozen of them had gone down before the guns'.[38] Terrified, riderless horses careered off at a gallop down the side streets.

Phil Jordan had hurried over from nearby Furshtatskaya and had seen it all, too, and soon afterwards wrote excitedly to Mrs Francis in St Louis:

The Cossacks and Soldiers had a terrible fight just one block from the embassy. The Cossacks as you know always fight on horseback. They made a charge on the soldiers who was in the middle of the street with machine guns and cannons. My oh my what a slaughter. After 30 minutes of fighting [I] counted in a half a block 28 dead horses. When the Cossacks made their charge the soldiers began to pump the machine guns and you could see men and horses falling on all sides.[39]

Half an hour later, when US ambassador David Francis visited the scene in the pouring rain, 'the street was literally and actually running with blood' and 'bodies were scattered for four blocks'. Louis de Robien also ventured out from his embassy later that evening to be greeted by 'a heartrending sight': 'dead horses, their skins taut and shining from the shower that had just fallen, lay in the wet roadway between the pools of water, some of which were tinged with red'. De Robien counted twelve of them in the road between Shpalernaya and Sergievskaya, but there were other dead horses further down towards Nevsky. People had already gathered round them and were stealing their bridles and saddles.[40] Around thirty horses were killed that day and ten Cossacks. But, as one gloomy Cossack told Leighton Rogers, 'We can get more men ... but such horses – no.' Another reporter saw a big, burly cab driver weeping over the dead horses. 'The loss of 12 good horses was too much for an izvoschik's heart to bear.'[41] As for the numbers killed and wounded during those days in July, official figures published by the Central Executive Committee of the Soviets talked of four hundred, but the central first-aid services in Petrograd estimated in excess of seven hundred, and on 6 July *Novoe vremya* claimed that more than one thousand were killed during the riots of 2 and 3 July alone.[42]★

That evening 'we went to bed wondering what would happen next,' wrote Lady Georgina Buchanan to her family in England. 'All night there was shooting so sleep was nearly impossible.'[43] She was grateful to be safely tucked up in her bed, but over at the American embassy, when the guns and cannons had begun roaring again around midnight, the irrepressible Phil Jordan had 'jumped out of bed and rushed to the Winter Palace Bridge' [the Palace Bridge] to see what was going on:

The Bolscheviks had Started to come on this Side of the town and the Soldiers was waiting for them at the foot of the bridge. Just as they was about on the middle of the bridge the soldiers opened fire with machine Guns and cannons. it was one grand Sight. the Sky was full of the prettiest fire works you Ever saw. you know during a Revolution or any kind of fighting every body has to lay flat on

---

★ Much like February 1917, the casualty figures cited were entirely arbitrary. Nobody had any idea of the numbers killed on those days and they ranged between four and five hundred, but are likely to have been much higher.

your Stomach. I was laying flat behind the man that was pumping the machine Gun.[44]

Later, when Francis was dictating his own version of events in a letter to Jane, musing on when he might return home, he observed that Phil rather hoped they would not leave too soon, as he had told him, 'we are having so many revolutions here now that it is too interesting for us to think of leaving'.[45]

Violent torrential rain all night kept most people off the streets and it persisted all through Wednesday 5 July. Shops were closed, no trams were running and only a few *izvozchiki* were in evidence. Bertie Stopford heard that all the bridges were to be raised to cut off the revolutionary strongholds in the Vyborg and Petrograd Sides. The Bolsheviks were to be 'polished off' tonight, he was reliably informed, for the government was determined to bring things under control, with the help of troops ordered back from the front by Kerensky, who was also returning to Petrograd.[46] Everyone was now expecting him to single-handedly bring the city back from the brink of catastrophe. Meanwhile the Bolsheviks were in control of the Peter and Paul Fortress and were directing operations, in so far as there was any coherent plan, from their stronghold at the Kschessinska Mansion.

The square in front of the Winter Palace had now been turned into a military camp, with armoured cars, artillery and Red Cross ambulances drawn up in front of the War Department nearby; there were guards posted on every street corner, stopping cars and questioning their drivers. On Suvorov Square, Meriel Buchanan heard troops coming and going all day and machine guns being dragged into position. The Buchanans were still being prevailed upon to leave the capital for their own safety, 'but naturally we could not and would not do so', wrote Lady Georgina, as it would set a bad example; after all, 'what would the colony say if we ran away?'[47] But at 6.00 a.m. on the 6th they were woken and asked to move down to the coach house, just as they were, in their slippers and dressing gowns, and be ready to leave at a moment's notice. Government troops had been ordered to seize both the fortress and the Kschessinska Mansion directly across the river. The British embassy was in the direct line of fire and it was feared that the Bolsheviks would turn the big guns of the fortress straight at them. Sir George, however, was not to be hurried: 'I wish,' "the old Man" sighed wearily, 'these people would put it off till a little latah'; and with that he 'turned on to his other side and relapsed into sleep'.[48]

When Sir George did finally emerge from his bedroom, he refused to budge from the embassy: 'Thanks very much, but my wife and daughter want to see it,' he insisted. When an alarmed Bertie Stopford rushed to the embassy on hearing of the coming assault on the fortress, he found the ambassador 'on the balcony surrounded by his secretaries – instead of sitting in the cellar, as they had been told to do – eagerly watching the troops advancing on their stomachs across the Troitzka Bridge'. Sir George later recorded that he had spent 'an exciting morning' watching, till around 1.00 p.m. From her vantage point in the corner drawing room, Lady Georgina had found it all rather thrilling: 'One really almost felt one was in the front trenches.'[49]

Leighton Rogers had seen the first reinforcements arrive, 'a regiment of soldiers on portable bicycles' from the front at Dvinsk, who were to take part in the assault on the Peter and Paul. He noted this was a different breed from the ill-disciplined and slovenly troops in the city:

That they were seasoned fighters was obvious from their rugged bronzed faces, the worn look of their equipment, which was complete and ready down to camp-kitchens cooking mess and carts with hay for the horses pulling them. Slowly and keeping the front wheels of their cycles in perfect alignment they rolled along the Quay and turned onto the [Liteiny] bridge. And in a methodical, business-like manner they made ready for an assault. It was a strange scene: these men so calmly preparing for a killing, the brooding Fortress with its red rag of a flag barely stirring in the warm summer air, the ranks of guns pointed across the unruffled Neva.[50]

As things turned out, little was required beyond a show of government strength; by around 11.30 a.m. the Kschessinska Mansion had capitulated without a fight and about thirty of Lenin's men were arrested (Lenin himself had been spirited away to a safe house); shortly after 1.00 p.m. the fortress, too, had surrendered. Donald Thompson was with the government forces when they entered the Kschessinska Mansion. They found it stashed with hardware: 'seventy brand new machine-guns and a great quantity of provisions and arms, as well as numerous commandeered cars in the yard'. Later that day he was shown 'a lot of what they said were important documents', which 'showed that Lenine was unquestionably connected with the Germans'.[51] It was now that the Provisional Government pulled its only trump card. The documents found at Lenin's headquarters showed that the Bolsheviks had been receiving funding from the German General Staff. Such evidence was political dynamite at a time of rampant public hatred of the German enemy. A statement was quickly published in the evening paper, *Zhivoe slovo* [The Living Word], and some of the details were also passed on to the mutinous regiments in the Petrograd garrison. This news turned the tide against the Bolsheviks and brought waverers over to the side of the government.

Throughout the 'July Days', as they became known, Donald Thompson had been out with his camera and tripod, sometimes on foot, but often racing up and down the streets in a hired car with the 'camera sticking up in the tonneau', looking 'not unlike a new kind of gun', as Florence Harper recalled. 'In fact it looked so dangerous that it gave us a clear passage up the Nevsky.' With reckless abandon, Thompson had set up his camera at every opportunity 'and proceeded to crank'.* But late that afternoon he had witnessed a final, sickening demonstration of mob savagery reminiscent of the February days, which he did not record on film. Out at the Tauride Palace he had seen three revolutionists dressed as sailors fire from a motor car on a group of officers on the steps of the building, after which they had driven away at speed, only to be stopped soon afterwards by a motor truck that blocked the road. The men had been dragged from the car and promptly lynched by the crowd that had gathered. It was a new kind of savagery that he hadn't seen before: 'they stretched them up to the cross arm of a telegraph pole, and didn't tie their hands. Then they drew them off the ground about three feet. All three of them as they were hanging tried to hold on to each other, but the mob knocked their hands away and they slowly strangled to death.' Hardly the most comforting story with which to conclude a letter to his wife Dot, back home in Kansas.[52]

With the disturbances now subsiding, Arthur Ransome, in a telegraph to his newspaper that night, summarised the chaos and futility of recent events in curt and dramatic form:

> Nothing could be sadder than events of these last few days stop soldiers brought out into streets by agitators on all kinds pretexts march along without slightest understanding what all trouble about stop ... whole town including soldiers in state of excited nerves stop single shot anywhere starts fusillade in which suffer innocent persons who fall victims to panic of others stop ... No visible object sought by demonstrators and none attained stop for twenty four hours town practically at their mercy and absolutely nothing done ... big number people killed wounded and all for no purpose stop this becoming obvious to many demonstrators

---

* One fellow newspaper correspondent apparently even claimed excitedly to Ambassador Francis that Thompson was 'taking pictures of the fight on the Nevsky with a gun in each hand and loaded down with ammunition'.

stop ... none of enthusiasm of revolution stop instead puzzled simple folk moving this way and that stirred up by contradictory agitation.[53]

'Petrograd is quiet now,' wrote Harold Williams in his own despatch to the *New York Times*, 'but there is a heavy and bitter feeling of humiliation and degradation in the air over this insane and preposterous adventure. Why was it allowed? Why was it not checked at the very outset?' He was appalled at the unscrupulous and cowardly behaviour of 'the Leninite plague' that had stirred up violence in 'these ignorant masses' with their 'criminal propaganda'.[54]

Kerensky was furious that the government had not been able to take control of the situation during his absence at the front. He was determined that its replacement, formed on 7 July, under his premiership and supplanting a demoralised Prince Lvov, would be allowed 'dictatorial powers in order to bring the army back to discipline', and he demanded new controls that did not kowtow to 'any interference on the part of soldiers' committees'.[55] Retaining his role as Minister of War, Kerensky appointed as commander-in-chief of the army General Kornilov, whose immediate response was to call for the restoration of courts martial and capital punishment for desertion at the front. The mutinous troops of the Petrograd garrison were to be disbanded and punished by being sent to the front; the Kronstadt sailors were disarmed and sent back to their base, although the government sadly lacked the will or the muscle to punish them.

Petrograders awoke on the 7th to discover that 'for a time, at least, the power of the Bolsheviki had been broken'.[56] A warrant had now been issued for the arrest of Lenin, Trotsky and the Bolshevik ringleaders. Trotsky was quickly held, but Lenin eluded the round-up. After spending a few days hidden away in a safe house in Petrograd, he travelled north to Razliv, where he hid out in a hay barn before shaving off his beard and donning a wig and workmen's clothes and escaping to the safety of Helsinki. 'This Lenine, who escaped ... and his confederate,

Trotzky, who was a hash slinger* in New York a few months ago, have done more to ruin Russia than any two men I know of in history,' Donald Thompson told his wife. 'I think that Kerensky's only solution is to catch these two and give them the limit. I know that if I had the chance I would take a good deal of pride in shooting both of them.' Ambassador Francis, rarely so emphatically critical, had no doubts either about the government's failure to seize the upper hand and arrest Lenin and Trotsky and the other Bolshevik leaders, try them for treason and execute them. Had they done so in July, he later wrote, 'Russia probably would not have been compelled to go through another revolution.'[57]

Ten days after the fighting, a day of mourning was set aside for the lavish funeral rites of seven of the twenty Cossacks killed in the street fighting.[58] In stark contrast to the secular funeral for the victims of the February Revolution, the ceremonial on 15 July was an intensely Orthodox one – designed, so one British observer was told, as a 'rebuke' to the socialist groups that had organised the Field of Mars burials without any religious ceremony. Apparently some of the relatives of victims buried there had subsequently paid for private services to be conducted over the graves. Kerensky, ever one for high drama and the exploitation of public sentiment, had wished to turn these obsequies into a moment of communal theatrics, thought Ernest Poole, proclaiming that the Cossack heroes should be 'buried in the graveyard where the Russian grand dukes lay'.[59]

At five on the afternoon of the 14th, the dead were brought in coffins covered with silver cloth surrounded by a Cossack guard of honour carrying black pennants on their lances, to lie in state in St Isaac's Cathedral. Heaped with flowers and surrounded by flaming candles, the coffins lay there overnight on catafalques raised high in a position of great honour before the 'holy gate' of the iconostasis and surrounded by the cathedral's

---

* A waiter in a cheap diner.

'towering columns of lapis lazuli and malachite'. An endless stream of mourners poured into the cathedral all night: 'Cossacks, soldiers, sailors, Red Cross nurses, priests and Tartars, Georgians and Circassians, in costumes and uniforms of a hundred kinds and hues.'[60] The cathedral was so dark inside 'you could see only human shadows pressing close around you,' recalled Ernest Poole, 'but on the stone-paved floor you heard the slow shuffle of thousands of feet.'

The following day, after a long and elaborate funeral service featuring the full Russian Orthodox panoply of gleaming icons and crosses, incense and two hundred choirboys – a 'triumphant symphony of grief', as Rheta Childe Dorr remembered it – the funeral procession left the cathedral.[61] Outside, the vast crowd that had gathered in the square and the surrounding streets awaited it, many weeping and carrying black mourning flags. For once there were no red revolutionary flags in sight. Great waves of music surged back and forth across the streets from numerous bands, as the coffins, 'borne on ornate canopied hearses drawn by black horses', passed rows of Cossacks, the horses 'standing at perfect attention', and were taken for burial at the Alexander Nevsky monastery at the far end of the Nevsky Prospekt.[62]

'Well, at least these were not buried like dogs, as ours were,' remarked a woman in the crowd, reflecting bitterly on the lack of religious ceremony for the victims of the February Revolution.[63] Louis de Robien was moved to see the parents of some of the dead Cossacks – simple peasants from as far away as the Urals or the Caucasus – who had come all this way to follow their sons' coffins. In Cossack tradition, the dead men's riderless horses followed the cortège, with stirrups crossed over the empty saddles. One of the horses had been seriously injured, noted De Robien, 'and was limping pitifully behind its master's coffin'. On another horse 'the dead man's son, a little Cossack of about ten years old, had been put up into the saddle'.[64]

Never one to miss such a spectacle, Phil Jordan was as always close by, awestruck by the immensity of the occasion: 'the press

Said Over one million people … think of such a large crowd and all frightened half to death. every time the man would strike his base drum the crowd would Shiver,' he told Jane Francis.[65] Rheta Childe Dorr saw the occasion as 'an hour of hope' – a demonstration by Kerensky's government designed to chasten the Soviet and serve as a warning to the extremists. 'The casual observer in Petrograd would have said that revolutionary disturbances were a thing of the past,' wrote Bessie Beatty after the Cossack funeral, 'that order had come to stay. But the casual observer would have failed to understand the breadth and depth of the movements stirring beneath the surface.' For thirty-year-old Beatty – a convinced socialist, who had covered miners' strikes in Nevada – the July Days had been 'only the beginning of the class struggle in Revolution'.[66]

The day of the Cossack funeral, in his first public appearance as Prime Minister, Alexander Kerensky, dressed in a plain khaki uniform and puttees, had swept up in a limousine as the last coffin was carried out of St Isaac's, to be greeted by 'a mighty cheer' as people rushed forward shouting his name. He had made a short speech on the steps of the cathedral and then 'waved the crowd to silence and bade them stand quietly back', before walking on hatless and with bowed head behind the procession. 'He would not have been human if he had not felt a thrill of triumph at this reception,' remarked Rheta Childe Dorr. Ernest Poole noted Kerensky's charismatic power: 'On that day the government seemed embodied in this one man', and in the first weeks after the July Days every foreign visitor to Petrograd had wanted to meet the new Prime Minister.[67]

But he was a difficult man to see, 'as he allow[ed] himself to be got at by everybody', noted Jessie Kenney, having been told that Kerensky's ministers were trying to 'guard him against dissipation of his energies'. On 21 July she and Emmeline Pankhurst were finally invited to the Winter Palace to meet him. 'People say that he wants to be another Napoleon,' Kenney had noted in her diary a few days before, and when they arrived that morning Kerensky seemed to be living up to the role, adopting the appropriate pose on cue and seated at a table formerly used by the Tsar, 'with the thumb of one hand in his coat'. 'I wondered at the time if this were the Napoleonic gesture.'[68] He then ushered Pankhurst to a seat by the fireplace where they chatted in French, with an interpreter occasionally adding things in Russian at Kerensky's behest. Kenney noted the animation with which he spoke, but:

> I did not have the impression of a man dedicated to one end, in the way that Lenin was … or Plekhanov, or Mrs Pankhurst. He had been a fine lawyer, was an enthusiast, an orator of eloquence, but did not have the restraint over himself that the others possessed. There was vacillation here, a man open to his passion and his moods … Quite obviously he was no match for Lenin, who, relentless and dominating, would ride mercilessly over everything and everyone in his path.

All in all, Kenney found Kerensky rather overbearing and noted an antipathy towards Pankhurst; perhaps, she wondered, he was jealous that so many people had asked to meet her. Before they left he made a point of indicating the ornate silver inkstand and quill pen placed on his desk: 'The Czar used to sign his documents with this pen,' he told them portentously.[69]

Kenney concluded that here was a man trapped between too many conflicting forces and the task was simply too much for him. He certainly did not lack the magnetism required for the role of Prime Minister, thought Rheta Childe Dorr, but even Kerensky could not 'take that huge, disorganized, uneducated, restless, yearning Russian mob by the scruff of the neck and compel it to listen to reason'.[70] Dorr's compatriot, Princess Cantacuzène-Speransky, had a similar view. Kerensky 'seemed to lose his grip on things' after the July Days – whether from ill health or the strain of his overwhelming responsibilities. She noticed that the 'man of the people' image of the early days of the revolution – a man whom people trusted for his honesty and patriotism – had receded; and now that he was living at the Winter Palace in rooms formerly occupied by Alexander III, 'sleeping in the emperor's bed, using his desk and his motors, giving audiences with much form and ceremony', he seemed to have lost that common touch and become ever more grandiloquent. Like Kenney, she saw a 'man struggling to maintain his personal popularity by being forced into uneasy compromises'.[71]

Kerensky 'dashes busily around, from rear to front and from one front to another, making impassioned speeches, but disintegration goes on', wrote Pauline Crosley on 13 July. She too remained unconvinced of his ability to pull things together: 'My Russian friends assure me matters will become "normal" (normally unsettled) for a time – that the anarchists will not make another serious attempt until they have completed their organization, that they now know how easy it is to take the city and the next time they capture it they will keep it.'[72]

In this continuing state of unease, Petrograd at the end of July 1917 remained a city in flux resembling an armed camp. It was also a city (half the size of New York) which the collapse of the old regime in February had left without any effective, organised police protection, bar a hastily created Militia.[73]* Although the unrest had been quelled for now, it did not feel any more secure than previously, and the rumours of further trouble continued to be 'large and varied'. 'A curious state of mind came over the Russian public,' recalled Willem Oudendijk of that late summer. 'Nothing good was expected any more, no hope filled anybody's heart, a dull sense of acquiescence in whatever further misfortune

---

* In parallel with the duality of the Petrograd Soviet and the Provisional Government both vying for political control, the Militia that replaced the old Tsarist police force was composed of two rival bodies: the city militia controlled by the Petrograd City Duma, established to serve everyone along democratic principles; and the autonomous workers' militia, formed to serve only the interests of the working classes and the objectives of the revolution.

the day might bring pervaded everywhere.' Government, such as it was, wrote Rheta Childe Dorr, continued to exist 'only at the will of the mob'.[74]

But the Bolshevik leadership, too, was in disarray, having proved unable to respond to the fast-moving demonstrations in July. Lenin had prevaricated on whether or not to steer the unrest towards a second revolution and in the end had opted for 'wait and see' tactics, as too had the Central Committee of the Petrograd Soviet. The truth was that the revolutionary vanguard in Petrograd had been as uncertain of the direction the demonstrations would take – proletarian revolution or *coup d'état*? – as anyone else. And with the Bolsheviks suffering the body blow of the damaging revelations about their links to German money, they had been forced into retreat. But for how long?

The crisis in the war had also escalated that month, with continuing Russian military disasters, including the surrender of two Army Corps and a major defeat at Tarnopol; extensive territories in Galicia and Bukovina had also been lost. By 22 July one million Russian troops were in retreat; many thousands had been captured and even more had deserted. There was now real fear of a German advance on the capital. Arthur Ransome was desperate to leave. He had had yet another bout of dysentery (his fourth that year) and was weak and hungry and longing for home. He could not expect his family – even living under wartime rationing in England – to have any comprehension of how difficult things currently were in Russia:

You do not see the bones sticking through the skin of the horses in the street. You do not have your porter's wife beg for a share in your bread allowance because she cannot get enough to feed her children. You do not go to a tearoom to have tea without cakes, without bread, without butter, without milk, without sugar, because there are none of these things. You do not pay seven shillings and ninepence a pound for very second-rate meat. You do not pay forty-eight shillings a pound for tobacco.*

'If ever I do get home,' he concluded, 'my sole interest will be gluttony.'[75]

Donald Thompson was equally despondent. He, too, had been losing a lot of weight. 'My stomach has the right to have a personal grudge against me,' he told his wife, 'for it is so seldom that I give it even a taste of proper food.' So hungry and exhausted was he that he now promised her this would be his last foreign assignment. 'Today [8 July] I feel as you always want me to feel – sick and tired of being a war photographer.'[76] On the 15th he started making plans to travel home; but he would not leave without first getting a permit, personally signed by Kerensky, to take his precious film footage and photographic images out of the country. On 1 August he finally caught the Trans-Siberian express to Vladivostok. From there he picked up a steamer to Japan and on across the Pacific to California.

Thompson had no regrets to be leaving at last. Five months previously he had seen the people of Petrograd march with a clearness of intent – for the idealistic revolutionary concepts of Liberty, Equality and Fraternity; but now he could find no more words of hope. 'I see Russia going to hell, as a country never went before.'[77]

---

* Around £20 ($29) and £120 ($172) respectively in today's money.

12

'This Pest-Hole of a Capital'

In the early hours of Tuesday 1 August, Nicholas Alexandrovich – formerly Tsar of All the Russias, but now just plain Colonel Romanov – was sent away from Tsarskoe Selo with his family, by rail to Western Siberia. They would be left to languish at the Governor's House in Tobolsk for the next nine months while the government debated what best to do with them.* Their former home, the Alexander Palace, was left empty; and the Tsar's private railway line that had linked Tsarskoe Selo to the capital was torn up, its rails and sleepers sent for reuse elsewhere. Few foreign observers in Petrograd had had much to say about the demise of the Romanov dynasty after more than three hundred years; the Tsar's removal – the details of which were not revealed, or his destination, either – left most of them indifferent, as people in the capital continued to struggle with desperate food shortages, unstable government and civil unrest. Tsarist Russia already seemed a long way in the past.

A few chosen members of the forty-strong US Red Cross Mission that had arrived in town on 25 July were, however, allowed sight of the interior of the deserted palace not long after the imperial family was taken away, prior to the palace's opening to the curious as a museum. They noticed many touching reminders of the Tsar's family: books open on tables, sheet music still propped up on the piano: 'Evidently it had been left in a great

---

* At the end of April 1918 they were transferred 365 miles south-west to a house in Ekaterinburg, where, on the night of 16–17 July, the entire family was brutally murdered by the Bolsheviks.

hurry, things lying around, toys of the children on the floor, an unfinished letter on the Empress's desk,' commented George Chandler Whipple.[1] 'Here and there on a table or mantelpiece lay a number of Kodak snapshots taken evidently by the children,' recalled his colleague, Orrin Sage Wightman. Perhaps most poignant of all was the sight of one of the Tsarevich Alexey's abandoned French exercise books, in which he had written his name at the top of the page 'and in his childish writing was inscribed in French, "The French lesson is very hard today."' This brief, private glimpse of a now-vanished era had been quite 'overwhelming', wrote Wightman. 'To get into the life of a deposed Czar, not long after the nation had fixed it up as a museum, but when the marks of his living presence were still fresh, was indeed a privilege the memory of which will never leave me.'[2]

The members of the Red Cross Mission had travelled to Petrograd from Vladivostok on the Trans-Siberian Railway, in the imperial train in which Nicholas II had signed the abdication. Accommodated in its nine sumptuous carriages, they had enjoyed the comforts of 'nickle-silver toilets, beautiful Russian leather seats, silk covered cushions' and had slept in 'beds of damask linen with pillow cases of silk and all marked with the double eagle and crest'.[3] Bessie Beatty was at the Nicholas Station to witness their arrival, which was greeted by Ambassador Francis and his staff. While she admired the group's demonstrable 'wealth of human sympathy', the expertise of its team of doctors and sanitary engineers, and the seventy tons of much-needed surgical supplies it had brought with it, she wondered 'what sort of a dent' it could possibly make in Russia at this late stage.[4*]

---

* The Mission also brought its own official film cameraman, Lieutenant Norton C. Travis, an experienced freelancer for Pathé, Fox and Universal. Like Donald Thompson, he was out filming in the thick of it: 'I could have ground all day at scenes of the populace looting stores, factories and residences. Freedom simply meant helping themselves to everything they wanted,' he later wrote. Like Thompson, Travis also filmed the Women's Death Battalion at the front, and spent most of his time in Russia filming near Minsk.

No sooner had the mission emerged from the station than Orrin Sage Wightman noticed how 'shot up' Petrograd's crowded, dusty streets looked. There was no sign of any police; no regulation of traffic, and you took your life in your hands trying to cross the street.[5] All the buildings were 'dingy and shabby and plastered over with bills and posters relating to the revolution'. They covered 'the stores, the churches, the palaces, the bases of statues, the telegraph poles, the fences. Wherever a poster would stick, there it was pasted. This gave the city a very unkempt appearance.' All sign of imperial splendour had been defaced or stripped away and there were red flags everywhere, including one 'placed in the hands of the bronze statue of Catherine the Great in the park on the Nevsky'. The only respite came when for three days small gala booths decorated with flowers, branches of yew and evergreens and bunting sprung up across the city, selling bonds for the government's recently launched Liberty Loan.[6]*

Some of the members of the mission were accommodated at the Hotel de France on Morskaya. 'A wretched place, but the best now available,' recalled civil engineer and pioneer of public health reform, George Chandler Whipple. The rooms were 'none too clean'; breakfast was chewy black bread and weak tea, reinforcing the realisation that 'we were in a war held city'. Indeed, such were the drastic food shortages that the hotel manager had warned them 'that sometimes he could give us a good meal and sometimes he could not'.[7] Whipple and some of his colleagues soon transferred from the dirty and vile-smelling 'Buggery', as they had nicknamed the infested Hotel de France, to the distinctly cleaner and more cheerful Hotel d'Europe, where they were thrilled to get coffee with boiled milk at breakfast. It did not take many days of Petrograd rations for the group to fall upon the hospitality offered at a reception in their honour at the American embassy, during which J. Butler Wright noted how the Red Cross Mission 'consumed tea, sugar, and white bread in an alarming manner'.[8]

---

* The bonds sold were for small amounts of twenty rubles ($4). Around four billion rubles ($1 billion) were raised.

Over at the Astoria – or the 'War Hotel' as she called it, and appropriately so, as its exterior was still battle-scarred – Bessie Beatty was pleased to note a distinct improvement in conditions, thanks to recent repairs and renovations. 'After living for a whole summer each unto himself alone, breakfasting, lunching, teaing, and dining in our own rooms, we suddenly came out of hiding and looked one another over':

> The bloodstains of the Revolution had been scoured from the rose-colored carpet in the drawing-room. The boards had come down from the broken windows, and new glass and gorgeous crushed mulberry curtains had taken their place. The dining-room, a few weeks ago the repository of armless chairs and legless tables, dumb victims of the vengeance of an angry mob, now fronted the world arrayed in white napery.[9]

The casual observer might have imagined that residents at the Astoria were living in the lap of luxury, 'but there was none'. The food was as dire as ever: at lunch the first course was 'chopped meat and *kasha* stuffed into cabbage leaves, and the second the same chopped meat and *kasha* inadequately hidden by the half of a cucumber'.[10]

Once the Red Cross Mission had unloaded and stored its precious medicines and food supplies under government protection, it had begun to evaluate their supply and distribution across Russia, and the setting up of mobile disinfection stations to counter the alarming spread of typhus. George Chandler Whipple had felt that it would have an uphill struggle: 'there will be no use to talk cleanliness to people who are threatened with starvation,' he noted in his diary.[11] The bread queues were alarming and he was struck by how the crude methods used for cutting and weighing the bread rations slowed things down, making the wait even more interminable for those who had already been queuing for hours. It was clear to him that the food crisis had been 'made doubly severe by the influx of soldiers, refugees and others', for war had brought an increase of the city's population from two to three million. 'The authorities fully expect a famine in Petrograd this winter, with the starvation of several hundred thousand perhaps, unless some drastic steps are taken.' Whipple noticed how huge stockpiles of wood were appearing everywhere, brought in to the quaysides by great flat-sided barges. Petrograd was a wood-burning city where little or no coal was available, and the price of wood was rocketing. There was nothing to buy in the shops and no shoes to be had anywhere – clothing, too, would become scarce in the coming winter, he noted. People might still be broiling in the heat of August, but come September when the rain set in, things would change dramatically.[12]

Fellow Americans whom Whipple met, and who had been working on welfare projects in the city, seemed beaten down by the losing battle. Franklin Gaylord, who had lived in Petrograd for eighteen years and had devoted himself to working with the Mayak (Lighthouse) – the Russian affiliate of the YMCA – had come to the grim conclusion that Petrograd was 'the worst, the rottenest, the stinkingest city in Europe, the streets are bad, labor is hopeless, there is no sanitation, we can't drink the water, we can't get food, the rooms are full of bedbugs, we don't see the sun all winter, it is cold and gloomy and the air isn't fit to breathe'.[13] It was a discouraging start, but the Red Cross Mission duly went about its fact-finding duties, visiting food shops, the Red Cross and other welfare storehouses, travelling to hospitals and nursing communities in and around the city, inspecting waterworks and sewage plants. Typhus, TB and scurvy were the mission's major medical concerns, and its members found working with the Russians a challenge. Dr Orrin Sage Wightman thought them 'like a lot of children, who, after a long period of oppression have suddenly acquired a liberty which has been turned to license'. He was shocked by the 'laziness and indifference' he saw everywhere: the 'supreme idea of the people' of Petrograd appeared to be to do nothing. 'The spirit of indolence, which they interpret as freedom, has so abased them that nothing short of intense suffering can bring them to their senses.'[14]

'All here is chaos!' wrote Raymond Robins, the most high-profile member of the mission and a distinguished economist and progressive politician back home.* As an evangelical Christian, he had travelled to Petrograd with a crusading attitude to the challenges facing them. But he had to admit that life in the capital was 'a day to day affair ... Uncertainty is everywhere ... the outlook is stormy in the extreme'.[15] This sense of uncertainty was further underlined in his mind when he met Kerensky on 1 August and found him utterly worn out, 'so busy with the mere task of keeping things together from day to day that we can see him for only formal moments. He seems so high strung and overworked as to make one wonder whether he can hold the line for the next six months' – that is, until a government could be formed by an elected Constituent Assembly.

Like his colleagues Robins saw the future of Russia hanging on the economic situation and the perilous food shortages. He was deeply concerned about the long lines for bread, meat, milk and sugar: 'As go these lines, so goes the Provisional Government. If they shorten, the Government lives; if they lengthen, it will die.'[16] But the Provisional Government seemed to him to be 'men who are dreamers with responsibility and no capacity to bring their dream into being now that they have the power'. Far too much, in his opinion, depended on one man – Kerensky – 'the only possibility of control this side of reaction or a military dictator'. But for now, at least, Robins was still clinging to a stubborn romantic idealism about Russia's future; 'the Russian will hold fast to a spiritual content and will bring back worship and reverence to the life of man,' he wrote hopefully to his wife Margaret on 6 August. 'He will found the great social democracy and give

---

* Robins's sister Elizabeth was well known in Britain as an actress notable for playing Ibsen, a writer and an ardent suffragette. She was also closely acquainted with Emmeline Pankhurst and Jessie Kenney.

to the race the best chance for the equality of opportunity, freedom and brotherhood.'[17]

On 21 August another blow to Russia's war effort came with news
that the strategically important Baltic port of Riga, 350 miles to
the south-west, had fallen to the Germans – or, rather, its Russian
defenders had simply abandoned it to them without a fight. Despite
this, a state of denial about the Russian army's disintegration persisted in the capital. Willem Oudendijk had gone to the opera that
evening with his wife to hear Chaliapin sing in Rimsky Korsakov's
Rusalka: the audience had been wildly enthusiastic, rushing forward
from their seats and 'recalling Chaliapin before the footlights over
and over again at the end of every Act. There seemed no thought
of revolution, or the Germans, or war that evening. Petrograd was
now in the war zone; but what did it matter? Here was Chaliapin
singing! Cheer! And applaud! Bravo, Chaliapin!'[18]

The fall of Riga had come soon after a last-ditch attempt had
been made at a conference held in Moscow to bridge the gap
between the warring bourgeois and socialist political groups and
unite them behind Kerensky's government. He himself had
appeared there in military tunic, flanked by two adjutants
and adopting his distinctive Napoleonic pose – which had now
earned him the sobriquet 'Napoleonchik' – and had made one
of his familiar emotional bids for support. But even Kerensky's
'brilliant but fiery improvisation', as Louis de Robien observed,
no longer sufficed. Russians might traditionally 'get even more
drunk than the French themselves on eloquence and empty
phrases', but mere words were no longer 'enough to feed the
people or put a stop to anarchy'.[19] Onstage Kerensky had been
challenged by the commander-in-chief he had appointed in
July – General Lavr Kornilov – who had given an uncompromising speech in which he laid out the draconian measures he
deemed necessary to bring Russia back from the brink of defeat
by the Germans; it had brought the conference to its feet.[20]

During her weeks in Petrograd, Bessie Beatty had observed
how Kerensky had struggled to 'follow a middle course' that

would satisfy both the reactionary right and the Bolshevik left, and how he had resisted calls to resort to force, as Kornilov would have wished. She felt that he had been right to do so and that 'the masses would regard any attempt to install a dictator as an attack on their Revolution and would desert the man responsible for it'. Emmeline Pankhurst had laughed at her when she had ventured this opinion at dinner. Russia must have a strong hand, she asserted, and Kerensky was a weakling. The only man who could 'save the situation' was Kornilov, who would 'rule with an iron hand'.[21] The appointment of the right-wing Kornilov after the disruption of the July Days, despite opposition from Mensheviks and Socialist Revolutionaries within the government, had been seen as a toughening up by Kerensky, an attempt to shore up the floundering fortunes of his government in the face of mounting Bolshevik opposition. Kornilov, from a humble Cossack background, was a self-taught career soldier, a patriot and, in the eyes of his men, 'a natural chieftain'.[22] But he was no conciliator; and no politician, either. He was, in the opinion of General Knox, who had observed him at close hand at the front, a 'hard-headed soldier of strong will and great courage' who had won respect by deeds and not words.[23] Violently opposed to the Soviets and their soldiers' committees, Kornilov was now demanding absolute control over the army, at the front and in the rear.

Sir George Buchanan could see that Kerensky had lost ground since the July Days and that Kornilov, 'were he to assert his influence over the army and were the latter to become a strong fighting force ... would be master of the situation'. But for now the two men needed each other: 'Kerensky cannot hope to retrieve the military situation without Korniloff, who is the only man capable of controlling the army; while Korniloff cannot dispense with Kerensky, who, in spite of his waning popularity, is the man best fitted to appeal to the masses and to secure their acceptance of the drastic measures which must be taken in the rear if the army is to face a fourth winter campaign.'[24]

The Moscow conference, which had ended in stalemate, had shown that there was clearly an irreconcilable level of antagonism between the two men. Frustrated by Kerensky's reluctance to accord him the dictatorial powers he needed to wrest back control over the army, Kornilov sent Kerensky an ultimatum on 27 August: that he should resign as Prime Minister and cede him full military control. To back up his claim, he began moving troops on Petrograd from the north-western front under General Alexander Krymov, intent on arresting anarchist and Bolshevik troublemakers, bringing the Petrograd garrison to heel and forestalling the Bolshevik coup against the Provisional Government that he knew would come sooner or later. 'It is time to hang the Germans' supporters and spies led by Lenin,' Kornilov had said. 'And we must destroy the Soviets so that they can never assemble again.'[25] This was the only way the army could be saved from dissolution, and the country from chaos.

Kornilov's challenge had 'thrown Petrograd into an uproar'. Everyone dreaded the city once more becoming a battleground.[26] The loss of Riga had already created panic, with people besieging the railway stations for any train out to the safety of the country-side. 'In the War Hotel, storm center of the storm center,' wrote Bessie Beatty, 'we sat and awaited the inevitable.' Arno Dosch-Fleurot advised her to get out before the trouble started: 'The hotel may still be here in the morning, but it may not, and there is no use in taking chances,' he told her. Military men to whom Beatty talked at the Astoria agreed that both Kornilov and Kerensky were determined characters, 'so it will be a fight to the finish'. Most of them were eagerly awaiting the arrival of Kornilov: 'For them it was all settled. Kerensky would be overthrown – Korniloff would capture the city. The death-penalty would be restored; the leaders of the Soviet would be hanged. Russia's troubles would be over.'[27]

Sunday 27 August dawned warm, cloudless and sunny; the Nevsky 'was crowded with the usual shifting masses of pedestrians, peopled impelled this way, drawn that, hurrying, loafing, hating, loving, living in spite of war and revolution,' recalled Leighton Rogers.[28] Sir George Buchanan had headed out to the golf course at Murino and it wasn't until his return in the evening that he was informed, when summoned to the Russian Foreign Office with the new French ambassador Joseph Noulens, that Kornilov was marching on Petrograd and Kerensky had declared him a traitor. Frantic preparations were now being made across the city to resist this advance. But to achieve this, Kerensky had been forced into the necessary compromise of appealing to the Bolsheviks of the Petrograd Soviet for support. Lenin was in hiding in Finland; from jail Trotsky advocated supporting Kerensky for now, in order to defuse the Kornilov threat. At their stronghold at the Smolny Institute, where they had been transferred from the Tauride Palace in July, the Petrograd Soviet marshalled the leaders of the garrison and the new workers' voluntary militia – the Red Guards, formed after the February Revolution – to organise workers, sailors from Kronstadt and ordinary civilians in the defence of the city.

Thousands of workers were given back weapons that had been confiscated from them after the July Days and, in what seemed an act of madness, supplied with additional guns and ammunition. All over the streets of Petrograd groups of militia began drilling. Bessie Beatty witnessed workers from the munitions factories, assisted by engineers and sappers, digging trenches and building barricades, in a dash to 'throw a trench around the city'. Phil Jordan described seeing 'thousands and thousands of Soldiers' at the Nicholas Station just arrived from the front, who were marched straight to the Nevsky to dig trenches. 'Just think of diging trenches in the heart of the city,' he crowed, as he anticipated yet more violence on the streets.[29]

The following day, word was out that General Krymov's 'Savage Division' was only two days away. Meriel Buchanan recalled people being as fearful of this – Kornilov's advance guard of four thousand largely Muslim Caucasian cavalry, legendary for its ferocity – as they were of the Kronstadt sailors.[30] Members of the diplomatic corps were advised to leave for Moscow or Finland, but once again Sir George Buchanan refused to leave the British colony without diplomatic protection, and his wife and daughter would not countenance evacuation, either. Instead, Lady Georgina's British Colony Hospital, which had recently closed down, was made ready to offer refuge to women and children from the community, should the need arise. Although US ambassador David Francis felt in no way threatened or worried about his personal safety, he acknowledged that many of his fellow nationals were, and in response he instructed J. Butler Wright to charter a small steamboat, 'upon which Americans who so desire can take refuge in the event disturbances should occur'. Meanwhile, as Wright noted in his diary, the diplomatic corps had found itself 'in the unacceptable situation of having to go through the motions of agreeing with and supporting the government while it secretly wish[ed] fervently that Kornilov might win'.[31]

Petrograd was now under martial law: 'The air is full of rumours,' wrote Raymond Robins, 'it is a wild time.'[32] At around five that morning Florence Harper had been woken by the sound of firing in the square outside the Astoria and heard a surge of people coming into the lobby below. Peeping out of her room, she saw sailors banging on the doors of several rooms and marching Russian officers away under guard. Bessie Beatty was disturbed by the noise, too, and when she ventured out of her room found a 'sea of cutlasses' in the hall outside. It was 'filled with Russian sailors, perhaps a couple hundred of them, husky chaps with rifles in their hands, and every rifle topped with the most bloodthirsty-looking blade I had ever seen'. 'Life holds no further terrors for the man or woman who has faced two hundred such weapons all gathered in one spot,' she observed. In comparison, 'an Atlantic Ocean submarine would seem like a friendly neighbor come to call'.[33]

At first she thought the men were Kronstadters; they had taken possession of the hotel and were now examining passports and searching rooms. It turned out they were from the Soviet and 'had decided to take things into their own hands and arrest all officers whom they suspected of counter-revolutionary tendencies' and who might side with Kornilov. In the process they had terrorised the female residents of the hotel, who were huddled in groups on the landings. Some of the men forced their way into Harper's room, searched it and walked away with her camera. At lunch she found everyone buzzing with a mix of excitement and fear. Forty Russian officers had been arrested and taken away from the hotel; seven more were arrested later. All were hauled off to the Peter and Paul Fortress on a charge of 'plotting against the revolution'.[34]

And then, as suddenly as the Kornilov threat had manifested itself, it evaporated. On Wednesday the 30th the papers published a note from Kerensky's government saying that the 'revolt' – if that indeed had been what it was – had failed. Kornilov's march on Petrograd was beaten before it even got started; beaten not by any military action to repel it, but by the pro-Bolshevik railway workers, who had refused to move his troop trains and had also sabotaged the rail network needed to get the trains to Petrograd, by jamming signal points, damaging bridges and tearing up or blocking the lines.* Troop trains full of Krymov's men had been left at a standstill. And when his advance guard did encounter opposition troops, they had refused to act against Kerensky and the Petrograd Soviet; indeed, they had openly fraternised with these troops and were persuaded by them to stand down.[35]

Kerensky now put out an order for Kornilov's arrest. His position throughout this debacle had been highly ambivalent. British embassy counsellor Francis Lindley felt that Kerensky – 'torn between his fear of aiding a counter-revolutionary movement and his honest desire to assert the authority of the Government' – had made the wrong decision. 'Like all socialists in a similar position he preferred his party loyalty to the good of his country. It was the end of him.'[36] Whether or not Kerensky had genuinely believed that Kornilov was intending a coup against him, rather than the suppression of the Bolshevik-led Soviet, remains unclear. Willem Oudendijk certainly felt that Kerensky's 'nervous fear of being replaced by Kornilov made him act with reckless and fateful impulsiveness'.[37]

US resident Pauline Crosley reported widespread rumours in diplomatic circles that it had been 'fully understood' that Kornilov had intended to establish a Military Government – 'with Kerensky's knowledge and approval' – to protect Russia from a Bolshevik

---

* Kornilov admitted this was what had stymied his march on Petrograd, to US diplomat DeWitt Clinton Poole when he met him in southern Russia in 1918.

coup; that a dramatic and triumphant entry into Petrograd had been planned for Kornilov's troops, but that 'during the night … some one or some thought suggested to Kerensky that he would lose power and prestige as Korniloff's increased'. Her conclusion was that Kerensky's ambition 'could not stand that pressure' and that he had 'foiled an honest attempt to save Russia', as a result of which Russia was 'worse off than ever before'.[38]

Either way, the Kornilov affair prompted an inevitable upsurge in support for the Bolsheviks, who quickly recovered the ground they had lost after the debacle of the July Days. On 1 September Kornilov was arrested and taken to jail. On 4 September, Trotsky and many of the Bolshevik leaders were released from prison on Kerensky's orders. Kerensky had now proclaimed Russia a republic, but nobody in the Soviet or the former government wanted to work with him in yet another doomed coalition. As a last desperate measure, and one guaranteed to further alienate public opinion, Kerensky assumed command of the army and imposed his own temporary French revolutionary-style Directorate of five, with himself as virtual dictator.

Florence Harper bumped into Arno Dosch-Fleurot in the lobby of the Astoria after news came of Kornilov's arrest. 'We both used language not exactly polite,' she recalled. 'I was filled with blind rage. We all knew it was the last chance. The Bolsheviki were armed; the Red Guard was formed. The split was definite; Kerensky was doomed.'[39] Everyone in diplomatic circles agreed that his government had been fatally weakened. David Francis's sympathies were with Kornilov, although he was obliged to preserve an impartial stance in public. Kornilov was 'a brave soldier and patriot whose mistake was making demands before public sentiment was sufficiently strong in their favor to force their acceptance.'[40] He felt that the Provisional Government could only save the situation if it took 'prompt and decisive steps to restore the discipline of the army and navy'. But within the US embassy he was the only person with any remaining hope that this might happen. 'Everyone, with only the exception of D.R.F., believes that a clash – and a serious one – is bound to occur soon,' wrote

J. Butler Wright. He and his colleagues were deeply despondent, having seen Kornilov as Russia's last hope. And they were beginning to doubt the sixty-seven-year-old ambassador's grip on the situation; he seemed tired, old and out of touch.[41]

The failure of the Kornilov march on Petrograd at the end of August did much to accelerate the departure, which had already begun after the July Days, of foreign nationals from Petrograd. All remaining embassies in the city now began making contingency plans for the evacuation of their staff and their colonies of expatriates. 'All those whose duties permit them to go are being sent away,' Pauline Crosley told her family. 'All Embassies are planning for the escape of those who must remain. There is no fear of the Germans coming soon, but a serious Bolshevik uprising is anticipated, and its success means *Anarchy*.'[42] At the end of August, J. Butler Wright was sent by David Francis to 'spy out a possible exit from this pest-hole of a capital in case the government blows up or we are forced to evacuate suddenly'.[43] Deciding he would take no chances, on 9 September Wright put his wife and son on a train to Moscow, further away from the German front, and where the internal situation was less fraught.

Naval attaché Walter Crosley, on Francis's instructions, had meanwhile chartered 'a steamer large enough to accommodate the entire American Colony', which had been anchored on the Neva. Plans were in place by 3 September for the evacuation of 266 people: the entire US colony, embassy and consulate staff and members of the Red Cross Mission; but this was a last resort, if their safe and orderly evacuation to Moscow by rail should prove impossible. The US consulate had also already evacuated a large amount of its archives to its counterpart in Moscow by special courier, and other important documents were sent out from the embassy with the Red Cross Mission when it left for there.[44]

The British had been making similar contingency plans, even discussing the possibility of mooring 'two of our submarines' in the Neva opposite the embassy for an emergency evacuation. British consul Arthur Woodhouse observed in a letter that 'you can size up the situation by the number of Britishers leaving the country. In a word, it is not a fit place for English ladies and children.' But his duty 'plainly requires my presence here,' he told his wife in response to her pleas that he should leave. 'I must stay on to the end ... The office is practically a tourist bureau now-a-days. Ordinary consular work is a thing of the past.'[45]

Some of the British families who had lived in Petrograd for generations and who had built homes and established businesses there were already preparing to return to England, forced to abandon their businesses and leave many of their treasured possessions behind and travel with only what they stood up in. 'I was wearing all my clothes, I couldn't bend my arms at all, and I had gold sovereigns stitched into my coat lining. Mother carried her precious silver-wedding teapot,' recalled Dorothy Shaw, who was thirteen at the time and whose father was a manager at Thornton's woollen mill in Petrograd; they were one of thirty-six English families who worked there and had settled in the vicinity of the mill. She and her mother made their way to Bergen where, after a three-week wait, they got on HMS *Vulture*, a British official despatch boat operating between England and Norway, escorted by two torpedo boats, which brought them and other British refugees back across a North Sea bristling with German U-boats.[46]

It had been a deeply dispiriting time for British families such as this, having to watch helplessly as their factories fell idle, irreparably damaged by punitive strikes or forced to close with the onslaught of impossible wage demands. Throughout 1917 British nationals saw the fortunes their ancestors had built up in imperial St Petersburg – some since the eighteenth century – haemorrhage away in the chaos of revolutionary Petrograd. 'Every Sunday the English Church along the quay grew emptier,' recalled Edward Stebbing. 'Familiar faces were missing from the weekly working parties in the Embassy, there was sadness, separation, dispersal everywhere.' The strain of holding things together was also telling on Sir George Buchanan. Stebbing was shocked to see 'how really ill he looked'. With the threat of another revolution growing, Sir George sent out a request to all British subjects to notify the consulate of their address, telephone number and full details of all family members. He wanted to ensure that British nationals should leave in safety, and with dignity, if and when the time came.[47]

Members of the Russian aristocracy, fearful of the virulent antipathy they now encountered, were also selling up and leaving Russia. 'Everyone would like to emigrate, but it is difficult because of the impossibility of taking money out, or of being sent sums of money from Russia,' noted Louis de Robien; his embassy was being besieged daily by Russians wanting to go to France.[48] Even Elizaveta Naryshkina, the Empress's former Mistress of the Robes and the most senior lady at court, was now selling off her valuables. She had a Sèvres porcelain bust of Marie-Antoinette, given by the Queen herself to her grandfather, which she was desperate for the Louvre to buy, in order that she might survive.[49] This option seemed infinitely preferable to the bust 'one day grac[ing] the parlour of a Transatlantic pork merchant'. Out on the streets, members of the old imperial aristocracy were increasingly required to run the gauntlet of public hostility. They tried not to look conspicuous, for fear of drawing attention to themselves, for a good deal of animosity was now directed against anyone – be they Russian or a foreigner – perceived as being representative of the bourgeoisie. 'Everyone who was well dressed looked anxious,' noted Princess Cantacuzène-Speransky; 'no one wore elegant clothes.' 'I discreetly cover any article of dress that *might* rouse their ire with something almost shabby when I go on the street,' wrote Pauline Crosley.[50]

French actress Paulette Pax made sure to turn in her fur collar so that it did not show, whenever she went out, and asked her maid to lend her back the worn-out boots she had given her some time previously.[51] Phil Jordan constantly worried when the ambassador went out on one of his grand walks through Petrograd: 'Boss, you've got to stop struttin' around in that fur hat, that fur collar on your coat, and those spats and cane,' he admonished him. He was right to do so, for foreigners were bawled out for even the most modest manifestation of smart dress.[52] Claude Anet was reprimanded for being a bourgeois on the Nevsky: 'You don't belong to us,' he was told. 'You are wearing gloves.' Ella

Woodhouse recalled being out wearing her ordinary overcoat and matching hat, when she boarded a crowded tram. 'The tram jolted, I was pushed against some strap-hanger, who turned on me angrily, and I heard another woman passenger say: *"Doloi shlyapku!"'* – 'Down with the hat!'– it being perceived as the insignia of a bourgeoise. 'Need I add,' she continued, 'that I got off at the next stop. After that, I went about in an old coat with a prominent button missing, and a shawl over my head.'[53] '*Think* of a country, a Capital, in which it is unwise to appear on the street "well dressed"!' summed up an exasperated Pauline Crosley. She was dismayed that she had not seen a single man 'wearing a silk hat' in 'this large Capital of a large country' in all the time she had been there.[54]

With panic spreading about a possible German advance, many of the civilian population of Petrograd were also now trying to leave the city. Thousands, 'driven by irrational fear' of impending disaster, were desperate to get back to their villages where they thought all would be well. Pauline Crosley could not see the sense in this mass exodus, 'for we hear of nothing but disorders all over Russia, and I can learn of no locality that is really *safe*'.[55] Louis de Robien saw the long queues of people waiting for train tickets, often for as long as two days. At Petrograd's Nicholas Station, 'the booking-hall, the platforms and the lines were full of people camping in the midst of their luggage, waiting to leave by any available train':

> Soldiers, *Tovariches*, and women with their children were either squatting on the platforms or sitting on their bundles, surrounded by bags, bursting packing-cases tied up with ropes, wooden trunks painted in bright colours, nondescript suitcases, Samovars, rolled-up mattresses, household utensils and gramophone horns.[56]

When a train finally did come in – often after another two days or more of waiting – the crowd stormed it and clawed their way on board; those with money offered huge bribes for a precious seat. But many of the desperate were trampled and injured as they struggled to get on board.

For those foreigners remaining in the city, life was becoming increasingly unstable by September, with belligerent crowds out protesting once more on the streets. From her bedroom window at the Astoria, Emmeline Pankhurst could see armed Bolsheviks marching up and down brandishing weapons.[57] Concerned for her safety, a group of Russian officers at the hotel had offered to act as her armed bodyguard when she needed to go out, but she had refused; nor would she and Jessie Kenney capitulate to suggestions that they disguise themselves as proletarians, in order to avoid the threat of attack on the streets as despised members of the bourgeoisie. A few precious gifts of English food had arrived for them, care of the British embassy, which they grate-fully enjoyed; but while they had been away on a visit to Moscow in August many of the things they had left behind at the hotel were stolen. 'The sleepless nights and bad food, the emotional strain' – all were taking their toll, wrote Kenney, and the service at the hotel was getting worse and worse.[58]

The truth was, that despite the best of intentions and her ener-getic commitment, Emmeline Pankhurst's mission to Russia had been a failure. She had had little or no comprehension of Russia's women, and many of those with whom she had sought to engage had found her manner patronising. Why should she – an English-woman from a position of relative comfort and privilege – preach to women such as they, who had spent their entire lives struggling to survive against political and social oppression of a kind that was way beyond her understanding or experience? When it came down to it, as Florence Harper observed, 'the women of Russia were too busy revolutionising to bother about being organised'.[59] For her own part, Jessie Kenney liked to think that, if nothing else, 'we did foster hope, and we did all we could to maintain courage and faith'.[60] What is more, Pankhurst had done so through considerable physical pain and exhaustion. 'She was now looking more aged and worn with one struggle after another, and the continual gastric trouble was wearing her down,' recalled Kenney, and they decided to head back to England. But Emmeline Pankhurst would leave with powerful memories of Petrograd, and especially of Maria Bochkareva, and she would take with her a warning that the situation in Russia was 'as bad as it can be'. The challenge traditional government in Russia was now having to face from revolutionary politics – which Pankhurst found arbitrary and brutal – offered in her view 'an object lesson for the democracies of the world'; and a 'very terrible object lesson' it was.[61]

Ahead of her departure from Petrograd with Pankhurst, Jessie Kenney arranged to have her diary of their visit smuggled out of Russia, having been advised that all uncensored reading matter was routinely confiscated at the border with Sweden at Torneo. On their way out through Finland and Sweden to the boat at Bergen, they once more shared the same train as Lady Muriel Paget.* Florence Harper was on board too, by now 'so fed up with Russia and black bread and machine-guns and riots and murder and discord' that she had 'shaken the mud of Petrograd from her shoes with more pleasure than [she] realized'. On arrival in London, Harper headed straight for her first decent breakfast in seven months: 'porridge, sole, kippers, bacon and eggs, toast, marmalade and tea'; but that night there was a German air raid.[62] She might have escaped revolutionary Petrograd, but she was still in the war zone.

A few dogged foreign journalists did, however, remain in the city, hanging on for the anticipated big news story of a Bolshevik takeover, holed up in the city's increasingly rundown hotels. At the Hotel de France, Americans Ernest Poole, William G. Shepherd and Arno Dosch-Fleurot had learned to fend for themselves. The hotel had been hostage to repeated strikes by waiters, cooks and chambermaids; there was refuse, dirt and dust everywhere; the sheets went unwashed and their beds unmade. One day, desperate for something to eat, they found their way down to the hotel's huge pantry, 'where from floor to ceiling were piled dirty cups and plates and coffee pots'. They picked out some crockery, washed it and went to the kitchen, where 'one old cook, who had not

---

* On their return, Pankhurst and Kenney spoke about their 'Russian Mission' at two big meetings held at London's Queen's Hall on 7 and 14 November.

gone on strike with the rest, gave us vile black coffee and big chunks of soggy rye bread', which they carried back to their room.[63] Such was the life of the foreign correspondent, they agreed with grim humour. Most couldn't wait to get out, but others were still arriving, even now.

In the last week of August, after taking the long sea journey from San Francisco to Yokohama, followed by an eleven-day rail journey from Vladivostok, an English writer slipped into Petrograd on an ambitious – and secret – mission. He had been sent, by the Secret Intelligence Service (now MI6), 'to prevent the Bolshevik Revolution', as he later rather grandly put it, 'and to keep Russia in the war'. It seemed a tall order for one solitary, tubercular, inexperienced British spy, recruited because he knew a bit of Russian from reading Chekhov stories and happened to be related by marriage to Sir William Wiseman, the SIS's man in New York. His code name was Somerville, and his cover that of a journalist reporting on the situation in Russia for the British press. His real name was Somerset Maugham.

He had already worked undercover as a British agent in Switzerland in 1915–16 and had been living in New York, when Wiseman recruited him to go to Petrograd to subvert German propagandising for Russia's withdrawal from the war and to offer support to Kerensky. Maugham arrived in Petrograd on 19 August with a generous $21,000 to cover his expenses for this purpose, and expected to be 'occupied there presumably till the end of the war'.[64] As an aesthete and member of the English literary set, his first view of the Nevsky – after having enjoyed the 'flamboyance' of the rue de la Paix and the 'splendour' of Fifth Avenue – was a depressing one. He found it 'dingy and sordid and dilapidated' and the displays in the shop windows 'vulgar', but the diversity of its dense crowds was quite new to him and he found it enthralling: 'walking along the Nevsky,' he recalled, 'you saw the whole gallery of the characters of the great Russian novels so that you could put a name to one after the other'.[65]

A personal introduction to Kerensky soon followed, thanks to Maugham's friendship with Alexandra Kropotkin, daughter of the legendary revolutionary, Prince Peter Kropotkin. 'I think Kerensky must have supposed that I was more important than I really was,' Maugham later wrote, 'for he came to Sasha's apartment on several occasions and, walking up and down the room, harangued me as though I were at a public meeting for two hours at a time.'[66] Maugham quickly installed himself on the expatriate social circuit, meeting Hugh Walpole of the Anglo-Russian Propaganda Bureau and dining with him and other friends – and Kerensky as well – on caviar and vodka, 'at the expense of two governments', at the popular Medved restaurant.[67] 'I don't think that Maugham knew very much about Russia,' Walpole recalled of him in a later memoir, 'but his refusal to be hurried into sentimental assumptions, his cynical pretence that "all was anyway for the worst" (he did not himself believe that for a single moment) gave him a poise and calm that some others of us badly needed'.

There was a quality about Maugham, the literary man and gentleman spy, that professional spies did not have: 'He watched Russia as we would watch a play, finding the theme, and then intent on observing how the master artist would develop it,' added Walpole.[68] He took time to soak up the culture – attending the ballet and theatre – and catching up on his reading of the Russian classics. He also made sure he mixed with the Allied agents staying at the Europa and the Astoria, returning to his hotel room in the evenings to carefully encrypt messages to his controller, Wiseman, in New York, in which Kerensky was 'Lane', Lenin 'Davis' and Trotsky 'Cole' and the British government took the sobriquet of 'Eyre & Co.'[69]*

Eighteen days after Maugham had installed himself discreetly in Petrograd's Hotel d'Europe, a new pair of American reporters

---

* Maugham's impressions of Petrograd in 1917 would later be immortalised in his 1928 collection of stories *Ashenden*, which include a withering portrait of the frigidly correct Sir George Buchanan, as Sir Herbert Witherspoon.

arrived in town. Unlike their pragmatic, experienced compatriots Florence Harper and Donald Thompson, who had arrived without fanfare in February, the charismatic socialist and professional rebel John Reed and his wife, the feminist journalist Louise Bryant, arrived in Petrograd with a reputation for leftist sentiment and brimming with high-minded socialist ideals that were guaranteed to attract attention.

Thirty-year-old Reed, from a well-to-do conventional Portland (Oregon) family, had been something of a playboy and a joker during his years at Harvard. Moving to Greenwich Village, he became a key figure in the bohemian avant-garde, working as a reporter for the radical New York magazine *The Masses*, where he had earned a reputation for his uncompromising political beliefs, tackling social issues and championing the working-class underdog, as a vigorous supporter of the militant Wobblies (Industrial Workers of the World). In 1913, during the Mexican Revolution, he had installed himself with rebel Pancho Villa's forces, from where his vivid reporting had further built his reputation. Reed's work for the liberal *Metropolitan Magazine* had sent him to Europe in 1914. He had wanted to report on the Eastern Front, but although in the summer of 1915 he had managed to get to Petrograd, where he was briefly detained by the authorities, he had been refused permission to operate in the Russian military zone. Back in New York, he continued to produce inflammatory articles criticising the war and America's involvement in it.[70]

In December 1915 in Portland, Reed had met Louise Bryant – an attractive, auburn-haired social reporter and fashion illustrator from Nevada, who was active in the women's suffrage movement. Soon afterwards she had left her dentist husband and followed Reed to New York, where they had married, after her divorce, the following November. After the February Revolution broke, Reed had been eager to go to Russia and see things for himself, but it was not till August that he had managed to raise the money for his trip, reporting for *The Masses* and another socialist weekly, the *New York Call*. Bryant travelled with him, Reed having wangled her accreditation to write for the *Metropolitan Magazine* and the Bell syndicate. In 1917 the mainstream press still did not acknowledge women war correspondents, and Bryant's function was therefore, nominally, to report on Russia 'from a woman's point of view'.[71]

Because of their tight budget, the Reeds found the Petrograd hotels were more than they could afford, so they set themselves up at a freezing cold rented apartment at 23 Troitskaya (where they slept in their overcoats). They were eager to meet Arno Dosch-Fleurot, whose reports from Petrograd they had been following since 1916, and soon hooked up with him and fellow American socialists and journalists Bessie Beatty and Albert Rhys Williams (a former Congregational minister whom Reed had known in Greenwich Village) – both of whom had been in the city since June and who provided valuable introductions, along with the shared services of an interpreter, Alexander Gumberg.

John Reed's defining account of the October Revolution would later become the gold standard of eyewitness reporting on revolutionary Russia, but in September 1917 he had arrived in this political cauldron with no knowledge of the language or experience of its culture and politics, and no personal contacts in government, society or the revolutionary movement. To compensate, he had all the brashness, drive and charisma, the literary powers and journalistic flair for taking on such a big, dramatic news story; and he sensed that the story now brewing would be the making of his career. Together, the like-minded Reed, Bryant, Beatty and Rhys Williams joined forces to tell Russia's story from their own committed socialist perspective, as partisans and *tovarishchi*, determined to 'feel its strength – unshackled' and, hopefully, bear witness to 'the dawn of a new world'.[72]

PART 3

THE OCTOBER
REVOLUTION

13

'For Color and Terror and Grandeur This Makes Mexico Look Pale'

Thanks to delays of a week at Halifax, Nova Scotia, and in Stockholm, John Reed and Louise Bryant had been travelling for almost a month when they finally arrived, bedraggled and exhausted in Petrograd. They had sailed from Hoboken, New Jersey, on 17 August 1917 (NS), to Kristiania in Norway on a Danish steamer, the *United States*. Most of the people on board were Scandinavians, but there were a few American businessmen, as well as a contingent of Jewish exiles returning to Russia to live – so they hoped – in freedom at last. From her first-class deck Louise could hear their voices singing revolutionary songs carried up from the steerage deck below.[1]

Among the American passengers there was a party of seven young college graduates, who had recently been recruited by the National City Bank to join Leighton Rogers, Chester Swinnerton and others at the Petrograd branch, so that some staff could be transferred to Moscow. Twenty-three-year-old trainee John Louis Fuller of Indianapolis was one of them. He had never been abroad before and had enjoyed the entertaining company of Reed and Bryant on the train from Kristiania to Petrograd, during which he had a 'good many' political arguments with them.[2] They had all been alarmed by the vigorous pilfering of their luggage when

soldiers ordered them off the train at Beloostrov, the last stop
before Petrograd's Finland Station, when everyone had rued the
loss of 'toilet articles, shirts, socks, collars, razors' that were confiscated as supposed 'contraband'. Worse, 'The John Reeds had
lost most of their things including their letter of credit' that had
been in Reed's wallet, which had been stolen too, and Louise
had been humiliated by being 'compelled to strip when they
searched her'.[3]

US ambassador David Francis was wary of the Reeds when
they first presented themselves at his embassy. They had arrived
with a letter of introduction from a federal official in New York,
requesting that Francis offer any help he could in their assignment to study social conditions in Petrograd. Francis might well
have had sight of the contents of Reed's stolen wallet, which was
miraculously 'returned' to the US consulate (though minus the
500 rubles in cash it contained) soon afterwards, possibly having
been pickpocketed to order, so that Reed's credentials could be
checked.[4] Either way, once he had ascertained that Reed had
been 'cordially welcomed by the Bolsheviks whom he apparently
advised of his coming', Francis was on his guard. 'I naturally
regarded Mr Reed as a suspicious character and had him watched
and his record and acts investigated,' he recalled. These suspicions
seemed to be confirmed when a few days later Reed turned up
at a mass meeting to protest at the arrest in the USA, and the
forthcoming trial on a conspiracy charge, of a Russo-American
anarchist named Alexander Berkman.[5] Leighton Rogers had seen
the posters plastered on billboards around the city announcing
meetings to protest at this punishment of 'Brother Berkman in
the Capitalistic Oligarchy of the United States'; such violent
sloganeering, and the fact that Reed supported it, was more than
enough to alarm Francis and his staff.[6]

Not long after his arrival, Reed wrote to an old friend that
he had 'more stuff than I can write'. 'We are in the middle of
things, and believe me it's thrilling. There is so much dramatic
to write that I don't know where to begin.' Petrograd had already
seized his imagination, Reed told him: 'For color and terror and

grandeur this makes Mexico look pale.' He was full of questions and restless to 'see everything at once', as his friend Albert Rhys Williams recalled, but was hampered by having only the barest smattering of Russian. It did not take him long to overcome this; with the help of his interpreter, Alexander Gumberg, he had soon mastered enough of the language to be able to work out the essentials.[7] Rhys Williams helped Reed get to know the city and introduced him and Bryant to his many Russian contacts – taking them on a walking tour of all the major places linked to recent events, describing to them the demonstrations and riots he had witnessed earlier in the year and together discussing what path the endgame of revolution might take from here.

Reed wanted to know who was the most impressive speaker: Lenin or Trotsky? Even as a committed and well-informed social- ist, he had been in ignorance of the elusive Bolshevik leader until the US press had finally begun picking up on Lenin after the July Days, and he was eager to see him.[8] Rhys Williams was sure that revolutionary Russia would be Reed's coming of age, just as it had been his own: 'The Revolution was not something you could play around with. You could not take it up and then drop it. It was something that seized hold of you, shook you, and pos- sessed you.' The Bolsheviks were working for the kind of social justice that both men believed in, and they wanted it 'more pas- sionately than any other group'. They saw the coming battle as a straightforward class war: 'No one shall eat cake until everyone has bread,' urged Rhys Williams. Such lofty ideals were wonderful in principle, from a safe distance, but as they would soon discover, revolutionary practice in Petrograd was quite another matter.[9]

Interception of inflammatory remarks by Reed, suggesting that if the Bolsheviks gained control the 'very first thing they would do would be to kick out all the Embassies and all those con- nected with them', suggested to Ambassador Francis that Reed openly supported the overthrow of Kerensky's government.[10] Reed and Bryant had already been predicting 'trouble in a couple of weeks when the combined soviets hold their meeting here', as John Louis Fuller noted. On the journey from America, Fuller had 'heard them prophesying many things that haven't come true so perhaps this is another of their false alarms'.[11] To most of the Americans who encountered him in Petrograd, the headstrong and outspoken Reed appeared provocative, but also politically blinkered – foolish even.[12]* His seemed a very limited and politically naive view of Petrograd to those expatriates who had lived there for many years. Russia, for the impressionable Reed and Bryant, was very much a political adventure, a chance to witness a socialist experiment in the making, but having arrived 'on the crest of a counter-revolution', at the tail end of the Kornilov affair, they soon were experiencing the full impact of a city under political and economic siege.[13]

Louise Bryant was shocked by the long lines of 'scantily clad people standing in the bitter cold' and by how 'pitifully empty' the shops were; to her horror, a small five-cent bar of American chocolate currently cost seven rubles – or about seventy-five cents.† She was struck by the absurd anomaly that although she was told the city had barely enough food to last three days and there were no warm clothes to be bought anywhere, she passed 'window after window full of flowers, corsets, dog-collars and false hair'.[14] Even more absurd was the fact that the corsets were of the 'most expensive, out-of-date, wasp-waist variety' and the women of the old aristocracy who might wear them had 'largely disappeared from the capital'. But 'Red Petrograd' itself impressed her, with its tremendous solidity and presence, 'as if it were built by a giant who had no regard for human life'. It had retained

---

* Leighton Rogers did not think much of Reed, as he noted in his diary: 'This young man … has been milling around Petrograd playing revolutionary. I've seen him riding in trucks tossing out Red handbills and posing conspicuously beside speakers at Bolshevik street corner meetings … It burns me up to see this arrogant poseur aiding the Bolsheviks on the grounds that the "American proletariat" is supporting them in their separate peace … When I think of the good young Americans who will have to bear the brunt of the massive German attack that is surely coming in France … of how many of them will be killed, my blood boils at the thought of John Reed.'

† In 1917 the exchange rate was about eleven rubles to the dollar.

the 'rugged strength' of Peter the Great, who had built it two hundred years previously with such despotic determination; and all the depredations of war heaped upon it still had not altogether stifled its spirit or its cultural life.

'The Nevsky after midnight was as amusing and interesting as Fifth Avenue in the afternoon,' Bryant remarked; 'the cafes had nothing to serve but weak tea and sandwiches but they were always full'. 'Champagne still sparkled in cabarets and night-clubs by candle-light, long after the electric supply was cut off.'[15] The Cinematograph, where you could see the latest American movies featuring the likes of Chaplin, Fairbanks and Pickford, were 'ablaze with lights till nightfall, and crowded to the doors'. You could still go to the opera at the Mariinsky – to see *Prince Igor* or *Boris Godunov* – and hear Chaliapin sing, or join the sell-out audiences watching the exquisite Karsavina dancing *Paquita*.[16] After an absence of several months, the French troupe had returned to the Mikhailovsky with a repertoire of light-hearted French comedies to counter the dramatic gloom of Meyerhold's production of Alexey Tolstoy's *Death of Ivan the Terrible*, which was running at the Alexandrinsky.[17] 'The only difference was the clientele', which was now 'a motley crowd smelling of boot-leather and perspiration' and had probably 'gone without bread to buy the cheap little tickets'.[18]

John Reed was similarly taken by surprise to see that 'gambling clubs functioned hectically from dusk to dawn, with champagne flowing and stakes of twenty thousand roubles. In the centre of the city at night prostitutes in jewels and expensive furs walked up and down, crowding the cafes'.[19] 'Like Pompeii of old, the city feasted and made merry' while the volcano rumbled, noted one eyewitness.[20] There was, nevertheless, considerable nervousness generated by rumours of a German advance, and the threat of Zeppelin and even aeroplane raids continued. Frequent drills were carried out 'in case of an attack, with the sounding of sirens, the mobilization of firemen, and the putting out of lights', but these seemed futile in a city where few buildings had cellars in which people could take refuge. Such was the current air of desperation that some people openly expressed the wish 'that the German armies might come and take possession – the sooner the better – in order that the distress might be ended, even by the occupation of a foreign power'.[21] Anything was better than this perpetual state of uncertainty. 'Each day Russian morale sinks lower, and soon it may settle to a point where Germany can do with it as she wills,' wrote Leighton Rogers. 'It seems to me that a few million dollars' worth of vigorous Allied propaganda, conducted by men who understand the situation, would be able to counter the Germans and save this great, generous people to us. But we have no such propaganda and are losing by default.'[22]

As the fractured political life of the city juddered on from one crisis to the next, a nine-day Democratic Congress opened on 14 September at Petrograd's Alexandrinsky Theatre, attended by around 1,600 delegates, at which the national leadership was to introduce a programme of revolutionary democracy for the new government to be voted in by the Constituent Assembly. Much as the Moscow Congress in August had been, it was a last-ditch attempt to build some kind of unity between the right-wing establishment, the liberal Kadets and the socialist left, in the midst of the continuing political chaos. But few held out any hope of success. 'The Democratic Conference is like a rough and hastily constructed lean-to, full of gaps and crevices,' wrote Harold Williams. 'People have crowded into it for warmth and shelter from the cold and bitter winds that are blowing over Russia in this autumn of the Revolution, but there is little comfort to be found.'[23] The American quartet of Beatty, Bryant, Reed and Rhys Williams were all there, as too were a few other foreign reporters and Allied diplomats, allowed in to observe the proceedings from the former imperial boxes, whose Romanov insignia had been hacked off and replaced with red flags and revolutionary banners.

For the sophisticated socialite Somerset Maugham, the experience of a volatile and combative socialist congress populated by plebeians of the kind with whom he would never normally associate was quite an eye-opener. He scanned the 'peasant' types in the audience with considerable disdain, his overall impression being of a 'backward, loutish people' with 'ignorant faces and a vacuous look'. Despite their lack of education, this assembly seemed happy to be subjected to lengthy speeches given with 'great fluency, but with a monotonous fervour' by orators who were the kind of men, Maugham thought, whom you might see 'addressing the meeting of the Radical candidate for a constituency in the South of London'. He found them, for all their fluency and table-thumping, mediocre; and thought it 'amazing' that such people should 'be in control of this vast empire'.[24]

Arthur Ransome was there too – on one of his last assignments before returning to England – and noted that 'the only real enthusiasm aroused in the meeting was by Kerensky', who took to the rostrum dressed in plain soldier's khaki. Maugham was struck by Kerensky's lack of physical strength. He seemed to be 'green in the face with fright' and to have 'a strangely hunted look' as he gave an intense, impassioned speech for over an hour without notes, in which he asked for a vote of confidence, insisting that only a coalition government could save the country.[25] Ransome, who was 'within a yard' of Kerensky, noticed that he seemed to be in an extremely stressed state. 'I saw the sweat come out on his forehead, I watched his mouth change as he faced now one, now another group of his opponents,' he wrote in his despatch to the *Daily News*, impressed by the 'tremendous effort' Kerensky made to deal with the 'constant interruption from the Left'.[26]

Reporting for the *Daily Chronicle*, Harold Williams could not warm to Kerensky's rasping declamatory style, always delivered at the same relentless pitch, and he winced at the contrived moments of 'painful emotionalism'. But he had to admit that 'whether Kerensky [was] a great or a small man', there was 'no other man in Russia' at that time who could take his place; certainly not his sneering Bolshevik detractors.[27] Ransome was dismayed by their behaviour: 'They alone at a moment of terrible difficulty brought to the assembly the irresponsible nonchalance of a debating society,' as they sat there 'smiling, indifferent to words that to their speakers represented blood and tears'.[28]

During his speech Kerensky had 'stood practically among the audience as though he sought to appeal to each man personally'; Somerset Maugham could see that his appeal 'was to the heart and not to the mind'. For him it was a 'facile expression of feeling' that he, as a reserved Englishman, found 'a little embarrassing', but which Kerensky manipulated so skilfully, and which clearly had an 'overwhelming effect' on the more openly susceptible Russians, who seemed easily won over by the power of words. At the end of his speech Kerensky received an ovation, but it would be his last. 'The final impression I had,' recalled Maugham 'was of a man exhausted.'[29] Kerensky's exhaustion proved symptomatic of a congress that had been ever more fraught with disunity, marred by a shambolic voting system and by endless, excruciating delays in proceedings. An extremely hostile Bolshevik response to all conciliatory gestures had prevailed, culminating in a mass walkout, allowing a resolution for Kerensky to form a pre-parliament prior to the election of a Constituent Assembly to be passed by a small majority.[30]

Arthur Ransome headed home by sea on 26 September with a very clear sense of approaching danger; what he had seen at the congress had convinced him that the Bolsheviks were preparing the ground to seize power. He hoped, however, that a brief respite in England, for much-needed rest and a spot of fishing, would allow him time to recoup his energies before returning to Petrograd for the final showdown. But he was wrong: events would not wait for him.* His friend and fellow journalist Harold Williams stayed in Petrograd to await the inevitable, feeling ever more gloomy about what was to come: 'It matters little what resolutions are passed,' he wrote soon after the congress. 'The fate of Russia is not to be decided here. Other forces are at work,

---

* Ransome missed the October Revolution, arriving back in Petrograd on Christmas Day (NS; 12 December OS). *Times* correspondent Robert Wilton missed it too, leaving in mid-September. With Wilton's departure there was no *Times* correspondent in Petrograd to cover events in October when they broke.

real, stern, inexorable, which are guiding Russia, to what destinies who in this bitter and tragical time can foresee or foretell?'[31] Sir George Buchanan, who had also observed some of the sessions, was emphatic about their impact: writing to the Foreign Office, he declared that 'the only result has been to split up the democracy into an infinite number of small groups, and to undermine the authority of its recognized leaders'. And he went on to issue a warning:

> The Bolsheviks, who form a compact minority, have alone a definite political programme. They are more active and better organized than any other group, and until they and the ideas which they represent are finally squashed, the country will remain a prey to anarchy and disorder … If the Government are not strong enough to put down the Bolsheviks by force, at the risk of breaking altogether with the Soviet, the only alternative will be a Bolshevik Government.[32]

In contrast to so much gloom and despondency, the energetic US Red Cross envoy Raymond Robins had remained defiantly optimistic. He had attended every session of the congress, even though it had proved to be 'a continuous performance of the most exacting nature', with sessions lasting till four in the morning on two occasions. He had been excited by this, the 'first Social-Democratic Conference in which the power of government was represented under socialist leadership in the history of the world'.[33] But while he noted Kerensky's undoubted gifts as a speaker, Robins had observed the charismatic Trotsky marshalling his Bolshevik supporters during the conference, and came away feeling that 'the most skillful and dangerous leader of the extreme left was Trotsky' – moreover, that the congress had brought nearer an inevitable clash between the Bolsheviks (the 'party of destructionist separate peace tendencies') and the moderates. Many people had already left Petrograd, 'believing that the commune and civil war with murder and looting are just a day or two ahead,' Robins told his wife on 24 September, but he remained convinced that the new Coalition Government would 'yet master the situation'. Despite all the uncertainties, he was bullish about the success of his mission: 'The fact that we live on the edge of a volcano and that we may be overwhelmed any day simply adds to the zest of the service ... I am satisfied that the Revolution will never turn backward, and that Russia will achieve a great realization of liberty and social progress.'[34]

The weary Sir George Buchanan, after many years in Russia, had no such optimism. Shortly after the Democratic Congress he called on his French, Italian and American colleagues to make a collective approach to Kerensky's government 'on the subject of both the military and internal situations'.[35] David Francis had declined to take part, a fact on which his aide J. Butler Wright commented with dismay: '*Everyone*, with only the exception of [Francis], believes that a clash – and a serious one – is bound to occur soon. We fervently wish that it would come and get it over with.'[36] On 25 September, Buchanan and his other colleagues met Kerensky to urge the government to 'concentrate all its energies on the prosecution of the war' and restore internal order, increase factory output and re-establish discipline in the army. But when Sir George read out their moderately stated joint declaration, Kerensky cut short their interview with 'a wave of his hand' and 'walked out exclaiming: "You forget that Russia is a great power!"' Sir George found such a petulant 'Napoleonic touch' unworthy of him. As fellow diplomat Louis de Robien neatly observed: 'The Tsar also refused to listen to Sir George in similar circumstances: a few weeks later he lost the crown!'[37]

As September turned to October, Petrograd life continued to be measured by the same, tedious factional infighting and sloganeering, by stultifying meetings, wildcat strikes, rumour and counter-rumour. 'The endless talk when action was needed, the vacillations, the apathy when apathy could only result in destruction, the high-flown protestations, the insincerity and half-heartedness that I found everywhere sickened me,' wrote Somerset Maugham wearily.[38] 'The agitators are persistently at it,' noted Leighton Rogers. 'Meetings are held every day in various sections of the city protesting against this and that, anything as long as it is a protest ... Just as you bolster up a little hope some disheartening rumor comes along and knocks it down. The level of spirit in the city is sinking slowly but inevitably.'* 'Always the same chaos, the same uncertainty,' wrote French resident Louise Patouillet. 'This revolution truly is the road to Calvary.'[39]

A distinct whiff of approaching winter now filled the air, as the starving city once more became a place of dank mists, bone-chilling winds, little or no sun and persistent rain. The streets were a sorry sight, with pavement blocks taken up and gaping holes left in their place. Grass was growing between the cobble-stones on the once imposing square in front of the Winter Palace. Petrograd's crowded thoroughfares in autumn, with their drab people drained of the colour of summer, gave out 'an intense impression of dirt and din and chaotic movement'.[40] Under rain-filled, leaden skies the city seemed ever more melancholy. 'Poverty and filth. These are my impressions on arrival here,' wrote the disconsolate new Belgian ambassador, Jules Destrée, when he got off the train in mid-October 1917:

In this late-autumn time, Petrograd is a revolting cesspool. Liquid, sticky mud covers the carriage-way and the cause-ways. It has splashed up onto the windows of the lower stories of buildings and spreads over the ruts in the road, squirting treacherously underfoot, making stepping onto loose cobblestones risky. I've never seen anything as horrible, except in certain muddy streets in Constantinople. The locals smile at my squeamishness as they flounder around in this quagmire with their customary resignation. It's one of the

---

* One of the positives of the removal of the tsarist ban on public meetings was the revival in Russia of the Salvation Army, with proselytisers from Finland returning to the city after Easter 1917 and holding a series of large public meetings. But it didn't last for long; the Soviet government banned the Salvation Army in 1923.

evils of the war – there are others, much worse. In days of old, the roadways were fine and well maintained, but the army has commandeered all manpower and filth has got the better of the defenceless capital.[41]

It was the faces of the starving, shabby population standing in line that most distressed Destrée, as they did all new visitors to the city: they seemed 'docile, submissive and, without any prompting by the police, they just fall in line, one behind the other … they just wait in the rain and the icy blast, shivering'. He concluded that they had 'the mindset of fatalistic slaves' and it mattered not which kind of government ruled over them.[42]

As Petrograd languished in an apathy induced by hunger and exhaustion, a new danger haunted the streets. With the domestic electricity supply reduced to the hours between 6.00 p.m. and midnight and the street lights not lit for fear of Zeppelin raids, there had recently been a dramatic rise in robbery, rape and murder at night. Very few people ventured out after 11.00 p.m.; those foreigners who did so kept to the middle of the street, away from dark recesses and corners and, if they had one, carried a revolver in their pocket.[43*] Arthur Reinke noted that his friends were buying revolvers to protect themselves – paying $125 apiece. 'I find it desirable at night to carry 30 roubles,' he added, 'ready to hand out to a hold-up man in order to avoid a painful and messy interview.' The dangers on the streets for foreign residents at that time were legion:

Women had their shoes taken from their feet; men had their clothes removed in the street. Three men entered a fur store opposite the hotel; one began to pack up some valuable furs he had not paid for; the owner called for help, which brought an angry mob; the three men were quickly surrounded by

---

★ One night John Reed was held up and robbed, but after managing to explain in a few Russian words that he was an 'American and a socialist', his possessions were 'promptly returned, his hand cordially shaken and he was sent off rejoicing'.

the mob and beaten to death; it afterwards developed that two were innocent customers. A friend of mine had his necktie pin removed on the Nevsky in broad daylight by a soldier … His mother had her leather bag taken from her lap while seated in a street car by a soldier; the latter turned at the door playfully threatening her with his finger, as one might a child, and jumped off … a guest from our hotel disappeared and his body was found a week later in the river – minus a large sum of money he was known to have carried.[44]

People were frequently stabbed and killed simply because they did not hand over their valuables quickly enough when confronted, and Reinke recalled that the thieves always wore soldiers' uniform and carried a rifle, stopping pedestrians on the pretext of asking to see their papers, upon which they would 'clean out the pockets' of their victims. Many items, meanwhile, ended up in the centre of the city at a 'Soldiers' Market', where hundreds of soldiers could be seen 'selling the spoils of their thieving': 'almost every conceivable article, including their uniforms, boots, weapons, jewelry, paintings, statuary and other things obviously stolen by them'.[45] Thieving was endemic, and not just in Petrograd. Supplies from the food-growing districts were constantly being disrupted because the trains carrying them to Petrograd were attacked and plundered long before they even reached the city. Such violence was symptomatic of what was now going on in the Russian countryside, where the long-suppressed genie of anarchy had finally been let loose with a terrifying, brutal vengeance. The peasants, particularly in southern Russia, were running riot on country estates, killing their landlords, sacking and vandalising their manor houses and setting them on fire, slaughtering livestock and burning the grain in their barns.

In the continuing absence of 'the arch-revolutionist Lenin', who was still lying low in Finland, the most compelling figure on the political stage in Petrograd in the autumn of 1917 was undoubtedly Leon Trotsky.[46] Although originally a Menshevik, and for a while something of a political dilettante, his organisation of strikes and rallies in the wake of the Bloody Sunday massacre of 1905 had marked the beginning of his political ascendancy. Escaping Siberian exile in 1907, he had spent time in France and Spain, before being deported and settling in New York. When the February Revolution broke, he hastily left his apartment in the Bronx to return to Russia, finally throwing in his lot with the Bolsheviks. With the neurotic Lenin still fearful of showing himself, Trotsky was becoming the public face of the Bolshevik leadership. Louise Bryant had found him 'Marat-like' when she saw him speak at the Democratic Congress. His fire-and-brimstone manner had been 'vehement, serpent-like' and he had 'swayed the assembly as a strong wind stirs the long grass'. No other speaker had created 'such an uproar' as Trotsky, or provoked 'such hatred at the slightest utterance' with his violent, 'stinging words', while retaining a cool head.[47]

On 25 September, Trotsky had underlined his ascendancy when he was elected chair of the Petrograd Soviet, in which the Bolsheviks now had a majority. Arno Dosch-Fleurot had been at the Smolny Institute to witness the meeting, which was held in the large lecture hall of this former girls' school:

> Except for a small group of workers, the floor was thick with soldiers – big, bearded, blond peasant-soldiers from the north of Russia, who had deserted the Riga front. On the stage were a dozen dark men with keen faces, most of them dressed in black leather breeches and jackets, such as worn by the motor cyclist couriers of the army. Seen over thousands of straw-blond heads, their black hair and black suits were in conspicuous contrast.[48]

Black leather had by now become the ubiquitous uniform of the Bolsheviks, Fleurot noted. Trotsky wore it, too – and it would henceforth be his trademark. Like Bryant, Fleurot had witnessed the violence of his invective, when Trotsky told his audience at the Smolny that the Russian Revolution was reaching the point where the French Revolution was 'when the Jacobins set up the guillotine'. Seeing Trotsky elected that day, Fleurot remembered it as being the moment when he was 'sure there would be a successful Bolshevik revolution'.[49] Leighton Rogers had also noted the power of Trotsky's rhetoric: 'This man Trotzky is the king of agitators; he could stir up trouble in a cemetery,' he wrote, having heard him speak outside the Kschessinska Mansion, where he was alarmed by the 'wild look in his eyes of a cat with fits'. Trotsky had spoken with 'the enthusiasm and verbiage of a fanatic unable to keep up with the flight of his ideas and without regard for accuracy'.[50] Rogers's Russian was pretty good and he had no difficulty getting the gist of the familiar, overblown Bolshevik rhetoric spouted by Trotsky. As far as Rogers was concerned, it boiled down to the same strident, rabble-rousing components, which he playfully paraphrased in his diary:

Comrades, in a few weeks, a week, a few days, we are going to rise from our slavery to the capitalistic Kerensky government, the tool of British and French Imperialists, and tear the power from his hands. We shall do this for you, so that you may be free men as the Revolution meant you to be. You must support the Soviet because we shall give you: first, peace; second, bread; third, land. Yes, we shall take all land from the rich and divide it among the peasants; and we shall reduce the hours of work, my comrades of the factories, to four, at double the wages you now receive. And you will see the criminal of the old regime and of the autocratic Kerensky government punished, along with the property-owning capitalists who have enslaved you and the peasants. So support us, comrades, and add your voices to our war cry of 'Long Live the international proletariat and the Russian Revolution!' Workers of the world, unite; you have only your chains to lose!

Rogers knew it was 'bunk', and admitted in his diary that 'something in the man stirred me to uneasiness'. 'He has a large following and is dangerous. These people are easily mesmerized by talk.' Trotsky was spreading his inflammatory message all over Petrograd, arguing that the Russian people could not save the revolution all the time they were still fighting in the war. They needed peace in order to be free to 'make war on the bourgeoisie'.[51]

In contrast to Trotsky's vigour, Kerensky was a very sick man. He had for some time been suffering from stomach, lung and kidney trouble and had become increasingly dependent on morphine and brandy to curb not just the physical pain, but also his profound tiredness.[52] When Louise Bryant and John Reed finally got a meeting with him at the Winter Palace, he seemed broken. They found him in Nicholas II's private library, '[lying] on a couch with his face buried in his arms, as if he had been suddenly taken ill, or was completely exhausted'. Bryant put much of this weariness down to the fact that Kerensky saw the 'approaching class struggle' as a long one, for which he perhaps did not have the stomach or the energy. 'Remember, this is not a political revolution,' he told her. 'It is not like the French revolution. *It is an economic revolution.*' It would require a 'profound revaluation of classes' and a realignment of Russia's many different nationalities. 'Remember, that the French revolution took five years and that France was inhabited by one people,' he told her, adding that 'France is the size of one of our provincial districts. *No, the Russian revolution is not over – it is just beginning.*'[53]

Unable to hold out any longer, Kerensky turned, in desperation, to British agent Somerset Maugham, summoning him to the Winter Palace. Maugham had by now sent a coded message to his controller Wiseman in New York that Kerensky's popularity was plummeting. In his view, the British government would be better advised to support the Mensheviks against the Bolsheviks, and invest money in a programme of espionage and propaganda to this end, conducted by Czech secret agents whom he knew in the city. At their meeting at the Winter Palace, Kerensky asked

Maugham to memorise a secret message to the British Prime Minister, David Lloyd George, and take it to England, requesting that he urgently send arms and ammunition and that he remove from his post Sir George Buchanan, whom Kerensky disliked. 'I don't see how we can go on,' he had told Maugham. He had to have something positive to tell the army, to keep it in the fight.[54]

Maugham left Petrograd that same evening on a British destroyer heading for Oslo. Kerensky's requests, when he presented them, were summarily rejected by Lloyd George, but Maugham was never able to return to Petrograd to pass on the message. Meanwhile Sir George Buchanan, still doggedly lobbying Kerensky to take an active stand and eradicate Bolshevism before it was too late, had once more been rebuffed. He couldn't clamp down on the Bolsheviks, Kerensky told him, 'unless they themselves provoked an armed uprising', for to do so might spark a counter-revolution.[55] Somerset Maugham had understood this crippling inability to take positive action – Kerensky was 'more afraid of doing the wrong thing than anxious to do the right one,' he wrote in his later memoirs, 'and so he did nothing until he was forced into action by others.'[56]* For Kerensky the appeaser, a reactive response to the coming Bolshevik coup was the only option left to him. Even at this late stage he still believed he could gain the upper hand: 'I only wish that they would come out,' he told Sir George, 'and I will then put them down.'[57]

By mid-October there were renewed reports of an increasing hostility towards foreigners in Petrograd. Rumours had been circulating since the beginning of the month of Bolshevik plans to 'slaughter Americans' or even initiate 'a general massacre of the foreigners' at any time.[58] 'There must be something in the threats,' Leighton Rogers wrote in his diary, 'because the Embassy has quietly informed all Americans that there is to be a river-boat at the Quay above the Liteiny Bridge ready to take them aboard in

---

* As John Reed had perceptively observed of Kerensky: 'Life is hideously swift for compromisers here.'

case an outbreak should come ... prepared to navigate up the river to Lake Ladoga and a shore town on the Murmansk Railway, where passengers can transfer to trains.' The steamer commandeered by Walter Crosley was ready and waiting and provided with navigation maps; in addition, two volunteer guards from the American colony were on board at all times.[59] Leighton Rogers and his colleague Fred Sikes had recently taken their turn on duty, bringing with them 'a can of beans, my alcohol stove, and a thermos bottle of coffee'. Supplied with one ancient Colt .38 with which to defend themselves, they had noted the sheet of instructions telling them to 'shoot to kill', should the need arise. They were appalled to find that the good ship 'Getaway' – so named by their bank colleague, John Louis Fuller – was not large enough 'to accommodate half the Americans in Petrograd' and had no supplies whatsoever of food. At best it might have squeezed 150–200 people on board. Yet, in the dark not far away, Rogers and Sikes could make out 'one of the largest and most luxurious river steamers, with adequate cabin space for hundreds in an emergency'; it turned out that it had been 'chartered to the French Embassy'.[60]

'Things are coming to a pretty pass here,' British consul Arthur Woodhouse wrote home on 11 October, when he heard that the Bolsheviks had announced they would soon start 'suppressing' the bourgeoisie. 'I confess I should like to be out of it, but this is not the time to show the white feather. I could not ask for leave now, no matter how imminent the danger. There are over 1,000 Britishers here still, and I and my staff may be of use and assistance to them in an emergency. Certain it is, judging by the numbers that still come to the Consulate, we are required here now.'[61] David Francis had heard the same rumours that 'the Bolsheviks had made a list of people whom they intended to kill, and that, while the British Ambassador heads the list, I am not many removes from the top'. 'I do not believe this,' he reassured his son back home, 'and consequently I am not regulating my actions or movement accordingly.'[62] The pragmatic Phil was, however, preparing himself for trouble:

Some days and nights you will See on the Nevsky Prospect ten or twenty thousand marching with black flags and banners reading we are on our way to kill all Americans and all rich people – that includes me and [whoever] has on a White shirt. I will tell the Gov. that they are on the way again to kill us. The Gov will Say all right are you ready. I will say yes I am all ready so the Gov will tell me to load the Pistol and see if She is in working order. he Says that he will get to or three before he goes.[63]

Despite so much gathering uncertainty, on 19 October Leighton Rogers and his colleague Fred Sikes were excited at the prospect of moving from their present cold and draughty accommodation to a swanky new flat that was being loaned to them rent-free for the next six months, by an American couple connected to the American International Corporation while they went back to the States. It was beautifully fitted out with 'fine rugs, handsome furniture, and tapestries and paintings that [were] a delight to the eye'. And there were books, too, and a 'full-sized Victrola [phonograph] with an extensive library of Gold Seal records', not to mention a modern bathroom and a cook and two maids to keep the whole thing running. It would be good to escape their present noisy accommodation: 'no more shall we hear the girl upstairs play "Get Out and Get Under" twenty times in succession, while members of the All-Siberian Salt Miners or whoever the heavy-footed guests are, dance till the ceiling plaster dusts our carpets.' They had set a date to move in on Sunday 22 October.[64]

Rogers did not of course know that about twelve days previously Lenin had crept back into Petrograd, clean-shaven and disguised in a wig and spectacles, and was now holed up in a flat on the Vyborg Side, plotting the final downfall of Kerensky's government. On the night of 10 October an enervating ten-hour meeting of the twelve members of the Bolshevik Central Committee had been held at which a vote had been carried, by 10–2 (with moderates Kamenev and Zinoviev voting against) for an immediate armed uprising. Lenin was incandescent with impatience; he had been insisting for weeks that the takeover must happen *now*, but several in the leadership were reluctant to strike too early. The people were worn out; would they respond to yet more upheaval, when simply surviving from day to day was arduous enough? The consensus, upheld by Trotsky who had come to dominate the planning of the uprising in Lenin's absence, was that they should exercise caution and wait until the 2nd All Russian Congress of Soviets, due to open on 25 October, which would give the coup greater legitimacy.

This decision was an open secret, and many in the city wished the Bolshevik seizure of power over and done with, 'to relieve this extraordinary situation'.[65] Not least among them was John Reed, who, with Albert Rhys Williams, had resumed his 'restless search' for a story after the Democratic Congress, 'going from the Winter Palace to [the] Smolny, from the US Embassy to Viborg, trying to be everywhere at once, seeking out translators to read the papers, sorting over wildly contradictory statements'. They were, Rhys Williams remembered, 'like the rest of the capital, wearily, doggedly waiting for something to happen. The suspense was like a fever.'[66]

14

'We Woke Up to Find the Town in the Hands of the Bolsheviks'

'The Bolsheviks have advertised trouble again, this time for the 21 or 22 of this month, Russian style,' bank clerk John Louis Fuller wrote in his diary on 11 October, but – like his colleagues, Rogers, Sikes and Swinnerton – he didn't take this latest announcement that seriously. They had heard it all before: 'every time they have advertised their intentions so widely nothing ever happens.' This time, however, there was, he admitted, an ominous atmosphere in the city, and the promise of a renewal of disturbances was reiterated a few days later. 'Trouble is going to come sometime with very little noise,' Fuller was convinced, 'and then it will be real trouble.'[1]

They had all been working flat out at the National City Bank since the recent transfer of twelve of their staff to the Moscow branch, each of them doing the work of four. That Saturday evening, 21 October, had found Fuller working late, one of the last to leave the bank. It was pitch-dark except for his desk lamp: 'If I didn't know there were a couple of soldiers standing guard up in front I'd think I was the only living soul around.'[2] They had run out of kerosene, which meant that during the day-long power cuts they had to struggle to see what they were doing, but once the light began fading, it was too difficult to continue working after 4.00 p.m. In the end, the 21st had passed quietly; Fuller had gone for his regular Russian lesson, and then in search of cherry jam to feed his insatiably sweet tooth; after much trudging around, he came home with seventeen pounds of it and some precious but horribly expensive English milk chocolate. But the jam would have to be eked out slowly, bearing in mind yet more imminent reductions in the bread and tea rations with which to enjoy it. They had all been trying to get hold of eggs, their ration cards entitling them to just one per week. Leighton Rogers had joked that such was the scarcity of eggs that even the hens had now gone on strike. 'Soon we may learn the answer to the question that has puzzled philosophers for centuries: "Which came first, the hen or the egg?" – by learning which will come last.'[3]

Like everyone else at the bank, Rogers had been watching the streets for signs of trouble, but was hopeful that the Provisional Government was merely biding its time and would nip the Bolshevik threat in the bud. While his friend Fuller had been preoccupied by his search for jam that Saturday, Rogers had been out watching parades on the streets – a token show of strength, first by young military cadets from the officers' training school, and then by one of the Petrograd Women's Battalions: 'In new, regulation Russian uniform, with long, belted coats, grey Astrakhan hats tilted at the proper angle and bayoneted rifles held at left shoulder arms, they moved up the street with the full arm swing of the Russian infantryman.' Rogers was impressed, especially when the women started singing. They reminded him of the Valkyries.[4]

The following day, the city remained tense but quiet, although there had been a huge gathering of around 10,000 people at the Cirque Moderne, a huge concert hall north of the Neva that had become a popular venue for political rallies; and at the People's House, another rallying point, Trotsky had given one of his usual lurid speeches, to a crowd who listened with almost religious fervour. The curious ventured out on the streets that Sunday to see what might happen, but the day passed off without disturbance, despite the presence on every corner, as Leighton Rogers noted, of political agitators who 'spoke in frenzied haste and moved on'.[5] Having postponed the move to their new flat for three days, in order for this latest promised explosion of revolutionary violence to be over and done with, he and Sikes had finally decided on a date: Wednesday 25 October. They were very soon rueing that decision.

'They've begun it; they're at it now as I write,' Rogers scribbled excitedly in his journal for 25 October. 'Machine-guns and rifles are snarling and barking all over the city. Sounds like a huge corn-popper. – And we picked this afternoon to move!'

Having left work early that morning to pack up the last of their things, the two colleagues had noticed 'an electric feeling in the air, as if the nerves of a million and a half people were taut'. But after three days of false alarms they had 'paid little attention to it', until they went outside to try and find three *droshkies* to convey their belongings to their new address and found the streets full of people, hurrying, 'almost running, towards the river and particularly towards the Palace Bridge'. They assumed this was because it was going to be raised, as it had been during the last few days, to keep pro-Bolshevik workers and soldiers on the Vyborg and Petrograd Sides out of the city centre. But they needed to cross that bridge to get to their new apartment, and by the time they had managed to corral three *droshkies* and haggle frantically with their drivers on an extortionate price of ten rubles each* to move their trunks, 'the roadways were black with people swarming towards the Palace Bridge'.[6] The *droshkies* were almost carried along by the mob as they set off in that direction. In the struggle to keep the three vehicles containing all their worldly possessions together (worsened by the fact that one of the drivers was dead-drunk), Rogers and Sikes didn't make it to the bridge in time: guards deployed across the road clubbed at

---

* $110 at the October 1917 exchange rate, which had increased from 6.20 rubles to the dollar in January, to eleven rubles to the dollar.

the horses with their guns and forced them back.⁷ The square in front of the bridge was now seething:

> Men and women ran this way and that, shouting and gesticulating; crowds gathered at corners, on the steps of neighbouring buildings, pressed into windows and doorways, massed on the platform and behind the Stock Exchange pillars, strained against the walls of buildings, waiting with that fearful anticipation with which you might watch pressure being applied to a huge rubber band, wondering when it will snap and how painful will be its sting.⁸

Then someone opened fire and, in response, shots rang out on all sides. There was pandemonium – motor cars hooting, tram bells clanging – as the crowd panicked, and their three *droshky* drivers caught in the middle of it 'sprang upright, yanked and sawed at the reins, howling; and with each howl demanded more and more roubles'.⁹ In desperation, Rogers and Sikes urged their drivers to head further along the embankment to the Troitsky Bridge opposite the British embassy, which had not yet been raised. At this point the drunken driver threatened to ditch their trunks in the street and run, 'saying he was a Bolshevik and could do as he pleased'. In response, recalled Rogers, 'Fred and I rose in wrath, brandished our fists in his face, said we ate Bolsheviks for breakfast and if he tried any monkey business we would beat the hell out of him.' That seemed to do the trick – the three *droshkies*, 'with one driver reasonable, another scared to death, and the third drunk', managed to extricate themselves from the mob and headed for the Troitsky Bridge and across to the Petrograd Side; but not without stopping off at their bank, located right opposite the bridge, where Fred dashed in to get more money with which to pay their rapacious drivers. On arrival the men were well rewarded with twenty-five rubles each for their trouble, 'influenced, I suppose, by the wave of religious feeling that had swept over us when the shooting started'. Rogers and Sikes had barely trundled their belongings upstairs to their swish new apartment when 'civil warfare erupted in all parts of the city, machine-guns ripped, and they were at it again'.[10]

It was not till the following morning, however, when walking to work at the bank, that Leighton Rogers finally realised that the government had actually fallen, 'and that my destiny in this country was to be guided from then on by a government of anarchists'.[11] It was a reaction echoed by other foreign residents, who on 26 October discovered that a second revolution had taken place while they had been slumbering in their beds. It had all passed off with so little drama compared to February, noted British embassy counsellor Francis Lindley. 'This morning we woke up to find the town in the hands of the B[olsheviks]' and the takeover appeared to have been fairly low-key: 'I am glad to say there is none of that infernal careering about and shooting in the air at present.' The Provisional Government 'seemed to have disappeared,' he added. 'We don't know where.'[12]

After months of alarms and predictions, the expected Bolshevik coup in Petrograd, when it came, was not the heroic workers' showdown of Soviet historiography, but more an exhausted capitulation of Kerensky's moribund and virtually defenceless government. There is no doubt that by mid-October the Bolsheviks had gained the upper hand in Petrograd, with about 50,000 party members and control of the Petrograd Soviet. They were well armed, and the soldiers and sailors who had gone over to them were increasingly belligerent. For once, Bessie Beatty was finding the city she had grown to love 'desolate, ugly, forbidding'. 'Death was in the air' and at times she tried to shut out her apprehension by curling up with a book of poetry at her hotel. For weeks people had been watching for signs of further turmoil: 'Has it come?' they constantly asked each other. 'Every time the electric light failed, the water was turned off, or some one banged a door or dropped a block of wood, Petrograd jumped automatically to the same conclusion: it has come!'[13]

'Day after day members of the British colony came to my father to ask what they should do,' recalled Meriel Buchanan.

'Was there any hope of the situation improving? Would it be safe for their wives and families if they remained?' It was a huge burden of responsibility for Sir George, but he could 'only advise them to cut their losses and leave'.[14] The Buchanans themselves were packing, for Sir George was scheduled to travel to Paris with the Russian Foreign Minister, Mikhail Tereshchenko, to attend an Allied Conference, and Meriel and her mother were going to travel with him and spend six weeks in England.

The first intimations of 'the approach of a storm', as Sir George put it, came when the embassy was given an armed guard of military cadets on the afternoon of the 22nd, having been told that the Bolsheviks were supposed to be going 'to do something' that day.[15] In response to increasing tension in the city, Kerensky had ordered the two leading Bolshevik newspapers, *Soldat* [Soldier] and *Rabochi put* [Workers' Path], which were openly fomenting trouble, to be closed down; the Provisional Government also passed a resolution to have Trotsky and the members of his newly created Military Revolutionary Committee – who now controlled the army and garrison in Petrograd – arrested, along with the leaders of the Petrograd Soviet. But once again, not wishing to provoke the Bolsheviks into making the first move, Kerensky prevaricated.

Instead, a nominal guard of his government HQ at the Winter Palace was put in place, composed of young and inexperienced cadets, a bicycle squad, a couple of companies of Cossacks and a contingent of about 135 women from the Petrograd Women's Battalion, whom Kerensky had reviewed only the previous day. In all there were about eight hundred troops guarding the palace,* along with six field guns, a few armoured cars and machine guns.[16] The women – some of whom were veterans of Bochkareva's original Death Battalion† – had been expecting to be sent to

---

* Figures vary considerably. The guard may have been a couple of thousand initially, but many deserted their posts in the hours that followed.

† Bochkareva, having recovered from her wounds in hospital in Petrograd, had gone to Moscow to try and get the Women's Battalion there to go with her to defend Riga. In 1919 Bochkareva was arrested by the Bolsheviks, accused of being 'on enemy of the people.' She was shot on 16 May 1920.

the front to fight the Germans and had no desire to defend Kerensky's government. Countess Nostitz had seen them take up their position early in the day. Crossing Palace Square, she 'looked curiously at these girl soldiers as they lounged round the Palace entrances, rifles in hand. They were a motley crowd. Strapping, healthy young peasants, factory workers, harlots recruited from the streets, with here and there slightly older women of another type – intellectuals, pale-faced, fanatical.'[17] Some of the women were busy carting faggots of wood back and forth to build a barricade at the main gateway.

On the afternoon of the 24th Louise Bryant, John Reed and Albert Rhys Williams had had no trouble getting past the cadets on guard at the palace, by showing their American passports and telling them they were on 'official business'. Inside they were greeted by the extraordinary anomaly of doormen still resplendent in their old imperial 'brass-buttoned blue uniforms with the red-and-gold collars', who 'politely took our coats and hats'.[18] They noted an air of nervous anticipation among the cadets, who had made up straw mattresses for themselves on the floor and were huddled up in blankets trying to get some rest; they looked at the Americans in astonishment. 'They were all young and friendly and said they had no objection to our being in the battle; in fact, the idea rather amused them.' Bryant felt sorry for them. They seemed so cultured; some even spoke French. But they had very little food and their ammunition supplies were low and they were already demoralised. With no sign, as yet, of any action at the Winter Palace, the Americans headed back to what, for them, was the real epicentre of the socialist revolution they had come to witness – the Smolny Institute.

A gracious Palladian building fronted by columns and a grand portico, the Smolny was located on the eastern edge of Petrograd and was approached by a broad driveway surrounded, at this time of year, by snow-covered lawns. The original group of five delicate blue cupolas was part of a convent that had been built by Empress Elizabeth in the mid-eighteenth century. Not far from this, a rather more austere three-storey, 600-foot-long structure had been added in the early 1800s as a finishing school for the daughters of the Russian nobility. It was here that the Petrograd Soviet had decamped after its members had succeeded in trashing their base at the Tauride Palace, which was now being redecorated. The arrival of hundreds of political activists and their dirty boots, along with the aroma of unwashed bodies and the stale reek of cigarettes, had soon transformed the Smolny into much the same kind of noisy, overcrowded transit camp, 'thick with the dirt of revolution', as the Tauride had been.[19] By the morning of 24 October the Smolny was the unofficial 'General Staff' of the Bolsheviks – its approach, by necessity, heavily guarded by double rows of sentries at its outer gates and great barricades of firewood. Two naval cannons and a couple of dozen machine guns were also positioned outside, with soldiers with fixed bayonets standing guard in the doorway.

Inside, with its one hundred rooms still bearing the signs of their previous life as classrooms, the Smolny had been hastily adapted to suit the needs of political agitators. Classrooms where daintily dressed girls once studied French and literature and learned needlework and the piano, as well as the dormitories where they had slept in neat rows of beds, were all now turned over to every kind of political committee. Upstairs in the elegant, pillared ballroom with its ornate crystal chandeliers, where until only recently the genteel young Smolny girls in their crisp white pinafores had learned to dance, the Petrograd Soviet was in constant, belligerent session.

For John Reed, Smolny was the place to be, the heartbeat of revolution: it was dynamic, visceral, exciting, invigorating and 'hummed like a gigantic hive'.[20] Albert Rhys Williams's vision was even more utopian; he saw it as a haven, the bastion of a brave new world. 'By night, glowing with a hundred lamp-lit windows, it looms up like a great temple – a temple of Revolution,' he wrote, fancifully seeing the two braziers by the front porticos as flaming 'like altar-fires'. This great new forum, 'roaring like a gigantic smithy with orators calling to arms', would be the place where all the 'issues of life and death' in the new Soviet Russia would be resolved by a superhuman breed of workers – 'dynamos of energy; sleepless, tireless, nerveless miracles of men, facing momentous questions'.[21]

These 'dynamos of energy' were arriving day and night with lorries full of supplies of food, arms and ammunition. Swarms of soldiers and workers trudged in and out of the building, fetching and carrying the huge batches of posters and propaganda being churned out for distribution across the city, and piling it high on trestle tables along the institute's long white corridors, which already languished unswept and littered with cigarette butts and other refuse. There was no formality, no organisation and no sense of precedence to the way the space was utilised; names of committees, scribbled out by hand on a slip of paper, were hastily tacked to walls and doors; meetings were ad hoc, loud, confused, combative and often exhaustingly protracted, as the quartet of American observers soon discovered. As work gathered to fever pitch, exhausted volunteers lay down and slept wherever they could, or grabbed what food was available – cabbage soup, a hunk of black bread, a bowl of *kasha* (porridge) or perhaps some meat of dubious provenance – in the huge refectory in the basement, before heading off for their next meeting.[22]

During the night of 24–5 October, with Smolny welcoming the hundreds of delegates for the 2nd All Russian Congress of Soviets, the Bolsheviks quietly – and almost unnoticed – seized the initiative. Lenin had finally re-emerged from hiding and appeared at the Smolny still wearing his disguise, and with the addition of a bandage round his face to look like someone with toothache. Here he closeted himself in a back room, where he took control, insisting that the Bolsheviks must make a move the following day, the 25th – the day the congress was due to open – 'so that we may say to it: "Here is the power! What are you going to do with it?"'[23] With their ranks bolstered by the defection to them on the Monday of the eight thousand troops of the Petrograd garrison, and with key government buildings lacking any effectual guards, that night Trotsky's Military Revolutionary

Committee sent armed detachments of Red Guards, soldiers and sailors to set up roadblocks with armoured cars and occupy the Central Telegraph Office, the Post Office and the Telephone Exchange. The Mariinsky Palace was surrounded; the State Bank and the Nicholas and Baltic railway stations were soon under Bolshevik control and the major electric power station also fell to them.[24] Finally, at 3.30 in the morning of the 25th, the naval cruiser *Aurora*, accompanied by three destroyers, steamed in from Kronstadt and dropped anchor broadside-on to the Winter Palace. It was clear that the endgame had come for this, the last symbolic bastion of old imperial Russia.

Locked in session with his ministers in the Winter Palace, Kerensky was well aware that he was losing control of the situation. The remaining loyal Cossacks on whom he depended for the defence of the city had refused to do so alone, still resenting his perceived betrayal of their leader, Kornilov, in July. There was no choice but to make a dash to the front for reinforcements. But when Kerensky came to leave, it was discovered that all the government cars parked at the General Staff had been sabotaged – the magnetos controlling their ignition systems had been removed. In desperation he was forced to abandon his ministers at the Winter Palace and commandeer a chauffeur-driven Renault from the American embassy, accompanied by a second car bearing the US flag, to take him to Pskov to rally what loyal troops he had left.[25] With the Provisional Government in disarray, Lenin could wait no longer to announce the triumph of the Bolshevik takeover.

At 10.00 a.m., without the backing of either the Military Revolutionary Committee or – as originally planned – the ratification of the 2nd Congress of Soviets, which would convene that evening, Lenin issued a press release. 'The Provisional Government has been deposed,' it declared; 'Government authority has passed into the hands of the organ of the Petrograd Soviet.'[26] By the time the delegates from all over Russia had finally gathered in the former ballroom of the Smolny that afternoon, a cordon of Bolshevik soldiers and Red Guards were in position surrounding the Winter Palace and manning barricades on the Moika River and the Ekaterininsky Canal approaching it. The telephone wires to the palace were cut (although one direct line was overlooked) and at 6.30 p.m. the Bolsheviks demanded the unconditional surrender of the Provisional Government. This ultimatum expired at 7.10 p.m., but as yet all remained quiet. Voices in the crowd grumbled, 'Why wait? Why not attack now?' Albert Rhys Williams heard the response of a bearded Red Guard: 'No,' he said, the cadets would only 'hide behind the women's skirts … Then the press would say we fired on women. Besides, tovarish, we are under discipline; no one acts without orders from the committee.'[27]

Even at this dramatic turning point, decision-by-committee prevailed and, leaving them to their discussion, the four Americans went back down to the Nevsky, which seemed curiously relaxed. People were out strolling, some clearly en route for the theatre, which is where the four of them should have been heading, for they had tickets for the ballet at the Mariinsky that evening. 'The whole town is out tonight,' remarked Reed – 'all but the prostitutes' – who seemed to have gauged the danger in the air. Eschewing a night at the ballet, the quartet decided to head back to the Smolny for the opening session of the 2nd Congress. 'A strange quiet, an easy quiet, almost a serenity seemed to have descended on the old gray city along with the fog,' noted Rhys Williams. He was taken with how 'orderly, and even rather gentle' this revolution seemed.[28]

Back at the Smolny, the great hall upstairs was crowded to capacity and seething with activity; there was no heating, bar 'the heat of unwashed human bodies', and despite frequent exhortations for the comrades to desist, the air was thick with the fug of cigarette smoke.[29] An interminable wait then ensued for the congress to begin. Eventually a delegate from the Menshevik group informed the delegates 'that his party was still in caucus, unable to come to an agreement'. 'Nerves were at trigger-tension,' recalled Beatty, and the audience grew angry and restive. And then, forty minutes later, 'Suddenly through the windows opening on the Neva came a steady *boom! boom! boom!*' It was the guns of the *Aurora* firing on the Winter Palace.[30]*

Everyone at the Smolny heard the reverberations and thereafter the opening session of the congress descended into chaos, with the more moderate Socialist Revolutionaries and Mensheviks (who had three colleagues serving as ministers in the Provisional Government trapped inside the palace) demanding that the congress's priority should be the urgent resolution of the current governmental crisis, which had brought the country to the brink of civil war. Two hours later, with the 'methodical boom' of the cannons of the Peter and Paul fortress joining in the bombardment of the Winter Palace with live shells and rattling the windows, the delegates were now 'screaming at each other' in discord.[31] In protest, a hundred or more of them walked out to head for the palace to try and secure the safe release of their colleagues. Beatty, Bryant, Reed and Rhys Williams followed. But first they each had to procure an all-important flimsy piece of paper from the office of the Military Revolutionary Committee allowing them 'free passage all over the city'. 'That scrap of paper,' with its blue seal, Beatty recalled, was to 'prove the open sesame to many closed doors before the gray dawn of morning'.[32]

It was now past midnight and the palace was two miles away; there were no trams running and no *izvozchiki* to be seen. Luckily, in the forecourt of the Smolny the group managed to clamber onto a motor truck full of soldiers and sailors who were about to leave for the Nevsky to distribute leaflets. They 'warned us gaily that we'd probably all get killed and they told me to take off a yellow hatband, as there might be sniping,' recalled Bryant.[33] As the truck rattled along at speed, with Bryant and Beatty ordered to lie on the floor and hold on tight, the men hurled sheaves of white leaflets out of the back into the dark and seemingly deserted streets, upon which 'people came darting mysteriously from doorways and courtyards to grasp them and

---

* The charge was actually a blank one, though a myth was subsequently perpetuated that the shots had been live.

read their dramatic announcement: "Citizens! The Provisional Government is deposed. State Power has passed into the organ of the Petrograd Soviet of Workers' and Soldiers' Deputies".'[34]

When the truck turned up into the Nevsky, it headed for the palace, but at the Ekaterininsky Canal the group was allowed no further and had to get off; there was firing going on up ahead and they were refused entry by armed sailors guarding a barricade under a huge arc-light.[35] After some persuasion and the production of their blue passes, they eventually found a Red Guard who allowed them through and up, past a cordon of sailors, to the Red Arch leading into Palace Square, from where all they could hear was the 'crunching of broken glass spread like a carpet over the cobblestones', from the many smashed windows of the Winter Palace.'[36]

It was then, at around 2.45 a.m., that a sailor suddenly emerged out of the darkness. 'It's all over,' he shouted. 'They have surrendered.' Ahead, the Winter Palace – despite the damage to its windows – was lit up 'as if for a fete' and the Americans could see people moving about inside. The four of them 'clambered over the barricades' behind the guards and sailors and followed them towards the great palace, now 'streaming with light', and entered the building through whatever doorway or window they could find.[37]* The remaining terrified young cadets on guard inside were quickly disarmed and seemed grateful to be allowed to leave unscathed. Waving their blue-sealed passes, the Americans entered and watched groups of sailors mount the stairs and begin a room-by-room search for the members of the Provisional Government, who were soon found in the Malachite Hall upstairs, and were led out under arrest.[38] 'Some of them walked with defiant step and heads held high,' recalled Beatty. 'Some were pale, worn, and anxious. One or two seemed utterly crushed and broken.' The Americans watched in silence as the men were

---

* John Reed's more dramatic version of the 'storming of the Winter Palace' (it wasn't) would become the stuff of legend, immortalised in Eisenstein's equally hagiographic 1928 film *October*.

marched away; they were taken to the Peter and Paul Fortress on the opposite side of the Neva. After this the Americans were allowed to go upstairs and take a look for themselves at the council chamber and the 'shattered rooms' scarred with bullets, where the silk curtains 'hung in shreds'.[39] Further on they were stopped by a group of suspicious soldiers muttering accusations that they were despised members of the 'bourgeoisie'. Once again the blue passes saved the day, but not before the men had duly conferred and taken a comradely vote on whether to let them pass.

As the group made its way through the upstairs rooms, it was clear that some of the insurgents had succumbed to the inevitable urge to go on the rampage and had started battering open the piles of packing cases filled with precious artefacts being readied for evacuation; others wreaked their fury by shattering mirrors, kicking in wall panels, rifling drawers – plundering and breaking whatever they did not loot. Offices were wrecked, their cabinets ransacked and papers scattered everywhere. Rhys Williams and Bryant both noted a concerted effort to stop the looting and saw soldiers exhorting the looters, 'Comrades, this is the people's palace. This is our palace. Do not steal from the people.' Upon which, a few were shamed into giving up their pathetic loot: 'a blanket, a worn sofa cushion of leather, a wax candle, a coat hanger, the broken handle of a Chinese sword'.[40]

For those less close to the action, which essentially had been concentrated up at the Winter Palace, 25 October had passed much like any other day. John Louis Fuller had been at his desk at the National City Bank and had noticed little change, beyond a constant toing and froing of men and motor trucks at the barracks nearby – 'Just like a ward head quarters in America at election time'.[41] True, there had been sporadic bursts of gunfire and skirmishes and a renewed presence of armoured cars on the streets, but everyone had become inured to that. 'No one stays at home simply because there is street fighting,' noted Pauline Crosley in a letter that day, and everyone had learned to dodge those parts of the city where they heard shooting. She had held another large dinner party during disturbances only the other evening. But she did admit that things outside were now hotting up: 'there *is* some excitement, and as I write the atmosphere is punctuated by all kinds of shots – rifle, pistol, machine guns, field pieces and large guns aboard ship!'[42] She had seen and heard the flashes of the field guns from the Peter and Paul Fortress, booming out with live shells, but remained unperturbed. Up at her apartment on the French Embankment she was actually more worried about her precious store of 'canned fruit, vegetables, condensed milk, cocoa, etc.', which she had recently received from the States. 'Nothing really worse than what has happened since we have been here can happen,' she added confidently.[43]

That evening the head of the British Chancery, Henry James Bruce, had closed the office early to go to the ballet to see *The Nutcracker* and had arrived there 'peacefully by tram', even though he had heard earlier that afternoon that 'the whole town was in the hands of the Bolsheviks'. Walking back from the theatre, he had thought the streets seemed quiet, until he and his lady companion encountered 'the Lord's own holy racket going on round the Winter Palace, where the government were putting up a last stand'. In the midst of this he had spotted the Chancery porter, Mr Havery, who was diligently walking his usual two miles to the Central Post Office, being stopped by a soldier, and heard him respond 'in his peerless Cockney Russian that he couldn't help him (the soldier's) troubles; he had some letters to post, battle or no battle'. Altogether, Bruce's walk home that evening was 'a very jumpy business', he admitted, but he had succeeded in escorting 'Madame B' to safety on foot 'to a machine-gun obligato'.[44]

The firing at the Winter Palace had in fact ceased at around 2.30 a.m. and the casualties were very few. Only seven had been killed – two cadets, four sailors and one female soldier; fifty had been wounded. 'I have never before seen a revolution in which the government put out of office has been defended by armed women and children alone,' remarked Walter Crosley in disbelief.[45]

In fact many of the hungry and dispirited cadets and Cossacks inside the palace had abandoned their posts well before the insurgents had even arrived, and most of the Women's Battalion, terrified by the bombardment, had taken cover in a back room. Stories later circulated about their maltreatment after they surrendered. Countess Nostitz saw them being manhandled out of the palace. 'Their screams echoed through the square as they fought and struggled in vain. The soldiers shouted with laughter at their efforts to escape, silenced them with the butt of a rifle when they grew too troublesome', as the women were taken across the river to the Grenadersky Barracks on the Petrograd Side, where they were subjected to 'a barrage of verbal abuse' and some were beaten up. Nostitz was right to fear the worst and rang the British embassy, entreating them to 'send someone to make an official protest against the rape of those unfortunate girls'.[46]*

A sense of unreality about what had happened in Petrograd persisted on the 26th. Looking out of the British embassy windows, Meriel Buchanan wondered 'if the thunder of the guns, which had kept us awake, had been for real, for everything looked much as usual. Crowded trams came across the bridge, the pigeons sheltered from the wind on the balustrades of the Marble Palace, and the lovely slender spire of St Peter and St Paul still shone as brightly as ever in a fitful gleam of sunshine.'[47] The streets were full of armed workmen and soldiers, but despite a feeling of unrest and uncertainty, 'the normal life of the town continued as if nothing had happened'. 'The city itself seems to regard the whole event in the light of a pleasant excitement,' remarked a Danish Red Cross worker.[48]

Curious crowds were gathering outside the Winter Palace simply to stand and stare at its smashed plate-glass windows and its walls pockmarked by machine-gun and rifle fire – 'like a case of the measles'. Foreign residents noted how relatively minor the

---

* The most reliable sources suggest there were three cases of rape and one suicide.

damage was, all things considered. 'We walked around the Winter Palace and saw the marks of the fray,' wrote Pauline Crosley, 'but in spite of all the firing *we heard* and the flashes of the guns *we saw*, as well as the short distances concerned, we could only see *two* places where anything larger than a rifle bullet had hit that perfectly enormous building.' A friend had seen the Bolsheviks open fire on the palace with a field gun – and miss several times.[49] In fact, although there were many bullet gouges in the green stucco façade and white columns on the south side facing Palace Square, the palace had only been hit by artillery in about three places on the north side facing the Neva. It turned out that the firing from the Peter and Paul Fortress about four hundred yards directly across the river had been inaccurate; according to French diplomat Louis de Robien, the gunners had managed to miss their target 'with almost every shot, sending their shrapnel either into the water, at their feet, or else to the devil'.[50]

Inside the Winter Palace it was a different story: damage from the occupation by the cadets and Women's Battalion and the subsequent takeover by the Bolsheviks was visible everywhere. Hundreds of muddy footprints had soiled the elegant parquet floors; silk hangings had been torn down and were now being used as bedding. But strangely enough, recalled Julia Cantacuzène-Speransky, 'the rabble had passed by furniture, paintings, porcelains, and bronzes of great value, and had even looked uncomprehendingly at a vitrine full of ancient Greek jewelry wrought in pure gold', although they 'hustled one another to cut leather coverings off seats of modern chairs in anterooms and in the emperor's sitting room' to make and patch boots, and to 'knock down gilded plaster from the walls, sure it must be real gold'. The great Malachite Hall was 'smashed beyond repair, and infinite damage was done to some of the apartments of ceremony.'[51]

On the afternoon of the 26th two anxious-looking officers who had been acting as instructors to the Women's Battalion arrived at the British embassy, begging Lady Georgina Buchanan to 'intervene on their behalf,' fearing, as Countess Nostitz had, that they were 'completely at the mercy of the Red Guards and the Kronstadt sailors'.[52] At Lady Georgina's request, Colonel Knox immediately headed over to the Smolny, where he spoke to 'one or two truculent Commissars and finally persuaded them that their inhuman treatment of these women soldiers would be condemned by England and France'. Shortly afterwards the women were released and escorted to the Finland Station, from where they travelled by train to rejoin their battalion at Levashovo. Before leaving, four of them came to the embassy to thank Knox and asked if they could be transferred to the British army.[53] The women were somewhat contemptuous of their assailants at the Winter Palace. 'As if the Red Guards are soldiers! They do not know how to hold a rifle; they can't even handle a machine gun' – a fact they felt was borne out by the number of shots that had gone wide of the palace.[54]

On 26 October, Lenin issued a proclamation announcing the creation of a new government. In the spirit of the *commissaires* of the French Directory, it was named the Council of People's Commissars, with Lenin as President and Trotsky as Commissar for Foreign Affairs. But this new government did not have the consent of the moderate Socialist Revolutionaries and Mensheviks in the Petrograd Soviet or the ratification of a Constituent Assembly; until then the government of Russia would devolve to a succession of ad hoc committees with no political legitimacy. Nevertheless, at the congress at the Smolny that evening, Lenin – having spent the entire revolution in a back room, rather than leading from the barricades – finally emerged triumphant.

'My eyes were riveted on the short stocky figure in the thick worn suit, a sheaf of papers in one hand, who walked quickly to the podium and swept the spacious hall with his rather small, penetrating, but merry eyes,' recalled Albert Rhys Williams. 'What was the secret of this man who was so hated and loved in equal measure?' he wondered. Lenin did not have the magnetism or commanding presence of Trotsky.[55] In comparison he seemed rather 'pedestrian' in his manner on the rostrum; even John Reed thought he looked faintly absurd, in trousers that were much too long for him. Yet here he was, 'the idol of the mob ... a strange, popular leader, a leader purely by virtue of intellect', whereas the mercurial Trotsky was a leader by oratory.[56] For Rhys Williams, Lenin's first appearance on the podium that evening had 'no more aplomb than a seasoned professor who has appeared daily before his class for months'; he heard a nearby reporter remark that if Lenin 'were spruced up a bit you would take him for a bourgeois mayor or banker of a small French city'.[57] But Lenin's speech, given in a hoarse voice, in which he called for peace without annexations and reparations and proposed a three-month armistice with Germany, received an ecstatic response and shouts of 'Long Live Lenin'. The social revolution begun in Russia, Lenin insisted, would soon break out across France, Germany and England. Let the Russian Revolution mark the end of the war! To which voices broke out in a rousing rendition of the Internationale.

Over-excited by the day's events, the quartet of Americans did not sleep all night. They sat talking and warming their hands at a bonfire in the courtyard outside; it was 7.00 a.m. before they finally got the tram home. In contrast, the more seasoned foreign residents of Petrograd found it hard to raise any sense of excitement, hope or expectation at this latest change of government. Willem Oudendijk had walked through the city with his wife and 'found everything quiet'. 'Thus the second Revolution had been accomplished,' he wrote later. 'We did not realize what a great historical day we were living in as we trod our way home through the perfectly tranquil streets filled with apathetic, indifferent looking people.'[58]

For a couple of days there had been no news of Kerensky. 'No one had the remotest idea' what was going to happen next, recalled Bessie Beatty. 'Where is Korniloff?* ... Where are the Cossacks?' Last and worst of all, 'Where are the Germans? Rumour

---

* Kornilov escaped from jail on 6 November and went south to join anti-Bolshevik Cossack forces in the Don region. He went on to command a volunteer unit against Bolshevik forces, but was killed in April 1918 in the Kuban region of southern Russia.

was riding a mad steed.'[59] In response to the arrest of Kerensky's ministers and the pre-emptive proclamation of power by the Bolsheviks, the moderates on the left had established their own 'Committee for Salvation of Country and Revolution' in order to try and rally anti-Bolshevik groups and ensure that a legitimate government would be voted in by the Constituent Assembly promised for November. By the night of the 27th rumours had begun circulating that Kerensky was on his way with the Cossacks and that they were now at Gatchina, twenty-nine miles to the south. The following day a proclamation was circulated that Kerensky had taken Tsarskoe Selo and would be in Petrograd on the Sunday, 29 October. In response to the news that reinforcements were on their way, and encouraged by the Committee for Salvation to take a stand, early that morning a company of cadets disguised as soldiers of the Semenovsky Regiment, and using false papers and the correct passwords, succeeded in getting past the few Red Guards at the Central Telephone Exchange on Morskaya, while others using the same ruse occupied the Astoria Hotel.[60] At the Astoria, Bessie Beatty was surprised by the youth of their leader, 'a boy officer, a cigarette hanging nonchalantly from the corner of his mouth and a revolver in his hand', who had 'lined the Bolshevik guards up against the wall and disarmed them'.[61]

The cadets – some of whom had been captured at the Winter Palace on the 25th and set free – certainly did not lack courage, but without reinforcements and with very limited supplies of ammunition, and even less sign of proper organisation or leadership, they could not hold out for long. Beatty and Rhys Williams had no difficulty – as '*Amerikanskie tovarishchi*' – getting into the Telephone Exchange two blocks from the Astoria to see for themselves. The cadets seemed to Beatty 'mere children in this business of war' and were building barricades of 'boxes and boards' supplemented with logs from a nearby woodpile to defend their position. Rhys Williams thought they seemed confident of the imminent arrival of Kerensky's troops.[62] From inside the building, he and Beatty watched them take up positions behind the woodpile barricade and a couple of motor trucks, as a 'gale of bullets' came from an attacking force of Red Guards and sailors.

Soon the cadets had retreated to a back room, where they had 'thrown down their guns and were waiting for the end'.[63] In a pantry, Beatty found 'a boy officer with a huge breadknife, trying to cut the buttons from his coat with hands that trembled so they made a long job of it'. Another was desperately trying to tear off his identifying epaulettes. She could not miss the irony: 'suddenly the thing for which these boys had striven – the coveted gold braid and brass buttons of an officer's uniform, symbol of their superiority – had become their curse'. She realised that at that point 'any one of them would have given the last thing he possessed on earth for the suit of a common working-man'. In a corridor she found Rhys Williams confronted by a desperate cadet officer, who was pleading with the American to let him have his coat so that he could try and make his escape in disguise. She saw the anguish in the boy's eyes, but it was clear that Rhys Williams, as a devout socialist, was gripped by a moral dilemma. He had won the respect and confidence of the Russian workers during his time in Petrograd: 'If I give him my coat they will recognize it and think me a traitor.' He couldn't bring himself to do it, and yet both he and Beatty recognised that 'the whole tragic situation was done up in the plight of this one feeble human being trying to save his life'.[64]

In the afternoon the building was stormed. As the cadets were taken away by Red Guards and sailors loudly 'shouting for vengeance', Rhys Williams appealed to them not to 'sully the ideals of your Revolution' by yielding to the temptation to kill them. In their memoirs, Rhys Williams and Beatty remained silent on the fate of the cadets but, as John Reed noted, although most of those from the Telephone Exchange 'went free', 'a few … in their panic tried to flee over the roofs, or to hide in the attic, and were found and hurled into the street'.[65]

All that day Reed had been listening to the 'volleys, single shots, and the shrill clatter of machine-guns [that] could be heard, far and near', as groups of cadets engaged in skirmishes with Red Guards across the city.[66] They also came under siege at two of their bases: the Alexandrovsky Military Academy on the Moika, and the Vladimirsky Military School on Grebetskaya on the Petrograd Side. Those at the Vladimirsky had put up stiff resistance and managed to repel two armoured cars with machine guns, but then the Bolsheviks brought up three field guns and began bombarding them. 'Great holes were torn in the walls of the school,' wrote Reed; the cadets put up a frantic defence as 'shouting waves of Red Guards, assaulting, crumpled under the withering blast'.[67] The firing did not let up until 2.30 p.m. when the cadets were forced to put up a white flag. 'With a rush and a shout,' Reed saw soldiers and Red Guards pour into the school, 'through windows, doors and holes in the wall'. Five of the cadets were savagely beaten and bayoneted to death, and the remaining two hundred who surrendered were taken away to the Peter and Paul Fortress. En route another eight cadets were set upon by a mob of Red Guards and murdered.[68] The Vladimirsky itself was almost reduced to rubble by the Bolshevik bombardment.

Countess Nostitz was horrified by the scenes that unfolded at the Alexandrovsky Military Academy. For her, the 'heroism of these boys, mere children of fifteen and sixteen', had been the 'one redeeming feature in that black day of horrors'. When the college was attacked, some of the cadets had taken cover in the huge woodpiles stacked in front of it, ready for winter:

Routed out, they clambered to the top and fired into the ranks of the Bolsheviks in a last desperate attempt to check their advance. Hopelessly outnumbered, they fought on until their ammunition gave out, then stood, their round childish cheeks chalk-white, waiting for death. It was horrible to watch the Bolsheviks playing with them as a cat plays with a mouse, prolonging the moment of suspense, carefully singling out their living targets till they had shot them all down, one by one.[69]

The cadets' bodies lay there for days untended, 'stacked one on top of the other on the woodpile'. As those inside the academy surrendered, a Red Cross worker recalled how 'at the Moika Canal a number of these young men were lined up, with their hands tied behind their backs, and shot down from behind, falling head-foremost into the water'.[70] Elsewhere, any identifiable cadets found on the streets for the next few days were attacked and murdered by marauding sailors and Red Guards, much as the police had been sought out in February; Louis de Robien saw how a car full of cadets trying to escape had broken down on Gogol Street, and Red Guards had pounced on it and massacred them all; their mutilated bodies were left lying on the pavement for hours.[71] Thankfully, the British had succeeded in safely smuggling out the eight cadets who had been guarding their embassy – and sent them home 'dressed up as civilians'.[72]*

For Bessie Beatty, the rout of the cadets had been 'a day of shame', 'a sacrifice of the innocents as needless as it was useless', and she laid much of the blame on the shoulders of those who had sent these young boys to fight for them while staying safely out of reach. The 'ill-starred Cadet rising' had marked a brief and unequal trial of strength between Lenin's new government and the Committee for Salvation.[73] 'Kerensky has again failed us, as he did at the time of the July rising and of the Kornilov affair,' Sir George Buchanan noted sadly in his diary on 30 October. Having briefly rallied support from eighteen Cossack companies under General Krasnov, Kerensky had accompanied their march on Tsarskoe Selo. But here he had once again prevaricated, and Krasnov had pulled back to Gatchina at the prospect of his

---

* Sir George Buchanan noted with some distaste, however, that while guarding the embassy the cadets had purloined some of its whisky and wine and had drunk themselves stupid and been sick.

1,200 men being sacrificed to a mixed force of 50,000 Bolsheviks and workers, which was now being rallied against them. Soon afterwards Kerensky fled – no one knew where – and went into hiding, before escaping to Finland in May 1918.*

On 2 November, Lenin's government announced the final defeat of the Provisional Government. But it had been a defeat without honour. The abandonment of the defence of Petrograd to 'a few Cossacks, a battalion of women and some children' had, as Louis de Robien concluded, 'only succeeded in alienating everyone'; it had made Kerensky's government 'an object of ridicule'.[74] It had also ensured that the demise of the old bourgeois government – and the inception of the new Soviet one – was 'ignominious, without fanfare, or heroics'.[75]

---

* Settling in France, Kerensky became embroiled in émigré politics and regularly criticised the new Soviet government from exile. He subsequently lived in Berlin and Paris, before settling in the USA in 1940, where he wrote his memoirs and broadcast regularly on Russian affairs. He died in New York in 1970.

15

'Crazy People Killing Each Other Just Like We Swat Flies at Home'

On 17 November, Phil Jordan sat down to write one of his long anecdotal letters describing recent events. It had been a harrowing time; the Bolsheviks, he told Mrs Francis's cousin Annie Pulliam, had 'shot Petrograd all to pieces'. 'We are all seting [sitting] on a bomb Just waiting for some one to touch a match to it,' he added, with his usual vivid sense of drama. 'If the Ambassador gets out of this Mess with our life we will be awful lucky.' For once the redoubtable Phil was anxious: 'These crazy people are Killing each other Just like we Swat flies at home.' Even his boss was admitting to his son Perry, 'I never knew of a place where human life is as cheap as it is now in Russia.' But sad to say, murder and robbery and acts of violent retribution were now so commonplace that he had found himself becoming 'accustomed' to it.[1]

In Moscow the October Revolution had been far more savage and bloody. The cadets there had been 'forewarned and forearmed' and had taken up strong defensive positions in the Kremlin and other strategic buildings.[2] It had taken ten days for the Bolsheviks to wrest power, with fierce battles on the streets and around the Kremlin leaving more than a thousand dead, and with atrocities against the surrendering cadets far more widespread than those in Petrograd. The US consulate had been badly damaged by gunfire; the Hotel Metropole, where many foreign nationals were staying, had been partially destroyed. Leighton Rogers's colleagues at the Moscow branch of the National City Bank – which was housed in Moscow's National Hotel – had had to take refuge in the potato bins in the cellar, where he heard tell they had held a three-day poker game during the worst of the fighting.[3]

In Petrograd both the British and American embassies, although not attacked, had been virtually cut off from the outside world; none of their telegrams were getting through, their diplomatic couriers were not allowed out and their mail was blocked as well. Officials at the US embassy were doing everything possible to induce their nationals to leave Russia the minute they could and, in particular, had been evacuating women and children by the Trans-Siberian Railway. With the first real ice and snow of the winter setting in, on 5 November thirty-five American men, women and children left the city by train, together with many of the members of the US Red Cross Mission who had decided to quit.[4] The problem of getting these nationals out of Russia was manifold: there were wives who did not wish to abandon their husbands; women fearful of travelling alone; people who did not have the money for the fare; even 'enemies who cannot stand the thought of ten days in the same car', as J. Butler Wright noted – not to mention the perilous nature of the journey itself, with trains being stopped and boarded by rabbles of Red Guards at many points along the line. For the British the situation had become even more strained, when Trotsky refused exit permits to members of the colony wishing to leave, in retaliation for the arrest and internment in England of two Bolsheviks who had come to spread anti-war propaganda. 'Britishers, at present, are virtually prisoners in Russia,' Consul Arthur Woodhouse told his twenty-year-old daughter Ella, now safely back in England:

We are having a lively time at this office. Frenzied H.H.H.s ['helpless, hopeless hystericals'] still come along as usual, and refuse to be comforted. I am thankful to say that the bulk of the Britishers has left. Those who are still here would like to do so, of course, but either cannot for lack of means, or, under present conditions, are not permitted to quit.[5]

It was a particularly difficult time for the ambassador, too. Assassination threats were being made against Sir George Buchanan in the Bolshevik press, which derided him as 'Tsar of Petrograd', and it was rumoured that Trotsky was going to have him arrested. Sir George's family begged the ambassador not to go out for his daily walks, but he refused, assuring them that he 'did not take Trotsky's threats too seriously'.[6] He stuck to his guns and, 'with great dignity and determination', also resolutely refused to receive Trotsky and declined his offer of Red Guards 'for the protection of the embassy'.[7] Buchanan informed London that 'the Government is now in the hands of a small clique of extremists, who are bent on imposing their will on the country by terroristic methods', and he would have no truck with them. The Foreign Secretary, Arthur Balfour, had telegraphed from England urging him to return home, but Sir George was adamant: 'It would not do for me to leave Petrograd, as my presence here reassures the colony,' he responded in early November. But his wife, fearful for her husband's failing health, had found it all a terrible strain and admitted they were 'having a horrid time'.[8]

Much like Buchanan and Woodhouse, David Francis had refused to be intimidated; 'I will never talk to a damn Bolshevik,' he had growled, also refusing the offer of Bolshevik guards for the US embassy. 'It evidently never occurred to him to leave his post whatever came,' wrote his friend Julia Cantacuzène-Speransky, 'though he spoke quite frankly of the threats and dangers to which he was constantly subjected.'[9] This was not to mention the strain Francis had been under recently, thanks to gossip within the embassy about his friendship with Russian resident Matilda von Cram, whom he had befriended on the boat from America, and who was still suspected of being a German spy. Separated from his family and increasingly isolated from his disapproving staff, many of whom seriously doubted his professional competence, Francis had doggedly clung to the charming company of Madame Cram – who still visited regularly to keep him company and teach him French – and his staunchest ally, Phil Jordan. But recently Francis's aide, J. Butler Wright, had become seriously worried about the ambassador's health, noting an increased mental and physical exhaustion (Francis often worked till two or three in the morning, as Phil Jordan knew). More worrying, however, was the fact that Francis had become muddled and inconsistent in his official dealings; he seemed to have 'lost his moorings'. On 22 November an encoded cable was sent to Washington, recommending 'that to prevent public humiliation formal orders be sent to [the] Ambassador to hasten to Washington'.[10]

For the many British and American expatriates who could not leave Petrograd there was nothing to do that winter but lie low and 'see how this new government of workers and peasants would be constituted ... and translate their dream into reality'.[11] Smolny remained a cauldron of political debate, rivalry and invective, but the masses had ceased to care and did their best to get on with their lives. As far as Louis de Robien was concerned, the people were 'bored with the whole question'. What did the leadership holed up at the Smolny have to offer them? Certainly not bread. Nothing but 'Theories, dogmas, opinions, doctrines, hypotheses – all expressed in words lacking any sense of proportion'. 'This,' wrote French resident Louise Patouillet, 'is the moral baggage that most of the revolutionary leaders carry with them':

> Meetings with an endless number of splinter groups or plenary sessions, interminable voting on points of order or corrections to the points of order. Useless, and consequently inevitable, debates that go on without a break, all day, all night. An endless stream of speakers whose hands are bound by the chains of party dogma, and who can only see things through their dead, doctrinaire eyes.[12]

What ordinary Russians needed, Patouillet wrote, were 'deeds not words'. Her compatriot Louis de Robien had also become deeply cynical of any prospect of a viable political solution in Russia: 'Parties are founded, cartels are established, people make mergers, Committees are formed, and so are committee Councils, and council Committees: they all claim to be saving the country and the world, but each day one hears of some new split and some sensational new patching-up.'[13]

In this continuing atmosphere of conflict and uncertainly Lenin had pushed ahead, unchallenged, with the Bolshevik programme of socialisation and the systematic destruction of all vestiges of the old imperial order. His first and most dramatic diktat was the Decree on Land, abolishing private ownership and confiscating all such lands for redistribution among the peasantry. The delegates at the Congress of Soviets had unanimously ratified it before the congress was dissolved on 27 October. Freedom of the press was also quashed, although many opposition papers went underground, just as the revolutionary press had done in tsarist times; the State Bank was taken over, and advertising became a state-controlled monopoly. Freedom of speech was remorselessly eroded – first the political clubs were closed, and then all public meetings apart from official government ones were banned.

The Municipal Duma of Petrograd, which till late November valiantly resisted Bolshevik intimidation, was forcibly dissolved at bayonet point and its mayor and councillors arrested.[14] All courts opposing the new Soviet regime were closed, replaced by the Military Revolutionary Tribunal, which proceeded ruthlessly to deal with 'counter-revolutionists', 'speculators' and any other perceived enemies of the new socialist state. 'Petrograd greeted the day of the tribunal's first sitting with apprehension,' recalled Bessie Beatty, pronouncing it 'the beginning of the terror'. On that sombre day 'press and populace discussed little besides the guillotine'.[15] In a final ominous act of official repression, on 7 December a new body for 'Combating Counter-Revolution' was created: the Chrezvychainaya Komissiya – better known by its acronym Che-Ka, and located unobtrusively on the fourth floor of a house on Gorokhovaya.[16] It was here that prominent members of the bourgeoisie and aristocracy (if they hadn't already fled Russia) were brought for interrogation. Sometimes, at night, the occasional crack of a rifle could be heard; there was talk of a trench along a rear wall of the building, where people were taken out and shot.

On 12 November, elections to the long-awaited Constituent Assembly had finally begun. Leighton Rogers found it an inter-esting exercise: there were nineteen political parties vying for seats, and the campaign was a veritable 'battle of posters'. Every-where across the city 'buildings, walls, and all available hoarding spaces [were] plastered with them, as much as ten deep', for as Rogers noted, it was 'considered clever indeed for members of a Party to sneak out at night and cover every opposition poster with one of its own'. One of the groups had an office in his apartment building and 'on three occasions' he had seen their representatives 'setting forth after midnight with rolls of posters and buckets of paste'. 'There may be some truth in the statement made the other day as a joke,' he added, 'that the Party with the most paste and posters will win.'[17]

At the end of the two-week voting period it was clear that the Bolsheviks had not gained the mandate they had confidently been expecting; far from it, they were very much in the minority, with only 24 per cent of the vote. Lenin was incensed and post-poned the opening of the Assembly scheduled for 28 November to the New Year; if he had had his way, he would have done away with it altogether.* The continuing political vacuum was marked by an inexorable increase in Bolshevik tyranny and the arrest and murder of political opponents. Winter 1917–18 inau-gurated what Willem Oudendijk called a 'bayonetocracy' – 'a soldiers' dictatorship', in the words of Louis de Robien – and with it the widespread imposition of summary justice. The rifle

---

* When the Constituent Assembly finally met at 4.00 p.m. on 3 January 1918, it lasted precisely twelve hours. It was dispersed by Lenin at 4.00 a.m. the next day.

and the bayonet ruled in a city swollen with idle soldiers returned from the front, who were noted for their unpredictable, anarchic behaviour. 'Our own bourgeois Revolution of 1789 lapsed into the excesses of the Terror, and ended with Bonaparte and his wars,' noted de Robien. 'But that was not enough to cure us.'[18] He held out little hope for the Russians, having lately witnessed a typical example of the ugly face of mindless, arbitrary violence when he saw 'two soldiers bargaining for apples with an old woman street vendor':

> Deciding that the price was too high, one of them shot her in the head while the other ran her through with his bayo-net. Naturally, nobody dared to do anything to the two soldier murderers, who went quietly on their way watched by an indifferent crowd and munching the apples which they had acquired so cheaply, without giving a thought to the poor old woman whose body lay in the snow for part of the day, near her little stall of green apples.[19]

Anxiety communicated itself wherever one went: 'Never, on any face one passed, did one see a smile,' remembered Meriel Buchanan, 'never, down any of the wide streets was there the sound of a laugh, a note of music, or even the ringing of bells from the churches.' 'By the time I left, this feeling of hatred towards anybody not obviously belonging to the proletariat was almost tangible. One literally felt it, whenever one went out into the street,' remembered Ella Woodhouse.[20]

For the Americans it was just the same; Phil Jordan admitted that the situation in Petrograd was 'something awful':

> Streets are full of all the cut throats and robbers that are in Russia. you can hear the machine guns and cannons roaring all night and day. thousands are being killed. why we are alive I can not tell. they break into private homes and rob and kill all the people. in a house not very [far] from the embassy they killed a little girl and 12 rifle baynets found

stuck through her body. oh the horrible Sights that is to be seen ... I have fond out that the best thing to do right now is keep your mouth shut and look as much like an American as you can ... All the thugs that have been turned out of prison was armed with a rifle ... we cant tell at what minute the Germans will take Petrograd. If they come right at this time I don't know what we would do because we cant get out. we are like a rat in a trap. the Bolshevicks have torn up all the rail roads. I cant tell but this Ford might be a life Saver. All the business houses and banks are closed. The city is pitch dark. At times we only have tallow candles for light, the plants have no coal and Very little wood. The Banks are in charge of the Boshevicks and escaped convicks and thieves are on guard with machine guns and rifles, the food question is growing worse every day ... the Ambassador told me two days ago to be packed with as little as possible because we might have to go and leave it all behind.[21]

The recent Decree on Land – and, with it, the dissemination of Lenin's favourite Marxist dictum that 'property is theft', implying that people should steal back that which had been stolen from them – 'had initiated a stampede'. 'Private property was at public mercy,' wrote Leighton Rogers, as the Bolsheviks urged that it be searched out and seized with whatever force was necessary.'[22] With looting, robbery and murder becoming the order of the day – and night – it was difficult for those foreign observers who had had a degree of sympathy for the ideals of the February Revolution to hang on to their convictions, when they now saw them betrayed daily by the aberrations of the new Bolshevik dictatorship.[23] Even Red Cross official Raymond Robins, who had so eagerly greeted the new dawn of October, telling his wife Margaret that 'This is the Great Experience', was beginning to have his doubts. 'Think of it,' he wrote to Margaret on 8 November, 'the most extreme Socialist-Peace-Semi-Anarchist Government in all the world maintaining its control by the bayonet, proscribing all publications except those that favor their program, arresting persons without warrant and holding them for weeks without trial and without charge.'[24]

The one ray of hope came when, on 2 December, Trotsky announced that the Bolsheviks had agreed an armistice with the Germans; peace negotiations would begin at Brest-Litovsk on the 9th. Everyone wanted an end to the war and a return to normality, for the next act in the drama was now staring Russia in the face: famine. Next to peace, the one and only topic of conversation – not just among ordinary people on the streets, but in the grandest drawing rooms of Petrograd – was 'the best way to get hold of a sack of flour or a few eggs'.[25] 'Even the foreign colony, whose members were far better off than the Russians,' recalled Bessie Beatty, 'heard the gray wolf howling. We were a hungry lot from morning until night. Most of us developed an appetite such as we had never known. We scraped the plates clean.'[26]

Phil Jordan had constantly risked his safety going out in the ambassador's Ford to distant street markets and outlying villages to try and find food. 'After living in a wild country like this for 18 months it makes you feel like there is only two decent places to live,' he told Annie Pulliam, 'one is heaven the other is America.'[27] Just recently, while out shopping, he had been gathering up his purchases ready to leave when 'about three hundred Bulsheviks rushed in the market with cocked rifles'. One of them told him no one was allowed to buy anything in the market any more because 'we are going to take it all for our friends'. 'You get out of here and be dam quick about it. I Said I will not leave this place until my money is returned. he then tol the Clerk to give me my money. they then began … shooting to frighten the people and took every thing in the market.'[28]

With the quest for food proving such a dangerous and costly exercise among the relatively privileged expatriate community, it was no wonder that when Robbie Stevens, director of the National City Bank, gave a Thanksgiving Dinner on 2 November for all twenty-four of his employees, everyone 'turned out in all their glad rags' to enjoy some good food while it was on offer.

While the 'gray wolf' of hunger remained a 'sleeping serpent' and had yet to foment further social unrest in Petrograd, the ever-present menace of alcohol was, as Bessie Beatty observed, far more serious.[29] All foreign observers had agreed that the tsarist ban on vodka sales had been the one thing that had saved the revolution in February from even worse savagery and violence, inflicted by mobs maddened by drink. But on the night of 23–4 November the revolutionaries finally laid their hands on the untapped alcoholic nirvana languishing in the cellars of the Winter Palace.

After the palace was taken, it was discovered that the Tsar's wine cellars were still intact, stashed full of wine, champagne and brandy. Indeed, Petrograd itself still retained more than eight hundred private wine cellars belonging to the clubs and former aristocracy, with one vault alone containing 1.2 million bottles. The alcohol stored in the Winter Palace included priceless bottles of champagne that had 'lain undisturbed for three hundred years', according to Bessie Beatty, all of which was valued at something like 'thirty million rubles'. Once word got out that it was all still sitting there, the Bolsheviks knew that the *tovarishchi* would come running. The Military Revolutionary Committee pondered what to do. They were badly in need of funds and the best and obvious option would be to sell it, perhaps to the British or Americans.[30] A safer option would have been to take it away and dump it wholesale – perhaps in the Neva, before the mob got their hands on it. In the end, the best solution seemed to be simply to send in a contingent of Red Guards 'whose revolutionary spirit was sufficiently strong to withstand the temptation of the liquor', to smash the bottles and then pump out all the alcohol, for the cellars would be awash with it.[31]

The night the Red Guards went in, Bessie Beatty thought 'the whole populace was going to be killed', for she heard the constant sounds of what she thought were rifles going off. But no, it was the sound of the 'popping of thousands of corks' up at the Winter Palace.[32] Inevitably, the men sent in to wreak this destruction could not resist the lure of rare vintage Tokay from the reign of

Catherine the Great, and happily proceeded to drink away 'the inheritance of Nicholas Romanov'.[33] Armed sailors were sent in to try to restore order – but a large crowd of drunken men was wreaking havoc by then, lurching around ankle-deep in the wine from the broken bottles, and would not be dispersed. Shooting and fighting broke out. Finally three companies of fire engines were sent to turn their hoses on the cellars – flooding them and smashing many more of the wine bottles in the process. Several who were too drunk to escape were drowned or froze to death in the ice-cold river water from the hoses.[34] Leighton Rogers heard tell of a soldier on a tram bemoaning the fact that 'sixty-three of his comrades had died in the carousal in the Winter Palace wine cellar, shot by their fellows in quarrels or too drunk to swim the flood created by fire engines'; upon which, a woman sitting across the aisle from him 'raised her eyes piously and sighed, "sixty-three, thank God"'.[35]

News spread fast across Petrograd about the rich pickings to be had up at the Winter Palace. Soon everyone was joining in, recalled Meriel Buchanan: 'Crowds, eager for a little booty, arrived on the scene. Soldiers in motor lorries drove up, and went away again with cases full of priceless wine. Men and women, with their bags and baskets heavy with bottles, could be seen selling them to passers-by in the streets. Even the children had their share of the booty, and could be met staggering under the weight of a magnum of champagne, or a bottle of valuable liqueur.'[36] For days the sour reek of alcohol hung over the Winter Palace.* Even as far along the embankment as the British embassy the air was redolent with it. Soldiers and sailors lay dead-drunk in the snow, which was stained red, not with blood this time, but with wine. 'In some places the crowds scooped it up in their hands, trying to get the last drop of flavour out of it, fighting each other for the remains,' recalled Meriel Buchanan; others lay down in the gutters trying to drink the wine that ran there from so many broken bottles.[37]

---

* What was left of the Winter Palace wine collection was eventually removed to Kronstadt, where loyal sailors smashed it up.

But the pillaging and the deaths did not stop at the Winter Palace; alcohol-lust caught fire among the Red Guards, as well as soldiers and sailors filling the city, and many went on the rampage, breaking into private wine cellars and drinking themselves into a bestial stupor. The English Club soon succumbed, as too did Yeliseev's emporium on the corner of the Nevsky, a favourite of the foreign diplomatic community. The only way that Contant's restaurant managed to protect its wine cellar was by 'installing twenty or so hefty chaps provided with rifles, machine-guns and grenades, whom it pays, feeds, and supplies with drink in abundance'. (By Christmas, Contant's would be the only restaurant still able to serve wine.)[38] Russian friends of the Buchanans started arriving at the British embassy because soldiers had broken into their homes and 'were not only drinking all their wine, but were breaking up the furniture, and, being too drunk to know what they were doing, were indulging in promiscuous shooting'.[39] One night Phil Jordan had heard an 'awful thumping' and breaking of glass three doors down from the embassy, and went out to discover that eight or nine soldiers had battered their way into a wine store and had 'all got as drunk as they could'. The temperature was 18–20 degrees below zero, and yet 'the next morning the Street for one block was full of drunken Soldiers Some Sleeping in the Snow Just as you could in bed'. 'And Mrs Francis think,' he added. 'No law not a policeman or any one to say Stop.'[40]

'The whole of Petrograd is drunk,' admitted the newly appointed People's Commissar for Enlightenment, Anatoly Lunacharsky, in a moment of exasperation.[41] 'Night after night came the sounds of bedlam,' wrote Leighton Rogers, as the drinking continued: 'talking, laughing, shouts, groans, flashes of light in the darkness, glimmerings of candles, shots and frantic stumbling about … the entire city seemed to have caught the carousel fever.'[42] From the British embassy, Meriel Buchanan could hear the pandemonium broken by 'interminable choruses of Russian folk songs'. A thriving trade in stolen booze soon sprang up, with some of the fine vintage wines still bearing the imperial crest being resold by looters. Even members of the British and American colonies admitted to buying some of it. Louis de Robien noted how some particularly enterprising fraudsters had been selling bottles of 'champagne' from the Winter Palace that they had secretly emptied of their original contents during their binges and replaced with 'water from the Neva'. The Bolshevik government meanwhile continued to try and destroy wine stores before the mob got to them: in the Duma cellars 36,000 bottles of brandy were smashed; three million rubles-worth of champagne was destroyed elsewhere. There was, however, one unforeseen consequence of the job of the official bottle-smashers: even if they piously refrained from drinking any of the wine themselves, they became hopelessly inebriated from all the fumes.[43]

As Christmas 1917 approached, life in Petrograd had never seemed more arbitrary, more dangerous. 'The Bolsheviks are nominally at the head of affairs,' wrote Denis Garstin, 'but in reality it's mob law – in which the mob is there but not the law. Trotsky and Lenin, hating the bourgeoisie more and more every day, issue new edicts destroying everything, repudiating debts, marriages, murders, alliances, enemy crimes – oh, they're having a great time.'[44] 'I am afraid of an intoxicated Russian with a gun,' admitted Pauline Crosley who, having opted to remain in Petrograd with her husband, avoided going out as much as possible, in common with most of her friends. Other foreigners who had decided not to leave, such as Paulette Pax, who was determined to fulfil her contract at the Mikhailovsky Theatre, 'for the prestige of France', stayed at home. But she found it hard to endure the endless days shut up in her apartment with her windows shuttered and, finally, took a chance and went out – simply to escape 'the stifling sense of entombment'.[45]

But there was little worth venturing out for, as yet another squalid winter drew in: a frozen Neva and snowbound streets; empty 'churches where nobody prayed'; few functioning trams, and those there were bursting to capacity; half the shops closed and shuttered; prolonged power cuts – made worse by serious shortages of coal, wood, kerosene and candles; bread made of straw; butter and eggs almost unheard of. And all the time the purchasing power of the ruble continued to plummet. 'Comparisons with former prices are beyond the arithmetical capacity of my brain,' Pauline Crosley wrote. 'I simply know that I would rather walk than to pay forty roubles (about $4.00 in our money just now) to an *izvozchik* for a 15 minute ride.' What more could she tell her family back home? 'In general the news is: Petrograd is still here; a part of Moscow is no longer there; many handsome estates are no longer anywhere; the Bolsheviki are everywhere.'[46] And now the banks were on strike. 'All business is running on momentum and nearing the point of immobility,' wrote Leighton Rogers on 29 November. 'So we drag along, hoping each day that the following one will disclose an improvement in the situation; but we have been hoping this for eight months now, and it has grown steadily worse.'[47]

At the beginning of December, Sir George Buchanan fell ill yet again. 'My doctor tells me that I am at the end of my tether,' he admitted. He was forced to agree that he must leave Russia. With the opening of the Brest-Litovsk peace conference on 9 December he had finally, reluctantly, given up all hope for Russia. It was clear to him that the war was 'more hated than even the tsar had been', and for the British mission in Petrograd to continue trying to keep Russia in it was futile.[48] His colleague David Francis, meanwhile, was adamant: 'I am willing to swallow pride, sacrifice dignity and with discretion do all necessary to prevent Russia from becoming an ally of Germany.' But it was too late; on 7 December Phil was writing to Mrs Francis: 'do you know that at the present time that Petrograd is … full of Germans [released POWs] Struting around the Streets as proud as peacocks. All the Russian people are quite happy that the Germans are here. They Say that when the Germans do take Petrograd that we Shall have some kind of law and order to live under.'[49]

On 12 December by the Russian calendar, the British, American and other remaining foreigners shut out the grim realities of starving Petrograd to celebrate Christmas – for by the European, Gregorian calendar it was 25 December. 'In the midst of war and revolution,' Bessie Beatty remembered, 'we not only celebrated Christmas, but we celebrated it twice.' And to her 'sunshine-fed California soul', that Christmas 'stepped ready-made from a fairy tale'.[50] Muddy Petrograd, made even more mournful by the tattered exteriors of the neglected and bullet-marked stucco buildings, was now transformed by the breathtaking beauty of a winter that came 'toppling out of the heavens', with snow piling up 'in billows on roofs and chimneys, and the icycles hang[ing] like crystal fringes from the woodwork'.

Against such a backdrop, Beatty wrote, even Christmas 1917 was magical, 'however empty the shops or troubled the people'.[51] The American Red Cross Mission held a lunch for American correspondents on Christmas Day; a crackling fire was lit and a decorated tree took pride of place. 'We pulled down the blinds and shut out war and revolution, while we laughed merrily over the Russian conception of mince pie.' At their palatial new fourteen-roomed apartment Fred Sikes and Leighton Rogers 'put out a mighty good meal' for some of their bank colleagues, recalled John Louis Fuller: roast goose, vegetables, a 'five layer cake', plus wine – some of it from the Winter Palace and bought on the black market. But the 'best was to come on Christmas night' at a party for the entire American colony, laid on at the National City Bank.[52] Bessie Beatty deemed it 'a triumph, taxing all the ingenuity of a clever woman and half a dozen resourceful men', explaining that 'the miracle of providing food for two hundred people with Petrograd's cupboard stripped almost bare was a real achievement'. The presiding genius of this 'conjuring trick' had been Mildred Farwell, Petrograd correspondent of the *Chicago Tribune*, married to a member of the Red Cross Mission, who organised the obtaining of 'baking powder from Vladivostok, six thousand *versts* away, to make American layer cakes. The eggs came from Pskoff, up near the Russian front. The Ambassador's pantry was robbed of its white flour. And the turkeys came from heaven knows where.'[53]*

That night, recalled Beatty, the old Turkish embassy 'took on all its former glory', decked out in flags and with its huge gilded mirrors reflecting 'a whirling company of women in shimmering frocks and men whose evening clothes had not been out of their creases for many a day'. 'Our plain, bare old counters, only used to having money handed across them were covered with good things to eat,' John Louis Fuller wrote in his journal. 'White bread sandwiches, turkey, chicken salad, cranberries, jam cakes of all kinds and apple pies ... another counter held the punch bowl made of about ten different kinds of wine.' Needless to say, 'before the party was more than half over [it] had all been consumed'. Everyone had a riotous time till 3.00 a.m., dancing to a balalaika band and a twelve-piece orchestra playing the one-step and American ragtime. A Russian guest who was an opera singer entertained with a marvellous rendition of the 'Star-Spangled Banner'. Leighton Rogers waltzed around, 'bumping ambassadors at every step and causing a great jingling of brass-work among the generals present with all their decorations', but he was a poor dancer and gave it up as a bad job.[54]

Over at the British embassy, Christmas night had been rather low-key in comparison, marked by the official farewell for Sir George Buchanan. The Allied Naval and Military Missions were invited, plus one hundred members of staff of the embassy and some Russian friends. It would be the last party held by the British diplomatic community in Petrograd. Luckily there had been no power cut that evening, 'so the crystal chandeliers blazed with light as they had done in the past' and, although he was very unwell, Sir George was there, standing 'at the top of the staircase receiving the guests as they came up, and with his monocle which dangled down from his neck and broad ribbon,

---

* Beatty makes no mention of whether her socialist colleagues Reed, Bryant and Rhys Williams joined in on any of the American colony's Christmas festivities, and their own memoirs are silent on the subject.

look[ing] as much an Ambassador as any Ambassador can look'. Embassy official William Gerhardie recorded the characteristic diffidence with which Sir George responded to a rousing chorus of 'For He's a Jolly Good Fellow' at supper, insisting that he was 'neither jolly nor good' and that 'all he could say of himself was that he was a "fellow"'.[55]

Meriel Buchanan never forgot that last sad party:

> Although the ballroom was stacked with tins of bully beef and other provisions, although every officer there had a loaded pistol in his pocket, and there were rifles and cartridge cases hidden in the Chancery, we tried to forget the desolate streets and the threat of constant danger. We played the piano and sang songs, we drank champagne and laughed to hide the sadness in all our hearts.[56]

Two days after these happy Christmas celebrations, the Bolsheviks put all of the foreign banks in Petrograd under direct state control and sent armed detachments of Red Guards to occupy them. That morning, 14 December, a 'loud commotion and raised voices erupted in the downstairs main entrance' of the National City Bank. The next thing Leighton Rogers and John Louis Fuller knew, 'metal-shod footwear thumped on the marble stairs as a squad of Bolshevik soldiers clattered into our banking rooms'. The men were led by a 'strutting little red-head in officer's uniform, black leather boots and all', who banged a long blue revolver on the counter, 'flourished a grimy document, and announced that by order of the People's Commissars he was seizing the bank and closing it'. The staff were ordered to hand over all keys, and their ledgers too were to be confiscated.* Despite their lack of Russian, the desk clerks got the gist of 'Red's' message (as Rogers nicknamed him) and closed up their ledgers and handed them

---

* According to Rogers, the National City Bank of New York was the first American financial or business institution to be taken over by the Bolshevik government.

over as the soldiers 'echeloned along the counter and rested their rifles on it, bayonets bristling'.[57] By now the manager, Steve, had emerged from his office to discover that his bank belonged to the Russian people, and to be told by 'Red':

> You will have to go with me to the State bank ... In your automobile.
> 'I haven't got one,' Steve protested.
> 'You're a bank Director – you must have an automobile.'

Fortunately Steve's Russian was good and he proceeded to explain in no uncertain terms that 'this was an American bank and Americans were democratic, unpretentious people who didn't always furnish their bank Directors with automobiles'.[58] Having pondered this, Red announced that all of the bank's cash would be confiscated. Unfortunately, with the State Bank closed, they only had a few thousand rubles in the tills at the time. Red was visibly disappointed. It turned out that it was a prearranged given that any Bolshevik units sent to 'nationalise' business institutions were allowed to divide between themselves whatever cash they found there. 'On the assumption that an American bank would be piled to the rafters with loose cash a lottery had been organized, with the winning squad drawing the American assignment.' Red was furious: 'What kind of a bank is this, anyway?' he shouted. 'No automobile for the Director and hardly any money in the cash-drawer ... I'll have to explain to them' – upon which he informed his men that the lack of cash was due to the trickery of the devious Americans, 'which just proved that we were dangerous people, the worst enemies the proletariat could possibly have'. 'Weren't we bankers,' he shouted, 'and didn't that make us capitalists; and weren't we foreigners, and therefore international capitalists? There wasn't any lower order of the human race, he said, in admonishing his men to keep close watch on us.'[59]

After taking the keys to the safe and strong boxes and informing the clerks that they were all under house arrest, Red carted

Steve off to the State Bank to release more funds. Meanwhile about a dozen '*soldati*' stayed on guard in the hall, 'sitting on our gold furniture', Fuller remembered, gorging on the bank's precious supply of bread, and lying down to take a nap on the period sofas and chairs. The young bank clerks sat there disconsolately until someone remembered the gramophone they had used for the Christmas party, brought it in and began playing American ragtime. One by one the Bolsheviks guarding them left their posts and gathered round to listen. When Red returned hours later with Steve, 'that's the way he found us,' recalled Rogers, 'with a couple of Russian Guards trying to dance to the Amerikansky capitalistical music'.[60] Red's occupation of the bank lasted well into the New Year; Rogers recalled him strutting around 'like a kingpin': it was 'the great moment of his life and he [was] making the most of it'. Such was his dictatorial behaviour, however, that Rogers feared Red was getting 'a bit Napoleonic'.[61]

Similar peremptory Bolshevik takeovers were made of British businesses across the city. Mechanical engineer James Stinton Jones had returned in September to wind up his business affairs and transfer his money to London, but had been very uneasy at the 'prison atmosphere' that he had found in Petrograd. The bank holding his money had now been taken over by Bolsheviks, but he demanded – and managed to get – 500 rubles (about £50) from his account. It was not enough, however, to pay the staff at his office and workshop, whom he was forced to sack. Then one morning the Bolsheviks came and demanded the keys to his workshop and stores, containing £20,000 worth of machinery and equipment. They returned soon afterwards for the keys to his flat:

'What do you want?' I asked …
'Hand over the key of your flat to Comrade ——, the bearer of this letter.'
'What do you mean? It is evening, it is cold, what am I supposed to do?'
'That is your business.' Then, looking at the coat rack, he enquired, 'Is that your cloak and galoshes?'

'Yes.'

'Take them.'

I turned to go into the room and he asked me where I was going.

'I am going to the bedroom to get the photograph of my mother.'

Again pointing to my coat, he said: 'Get your coat and galoshes.' As I gave the key to him, I was left with only the clothes I was wearing.

Stinton Jones returned to England after having spent most of the last thirteen years in Russia, taking with him only those clothes and what remained of the 500 rubles.[62]

During her final two weeks in Petrograd, Meriel Buchanan found it very hard not to cry. In leaving Russia, she felt as if she was 'deserting somebody I had loved very dearly, and abandoning them to die in utter misery. Day after day I went to say goodbye to one more building, to one more place which had become dear and familiar: the Kazan Cathedral on the Nevsky … the Alexander column in the Winter Palace square; the beautiful equestrian statue of Peter the Great by Falconet.'[63] She felt far more pain at leaving the city than at making choices about which possessions to pack in the one small trunk allotted her. Her heavy white Russian *shuba* lined with grey squirrel and with a fox-fur collar, her ornate court dress and train of silver brocade had to be left; her Siamese cat, too. The embassy silver was sent on by sea from Archangel, but much of the beautiful furniture collected by her parents during their long years in diplomatic service in Europe – the antique Dutch cabinet, French Empire chairs, Marie Antoinette's writing table, the Aubusson carpet – all had to be left behind.[64] The day before their departure she walked 'rather sadly through the desolate silent streets of the town which had become, after so many years, almost a home to me, and which I felt I would never see again'. It was intensely cold, with an icy wind blowing from the river, the snow piled high by the

24. An artist's rendering of the attack on the Hotel Astoria, 28 February 1917.

25. The lobby of the Astoria after the attack, its floor bloodstained, a revolutionary sentry on guard.

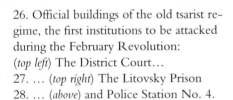

26. Official buildings of the old tsarist regime, the first institutions to be attacked
during the February Revolution:
(*top left*) The District Court...
27. ... (*top right*) The Litovsky Prison
28. ... (*above*) and Police Station No. 4.

29. A burnt fragment of a secret police record picked up on the street by
American bank clerk Leighton Rogers.

30. Soldiers digging the mass grave for the victims of the February Revolution at the Field of Mars.

31. The funeral procession for the dead of February.

32. A crowded session of the Petrograd Soviet in the Tauride Palace.

33. Romanov coats of arms are burned in Petrograd, May 1917.

41. Сожженіе гербовъ въ дни революціи

4. Troops of the Petrograd Women's Death Battalion.

35. Commander of the Women's Death Battalion Maria Bochkareva with Emmeline Pankhurst, their mutual regard clear.

36. Jessie Kenney, suffragette and former mill worker who accompanied Emmeline Pankhurst to Russia.

THE DAILY MIRROR, Wednesday, September 19, 1917.

"THE VICTORY IS OURS," SAYS GENERAL SMUTS

The Daily Mirror

CERTIFIED CIRCULATION LARGER THAN THAT OF ANY OTHER DAILY PICTURE PAPER

No. 4,338.   Registered at the G.P.O. as a Newspaper.   WEDNESDAY, SEPTEMBER 19, 1917.   One Penny.

CROWD MOWN DOWN BY MACHINE GUNS AT PETROGRAD

A terrible scene which occurred in the Nevsky Prospect, Petrograd's famous thoroughfare, during the Revolution: There were deadly encounters between the Leninites, the tools of German agents, and those who wished the war to be fought to a finish. The photograph shows the panic which occurred when the Leninites opened fire with machine guns on the crowd. The people are rushing wildly in all directions, while in the centre of the roadway a mother can be seen trying to shield her child.

D.S.O. A BRIDEGROOM.	FATHER'S COME HOME FROM CAPTIVITY.	A COLONEL'S WEDDING.

Major C. H. Fair, D.S.O., of Winchester, and Miss Marjorie Secretan, of Hemel Hempstead, were married in London yesterday.

Major the Earl of Stair, Scots Guards, who was recently repatriated, is now at Lochinch Castle, his seat in Wigtownshire, and here he is seen in the grounds with his five children. He was accorded a great reception by the tenantry.—(Exclusive to The Daily Mirror.)

Lieutenant-Colonel H. Cecil Batcher, D.S.O., and his bride (Miss Hester MacLeod) leaving St. Margaret's, Westminster, yesterday.

37. The *Daily Mirror* front page reports the July Days violence in Petrograd.

38. The American journalist John Reed, a 'charismatic socialist and professional rebel'.

39. Feminist journalist Louise Bryant, who travelled to Russia with Reed, her husband.

40. People run for cover during a gun battle on Nevsky Prospect in October 1917.

41. A room in the Tsar's Winter Palace, ransacked by the Bolsheviks after they took the Palac with little or no resistance.

roadsides. In an empty St Isaac's Cathedral she lit a candle at the icon of the Miraculous Mother of St George. That evening she dined at the Military Club on the Millionnaya with Colonel Knox and other military attachés who would be leaving Petrograd with them.[65]

Her father was equally melancholy: 'Why is it that Russia casts over all who know her such an indefinable mystic spell that, even when her wayward children have turned their capital into a pandemonium, we are sorry to leave it?' he asked in his diary.[66] On Tuesday 26 December 1918, at 7.45 a.m., the Buchanans left the embassy in the darkness of another power cut, making their way downstairs by the light of a flickering kerosene lamp, past the portraits on the landing of Queen Victoria, King Edward and Queen Alexandra, King George and Queen Mary. Their sobbing Russian maids saw them into their car, which jerked off slowly through piled-up banks of snow to the bleak and freezing Finland Station, where they were waved off by a few diplomatic colleagues and members of the British colony. A bribe of two bottles of finest embassy brandy had secured them a sleeping car to themselves.

Willem Oudendijk had gone to the embassy the previous day to wish his colleague farewell. 'Seldom,' he wrote, 'has any British diplomat left his post under more dramatic circumstances than Sir George Buchanan did on that occasion. He had been an extremely popular figure in Russian society; he had succeeded in making himself the most important member of the whole diplomatic body.' From the outbreak of war in 1914, when Sir George had been looked up to for his moral support of the Russian nation, he had been forced to watch in dismay the slow, inexorable 'crumbling of everything that held the Russian nation together' and to find himself the object of Bolshevik hatred as an enemy, a representative of 'the English bankers, generals and capitalists who desired nothing else but to feast on the blood of Russia's toiling masses'. 'What diplomat has ever lived through such heart-breaking changes during his tenure of office?' asked Oudendijk. 'In the midst of all this turmoil Sir George Buchanan stood like a rock, unperturbed; in looks, in words, in deeds a perfect British gentleman.'⁶⁷*

Buchanan's American colleague, David Francis, remained in Petrograd, however, under instructions from Washington (which had thought better of recalling him at this critical time) to do his best to effect a rapprochement with the Bolsheviks. The faithful Phil had been hoping to see his boss (whose health, too, was failing) home to safety. 'I am all packed up ready to fly at a minutes Notice,' he told Mrs Francis, adding that 'At times I wish the Ambassador did not have So much of that Kentucky blood in him and then mabe he would not take Such chances.' He was worried that the ambassador seemed intent on remaining in Petrograd 'Just a little longer than he ought to'.⁶⁸

As Russia saw out its old, Orthodox year, over at the French Embankment, with a blizzard raging outside, Pauline Crosley had been able to get enough wood to have an open fire in one room, lit by candlelight and kerosene lamps, where she and her husband had managed to entertain a few visitors. But they were only too aware of the 'evident effort to drive foreigners out'. It was so disheartening. 'Russia is a wonderful country,' she wrote, 'full of lights and shadows, though just now the shadows have the advantage. It is too bad that the world must lose so much that was beautiful in Russia to receive – what? Something much worse than nothing.'⁶⁹

Leighton Rogers had seen out the old year by taking a walk up the Nevsky, but it had only convinced him 'beyond doubt' of Russia's present economic and social disintegration. He could see it on every face he passed:

the frantic throng on the sidewalks, ragged, gaunt, worried, with the look of the fugitive imprinted on their pallored

---

* British chaplain Bousfield Swan Lombard wrote to his wife that he was 'pretty certain that Georgie Porgie only got away just in time' and that had he remained in Petrograd he would have been arrested by the Bolsheviks, as was the Romanian minister, Count Diamandi, early in the new year.

faces, hurrying along as though driven before a storm of unknown forces. People with rude bundles, some with hard-won loaves under their arms, and others with neither bundles nor bread, only the hunger for it. Thin, aged children forced to labor before their time; crippled soldiers turned out of hospitals by their native country with no other payment for their sacrifice than the privilege of begging on its streets; and professional beggars everywhere – blind, you say? Absolutely eyeless. The whole thing more like a conception of Doré than reality – a panorama of 'les miserables'.[70]

As the last day of 1917 turned, there was one comfort at least for Rogers: 'a letter from home – the first in a long time'. Written in September, it had taken four months to reach him. He was sad and dispirited, and thinking more and more about friends back home who had left for the Western Front. Petrograd had worn him down. After more than a year he had decided to quit the bank and join them. 'The Bolsheviks have stolen the Russian Revolution and may endure,' he wrote as he looked back on his time in the city. 'I hope not, fervently, but it is a possibility that must be faced … The future in Russia is dreadful to contemplate. Not only is she out of this war but she is out of our world for a long time to come. We had better make up our minds to that and concentrate on our own fight.'[71]

POSTSCRIPT

The Forgotten Voices of
Petrograd

Sir George Buchanan and his family arrived by boat at Leith in Scotland on 17 January 1918 and travelled back to London, to congratulatory messages from the British government and lunch at Buckingham Palace. But his health collapsed entirely soon afterwards and he took an extended rest in Cornwall. By now committed to the idea that only an armed Allied intervention would save Russia, he gave numerous talks on the subject and was deeply despondent when that intervention (of 1918–19) failed. Sir George was also bitterly disappointed not to be offered a peerage for his long years of service to British diplomacy, and felt humiliated by the derisory compensation offered him by the government for the loss of his property and investments in Russia. The invitation to take up the ambassadorship to Rome in 1919 for only two years seemed a clear indication that his services would no longer be required thereafter.[1]

On her return to England, Lady Georgina continued to work tirelessly for British and Russian refugees of the revolution, but in Rome she fell terminally ill with cancer and her suffering blighted the family's time there. She died in April 1921, shortly after they returned to England.[2] With the help of an editor, Sir George turned his Petrograd diaries into a book, *My Mission to Russia and Other Diplomatic Memories*, published in 1923; he died the following December. His daughter Meriel wrote several books about her time in Russia, including *Petro-grad, The City of Trouble* in 1918 and, in 1932, *Dissolution of an Empire*, in which she defended her father's reputation after he had come under unjustified attack for not doing enough to effect the evacuation of the imperial family to the safety of the UK in 1917.[3]

After the departure of the Buchanans, the British embassy in Petrograd was left with a skeleton staff of 'Last-Ditchers', headed by the consul Arthur Woodhouse, who was entrusted with the increasingly onerous responsibility for the well-being of the several hundred British subjects, mainly women, who remained in the city. Together with members of the British military mission, Woodhouse managed to get much-needed supplies of food to them as the situation got ever more desperate. But on 31 August 1918 a group of Red Guards forced their way into the embassy and, during the ensuing mêlée, naval attaché Captain Francis Cromie was killed.[4] Thirty embassy staff and officials were arrested, including the chaplain, Rev. Bousfield Swan Lombard, and Consul Woodhouse. They were incarcerated in the Peter and Paul Fortress until October, when they were finally released and evacuated to England via Sweden. For some time the embassy stood empty and neglected; by 1920 it was in use as a storehouse for confis-cated works of statuary, furniture and art, 'like some congested second-hand art shop in the Brompton Road', before they were sold off by the Bolsheviks.[5]

In February 1918, with Russian peace negotiations with Germany having ground to a stalemate, the German army had advanced to within one hundred miles of Petrograd. On 11 March the Bolshe-viks therefore transferred the seat of government to Moscow and the remaining members of the diplomatic community were evacu-ated to Vologda, 350 miles south. Many of David Francis's American colleagues left Russia at this time but, with the departure of Sir George Buchanan, Francis had become dean of the Allied dip-lomatic corps and was determined to hang on, claiming he did not want 'to abandon the Russian people, for whom I felt deep sympathy and whom I had assured repeatedly of America's unselfish interest in their welfare'.[6] Phil Jordan was, however, now anxious to leave; after several break-ins at other embassies in Petrograd he had come to the conclusion that the Bolsheviks 'don't respect foreign embassies any more'.[7]

On 26 February 1918* the American diplomats left Petrograd by special train for Vologda. Here Francis and Phil settled in surprisingly happily, making themselves at home in a simple but 'dandy' (so thought Phil) two-storey wooden house on the main high street where, for the next five months, visitors could enjoy the informal 'clubhouse atmosphere' and the stranded diplomats spent their evenings playing poker and smoking cigars. They drank bourbon when they could get it or otherwise 'plumped for vodka'. They had taken the good old Model T Ford with them and Francis used it to drive around seeking out potential sites for a golf course in the area.[8] But in October 1918, with civil war now raging in Russia, Francis fell ill with a severe infection of the gall bladder and had to be evacuated by US cruiser from Murmansk. Phil nursed him through a high fever during an extremely stormy sea crossing.

After recovering at a naval hospital in Scotland, Francis was transferred to London. Shortly after Christmas 1918 the proud Phil Jordan accompanied him as valet to a dinner with King George and Queen Mary at Buckingham Palace. When they finally returned to the States in February 1919, Phil was again accorded the ultimate accolade – an invitation to the White House. 'I was born in Hog Alley,' he later remarked, 'and I think you know that a kangaroo can jump further than any other animal, but I don't believe he could jump from Hog Alley to the White House – that was some jump.'[9] In 1922 Francis suffered a stroke and never really recovered his health. He died in St Louis in January 1927, having ensured that his sons would take care of the ever-present Phil, who was provided with rent-free

* New Style; the Bolsheviks finally adopted the Western calendar on 1 February OS, instantly adding thirteen days to make it 14 February.

accommodation and a small trust fund until his death from cancer in Santa Barbara in 1941.[10]

With Russia's withdrawal from the war, the Allied hospitals in Petrograd were closed down. Lady Georgina Buchanan's British Colony Hospital had already closed in July 1917, partly due to a loss of morale at the erosion of good manners and respect shown for its work by the Russian patients, but also because there were fewer of them – mainly cases of scurvy. Those wounded who remained had, since the revolution, become increasingly obstreperous.[11] The committee of the American colony hospital also voted to close its establishment – the only wounded Russian soldiers left, as Pauline Crosley noted, 'were those wounded fighting amongst themselves' and it had become 'too dangerous for the colony women to work there'.[12] Their unused supplies were handed over to the Salvation Army to distribute.

The days of the Anglo-Russian Hospital's usefulness had also come to an end, and in November 1917 the London committee that funded it voted to withdraw its hospital facilities on 1 January 1918. There was, however, the question of 'what was to happen to the hundreds of pounds worth of beautiful instruments and equipment' that it contained. Francis Lindley reported that a Red Cross commissioner 'suggested that it should be made over to the Soviets', but the administrators were loath to do this, knowing that it would either be purloined or wilfully destroyed. Instead everything was secretly packed up and taken to the Finland Station, and from there sent to Archangel under the protection of a British Armoured Car Division. It eventually arrived back at Red Cross HQ in London, 'which was better than being left to be wasted by incompetent Soviets'.[13] In 1996 the Russians placed a plaque commemorating the ARH at the front entrance of Grand Duke Dmitri Pavlovich's palace,* which can still be seen today.

The ARH's founder, Lady Muriel Paget, stubbornly refused to give up on her Russian relief work, however, and remained in

---

* Now known as the Beloselsky-Belozersky Palace.

Kiev, organising famine relief and running soup kitchens for six thousand people – eventually leaving in February 1918 via Siberia, Japan and the USA. In 1924 she set up the British Subjects in Russia Relief Association to help those still stranded in Russia, many of whom were eventually evacuated to Estonia. Of the many nurses and VADs who worked at the ARH, aside from the well-connected Lady Sybil Grey and Dorothy Seymour, we know virtually nothing of their later lives, though one or two of their memoirs and letters have surfaced, thanks to an extensive search in the course of research for this book.

While the careers of some of the British and American diplomats in Russia have already been written about and their archives survive (if scattered across the UK and USA), we know almost nothing, after they left Petrograd, of the many still-unsung and now long-forgotten expatriates – the nannies and governesses, engineers, businessmen and entrepreneurs, their wives and children – who lived and worked in the capital and wrote so vividly and movingly of their experiences in their diaries and letters home. Some, like Bousfield Swan Lombard, chaplain of the English Church in Petrograd, suffered persecution under the Bolsheviks. Bousfield remained loyally at his post after many in the British community had left, driven by a strong sense of responsibility for the 400 or so fellow nationals still stranded in the city – many of them teachers and governesses who had been in Russia all their lives and had 'sunk all their savings in some bank'. But Petrograd was such a dispiriting place to be, 'like a city of the dead', a place of 'lawless stagnation', as he told his wife back home, and he was hugely relieved to finally leave Russia in October 1918 after his release from prison.[14] Having lost virtually everything, Bousfield was compensated by the government for his eight years of loyal service in Russia to the measly tune of £50, upon which £43 16s. 7d. was immediately clawed back for the cost of his repatriation to Britain. Bousfield's and other valuable testimony relating to Petrograd in 1917 is held at the Leeds Russian Archive, which is a treasure trove of memory of the British colonies in Russia from the nineteenth century.

It is hard to be certain exactly how many British, American and French newspaper correspondents (not to mention other foreign reporters) came and went in Petrograd during 1917, as many were not given bylines in their press articles and only a small proportion of them published memoirs. But what is striking is how many there were of them, and how doggedly – cheerfully even – they endured the terrible privations of cold and hunger along with the rest of the population. These journalists often mention each other, in passing, in their own writings, but because of the jobbing nature of their work, always on the move from story to story, virtually nothing has survived of their archives – and, more disappointingly, of the photographs that several of them took.

Arno Dosch-Fleurot spent the rest of his life working as a newspaper correspondent in Europe, and was one of the first reporters to enter Germany at the end of World War I; he tried several times to return to Russia to write on the new Soviet state, but was refused permission. He later married a Russian and lived in Berlin in the 1930s, where he witnessed the rise of Hitler; on the outbreak of World War II, the Nazis arrested him and he was held in detention for fifteen months. For the remainder of his life he was Spanish correspondent for the *Christian Science Monitor*, dying in Madrid in 1951.[15] His book *Through War to Revolution* – poignantly dedicated to 'The Unknown Russian Soldier over whose tomb burns no flame' – describing his experiences on the Eastern Front and in Russia, came out in 1931, but is one of many accounts of Petrograd in 1917 that has been too long overlooked.

A similar fate has been shared by Isaac Marcosson's *The Rebirth of Russia*, published soon after he left Petrograd, as well as his other journalism on the subject. Marcosson returned to Russia in 1924, shortly after the death of Lenin, to see the extent to which 'the iron hand of Bolshevism had strangled freedom'. He found the country in an alarming state of 'dilapidation' and its beautiful, historic churches 'converted into stables'. It was a chilling experience and he was glad to bid farewell 'to espionage, tapped telephones, opened mail, incessant smells, and the oppression that attends constant surveillance'. On his return he wrote an excoriating indictment of the Soviet Union in a series of twelve articles for the *Saturday Evening Post* entitled 'After Lenin – What?' The Soviets promptly banned the newspaper, and Marcosson, from Russia.[16]

The most notable journalists – aside from British newspaperman Arthur Ransome, who went on to enjoy a celebrated career as a writer – remain the 'Four Who Saw the Sunrise', as Bessie Beatty alluded to herself and her companions John Reed, Louise Bryant and Albert Rhys Williams in the dedication to her 1918 book *The Red Heart of Russia*. Beatty returned home to a successful career in journalism and for many years hosted a popular New York radio show, before dying in 1947. Rhys Williams remained a committed communist activist and, unlike many of his anti-Bolshevik fellow journalists, was welcomed back to the Soviet Union on many occasions between 1922 and 1959; he died in 1962. His unrepentant support for the new Bolshevik Russia was in stark contrast to the utter dismay of Harold Williams, who had shown such passionate support for the ideals of February, only to see everything he hoped for stripped away and destroyed in the early months of 1918. 'If you lived here you would feel in every bone of your body, in every fibre of your spirit, the bitterness of it,' he wrote in the *Daily Chronicle* of 28 January 1918:

> I cannot tell you all the brutalities, the fierce excesses, that are ravaging Russia from end to end and more ruthlessly than any invading army. Horrors pall on us – robbery, plunder and the cruellest forms of murder are grown a part of the very atmosphere we live in. It is worse than Tsarism … The Bolsheviks do not profess to encourage any illusions as to their real nature. They treat the bourgeoisie of all countries with equal contempt; they glory in all violence directed against the ruling classes, they despise laws and decencies that they consider effete, they trample on the arts and

refinements of life. It is nothing to them if in the throes of the great upheaval the world relapses into barbarism.[17]

Although the American quartet of fellow socialists all produced memoirs of their own, more optimistic experience of Russia in revolution, it is John Reed's account, *Ten Days that Shook the World*, published in 1919, that eclipsed them all, further aggrandised by Warren Beatty's 1981 Hollywood film *Reds*. History has since criticised the four friends for playing into the hands of the Bolshevik propaganda machine as Lenin's 'useful idiots' – a term frequently applied to fellow travellers of the revolution. The brash and charismatic Reed lived fast and hard, pushing his health in the face of chronic kidney disease, and paid the inevitable price. He died young, of spotted typhus, in Moscow, after being persuaded back to Russia in 1920 to attend a congress in Baku. He was accorded a hero's burial in the Kremlin Wall, and Eisenstein's later film *October* was renamed after the title of his book, but Stalin was none too happy with Reed's account and ordered the bowdlerisation of the Russian translation, to diminish Trotsky's role and accentuate his own.

Reed's widow Louise Bryant, who made it to Russia just in time to sit by her husband's deathbed, continued with a sporadic career in journalism and remarried in 1923, but her drinking and ill health led to her early death in 1936. Her third husband, diplomat William Bullitt, laid a wreath on Reed's grave on a visit to the Soviet Union in 1932, but when the plaque commemorating Reed at the Wall was sought out by visitors in the early 1960s, it was discovered that it had been quietly removed and his ashes reburied in a new, collective site behind the Lenin Mausoleum, reserved for 'fallen heroes' of the revolution.

As for the intrepid duo of Florence Harper and Donald Thompson, it is greatly regretted that nothing is known of Harper's subsequent career after leaving Petrograd, aside from a handful of articles about her time in Russia that she published soon afterwards, including one for the *Daily Mail* in which she vividly described her own and Thompson's 'mad chase' following the story of the 'B-V (Bolshi-Viki)'.[18] Back in the USA, she featured in an interview with the *Boston Sunday Globe* in June 1918, in which she talked of her good fortune in coming through the February Revolution 'without a scratch':

> I have been in Petrograd during the Bolsheviki uprisings, sometimes out all night. I have been in street riots in Moscow, I nursed at the front, got trench fever, and trench foot, crossed the North Sea, sailing on a transport that four submarines chased, and am still alive and well. My friends say that they will have to tell off a firing squad for me on Judgment Day.[19]

Beyond this, Florence Harper simply disappears from view, and from the record.

Despite vowing he would never enter a war zone again, Donald Thompson was back in Russia the following summer – trailing the US intervention forces in Siberia. Like many others, he optimistically hoped that the Allied Intervention would bring about a counter-revolution and the end of Bolshevik tyranny, but after several months filming in Russia and watching the disarray in the Allied forces, he returned home disappointed. Nevertheless he became something of a celebrity in the USA when he released his five-reel silent film *The German Curse in Russia* in January 1918* – a virulently anti-German, anti-Bolshevik propaganda exercise in support of the US press campaign to discredit the new Russian government – which was well received in the American trade press. Thompson continued to work as an independent film-maker during the 1920s and 1930s; he died in Los Angeles in 1947.

In 1918 Harper and Thompson both brought out extremely vivid memoirs of their time in Petrograd; Thompson also published a valuable book of his photographs. It is a matter

---

* It was also known as *Blood-Stained Russia, German Intrigue, Treason and Revolt* in the USA and was premiered under that title in New York in December 1917.

of considerable regret, not to mention a loss to history and scholarship therefore, that Thompson's original photographic negatives do not appear to have survived; there is no archival paper trail for him, or for Harper, like so many other of those groundbreaking journalists.* Three of Thompson's films survive in whole or in part,† but, at the time of writing, no prints of *The German Curse in Russia* – shot partly in Petrograd during the revolution, and which was distributed by Pathé – seem to have survived, although the author has ascertained that the film was later cannibalised and some of the footage re-used in Hermann Axelbank's 1937 documentary film *From Tsar to Lenin*.‡

As for the most unlikely heroes of this tale – the young, green college graduates of the National City Bank of New York – there is little known about any of them, except Leighton Rogers.§ Having made the decision to leave, Rogers had considerable difficulty getting out of Russia to enlist for the US army. The Russians refused to give him a exit visa and eventually the British helped get him, by subterfuge, onto a freight train that was travelling out of the city to the port of Murmansk. For the next long and terrifying fourteen days Rogers endured a hair-raising journey to the Russian coast, barely surviving the bone-chilling cold and hunger; it was only the store of canned food that he

---

* Some, like Rheta Childe Dorr, lost all their notes and materials, which were confiscated at the border by the Bolsheviks when they left. Dorr had to write the whole of her book, *Inside the Russian Revolution*, from memory.

† *With the Russians at the Front*; *Somewhere in France*; and *War As It Really Is*. Nothing is known either of the whereabouts of the 75,000 feet of film shot by Lieutenant Norton C. Travis in Petrograd over eighteen days, or whether any of it has survived.

‡ The Axelbank film may also have used footage shot by Lieutenant Travis, among uncredited footage from numerous other cameramen, including Russians, who filmed in Petrograd and whose work was recycled for this film.

§ Fred Sikes rose through the ranks of the NCB, retiring as Vice President, and died in 1958. Chester Swinnerton also stayed with the bank and managed its South American branches; he died in New Hampshire in 1960.

had brought with him in a knapsack that kept him going.[20] Arriving in London on April Fool's Day 1918, he enlisted for the American Expeditionary Forces and served in army intelligence in England and France during 1918–19. In 1924 he published *Wine of Fury*, a fascinating novel based on his Petrograd experiences, and later worked in aeronautics. Sadly, his account of his time in Russia, 'Czar, Revolution, Bolsheviks', based on his diaries, was never published, but the typescript is preserved in the Library of Congress. Rogers never married and lived quietly with his sister Edith until his death in Greenwich, Connecticut in 1962.[21]

These are but a few conclusions to so many forgotten stories; the last echoes of a generation of lost voices. But if one had to single any one out, there is one voice above all others that strikes a nerve in its own inimitable way: the utterly truthful, ingenuous voice of an obscure African American, Phil Jordan, an unlettered man and political innocent, and a loyal servant of US diplomacy, who lived to tell the tale. His glorious letters, written in his vivid vernacular style, and reflecting an enduring sense of being 'a stranger in a strange land', remain the only known published account of the revolution by an African American.[22]* They provide us with an unforgettable sense of exactly what it was like to be caught, in Petrograd, in the Russian Revolution of 1917.

---

* Fleeting sightings of other African Americans in Russia at the time of the revolution all leave us frustrated at the lack of a paper trail on their lives there. One such is Jim Hercules, one of the possibly four black American 'Nubian guards' at the Alexander Palace, who served Nicholas and Alexandra and their family right up until the revolution, and who may well have been stranded in Russia for some time afterwards.

Acknowledgements

I cannot remember exactly when it was that I first started collecting foreign eyewitness accounts of the Russian Revolution of 1917, but my interest mushroomed during my days as a freelance copy editor in the 1990s. At the time, I was handling a lot of history manuscripts and it struck me how much seemed to have been written about the revolution by Russians, but how relatively little I had come across that was said by those many non-Russians who, for various reasons, were stranded in the city that year. I knew there had to be more to the story than just the over-hyped account of the one man, John Reed, who had always seemed to dominate, with his *Ten Days that Shook the World*.

I also knew there had to be plenty of women, aside from Reed's partner Louise Bryant, who had watched events unfold. And what about all those other journalists, not to mention the diplomats, businessmen, industrialists, nurses and doctors, aid workers and the wives and children they often took with them? What about the British governesses and nannies who, I knew, were well in evidence in Russia at the time? I was aware that the capital had had a thriving British colony going back to the eighteenth century (as, too, had Moscow) and that the Leeds Russian Archive at my old university held some fascinating material on some of them.

So, beginning with the people I had gathered at the LRA, I began to seek out other lost and forgotten eyewitnesses of Petrograd in 1917, in particular from the American and French diplomatic communities. Along the way I picked up an assortment of other nationalities, and an interest that had begun as something of a hobby grew into a serious pursuit. Ten years ago I realised there might be a book in it. But I had to bide my time, because I knew that the best possible moment for such a book would be the centenary of the revolution in 2017.

In the course of my happy but increasingly obsessive collecting of people who had witnessed the convulsions in Petrograd, many friends – old and newly acquired – helped along the way by offering suggestions, seeking out material for me and helping me track down some of my more stubborn subjects. I am most grateful to all of them, for the many and varied ways in which they contributed to the writing of this book, as follows: my fellow Russianists Doug Smith and Simon Sebag Montefiore for a dialogue on Russia, the Romanovs and much sage advice; my good friend Candace Metz-Longinette Gahring in St Louis for helping me access documents in the Missouri archives and elsewhere; Roger Watson for filling me in on the cameras used by Donald Thompson; Mark Anderson of the Chicago Public Library, a genius at winkling out difficult-to-find articles from old magazines; Ilana Miller for doing likewise in California; Marianne Kouwenhoven for help with tracking down Belgian and Dutch diplomats; Ken Hawkins for kindly sharing his thesis on Arno Dosch-Fleurot; Amy Ballard at the Smithsonian; and Griffith Henniger, Henry Hardy, June Purvis, Jane Wickenden and William Lee for their helpful contributions.

My special thanks must go to Harvey Pitcher, author of *Witnesses of the Russian Revolution* (John Murray, 1994), who offered valuable advice when I visited him in Norwich and most generously passed on all his research material to me; to Sue Woolmans for checking out material held in the BBC Radio archives and being such a stalwart friend and supporter of my work; to film historian Dr David Mould at Ohio University for sharing both his knowledge of Donald Thompson and an ongoing and stubborn desire to track down Thompson's lost films; to the stalwart Phil Tomaselli for once again providing scans of sources at the National Archives; to Charles Bangham and Brian Brooks for sharing their family memoir of Edith Kerby; and to John Carter for letting me see his grand father Bousfield Swan Lombard's letters from Petrograd. I also owe a huge thank-you to my friend David Holohan for his excellent translations of French eyewitness material and for photocopying some hard-to-find sources for me in London. Finally, once more I am deeply grateful to Rudy de Casseres in Finland, a superb Russianist, who read and commented on the text and helped me obtain some important research material in Russian, checking through many issues of the newspaper *Novoe vremya* for material for me — a task that defeated my eyesight.

In order to offer new insights on the revolution from previously uncited sources, I searched long and hard in forgotten books and online library and archive catalogues and was gratified to uncover a wealth of new material, particularly in US archives. Sadly, I was not able to use it all, but I would like to express my gratitude to the following archives and archivists for the material with which they so promptly and generously provided me: the Falers Library & Special Collections, New York; the Indiana Historical Society; the State Historical Society of Missouri and the Missouri History Museum, St Louis; the Library of Congress; the Seeley G. Mudd Manuscript Library, Princeton University, and Harvard University Archives. In California, Ron Basich once more sought out sources for me at the Hoover Institution and arranged for photocopies and scans. In all cases every attempt has been made to contact copyright holders for permission to quote material held in these archives.

During the writing of *Caught in the Revolution* I drew on a wealth of other material held in archives in the USA, which, although not quoted in this book, provided very useful background, and my thanks are due to: Carole Hsin at Yale; Robin Carlaw at Harvard; Dale Stieber at Occidental College; Lee Grady at the Wisconsin Historical Society; Karen Kukil at Smith College; Thomas Whittaker at the University of Chicago Library; and Tanya Chebotarev at the Bakhmeteff Archive.

In the UK I am deeply indebted to my friend and fellow Russianist, Richard Davies, archivist of the Leeds Russian Archive for his considerable and unflagging support in this project, and for his patience and good humour in sorting out a long request list of sources that I wished to consult when I visited, and for his continuing sage advice. Richard's dedicated work at the LRA over many years has ensured that this wonderful resource now holds a unique place in the UK for those researching the British in Russia before the revolution, and I would like to take this opportunity to urge anyone holding such family papers to consider donating them to it. All LRA sources quoted are with the kind permission of rights owners, where it has been possible to trace them. My thanks also must go to the Arthur Ransome Literary Estate; to Bridget Gillies and the University of East Anglia for the use of material from the wonderful Jessie Kenney archive; to the John Rylands Library and the University of Manchester; the National Library of Wales for Sir George Bury's 1917 report; Peter Rogers at the Stewart Museum, Burnby Hall; and the National Archives and the Imperial War Museum for access to manuscripts that they hold. There is a wealth of untapped material in the BBC Radio 4 archives dating back to the 1950s, and in its TV archives as well. I am grateful to Vicky Mitchell and to the BBC Radio Archives for permission to quote from the Louisette Andrews TV interview. I should also like to make a particular point of singling out the valuable leads I gained from Lyubov Ginzburg's fascinating thesis 'Confronting the Cold War Legacy: The Forgotten History of the American Colony in St Petersburg' (University of Kansas, 2010), which pointed me in the direction of one of the heroes of my book – Leighton Rogers.

My thanks are also due to David Mould for sharing photographs of Donald Thompson; to Amanda Claunch at the Missouri History Museum for providing photographs of David R. Francis and Philip Jordan; to Ulysses Dietz for a photograph of his great-aunt Julia Cantacuzène-Speransky and to Bruce Kirby at the Library of Congress for seeking out and providing a scan of a much sought-after photograph of Leighton Rogers.

As always, dedicated editorial and publicity teams were involved in the production of this book on both sides of the Atlantic. In the UK, Jocasta Hamilton, Sarah Rigby, Najma Finlay, Richard T. Kelly and the team at Hutchinson all offered unfailing commitment to, and encouragement in, the research and writing of this book. Richard has been a first-class editor and I am most grateful for his sensitive response to the manuscript and to what I was trying to achieve. My thanks also go to my diligent copy editor Mandy Greenfield and proof reader Mary Chamberlain.

In New York, my dear friend Charlie Spicer at St Martin's Press has remained a stalwart ally and advocate of my work. This has been our fifth book together and I truly value his guiding hand. I am also grateful to April Osborn, Karlyn Hixson, Kathryn Hough and the tremendously hard-working PR and marketing team at St Martin's Press for their commitment and indomitable energy.

Throughout the research and writing of *Caught in the Revolution* I had the unfailing encouragement of my family and also a wonderful agent, to whom this book is dedicated. Caroline Michel at Peters, Fraser & Dunlop has been a true friend, wise counsel and advocate from the moment I joined the agency and I count myself enormously lucky to have her representing my work. But I also enjoy the valuable support of Rachel Mills, Alexandra Cliff, Marilia Savvides and the Foreign Rights team at PFD, who work so hard at selling my books in other markets. Jon Fowler and James Carroll have also been great friends and supporters of my public speaking and my work in broadcast media.

I always find it very difficult to let go of my subjects at the end of any book. The colourful cast of characters in *Caught in the Revolution* has lived in my head for the last three years – some of them for far longer – and they have left an indelible impression on me. They have also left me frustrated, because I want to find out more about their time in Russia and their lives after they left. With this is mind, I would be delighted to hear from any descendants or relatives of any of my subjects, who might hold letters, photographs or other material relating to their time in Petrograd in 1917. I can be contacted via my agents, Peters,

Fraser & Dunlop at www.petersfraserdunlop.com or my own website, www.helenrappaport.com.

It goes without saying that I would also be thrilled to hear from anyone with material relating to this story, written by people who were there, but about whom I do not know! Finally, and most particularly, I would dearly love to see any other letters written from Russia by Philip Jordan, or to hear from anyone with further memories of him or his life. The ultimate serendipity would be to rediscover a complete copy of Donald Thompson's 1919 silent film *The German Curse in Russia*, which I fear has, sadly, long since been lost. But I live in hope.

Helen Rappaport
West Dorset, 2016

Notes

ABBREVIATIONS

Anet	Claude Anet, *Through the Russian Revolution*
Barnes	Harper Barnes, *Standing on a Volcano*
Beatty	Bessie Beatty, *The Red Heart of Russia*
Bryant	Louise Bryant, *Six Red Months in Russia*
Crosley	Pauline Stewart Crosley, *Intimate Letters from Petrograd*
Dissolution	Meriel Buchanan, *Dissolution of an Empire*
Fleurot	Arno Dosch-Fleurot, *Through War to Revolution*
Francis	David R. Francis, *Russia from the American Embassy*
Harper	Florence Harper, *Runaway Russia*
Heald	Edward Heald, *Witness to Revolution*
Houghteling	James Houghteling, *Diary of the Russian Revolution*
Mission	Sir George Buchanan, *My Mission to Russia*, vol. 2
Paléologue	Maurice Paléologue, *An Ambassador's Memoirs, 1914–1917*
Patouillet	Patouillet, Madame [Louise]: TS diary, October 1916–August 1918, 2 vols

Petrograd	Meriel Buchanan, *Petrograd, The City of Trouble*
Reed	John Reed, *Ten Days that Shook the World*
Robien	Louis de Robien, *The Diary of a Diplomat in Russia 1917–18*
Rogers	Leighton Rogers Papers, 'Czar, Revolution, Bolsheviks'
Stinton Jones	James Stinton Jones, *Russia in Revolution*
Stopford	Anon. [Albert Stopford], *The Russian Diary of an Englishman*
Thompson	Donald Thompson, *Donald Thompson in Russia*
Williams	Albert Rhys Williams, *Journey into Revolution*
Wright	J. Butler Wright/William Thomas Allison, *Witness to Revolution: The Russian Revolution Diary and Letters of J. Butler Wright*

Prologue: 'The Air is Thick with Talk of Catastrophe'

1 Violetta Thurstan, *Field Hospital and Flying Column*, 94. Thurstan, like many visitors to Petrograd at the time, was overwhelmed by Petrograd's scale and seductive power: 'It is one of those cities whose charms steal upon you unawares. It is immense, insistent, arresting, almost thrusting itself on your imagination … everything is on such an enormous scale, dealt out in such careless profusion … the palaces grandiose, the very blocks of which they are fashioned seem to have been hewn by Titans'. Rogers, Box 3: Folder 7, 12–13 (hereafter styled as 3:7, etc.).
2 Dearing, unpublished MS memoirs, 88.
3 Almedingen, *I Remember St Petersburg*, 120–2; see also an atmospheric evocation of Petrograd in 1916 in Walpole, *The Secret City*, 98–9, 134, and in Leighton Rogers, *Wine of Fury*.
4 Almedingen, *Tomorrow Will Come*, 76.
5 Steveni, *Things Seen in Russia*, London: Seeley, Service & Co., 1913, 80. Steveni's *Petrograd Past and Present*, published in 1915, has an excellent Chapter XXXI on the history of the British

colony; see also Cross, 'A Corner of a Foreign Field' and 'Forgotten British Places in Petrograd'.

6 Lombard, untitled TS memoirs, section headed 'Things I Can't Forget', 64.

7 Ibid., untitled TS memoirs, section VII, n.p.

8 Stopford, 18.

9 Farson, *Way of a Transgressor*, 150.

10 Nathaniel Newnham-Davis, *The Gourmet's Guide to Europe*, Edinburgh: Ballantyne, Hanson & Co., 1908, 'St Petersburg Clubs', 303.

11 Farson, *Way of a Transgressor*, 95.

12 *Dissolution*, 9.

13 Ibid., 5–7.

14 Bruce, *Silken Dalliance*, 174, 159; Pares, *My Russian Memoirs*, 424. For a profile of Sir George by a contemporary in Petrograd, see Pares, 'Sir George Buchanan in Russia', *Slavonic Review*, 3 (9), March 1925, 576–86.

15 Lockhart, *Memoirs of a British Agent*, 121.

16 Farson, *Way of a Transgressor*, 95.

17 Blunt, *Lady Muriel Paget*, 62; Lockhart, *Memoirs of a British Agent*, 118.

18 Meriel Buchanan, *Ambassador's Daughter*, 130.

19 Barnes, 182, 206.

20 Francis to Senator William J. Stone, 13/26 February 1917, quoted in Ginzburg, 'Confronting the Cold War Legacy', 86.

21 See Barnes, 406–7; 'D. R. Francis Valet Dies in California', *St Louis Post Dispatch*, 1941; Bliss, 'Philip Jordan's Letters from Russia', 140–1; Barnes, 69.

22 Barnes, 186; Samuel Harper, *The Russia I Believe In*, 91–2; Harper, 188.

23 Francis, 3.

24 Salzman, *Reform and Revolution*, 228.

25 Dorr, *Inside the Russian Revolution*, 41.

26 Saul, *Life and Times of Charles Richard Crane*, 134; Lockhart, *Memoirs of a British Agent*, 281–2.

27 Rogers, 3:9, 153.

28 Houghteling, 5.

29 Barnes, 194.

30 Ibid., 195.

31 Cockfield, *Dollars and Diplomacy*, 23.

32 For a discussion of allegations that Matilda de Cram was a spy, see e.g. Allison, *American Diplomats in Russia*, 66–7. General William V. Judson's report to the US Secretary of War, in Salzman, *Russia in War and Revolution*, 267–70, is a contemporary evaluation from the point of view of someone working at the US embassy. Barnes (*passim*) also discusses their relationship.

33 Barnes, 199, 200–1.

34 'Missouri Negro in Russia is "Jes a Honin" for Home', *Wabash Daily Plain Dealer*, 29 September 1916.

35 Ibid., 207.

36 Ibid.

37 Cockfield, *Dollars and Diplomacy*, 56.

38 Wright, 4.

39 Dearing, unpublished memoirs, 219.

40 Cockfield, *Dollars and Diplomacy* 32.

41 Ibid., 31.

42 Quoted in Noulens, *Mon Ambassade en Russie Soviétique*, 243.

43 Kennan, *Russia Leaves the War*, 38.

44 Lindley, untitled memoirs 5.

45 Dearing, unpublished memoirs, 144.

46 Heald, 25; Barnes, 207; Cockfield, *Dollars and Diplomacy*, 70; Wright, 10.

47 Farson, *Way of a Transgressor*, 94; Steveni, *Petrograd Past and Present*, Chapter XIII, 'The Modern City and the People'.

48 According to Louise Patin, *Journal d'une institutrice française*, 19, French residents were given special permits to obtain wine.

49 Suzanne Massie, *Land of the Firebird: The Beauty of Old Russia*, Blue Hill, Maine: Heart Tree Press, 1980, 407.

50 http://thegaycourier.blogspot.co.uk/2013/06/legendary-hotel-celebrates-100-years.html

51 Vecchi, *Tavern is My Drum*, 96.

52 Rogers, 3:7, 21–2.

53 Ibid., 23.

54 Farson, *Way of a Transgressor*, 180.
55 Ibid., 181.
56 See the memoirs of Ella Cordasco (née Woodhouse), which are only available online at: https://web.archive.org/web/20120213165523/http://www.zimdocs.btinternet.co.uk/fh/ella2.html
57 Farson, *Way of a Transgressor*, 180.
58 Dearing, unpublished memoirs, 87.
59 Oudendyk, *Ways and By-Ways in Diplomacy*, 208.
60 Garstin, 'Denis Garstin and the Russian Revolution', Walpole 589.
61 Grand Duke Nikolay Nikolaevich, quoted in Pipes, *Russian Revolution*, 256; Memorandum to Foreign Office 18 [5], August 1916, *Mission*, 19.
62 *Petrograd*, 78.
63 Salisbury, *Black Night, White Snow*, 311; *Petrograd*, 70.
64 Paléologue, 733.
65 Lockhart, *Memoirs of a British Agent*, 158.
66 Arthur Bullard, *Russian Pendulum*, London: Macmillan, 1919, 21; see also Houghteling, 4–5.
67 Rogers 3:7, 17, 7–8.
68 Buchanan, *Ambassador's Daughter*, 138.
69 *Petrograd*, 50.
70 Gordon, *Russian Year*, 35.
71 Ibid., 40.
72 Figures in many sources vary, but see: http://rkrp-rpk.ru/content/view/10145/1/
73 Cockfield, *Dollars and Diplomacy*, 69.
74 Wright, 15.
75 Lockhart, *Memoirs of a British* Agent, 119.
76 *Dissolution*, 151; Buchanan, *Ambassador's Daughter*, 141.
77 Stopford, 94.
78 Barnes, 213.
79 Paléologue, 755.
80 Christie, 'Experiences in Russia', 2; MacNaughton, *My Experiences in Two Continents*, 194.
81 http://alphahistory.com/russianrevolution/police-conditions-in-petrograd-1916/

1 'Women are Beginning to Rebel at Standing in Bread Lines'

1 Fleurot, 96.
2 Ibid., 99, 100; Hawkins, 'Through War to Revolution with Dosch-Fleurot', 20. Dosch-Fleurot finally left in March 1918.
3 Fleurot, 99, 100.
4 Ibid., 101.
5 Hawkins, 'Through War to Revolution with Dosch-Fleurot', 22; Fleurot, 103–4.
6 Thompson, 30. For Thompson's wartime career prior to Petrograd, see Mould, 'Donald Thompson: Photographer at War', and Mould, 'Russian Revolution', 3.
7 Heald, 23.
8 Thompson, 17.
9 Harper, 19.
10 Houghteling, 14, 4.
11 Cahill, *Between the Lines*, 217, 221.
12 Ibid., 218.
13 Ibid., 219.
14 Mason, 'Russia's Refugees', 142.
15 Ibid.
16 *Petrograd*, 48.
17 For details of her life and career, see Blunt, *Lady Muriel*, and Sybil Oldfield, *Women Humanitarians*, London: Continuum, 2001, 160–3; Powell, *Women in the War Zone*, 296–7.
18 Blunt, *Lady Muriel*, 59.
19 Jefferson, *So This Was Life*, 85.
20 Several of the other diplomatic communities funded hospitals in Petrograd during the war: the US colony's hospital was at 15 Spasskaya; the Belgians had one named for their King Albert; the Dutch had a hospital at 68 English Embankment; the Danes ran two hospitals, one at 11 Sergievskaya and another for lower ranks named after the Danish-born dowager Maria Feodorovna, at 13 Pochtamskaya. There were also French, Swiss and Japanese hospitals for the wounded. See Yuri Vinogradov, 'Lazarety Petrograda', http://www.proza.ru/2010/01/30/984

21 Lady Georgina Buchanan, letter 16 December 1916, Glenesk-Bathurst papers.
22 *Novoe vremya*, 6 February 1917.
23 Lady Georgina Buchanan, letters of 7 October 1916 and 20 January 1917, Glenesk-Bathurst papers.
24 Jefferson, *So That Was Life*, 84–6; Harmer, *Forgotten Hospital*, 67–8.
25 Letter to mother, 19 [6] September, quoted in Wood, 'Revolution Outside Her Window', 74; Powell, *Women in the War Zone*, 301.
26 Wood, 'Revolution Outside Her Window', 75; letter 23 [10] September, Powell, *Women in the War Zone*, 301.
27 Seymour, MS diary for 4 October [22 September], IWM ; Powell, *Women in the War Zone*, 301; Moorhead, *Dunant's Dream*, 64.
28 Blunt, *Lady Muriel*, 66.
29 Farson, 'Aux Pieds de l'Impératrice', 17.
30 Harmer, *Forgotten Hospital*, 57; Powell, *Women in the War Zone*, 302.
31 Harmer, *Forgotten Hospital*, 25; Powell, *Woman in the War Zone*, 303.
32 Violetta Thurstan's view of the three women, quoted in Moorhead *Dunant's Dream*, 235.
33 Jefferson, *So That Was Life*, 92. Lady Sybil Grey's diary, quoted in Harmer, *Forgotten Hospital*, 67. It is regretted that Lady Sybil's diary is in private hands and is not yet available for research.
34 Harmer, *Forgotten Hospital*, 118.
35 Cordasco (Woodhouse), online memoir.
36 Wright, 21.
37 Armour, 'Recollections', 7. For his account of the reception, see 7–9.
38 Chambrun, *Lettres à Marie*, 42.
39 Wright, 21, 22.
40 Armour, 'Recollections', 8.
41 Chambrun, *Lettres à Marie*, 42.
42 Francis, 49.
43 Wright, 22; Paléologue, 764.
44 Weeks, *American Naval Diplomat*, 106.
45 Francis, 50–1.
46 Chambrun, *Lettres à Marie*, 43.
47 Paléologue, 764; Chambrun, *Lettres à Marie*, 42; Wright, 22.

48 Wright, 26.
49 Ibid.
50 Buchanan, *Ambassador's Daughter*, 141; *Petrograd*, 89–90; Stopford, 100.
51 Paléologue, 776.
52 Nostitz, *Romance and Revolutions*, 178; see also Wright, 33.
53 Lockhart, *Memoirs of a British Agent*, 163; Paléologue, 783.
54 Lockhart, *Memoirs of a British Agent*, 162–3; Buchanan, *Ambassador's Daughter*, 142.
55 Paléologue, 793.
56 Buchanan, *Ambassador's Daughter*, 142; *Mission*, 57; Buchanan, *Ambassador's Daughter*, 138.
57 Salisbury, *Black Night, White Snow*, 321; Bury, 'Report Regarding the Russian Revolution', II.
58 Wharton, 'Russian Ides of March', 22.
59 Ibid. Chadbourn published his valuable account of the February Revolution under the pseudonym Paul Wharton.
60 Emily Warner Somerville, 'A Kappa in Russia', 123.
61 Wright, 33, 34.
62 Thompson, 334.
63 Almedingen, *I Remember St Petersburg*, 186–7.
64 Wright, 34.
65 Ibid.; Thompson, 37; Salisbury, *Black Night, White Snow*, 322.
66 *Mission*, 59. The Whishaws were an old established family in the British colony, whose company Hills & Whishaw was involved in the exploitation of oilfields at Baku. Stella Arbenina (aka Baroness Meyendorff), who features in this book, was a member of the Whishaw family.

2 'No Place for an Innocent Boy from Kansas'

1 Thompson, 33.
2 Ibid., 37; Harper, 24.
3 Paléologue, 796.
4 Ibid., 797.

5 British embassy counsellor Francis Lindley noted in his memoirs that a report on the mission prepared for the British Foreign Office, and far more optimistic in tone than those sent from the embassy, had only just been printed and reached the FO when the revolution broke. It had to be hastily retrieved and suppressed. Lindley, untitled memoirs, 28.

6 Paléologue, 808.

7 Weather statistics for 1917 in Russia show that the average temperature was -13.44 Centigrade and that the significant rise in temperature so often given (e.g. Figes, *People's Tragedy*, 308, and Pipes, *Russian Revolution*, 274) as occurring on Friday 24th did not in fact happen until Monday 27th, when the temperature finally rose above zero, to 0.03 degrees C. It was not until 13 March that it finally climbed well above zero and reached 8 degrees C. For a detailed discussion, see: *Ezhenedelnik statisticheskogo otdeleniya petrogradskoy gorodskoy upravy*, 1917, no. 5, p. 13.

8 Wilton, *Russia's Agony*, 104; Fleurot, 118; Wright, 42.

9 Thompson, 39.

10 Fleurot, 118; Gordon, *Russian Year*, 97.

11 Thompson, 41.

12 Ibid., 43.

13 Hasegawa, *February Revolution*, 217; Rochelle Goldberg Ruthchild, 'Women's Suffrage and Revolution in the Russian Empire 1905–1917', *Aspasia*, 1, 2007, 18; Thompson, 43.

14 Harper, 26.

15 Ibid., 27.

16 Thompson, 43; Harper, 27.

17 Thompson, 44.

18 Salisbury, *Black Night, White Snow*, 337.

19 Wilton, *Russia's Agony*, 105.

20 Thompson, 44; May Pearse, diary, 24 February 1917.

21 Thompson, 46–7.

22 Rivet, *Last of the Romanofs*, 171; Hart-Davis, *Hugh Walpole*, 159; Pocock MS diary, n.p.

23 Wright, 43. Figes, *People's Tragedy*, 308.
24 Ransome, despatch 48, 23/24 February 1917.
25 Thompson, 47.
26 Hasegawa, *February Revolution*, 224–5; Bury, 'Report Regarding the Russian Revolution', IV; Fleurot, 'In Petrograd during the Seven Days', 258. Fleurot, 118.
27 See Salisbury, *Black Night, White Snow*, 336–7. The poor quality of the northern capital's water precluded top-quality baking in the vicinity of the Winter Palace and necessitated daily rail deliveries from Filippov's bakeries in Moscow. See: http://voiceofrussia.com/radio_broadcast/2248959/18406508/
28 Anon., 'The Nine Days', 213, 214. It has, sadly, proved impossible to ascertain who wrote this article, but the author talks of working in the Singer Building, so it was probably a member of staff at the US consulate, or possibly an employee of Westinghouse, which was also based there.
29 Thompson, 48.
30 Gordon, *Russian Year*, 97.
31 Ransome, Despatches 49 and 48; Golder, *War, Revolution and Peace in Russia*, 34.
32 The Tsaritsa punctiliously recorded the temperature in her diary each day. Throughout the whole of February she records it as ranging from -19 degrees Centigrade on 5 February to -4.5 on the 24th. See e.g. V. A. Kozlov and V. M. Khrustalev, eds, *The Last Diary of Tsaritsa Alexandra*, London: Yale University Press, 1997.
33 Anon., 'The Nine Days', 213.
34 Ibid.
35 Golder, *War, Revolution and Peace in Russia*, 334.
36 Fleurot, 'Seven Days', 258.
37 Robien, 8.
38 Hasegawa, *February Revolution*, 233.
39 Ibid., 235.
40 Robien, 8; Chambrun, *Lettres à Marie*, 55.
41 Hasegawa says 36,800, see *February Revolution*, 238.
42 Markovitch, *La Révolution russe*, 17.

43 Bury, 'Report Regarding the Russian Revolution', V.
44 Heald, 50; 'From Our Own Correspondent [Robert Wilton], "The Outbreak of the Revolution"', *The Times*, 21 [8] March 1917.
45 Hall, *One Man's War*, 267, 263.
46 Hegan, 'Russian Revolution from a Window', 556.
47 Harmer, *Forgotten Hospital*, 119; Poutiatine, *War and Revolution*, 45–6.
48 Dorothy Cotton, letter, 4 March 1917, Library Archives of Canada; Blunt, *Lady Muriel*, 104.
49 Thompson, 50.
50 Patouillet, 1:55.
51 Grey, 'Sidelights on the Russian Revolution', 363.
52 Harper, 29; Thompson, 49.
53 Harper, 28–9.
54 Stinton Jones, 62.
55 Fleurot, 123.
56 [Wilton], 'Russian Food problem', *The Times*, 9 March 1917; [Wilton], 'The Outbreak of the Revolution, *The Times*, 21 March 1917.
57 Heald, 50.
58 Rogers, 3:7, 43–4.
59 Thompson, 51.
60 Chambrun, *Lettres à Marie*, 55.

3 'Like a Bank Holiday with Thunder in the Air'

1 Patouillet, 1:56.
2 Rogers, 3:7, 44.
3 Rogers, 3:7, 45–6; see also the account by Swinnerton, 'Letter from Petrograd', 2, which had been wrongly dated as 12 March OS, instead of 14 March OS.
4 Hasegawa, *February Revolution*, 248; Wright, 43.
5 Hasegawa, *February Revolution*, 249.
6 Ibid., 251; Salisbury, *Black Night, White Snow*, 342.
7 Markovitch, *La Révolution russe*, 19; Salisbury, *Black Night, White Snow*, 342.
8 Anet, 12.

9 Rogers, 'Account of the March Revolution', 7.

10 Thompson, 53.

11 Gordon, *Russian Year*, 103.

12 Thompson, 54, 57; Harper, 29–30.

13 Harper, 31.

14 Thompson, 58, Harper, 31.

15 Patouillet, 1:60; Anon., 'Nine Days', 214; Thompson, 58.

16 Harper, 32, 33.

17 Rogers, 3:7, 46.

18 Reinke, 'My Experiences in the Russian Revolution', 9.

19 Anet, 13.

20 Thompson, 59; Rogers, 3:7, 46.

21 Rogers, 'Account of the Russian Revolution', 8–9; Rogers, 3:7, 46; see also Stopford, 102.

22 Hegan, 'Russian Revolution from a Window', 556.

23 Fleurot, 122; Thompson, 60–1.

24 Stopford, 103. A document in The National Archives, KV2/2398, reveals the details of Stopford's original trip to Russia in 1916 and implies that he did some unofficial spying/snooping for Buchanan. In Russia he was well acquainted with the bisexual Felix Yusupov (the NA document alludes to Stopford's homosexuality in a veiled comment about him being 'a moral eccentric'). Stopford also had considerable experience in buying artworks from Fabergé for Cartier in Paris. In July 1917 he managed to get into Grand Duchess Vladimir's palace unseen, rescue the best of her jewels from the safe and get them safely out of Russia; of these, her tiara was eventually bought by King George V and is still worn by Queen Elizabeth II. In 1918 Stopford was prosecuted for homosexual offences and jailed for a year in Wormwood Scrubs, after which he settled in Paris. For further details on his life – much of which remains sketchy – see Clarke, *Hidden Treasures of the Romanovs*.

25 Thompson, 60–1.

26 Some later accounts of the February Revolution deny the presence of machine guns, but far too many eyewitnesses testify to their presence on rooftops. See, for example, John Pollock's

account, 'The Russian Revolution', written from first-hand experience, which claims that Protopopov 'had the roofs at every important street corner garrisoned by police with machine-guns' and goes on to observe that the revolution had succeeded thanks to this misjudgement: 'Had they been properly posted in the streets at strategic points and a sound scheme of coop-eration arranged among the police and gendarmes, some fifty thousand in strength, they could have swept every living thing from the streets: placed in dormer windows and behind para-pets, the mitrailleuses were extremely difficult to train on their objective'; 1070–1. Sir George Bury's 'Report' also contains numerous references to the deployment of machine guns.

27 Hasegawa, *February Revolution*, 252; Gordon, *Russian Year*, 101, 102.
28 Hasegawa, *February Revolution*, 263; Pipes, *Russian Revolution*, 276; Joseph Fuhrman, ed., *The Complete Wartime Correspondence of Tsar Nicholas II and the Empress Alexandra*, Westport, CT: Greenwood Press, 1999, 692.
29 Thompson, 62.
30 Pax, *Journal d'une comédienne française*, 11–12.
31 Ransome, Despatch 50, 25 February, 11.00 p.m.
32 Reinke, 'My Experiences in the Russian Revolution', 9.
33 Butler Wright's report to Francis, 10/23 March 1917, is included in Cockfield, *Dollars and Diplomacy*, 113.
34 Thompson, 63.
35 Wharton, 'Russian Ides of March', 22–3.
36 Hasegawa, *February Revolution*, 265.
37 Ibid., 267.
38 Gordon, *Russian Year*, 105.
39 Thompson, 64.
40 See Patouillet, 1:59–60.
41 Keeling, *Bolshevism: Mr Keeling's Five Years in Russia*, 76.
42 Harper, 37; Patouillet, 1:162.
43 Anon., The Nine Days', 215.
44 Whether Thompson was actually able to grab any success-ful shots of the street fighting seems unlikely, as none were included in his collection of photographs of the revolution

published as *Blood-Stained Russia* in 1918. He did manage to catch some static shots of bodies in morgues and of the funerals of the victims, but his major photographic coup came in May/June with his extensive coverage of Emmeline Pankhurst's visits to Maria Bochkareva and the Women's Death Battalion, which was widely reproduced in the Western press.

45 Thompson, 64, 67; Harper, 37–8.
46 Harper, 39–40; Thompson, 69–70.
47 Dorothy Cotton, letter of 4 March OS – though within the letter she reverts to NS; Grey, 'Sidelights on the Russian Revolution', 363; Wilton, *Russia's Agony*, 109, which claims that 100 people were killed during this incident alone.
48 Poutiatine, *War and Revolution*, 47–8; Hegan, 'Russian Revolution from a Window', 557.
49 Hegan, 'Russian Revolution from a Window', 558.
50 Wharton, 'Russian Ides of March', 24.
51 Hegan, 'Russian Revolution from a Window', 558.
52 Hasegawa, *February Revolution*, 268; Grey, 'Sidelights on the Russian Revolution', 364; Anet, 16.
53 'From Our Own Correspondent' – Robert Wilton's report for *The Times*, 16 March (NS) – his first major despatch to get through and be published in the UK; see also Wilton, *Russia's Agony*, 110.
54 Clare, 'Eye witness of the Revolution', n.p.
55 Wilton, *Russia's Agony*, 110; Markovitch, *La Révolution russe*, 24; Anon., 'The Nine Days', 215; Hasegawa, *February Revolution*, 268–9.
56 Wharton, 'Russian Ides of March', 24.
57 Swinnerton, 'Letter from Petrograd', 3.
58 Ransome, Despatch 52.
59 Harper, 41–2.
60 Wilton, *Russia's Agony*, 109; see also Wilton's report in *The Times*, 16 March 1917.
61 Wilton in *The Times*, 16 March 1917; Lady Georgina Buchanan, 'From the Petrograd Embassy', 19.
62 Wilton, *Russia's Agony*, 109.
63 Hasegawa, *February Revolution*, 272–3.

64 Pax, *Journal d'une comédienne française*, 16–18.
65 Fleurot, 124–5; Arbenina, *Through Terror to Freedom*, 34.
66 Anet, 11; Stopford, 108.
67 Paléologue, 811; Chambrun, *Lettres à Marie*, 57. In an uncanny parallel with Petrograd 1917, a demonstration by Frenchwomen on that same date in 1789, over the high price of bread and escalating hunger in Paris, had led to a mass march on the palace at Versailles.
68 Arbenina, *Through Terror to Freedom*, 34–5; Anet, 15.
69 Armour, 'Recollections', 5.
70 Rogers, 'Account of the March Revolution', 11; Anet, 11; Chambrun, *Lettres à Marie*, 57.
71 Marcosson, *Rebirth of Russia*, 47–9; Wilton, *Russia's Agony*, 112; Hasegawa, *February Revolution*, 275.
72 Thompson, 72, 73.

4 'A Revolution Carried on by Chance'

1 Rogers 3:7, 48.
2 Swinnerton, 'Letter from Petrograd', 4; Rogers 3:7, 46–7.
3 For descriptions of the bank, see Fuller, 'Journal of John L. H. Fuller', 9–10, and letter to his brother of 19 [6] September, in Fuller, 'Letters and Diaries', 20.
4 Rogers, 3:7, 46–7.
5 Cockfield, *Dollars and Diplomacy*, 89.
6 Marcosson, 'The Seven Days', 262.
7 *Petrograd*, 96.
8 Ibid., 97; Wharton, 'Russian Ides of March', 24.
9 Butler Wright report, in Cockfield, *Dollars and Diplomacy*, 115.
10 *Mission*, 63; Paléologue, 814–15.
11 Paléologue, 816.
12 Fleurot, 'In Petrograd during the Seven Days', 260; Fleurot, 126; see also Hasegawa, *February Revolution*, 278–81.
13 Paléologue, 813.
14 Marcosson, *Rebirth of Russia*, 52.
15 Thompson, 78.

16 Hasegawa, *February Revolution*, 286.

17 Marcosson, 'The Seven Days', 35; Marcosson, *Rebirth of Russia*, 52; Hart-Davis, *Hugh Walpole*, 458.

18 Knox, *With the Russian Army*, 553–4; as Sir George Buchanan observed in a ciphered telegram to the Foreign Office: 'The danger is that men have no proper leaders. I saw about 3000 to-day with only single young officer'. FO report, 12/27 March, 299, The National Archives.

19 Knox, *With the Russian Army*, 554–5; Stinton Jones, 107–8.

20 Stinton Jones, 108–9.

21 Gordon, *Russian Year*, 110; Anet, 23.

22 Thompson, 81.

23 Anet, 19–20.

24 Thompson, 81–2.

25 Paléologue, 814; Gordon, *Russian Year*, 110; Robien, 12.

26 Anet, 22; Butler Wright report to Francis in Cockfield, *Dollars and Diplomacy*, 114–15.

27 Wharton, 'Russian Ides of March', 24.

28 Hart-Davis, *Hugh Walpole*, 454.

29 Stinton Jones, 120.

30 Reinke, 'My Experiences in the Russian Revolution', 11; Gordon, *Russian Year*, 109.

31 Hegan, 'Russian Revolution from a Hospital Window', 558–9.

32 Fleurot, 130.

33 Stinton Jones, 131.

34 See Poutiatine, *War and Revolution*, 50–1; Marcosson, *Rebirth of Russia*, 56; Fleurot, 'In Petrograd during the Seven Days', 262.

35 Knox, *With the Russian Army*, 554–5; see also Stinton Jones, 107–8.

36 Gibson, *Wild Career*, 127.

37 Vecchi, *Tavern is My Drum*, 122; Stinton Jones, 110.

38 Hasegawa, *February Revolution*, 287; Keeling, *Bolshevism*, 86, 85.

39 Lombard, 'Things I Can't Forget', 92, 90; Stinton Jones, 144.

40 Farson, *Way of a Transgressor*, 187.

41 Stinton Jones, 'Czar Looked Over My Shoulder', 97; Gibson, *Wild Career*, 135.

42 Fleurot, 'In Petrograd during the Seven Days', 261.
43 Springfield, 'Recollections of Russia', n.p.
44 Lindley, untitled memoirs, 29.
45 Pearse, diary, 27 February/12 March; Swinnerton, 'Letter from Petrograd', 4.
46 Stinton Jones, 134, 132–3.
47 Seymour, MS diary for 12 March [27 February].
48 Lombard, 'Things I Can't Forget', 92–3.
49 Seymour, MS diary for 12 March [27 February]; Hegan, 'Russian Revolution from a Hospital Window', 558.
50 According to Poutiatine, *War and Revolution*, 55, it turned out that machine guns had been firing on the street from a window of the house next door to the ARH on the Fontanka side, and there were two more firing 'from the attic of a tall house on Nevskii, diagonally across from us'.
51 Sybil Grey diary, quoted in Blunt, *Lady Muriel*, 104.
52 Cotton, letter of 4 March, 3; Seymour, quoted in Wood, 'Revolution Outside her Window', 80; see also Pocock, MS diary for Monday 27 February.
53 Pax, *Journal d'une comédienne française*, 18–23.
54 Marcosson, *Rebirth of Russia*, 56.
55 Hasegawa, *February Revolution*, 296; Stinton Jones, 153.
56 Walpole, *Secret City*, 255.
57 See Keeling, *Bolshevism*, 82, 85; Stinton Jones, 124–5, 164; Marcosson, *Rebirth of Russia*, 35, 54; Hart-Davis, *Hugh Walpole*, 460.
58 Anet, 23; Pollock, 'The Russian Revolution', 158.
59 Metcalf, *On Britain's Business*, 47.
60 Stinton Jones, 'Czar Looked Over my Shoulder', 97; Clare, 'Eye Witness of the Russian Revolution'.
61 *Dissolution*, 166.
62 Quoted in Sandra Martin and Roger Hall (eds), *Where Were You? Memorable Events of the Twentieth Century*, Toronto: Methuen, 1981, 220.
63 Walpole, 'Official Account of the First Russian Revolution', 460; Stinton Jones, 142.
64 Fleurot, 128.

65 Ibid.

66 Ibid.

67 Fleurot, 'In Petrograd during the Seven Days', 262; Marcosson, *Rebirth of Russia*, 60.

68 Fleurot, 128–9.

69 Vecchi, *Tavern is My Drum*, 125; see also Stinton Jones, 150–1.

70 Anon., 'The Nine Days', 215.

71 See his report in Francis, 60–2.

72 Hasegawa, *February Revolution*, 292–3; Vecchi, *Tavern is My Drum*, 124; Wilton, *Russia's Agony*, 122–3.

73 Stinton Jones, 140–1.

74 Bert Hall, *One Man's War*, 269–70.

75 Wharton, 'Russian Ides of March', 26.

76 Ibid.

77 Swinnerton, 'Letter from Petrograd', 4, 5.

78 Locker Lampson, 'Report on the Russian Revolution', 240, Kettle, *Allies and the Russian Collapse*, 14.

79 Gibson, *Wild Career*, 129; Knox, *With the Russian Army*, 560.

5 Easy Access to Vodka 'Would Have Precipitated a Reign of Terror'

1 Bury, 'Report', XIII.

2 *Dissolution*, 168.

3 Wharton, 'Russian Ides of March', 26–7.

4 Dearing, unpublished memoirs, 242; *Dissolution*, 167.

5 *Dissolution*, 170.

6 Swinnerton, 'Letter from Petrograd', 7.

7 Paléologue, 819.

8 *Dissolution*, 169–70; *Mission*, 66.

9 North Winship telegram to the American Secretary of State, 20 [3] March 1917; https://history.hanover.edu/texts/tel2.html

10 Houghteling, 115.

11 Locker Lampson, 'Report on the Russian Revolution', 240; Poutiatine, *War and Revolution*, 52.

12 Locker Lampson, 'Report on the Russian Revolution, 241, 214.

13 Heald, *Witness to Revolution*, 57–8.
14 Locker Lampson, 'Report on the Revolution', 242.
15 Thompson, 89–90.
16 Locker Lampson, 'Report on the Revolution', 243.
17 Bury, 'Report', XV–XVI.
18 Grey, 'Sidelights on the Russian Revolution', 365.
19 Harper, 50.
20 Stinton Jones, 165.
21 Harper, 51.
22 Wilton, *Russia's Agony*, 124; Grey, 'Sidelights on the Russian Revolution', 365; Walpole, 'Official Report', in Hart-Davis, *Hugh Walpole*, 464–5.
23 Stinton Jones, 165; Poutiatine, *War and Revolution*, 53.
24 Swinnerton, 'Letter from Petrograd', 6; Rogers, 'Account of the March Revolution', 16.
25 Lampson, 'Report on the Russian Revolution,' 244.
26 Vecchi, *Tavern is My Drum*, 130–1.
27 Walpole, 'Official Report', in Hart-Davis, *Hugh Walpole*, 465.
28 Locker Lampson, 244.
29 Ibid.; Harper, 52.
30 Vecchi, *Tavern is My Drum*, 131.
31 Grey, 'Sidelights on the Russian Revolution', 366.
32 Harper, 56; Stinton Jones, 166.
33 Houghteling, 149. In an article for the *World's Work* on 21 April (NS) entitled 'How Tsardom Fell', Arno Dosch-Fleurot also commented on the mercy of the alcohol ban: 'None but a sober people could have carried out the Revolution. Had the populace of Petrograd and other cities been besotted by drink, the Revolution would never have been so remarkably free from sanguinary excesses on a large scale.'
34 Vecchi, *Tavern is My Drum*, 130–1; Harper, 53; Ysabel Birkbeck, quoted in Cahill, *Between the Lines*, 227.
35 Houghteling, 115.
36 Harper, 56, 59.
37 Harper, 54, 53; Wilton, *Russia's Agony*, 126.
38 Harper, 52, 54.

39 Walpole, 'Denis Garstin and the Russian Revolution', 591.
40 Louisette Andrews, BBC2 interview with Joan Bakewell in 1977.
41 Hegan, 'Russian Revolution from a Hospital Window', 559, 560.
42 Hasegawa, *February Revolution*, 289–90.
43 Seymour, MS diary for 13 March [28 February].
44 Rogers, 'Account of the March Revolution', 14; Rogers, 3:7, 52.
45 Swinnerton, 'Letter from Petrograd', 8–9; see also Leighton Rogers's account, in Rogers, 3:7, 59; and Stopford, 118.
46 Rogers, 3:7, 57; Chambrun, *Lettres à Marie*, 63.
47 Nostitz, *Romance and Revolutions*, 187. In *Dissolution*, 172, and *Petrograd*, 105, Meriel Buchanan refutes this; see also Stopford, 110. For Bousfield Swan Lombard's account, see 'Things I Can't Forget,' 97.
48 Nostitz, *Romance and Revolutions*, 185.
49 Cordasco (Woodhouse), online memoir.
50 Houghteling, 77.
51 Margaret Bennet, MS letter 2/15 March.
52 Bury, 'Report', XII–XIV; Ransome, Despatch 54; Houghteling, 76.
53 Stinton Jones, 167, 267–8; Markovitch, *La Révolution russe*, 42.
54 Markovitch, *La Révolution russe*, 64.
55 Stinton Jones, 264; Seymour, MS diary for 2 March; Rogers, 'Account of the March Revolution', 15.

6 'Good to be Alive These Marvelous Days'

1 Walpole, 'Official Account', 464–5.
2 See Paléologue, 824.
3 Wilton, *Russia's Agony*, 127.
4 Houghteling, 80, 82; Markovitch, *La Révolution russe*, 62.
5 Anet, 28.
6 Rogers, 'Account of the March Revolution', 21.
7 Houghteling, 80, 81.
8 Bury, 'Report', XXIII–IV; Hunter, 'Sir George Bury and the Russian Revolution', 67.
9 Bury, 'Report', XXIV; Hart-Davis, *Hugh Walpole*, 257–8.

10 Walpole, *Secret City*, 257–8; see also Anet, 29.

11 Pipes, *Russian Revolution*, 291.

12 Knox, *With the Russian Army*, 561, 562.

13 Gordon, *Russian Year*, 124; Bury, 'Report', XXV.

14 Anet, 23, 30; Rivet, *Last of the Romanofs*, 176; Sukhanov, *Russian Revolution*, 88.

15 Anet, 31.

16 Rivet, *Last of the Romanofs*, 216.

17 Pollock, 'The Russian Revolution', 1075.

18 Houghteling, 100. Re Protopopov's plans, see Grey, 'Sidelights on the Russian Revolution', 368.

19 Walpole, 'Official Account', 463; Walpole, *Secret City*, 228, 258–9.

20 Walpole, *Secret City*, 258–9.

21 Paléologue, 820.

22 Pollock, 'The Russian Revolution', 1076.

23 See Pipes, Russian Revolution, 304–7.

24 Pitcher, *When Miss Emmie Was in Russia*, 13; Dawe, *Looking Back*, 19.

25 Harper, 59–60.

26 Rogers, 3:7, 54–5.

27 Swinnerton, 'Letter from Petrograd', 7.

28 Harper, 66.

29 Hall, *One Man's War*, 272.

30 Stinton Jones, 185; Markovitch, *La Révolution russe*, 76.

31 Barnes, 226; Francis, 72.

32 Letter to Edith Chibnall, 14 March 1917, at: http://spartacus-educational.com/Wbowerman.htm; Anon., 'Nine Days', 216.

33 Heald, 61, 64.

34 Pollock, 'The Russian Revolution', 1074.

35 Locker Lampson, quoted in Kettle, *The Allies and the Russian Collapse*, 45.

36 Springfield, 'Recollections of Russia'.

37 Anon., 'The Nine Days, 216.

38 Markovitch, *La Révolution russe*, 60; Patouillet, 1:72–3; Paléologue, 823.

39 Swinnerton, 'Letter from Petrograd', 6.

7 'People Still Blinking in the Light of the Sudden Deliverance'

1 Wharton, 'Russian Ides of March,' 28.
2 Ibid.
3 Anet, 39–40.
4 *Dissolution*, 175.
5 Pipes, *Russian Revolution*, 310–13.
6 Ransome, Despatch 67, 18 [5] March.
7 Paléologue, 830; Hegan, 'Russian Revolution through a Hospital Window', 559; Anet, 63; Anon., 'The Nine Days', 217.
8 Thompson, 114; 123, 124.
9 Anet, 53.
10 Chambers, *Last Englishman*, 136. Pipes, *Russian Revolution*, 300. Figes, *People's Tragedy*, 336.
11 Golder, *War, Revolution and Peace in Russia*, 54; Oudendyk, *Ways and By-ways in Diplomacy*, 218.
12 Walpole, 'Official Account', 468.
13 Wharton, 'Russian Ides of March', 30; Anet, 55.
14 Anet, 96.
15 Houghteling, 130; Golder, *War, Revolution and Peace in Russia*, 53.
16 Paléologue, 835, 837, 838.
17 Fleurot, 139.
18 Anet, 106, 107; Hall, *One Man's War*, 273.
19 Marcosson, *Rebirth of Russia*, 121; Buchanan, FO report no. 374, 9/22 March, 121, TNA; Hall, *One Man's War*, 273.
20 See *Petrograd*, 107; Harmer, *Forgotten Hospital*, 123; Blunt, *Lady Muriel*, 105.
21 Long, *Russian Revolution Aspects*, 108–9; Hegan, 'Revolution from a Hospital Window', 561; Jefferson, *So That Was Life*, 101; Poutiatine, *War and Revolution*, 58.
22 Houghteling, 139; Stinton Jones, 223; Wharton, 'Russian Ides of March', 28.
23 Marcosson, *Rebirth of Russia*, 123; also in Heald, 64.
24 Long, *Russian Revolution Aspects*, 108–9.
25 See *Petrograd*, 107.
26 Robien, 22; Golder, *War, Revolution and Peace in Russia*, 39; Marcosson, *Rebirth of Russia*, 123.

27 Heald, 66.

28 *Dissolution*, 201; Crosley, 16.

29 *Dissolution*, 201–2.

30 Heald, 67; Cockfield, *Dollars and Diplomacy*, 100.

31 Ransome, Despatch 67, 18 [5] March; Marcosson, *Rebirth of Russia*, 114, 119.

32 Oudendyk, *Ways and By-ways in Diplomacy*, 213–14, 216.

33 Paléologue, 847–8.

34 Stinton Jones, 275–6, 278.

35 Ibid., 246; Houghteling, 162.

36 Houghteling, 142; Anet, 48.

37 21 March NS, quoted in Pitcher, *Witnesses of the Russian Revolution*, 51, 52.

38 Long, *Russian Revolution Aspects*, 5.

39 Marcosson, *Rebirth of Russia*, v.

40 Ibid., *Adventures in Interviewing*, 164.

41 Ibid., *Rebirth of Russia*, 125–6.

42 Farson, *Way of a Transgressor*, 276.

43 Stebbing, *From Czar to Bolshevik*, 89–90.

44 Thompson, 125; Oudendyk, *Ways and By-ways of Diplomacy*, 216.

45 Metcalf, *On Britain's Business*, 48.

46 Marcosson, *Rebirth of Russia*, 129.

47 Anet, 71.

48 Keeling, *Bolshevism*, 90–1.

49 See Houghteling, *Diary of the Russian Revolution*, 144–7.

50 Pitcher, *Witnesses of the Russian Revolution*, 63.

51 Foglesong, 'A Missouri Democrat', 28; Barnes, 229.

52 Houghteling, *Diary of the Russian Revolution*, 165.

53 Quoted in Kennan, *Russia Leaves the War*, 38.

54 Houghteling, 166.

55 Wright, 48, 49.

56 Knox, *With the Russian Army*, 584.

57 Stopford, 133; Knox, *With the Russian Army*, 585; Paléologue, 858–9.

58 Paléologue, 859, 860.

8 The Field of Mars

1 Harper, 67–8.
2 Ibid., 68–9.
3 *Petrograd*, 112; Walpole, *Secret City*, 331.
4 Harper, 70.
5 Rogers, 3:8, 66.
6 Heald, 77; Dawe, 'Looking Back', 20.
7 Anet, 113; Rogers, 3:8, 66; Paléologue, 875.
8 Wright, 62.
9 Walpole, *Secret City*, 331; Anet, 112; Heald, 76; Stopford, 146.
10 Harper, 71; Recouly, 'Russia in Revolution', 38.
11 Metcalf, *On Britain's Business*, 48.
12 Walpole, *Secret City*, 331; Heald, 77.
13 Golder, *War, Revolution and Peace in Russia*, 53.
14 *Dissolution*, 200; Heald, 77.
15 Rogers, 3:8, 67; see also Heald, 76–7.
16 Rogers, 3:8, 67–8; see also Anet, 114–15.
17 Marcosson, *Rebirth of Russia*, 116.
18 Stinton Jones, 268; Stopford, 147–8; Anet, 114; Chambrun, *Lettres à Marie*, 83. Lyndall Pocock, a Red Cross orderly at the ARH, counted the coffins in the six different processions as they passed and noted: four from the Vasilievsky Side; eight from the Petrograd Side; fifty-one from the populous Vyborg Side, suggesting a majority of casualties among the workers; twenty-nine and forty in two processions from the Nevsky Side; and forty-five from the Moskovsky – making 177 in all. See Pocock, diary entry for 25 March 1917.
19 For a full discussion of the figures, see Chapter 2, '*Beskrovnaya revolyutsiya?*', p.8, of a thesis by Ilya Orlov: '*Traur i prazdnik v revolyutsionnoi politike*', http://net.abimperio.net/files/february.pdf
20 Anet, 100.
21 Patouillet, 1:108, 109.
22 Walpole, 'Official Report', 467; Reinke, 'My Experiences in the Russian Revolution', 9; Marcosson, *Rebirth of Russia*, 115; Harper, 198; Houghteling, 156; Thompson, 124.

23 Pollock, 'The Russian Revolution', 1074; Pollock, *War and Revolution in Russia*, 163.
24 Paléologue, 875, 876.
25 Ibid., 876.
26 Ibid., 880–1.

9 *Bolsheviki!* It Sounds 'Like All that the World Fears'

1 Farson, *Way of a Transgressor*, 205; Jefferson, letters from Petrograd, 6.
2 Wright, 60.
3 Marcosson, *Before I Forget*, 247.
4 For an account of Lenin's life in exile 1900–17, see Rappaport, *Conspirator*.
5 *Mission*, 115; Lady Georgina Buchanan, 'From The Petrograd Embassy', 20.
6 Francis, 105–6.
7 Heald, 88, 89.
8 For an account of Lenin's journey from Zurich to Petrograd, see Rappaport, *Conspirator*, Chapter 18.
9 Fleurot, 145, 146.
10 Gordon, *Russian Year*, 145.
11 In exile in France, Kschessinska (1872–1971) married Nicholas II's cousin, Grand Duke Andrey Vladimirovich, and set up a ballet school where she taught, among others, the British ballerinas Margot Fonteyn and Alicia Markova. In 1955 the mansion became the location for the Museum of the October Revolution, now known as the State Museum of Political History.
12 Buchanan, *Ambassador's Daughter*, 165; Wright, 68.
13 Farson, *Way of a Transgressor*, 204.
14 *Mission*, 119.
15 Golder, *War, Revolution and Peace in Russia*, 57; Anet, 135; Farson, *Way of a Transgressor*, 203–4.
16 Quoted in Brogan, *Life of Arthur Ransome*, 126; Heald, 89.
17 Robien, 39–40.
18 Shepherd, quoted in Steffens, *Autobiography*, 761.

19 Gibson, *Wild Career*, 150; Fleurot, 146

20 Anet, 164.

21 Long, *Russian Revolution Aspects*, 126.

22 Paléologue, 892–3; Thompson, 160.

23 Robien, 33.

24 Heald, 81.

25 Paléologue, 887.

26 Wright, 63, 68.

27 Salzman, *Russia in War and Revolution*, 89–90; see also Crosley, 45, where she talks of many Russian officers coming to her naval attaché husband Walter – some even in disguise – asking to be sent to the US to join the American navy or army.

28 Wright, 68.

29 Lindley, untitled memoirs, 32.

30 Paléologue, 895–6; Robien, 40.

31 Robien, 40–1; Lockhart, *Memoirs of a British Agent*, 185.

32 Cantacuzène, *Revolutionary Days*, 275.

33 Paléologue, 897; Chambrun, *Lettres à Marie*, 98.

34 See Paléologue, 898; Robien, 50.

35 Francis, 101, 102; 'D. R. Francis Valet', *St Louis Post-Dispatch*.

36 Fleurot, 151.

37 See Foglesong, 'A Missouri Democrat', 34.

38 Paléologue, 910; Robien, 48; Anet, 161; Brown, *Doomsday*, 102.

39 Rogers, 3:8, 73.

40 Philips Price, *My Reminiscences of the Russian Revolution*, 21.

41 Ibid.; Heald, 86.

42 Heald, 87, 88.

43 Anet, 163–4.

44 Ibid., 163.

45 Paléologue, 912.

46 Rogers, 3:8, 73, 81.

47 Fleurot, 153.

48 Anet, 166, 167.

49 Thompson, 167–8.

50 Ibid., 169, 170.

51 Dosch, 153; Cordasco (Woodhouse), online memoir.

52 Golder, *War, Revolution and Peace in Russia*, 65; Paléologue 917.

53 Lockhart, *Memoirs of a British Agent*, 175.
54 Steffens, 'What Free Russia Asks of Her Allies', 137; Heald, 89.
55 Farson, *Way of a Transgressor*, 199.
56 Ibid., 201.
57 Fleurot, 155–6.
58 Paléologue, 925, 930; Robien, 54.
59 Chambrun, *Lettres à Marie*, 142.
60 Hughes, *Inside the Enigma*, 97.
61 Ibid., 98. Henderson's visit was also described in detail by Meriel Buchanan in *Dissolution*, 209–15, and in her *Diplomacy and Foreign Courts*, London: Hutchinson, 1928, 222–4.
62 See *Dissolution*, 211–12.
63 Hughes, *Inside the Enigma*, 99; see also Buchanan, *Ambassador's Daughter*, 169, 172, and *Mission,* 144–7.
64 Pares, *My Russian Memoirs*, 471.
65 Gordon, *Russian Year*, 154–5.
66 Robien, 58–60; Heald, 92.
67 Robien, 62, 65; Hall, *One Man's War*, 281.
68 Crosley, 60, 58.
69 Stinton Jones, 'Czar Looked Over My Shoulder', 102.
70 Marcosson, *Before I Forget*, 244.
71 Vandervelde, *Three Aspects of the Russian Revolution*, 31.
72 Ransome, letter 27 May 1917.
73 Dorr, *Woman of Fifty*, 332.

10 'The Greatest Thing in Hstory since Joan of Arc'

1 Mackenzie, *Shoulder to Shoulder*, 313.
2 Mitchell, *Women on the Warpath*, 65–6; Harper, 163.
3 Purvis, *Emmeline Pankhurst*, 292. See ibid., n.2, Chapter 20, 293.
4 Harper, 162.
5 Ibid., 163.
6 Kenney, 'The Price of Liberty', 12–13.
7 Ibid., 13.
8 Ibid., 19.
9 Ibid.

10 Rappaport, *Women Social Reformers*, vol. 2, Santa Barbara: ABC-Clio, 2001, 635.
11 Kerby, 'Bubbling Brook', 22.
12 Rogers, 3:8, 84.
13 Harper, 252; Armour, 'Recollections', 7.
14 Rogers, 3:8, 85.
15 Beatty, 38.
16 Rogers, 3:8, 86; Beatty, 35.
17 Kennan, *Russia Leaves the War*, 22, 21.
18 Harper, 164, 162.
19 Kenney, 'Price of Liberty', 27.
20 Ibid.
21 Mackenzie, *Shoulder to Shoulder*, 313; see also Mitchell, *Women on the Warpath*, 67, 69.
22 Kenney, 'Price of Liberty', 42, 43.
23 See Botchkareva, *Yashka*, Chapter 6, 'I Enlist by the Grace of the Tsar'.
24 Beatty, 93.
25 Dorr, 'Maria Botchkareva Leader of Soldiers', *La Crosse Tribune and Leader-Press*, 9 June 1918.
26 Botchkareva, *Yashka*, 162.
27 Vecchi, *Tavern is My Drum*, 79; see also Bochkareva's 'Deposition about the Women's Battalion', which describes how it was formed; in Rovin Bisha et al., *Russian Women, 1698–1917, Experience & Expression*, Bloomington: Indiana University Press, 2002, 222–31.
28 Vecchi, *Tavern is My Drum*, 79.
29 See Botchkareva, *Yashka*, 165–8.
30 Russell, *Unchained Russia*, 210–11.
31 See also 'Russia's Women Soldiers', *Literary Digest*, 29 September 1917, written by an Associated Press Correspondent; Long, *Russian Revolution Aspects*, 98.
32 Beatty, 100–1.
33 Thompson, 271; see also Dorr, *Inside the Russian Revolution*, 54–5.
34 Thompson, 272–3; Stites, *Women's Liberation Movement in Russia*, 296; Beatty, 107.

35 Botchkareva, *Yashka*, 168.

36 Thompson's coverage of the Women's Death Battalion attracted considerable press notice in the USA. See Mould, 'Russian Revolution', n. 16, p. 9.

37 Mackenzie, *Shoulder to Shoulder*, 315; Kenney, 'Price of Liberty', 35.

38 See Botchkareva, *Yashka*, 189–91.

39 Dorr, 'Marie Botchkareva, Leader of Soldiers'; Kenney, 'Price of Liberty', 49.

40 Harper, 170.

41 *Dissolution*, 217; Vecchi, *Tavern is My Drum*, 79; Harper, 172.

42 Mackenzie, *Shoulder to Shoulder*, 314.

43 Thompson, 274.

44 Poutiatine, *War and Revolution in Russia*, 73–4.

45 Patouillet, 1:147.

46 Shepherd, 'The Soul That Stirs in "Battalions of Death"', *Delineator*, XCII:3, March 1918, 5.

47 Harper, 173, 174; see Chapter X for the Women's Death Battalion.

48 See Botchkareva, *Yashka*, 217.

49 Mackenzie, *Shoulder to Shoulder*; *Britannia*, 3 August 1917.

50 Kenney, 'Price of Liberty', 37. Pankhurst relayed Yusupov's version of events to Rheta Childe Dorr, who was one of the first to publish this account from the horse's mouth.

51 Kenney, 'Price of Liberty', 53, 54.

52 Mitchell, *Women on the Warpath*, 66.

53 Harper, 163, 165, 166.

54 Ibid., 180.

55 Ibid., 187, 183.

56 Ibid., 182, 192.

57 Ibid. 253, 185; Francis, 145.

58 Harper, 188, 189, 192.

59 Rogers, 3:8, 87.

60 Wright, 93.

61 Ibid., 91.

62 Gerda and Hermann Weber, *Lenin, Life and Works*, New York: Facts on File, 1980, 134.

63 Harper, 254.

11 'What Would the Colony Say if We Ran Away?'

1 See Figes, *People's Tragedy*, 396.
2 Harper, 194–5.
3 Harper, 199; Ransome, quoted in Pitcher, *Witnesses of the Russian Revolution*, 120.
4 Harper, 202.
5 Thompson, 284, 283. Morgan Philips Price also visited in June and wrote a piece published in the *Manchester Guardian* on 17 July, see Pitcher, *Witnesses of the Russian Revolution*, 103–10.
6 Crosley, 79–80.
7 Pipes, *Russian Revolution*, 419; Figes, *People's Tragedy*, 426–8.
8 Dorr, *Inside the Russian Revolution*, 25; Thompson, 288.
9 *Dissolution*, 219; *Mission*, 152; Robien, 82.
10 *Dissolution*, 220, and *Petrograd*, 134; Lady Georgina Buchanan, 'From the Petrograd Embassy', 20, letter of 22/9 July.
11 Robien, 83; Noulens, *Mon Ambassade en Russie Soviétique*, 65, has a drawing of de Buisseret's motor car loaded down with heavily armed Bolsheviks. Thompson, 287.
12 Nellie Thornton, 'Englishwoman's Experiences during the Russian Revolution', 2–4.
13 Garstin, 'Denis Garstin and the Russian Revolution', 593.
14 Patin, *Journal d'une institutrice française*, 48.
15 Stopford, 171; Poole, *Dark People*, 4, 5.
16 Crosley, 90–2.
17 Blunt, *Lady Muriel*, 109.
18 Stopford, 175.
19 *The World*, 19 July 1917, quoted in Hawkins, 'Through War to Revolution with Dosch Fleurot', 70–1.
20 Harold Williams, *Shadow of Tyranny*, 57.
21 *New York Times* despatch for 4/17 July in ibid., 57, 58–9.
22 Poole, *Dark People*, 5.
23 Poole, *The Bridge*, 276; Poole, *Dark People*, 8; see also Thompson, 296.
24 Robien, 83.

25 Beatty, 115.

26 Ibid., 118.

27 Robien, 83; *Petrograd*, 136.

28 Harold Williams, *Shadow of Tyranny*, 63.

29 Ibid.

30 Lady Georgina Buchanan, 'From the Petrograd Embassy', 21.

31 *Petrograd*, 136–7.

32 *Dissolution*, 222; Poole, *The Bridge*, 275.

33 Beatty, 119, 121.

34 Wright, 101.

35 Rogers, 3:8, 98.

36 Ibid., 3:8, 99–100.

37 *Dissolution*, 222–3.

38 Beatty, 122.

39 Bliss, 'Philip Jordan's Letters from Russia', 143.

40 Francis, 137; Robien, 85.

41 Rogers, 3:8, 101; Williams, 88.

42 Francis, 138; See Chapter 6; P. N. Pereverzev, 'Lenin, Ganetsy, I Ko. Shpiony!', http://militera.lib.ru/research/sobolev_gl/06.html

43 Lady Georgina Buchanan, 'From the Petrograd Embassy', 21.

44 Bliss, 'Philip Jordan's Letters from Russia', 143.

45 Barnes, 249, letter of 9/22 July.

46 Stopford, 176.

47 *Dissolution*, 225; Lady Georgina Buchanan, 'Letters from the Petrograd Embassy', 21.

48 Gerhardie, *Memoirs of a Polyglot*, 125.

49 *Mission*, 154; *Dissolution*, 226; Buchanan, *Ambassador's Daughter*, 174–5; Stopford, 177; Lady Georgina Buchanan, 'Letters from the Petrograd Embassy', 21.

50 Rogers, 3:8, 102–3.

51 Thompson, 308, 309.

52 Ibid., 312; Harper, 'Thompson Risks Life'.

53 Ransome, Despatch 184, 5 [18] July 1917.

54 Williams, *Shadow of Tyranny*, 65.

55 Knox, *With the Russian Army*, 662–3; *Mission*, 156.

56 Dorr, *Inside the Russian Revolution*, 28.

57 Thompson, 315; Francis, *Russia from the American Embassy*, 141.

58 Overall about twenty Cossacks were killed and seventy wounded in the July Days; around a hundred horses were killed. See B.V. Nikitin, '*Rokovye gody*' (*Novye pokazaniya uchastnika*), http://www.dk1868.ru/history/nikitin4.htm

59 Stebbing, 'From Czar to Bolshevik', 44; Poole, *The Bridge*, 280.

60 Beatty, 129; Crosley, 110–11; Poole, *The Bridge*, 280–1.

61 Dorr, *Inside the Russian Revolution*, 32.

62 Beatty, 130.

63 Patin, *Journal d'une institutrice française*, 50.

64 Robien, 90.

65 Bliss, 'Philip Jordan's Letters from Russia', 146.

66 Beatty, 131.

67 Dorr, *Inside the Russian Revolution*, 32–3, Poole, *Dark People*, 12.

68 Kenney, 'Price of Liberty', 74, 75.

69 Ibid., 76.

70 Kenney papers, JK/3/Mitchell/5, UEA, 20; Dorr, *Inside the Russian Revolution*, 34.

71 Cantacuzène, *Revolutionary Days*, 315.

72 Crosley, 99–100.

73 Ibid., 105. For the two militias operating in Petrograd, see Hasegawa, 'Crime, Police, and Mob Justice', 58–61.

74 Oudendyk, *Ways and By-ways in Diplomacy*, 223; Dorr, *Inside the Russian Revolution*, 29.

75 Ransome, letter to his mother, 23 [10] July 1917.

76 Thompson, 324.

77 Ibid., 313.

12 'This Pest-Hole of a Capital'

1 Whipple, Petrograd diary, 133.

2 Wightman, *Diary of an American Physician*, 64–5, 63.

3 Robins, letter 13 [26] July, Falers Library.

4 Beatty, 149. For Travis see 'Tragedy and Comedy in Making Pictures of the Russian Chaos,' *Current Opinion*, February 1918, 106.

5 Wightman, *Diary of an American Physician*, 35.

6 Whipple, 'Chance for Young Americans', *Literary Digest*, 26 January 1918, 47; Whipple, Petrograd diary, 85.

7 Whipple, Petrograd diary, 79, 80–1.

8 Ibid., 97; Wright, 111.

9 Beatty, 146–7.

10 Ibid., 147.

11 Whipple, Petrograd diary, 90.

12 Ibid.

13 Ibid., 95.

14 Wightman, *Diary of an American Physician*, 38, 39, 41, 44.

15 Letter 15 August, in Salzman, *Reform and Revolution*, 182.

16 Letter 1/14 August, Falers Library; 5/18 August, Falers Library.

17 Letter 9/22 August and 6/19 August, Falers Library.

18 Oudendyk, *Ways and By-ways of Diplomacy*, 234.

19 Robien, 100.

20 See Pipes, *People's Tragedy*, 448; Long, *Russian Revolution Aspects*, Chapter XIII.

21 Beatty, 148.

22 Fleurot, 174.

23 Knox, 679.

24 *Mission*, 171–2.

25 John Shelton Curtiss, *The Russian Revolutions of 1917*, Malabar, FL: R. E. Krieger Publishing Co., 1957, 50.

26 Rogers, 3:8, 139.

27 Beatty, 153, 154, 155.

28 Rogers, 3:8, 136.

29 Beatty, 159; Bliss, 'Philip Jordan's Letters from Russia', 143.

30 Buchanan, *Ambassador's Daughter*, 179.

31 Francis, 162; Wright, 123.

32 Salzman, *Reform and Revolution*, 193.

33 Beatty, 156.

34 Beatty, 157; Harper, 278–9, 280–1.

35 Poole, *An American Diplomat in Bolshevik Russia*, 15–16; Gordon, *Russian Year*, 213.
36 Lindley, untitled memoirs, 14–15.
37 Oudendyk, *Ways and By-ways in Diplomacy*, 236.
38 Crosley, 192, 193.
39 Harper, 287.
40 Foglesong, 'Missouri Democrat', 37; Francis, 160–1.
41 Wright, 129.
42 Crosley, 174; see also Wright, 108.
43 Wright, 122.
44 Crosley, 173-4; Wright, 121, 122.
45 Woodhouse, FO 236/59/2258, 2 October.
46 Bosanquet letters, 28 December 1916, 193; Jennifer Stead, 'A Bradford Mill in St Petersburg', *Old West Riding*, 2:2, Winter 1982, 20.
47 Buchanan, *Dissolution of an Empire*, 242; Stebbing, *From Czar to Bolshevik*, 104.
48 Robien, 104.
49 Ibid., 123.
50 Cantacuzène, *Revolutionary Days*, 352–3, 354; Crosley, 135–6.
51 Pax, *Journal d'une comédienne française*, 77.
52 *Lubbock Morning Avalanche*, 13 March 1919.
53 Anet, 164; Cordasco (Woodhouse), online memoir.
54 Crosley, 135–6; see also 197.
55 Robien, 106; Crosley, 153.
56 Robien, 106.
57 Purvis, *Emmeline Pankhurst*, 297.
58 Kenney, 'Price of Liberty', 122.
59 Harper, 162, 166.
60 Kenney, 'Price of Liberty', 127.
61 Harper, 167; Kenney, 'Price of Liberty', 133.
62 Harper, 167, 293. For Harper, Pankhurst and Kenney's rail journey out of Russia, see Harper, Chapter XIX.
63 Poole, *The Bridge*, 271.
64 Morgan, *Somerset Maugham*, 227.
65 Maugham, *Writer's Notebook*, 137–8.

66 Maugham, 'Looking Back', Part III, *Show: The Magazines of the Arts*, 2, 1962, 95.
67 Hastings, *Secret Lives of Somerset Maugham*, 226.
68 Hugh Walpole, 'Literary Close Ups', *Vanity Fair*, 13, January 1920, 47.
69 Hastings, *Secret Lives of Somerset Maugham*, 227.
70 For Reed's career prior to Petrograd, see Bassow, *Moscow Correspondents*, 22–5; Service, *Spies and Commissars*, 50–4; Dearborn, *Queen of Bohemia*; Seldes, *Witness to a Century*, 42–5.
71 Dearborn, *Queen of Bohemia*, 75.
72 Bryant, 21, xi.

13 'For Color and Terror and Grandeur This Makes Mexico Look Pale'

1 Bryant, 19–20.
2 Fuller, Letters, 16.
3 Fuller, Journal, 7, 8–9.
4 See Rosenstone, *Romantic Revolutionary*, 289.
5 Francis, 167, 168, 165–6.
6 Rogers, 3:9, 147.
7 Homberger, *John Reed*, 105; Williams, 22.
8 See Williams, 30–1.
9 Ibid., 35, 36.
10 Francis, 169.
11 Fuller, Journal, 15.
12 Rogers, 3:10, 241. George F. Kennan, who was a friend of Reed and was interviewed for Warren Beatty's 1981 film *Reds*, agreed that Reed could be 'inconsiderate, intolerant, needlessly offensive … he could be grievously wrong about many things'. But there he was, with all that energy, in the centre of things in Petrograd, 'flaming like a human torch with its contagious enthusiasm, absorbing into his youthful frame the immense, incipient antagonism that was eventually to separate two great people and to devastate his own life and so many others. His was *one* American way of reacting to the Revolution. It deserves

to be neither forgotten nor ridiculed.' Kennan, *Russia Leaves the War*, 68, 69.

13 Bryant, 25.

14 Ibid., 42, 43, 37.

15 Ibid., 39–40.

16 Gordon, *Russian Year*, 219.

17 See Pax, *Journal d'une comédienne française*, 43–6. Pax had actually returned to France for several months.

18 Oudendyk, *Ways and By-ways in Diplomacy*, 227; Bryant, *Six Red Months in Russia*, 44; see also Reed, 38–40.

19 Reed, 61.

20 Gordon, *Russian Year*, 219.

21 Brun, *Troublous Times*, 2.

22 Rogers, 3:9, 159.

23 Harold Williams diary, quoted in Tyrkova-Williams, *Cheerful Giver*, 193.

24 Maugham, *Writer's Notebook*, 145.

25 Ibid., 146.

26 Ransome report to *Daily News*, quoted in Pitcher, *Witnesses of the Russian Revolution*, 174.

27 Williams, *Shadow of Tyranny*, 125; Wright, 130.

28 Brogan, *Life of Arthur Ransome*, 144, 145.

29 Maugham, *Writer's Notebook*, 150.

30 Pitcher, *Witnesses of the Russian Revolution*, 177.

31 Williams, *Shadow of Tyranny*, 28; published in *New York Times*, 6 October NS.

32 *Mission*, 188–9.

33 Salzman, *Reform and Revolution*, 197.

34 Ibid.

35 *Mission*, 191; see also Robien, 121.

36 Wright, 129.

37 *Mission*, 193; Robien, 122.

38 Hastings, *Secret Lives of Somerset Maugham*, 228.

39 Rogers, 3:9, 149, 148; Patouillet, 2:194. For the return of the Salvation Army to Petrograd, see Aitken, *Blood and Fire, Tsar and Commissar*, Chapter 8: '1917: A Transient Freedom'.

40 Cantacuzène, *Revolutionary Days*, 352–3.

41 Destrée, *Les Fondeurs de la neige*, 27.

42 Ibid.

43 Bruce, *Silken Dalliance*, 163; Reed's experience was also described in Madeleine Doty's *Behind the Battle Line*, 46. Doty, a Greenwich Village friend of Louise Bryant and a trained lawyer, arrived in Petrograd in November 1917, returning to the USA with Bryant and Beatty the following January.

44 Reinke, 'Getting On Without the Czar', 12.

45 Crosley, 190.

46 Wright, 129.

47 Bryant, 67.

48 Fleurot, 177.

49 Ibid.

50 Rogers, 3:9, 162.

51 Ibid., 162–3.

52 Gordon, *Russian Year*, 217–18.

53 Bryant, 120.

54 Hastings, *Secret Lives of Somerset Maugham*, 230.

55 *Mission*, 196.

56 Maugham, *Writer's Notebook*, 150; Reed's verdict on Kerensky, quoted in John Hohenburg, *Foreign Correspondence: The Great Reporters and Their Times*, Columbia University Press, 1995, 105.

57 *Mission*, 201; Noulens, *Mon Ambassade en Russie*, 116.

58 Fuller, Journal, 18–19.

59 Rogers, 3:9, 154.

60 Ibid., 155–6; Fuller, Journal, 20.

61 Cordasco (Woodhouse), online memoir.

62 Francis, 169–70.

63 Bliss, 'Philip Jordan's Letters from Russia', 142–3.

64 Rogers, 3:9, 164, 167. For a description of the flat, see Fuller, Journal, 47.

65 Wright, 141.

66 Williams, 87–8.

14 'We Woke Up to Find the Town in the Hands of the Bolsheviks'

1 Fuller, Journal, 23.
2 Ibid., 26
3 Rogers, 3:9, 186.
4 Ibid., 187.
5 Ibid., 186.
6 Ibid., 187.
7 Ibid., 188–9.
8 Ibid., 189.
9 Ibid., 190.
10 Ibid., 190–1.
11 Ibid., 191.
12 Lindley letter, entry for 25 October, LRA, MS 1372/1.
13 Beatty, 179–80.
14 Buchanan, *Ambassador's Daughter*, 180.
15 *Petrograd*, 187–8, 190.
16 See Pipes, *Russian Revolution*, 489, 495; Figes, *People's Tragedy*, 486.
17 Nostitz, *Romance and Revolutions*, 193.
18 Reed, 91, 92.
19 Knox, *With the Russian Army*, 712. For descriptions of the Smolny at this time, see: Gordon, *Russian Year*, 231–2; Reed, 54–5, 76–7, 96–9; Doty, *Behind the Battle Line*, 74–6; see also Robien, 140–1.
20 Reed, 87.
21 Williams, 128–9.
22 Doty, *Behind the Battle Line*, 76.
23 Reed, 73.
24 According to the *History of the Times*, Vol. 4, 146, 'very few correspondents' witnessed any of these events during the night; in fact most of what happened during 24–6 October was little reported as it occurred, because of the impossibility of getting telegraphed reports out. Before he left, *The Times*'s own Petrograd correspondent, Robert Wilton, had warned of a second impending revolution. See Philip Knightley, *The First Casualty*, London: Quartet, 1978, 138.

25 For accounts of this episode, see: Wright, 143; Gordon, *Russian Year*, 254–5; Barnes, 266–7; Francis, 179; see also Kennan, *Russia Leaves the War*, 71–2.

26 Pipes, *Russian Revolution*, 492.

27 Williams, 100–1.

28 Ibid., 101, 102, 103.

29 Reed, 98.

30 Beatty, 193.

31 Reed, 100.

32 Beatty, 202.

33 Williams, 11; Bryant, 83.

34 Beatty, 204; Reed, 105.

35 Bryant, 84–6.

36 Beatty, 210; Bryant, 86.

37 Beatty, 210; Bryant, 86–7; Rhys Williams, 119; Reed, 108.

38 Bryant, 87; Beatty, 211; Williams, 119.

39 Beatty, 212, 213, 215.

40 Williams, 122; see also Bryant, 88; Reed, 109.

41 Fuller, Journal, 29.

42 Crosley, 202, 200.

43 Ibid., 204.

44 Bruce, *Silken Dalliance*, 163–4.

45 Crosley, 208.

46 Nostitz, *Romance and Revolutions*, 195–6; see also Stites, *Women's Liberation Movement in Russia*, 299–300; Tyrkova-Williams, *From Liberty to Brest-Litovsk*, 256–9.

47 Buchanan, *Ambassador's Daughter*, 183.

48 *Dissolution*, 251; Brun, *Troublous Times*, 14.

49 Buchanan, *Ambassador's Daughter*, 183; Crosley, 209, 210.

50 Robien, 136.

51 Cantacuzène, *Revolutionary Days*, 413.

52 Buchanan, *Ambassador's Daughter*, 183; *Dissolution*, 251.

53 Buchanan, *Ambassador's Daughter*, 184; *Dissolution*, 251; Knox, *With the Russian Army*, 713.

54 Tyrkova-Williams, *From Liberty to Brest-Litovsk*, 25.

55 Williams, 126, 129.

56 Reed, 128.

57 Williams, 130.

58 Oudendyk, *Ways and By-ways in Diplomacy*, 241.

59 Beatty, 217.

60 Williams, 144; Beatty, see Chapter 12; Philips Price, 151–4; Crosley, 211.

61 Beatty, 226.

62 Ibid., 229, 237; Williams, 149.

63 Beatty, 235; Williams, 149.

64 Beatty, 233–4.

65 Ibid., 237; Williams, 149; Reed, 184.

66 Reed, 182.

67 Ibid., 183.

68 Ibid., 183, 184.

69 Nostitz, *Romance and Revolutions*, 195–6.

70 Brun, *Troublous Times*, 18, 20.

71 Robien, 137.

72 *Petrograd*, 200; *Mission*, 212.

73 Beatty, 225. Forty-four boys and three of their officers captured at the Vladimirsky were taken away to the fortress at Kronstadt; 129 cadets from the Telephone Exchange were locked up in the Peter and Paul Fortress. See A. Mitrofanov, *Za spasenie rodiny, a ne revolyutsii: Vosstanie yunkerov v Petrograde 29 Oktyabrya 1917 g.*, http://rusk.ru/vst.php?idar=419873

74 Robien, 142.

15 'Crazy People Killing Each Other Just Like We Swat Flies at Home'

1 Bliss, 'Philip Jordan's Letters from Russia', 146–7; Francis, 188–9.

2 Rogers, 3:9, 181.

3 Ibid., 181-2.

4 Wright, 149–50.

5 Letter of 21 November (4 December), quoted in Cordasco (Woodhouse), online memoir.

6 *Dissolution*, 263; *Mission*, 239; Buchanan, *Ambassador's Daughter*, 187.

7 Cantacuzène, *Revolutionary Days*, 424.
8 *Mission*, 218, 219; Lady Georgina Buchanan, 'From the Petrograd Embassy', 21.
9 Barnes, 277; Cantacuzène, *Revolutionary Days*, 425.
10 Barnes, 281; Wright, 283; Barnes, 283.
11 Robien, 147.
12 Patouillet, 2:368.
13 Robien, 147.
14 For a description of this, see Doty, *Behind the Battle Line*, 77–9, and Keeling, *Bolshevism*, 111–15.
15 Beatty, 293.
16 Rogers, 3:9, 182; Rogers, *Wine of Fury*, 262–3.
17 See Rogers, 3:9, 191, 190.
18 Robien, 160, 177.
19 Ibid., 166.
20 Buchanan, *Ambassador's Daughter*, 185–6; Cordasco (Woodhouse), online memoir.
21 Bliss, 'Philip Jordan's Letters from Russia', 144–5.
22 Crosley, 213; Rogers, *Wine of Fury*, 261.
23 Robien, 170.
24 Salzman, *Reform and Revolution*, 198, 383.
25 Robien, 147.
26 Beatty, 322.
27 Letter to Annie Pulliam, quoted in Barnes, 271–2.
28 Ibid.
29 Beatty, 330, 332.
30 Ibid., 331; De Robien, 163–4.
31 Beatty, 332.
32 Ibid., 331.
33 Oudendyk, *Ways and By-ways in Diplomacy*, 249.
34 Robien, 164; Buchanan, *Ambassador's Daughter*, 188.
35 Rogers, 3:9, 205.
36 *Dissolution*, 266; Buchanan, *Ambassador's Daughter*, 188.
37 Buchanan, *Ambassador's Daughter*, 188; Rogers, 3:9, 199.
38 Robien, 176.
39 Buchanan, *Ambassador's Daughter*, 189–90.

40 Bliss, 'Philip Jordan's Letters from Russia', 150.
41 Lunacharsky, quoted in Mark Schrad, *Vodka Politics: Alcohol. Autocracy, and the Secret History of the Russian State*, New York: OUP, 2014, 202.
42 Rogers, *Wine of Fury*, 216; Rogers, 3:9, 199; Robien, 164.
43 Robien, 164, 175, 166–7.
44 Garstin, 'Denis Garstin and the Russian Revolution', 596.
45 Crosley, 210; Pax, 44, 72–3.
46 Crosley, 230, 231.
47 Rogers, 3:9, 203.
48 *Mission*, 239.
49 Bliss, 'Philip Jordan's Letters from Russia', 150.
50 Beatty, 386.
51 Ibid., 387.
52 Fuller, Journal, 47.
53 Beatty, 390; Fuller, Journal, 47. Mildred Farwell, another unsung American female journalist, was based on the Eastern Front during World War I. She published articles for the *Public Ledger* on Serbia and elsewhere in the Balkans, and on Petrograd for the *Chicago Tribune*.
54 Fuller, Journal, 47–8, Fuller, Letters, 52; Rogers, 3:9, 211.
55 Gerhardie letter, quoted in Pitcher, *Witnesses of the Russian Revolution*, 263.
56 Buchanan, *Ambassador's Daughter*, 191; see also *Dissolution*, 273.
57 Rogers, 3:10, 213; Fuller, Journal, 48.
58 Rogers, 3:10, 214.
59 Ibid., 214–15.
60 Ibid., 215; Fuller, Letters, 54.
61 Rogers, 3:10, 218, 220. The Bolsheviks were still occupying the bank when Rogers finally left Petrograd in February 1918.
62 Stinton Jones, 'The Czar Looked Over My Shoulder', 106–8.
63 Buchanan, *Ambassador's Daughter*, 191.
64 Ibid., 192; *Dissolution*, 276–7.
65 *Dissolution*, 275.
66 *Mission*, 247.

67 Oudendyk, *Ways and By-ways in Diplomacy*, 253–4; Bousfield Swan Lombard, letter to his wife 2 January 1918, courtesy John Carter.

68 Bliss, 'Philip Jordan's Letters from Russia', 150.

69 Crosley, 264.

70 Rogers, 3:10, 223.

71 Ibid., 224.

Postscript: The Forgotten Voices of Petrograd

1 See *Mission*, Chapter XXXV; *Ambassador's Daughter*, 201–8.

2 For their life in Rome, see Buchanan, *Ambassador's Daughter*, Chapter XVII.

3 For a discussion of the Romanov asylum issue, see Helen Rappaport, *Ekaterinburg: The Last Days of the Romanovs*, London: Hutchinson, 2008, 147–51.

4 See Roy Bainton, *Honoured by Strangers: Captain Cromie's Extraordinary First War*, London: Constable & Robinson, 2002, Chapter 22; Oudendyk, *Ways and By-Ways of Diplomacy*, Chapter XXVII.

5 Cross, 'Corner of a Foreign Field', 354.

6 Francis, 235.

7 Letter of 18 January 1918 (NS), quoted in Barnes, 300.

8 See Harper Barnes, 'Russian Rhapsody: A Small City North of Moscow Opens a Museum to Honour a Former St Louis Mayor', *St Louis Post-Dispatch*, 24 August 1997. Some photographs of the interior and the museum's exhibits can be seen at http://ruspics.livejournal.com/572095.html

9 Barnes, 373. For Francis and Jordan in Russia after Petrograd, see Barnes, Chapters 19–21.

10 See Barnes, 405–7; 'D. R. Francis Valet Dies in California, *St Louis Post-Dispatch*, 1941.

11 Buchanan, *Ambassador's Daughter*, 166–7.

12 Crosley, 221.

13 Lindley, untitled memoirs, 96.

14 Bousfield Swan Lombard, letters to his wife 26 June, 17 March, 19 February 1918, courtesy John Carter.

15 Hawkins, 'Through War to Revolution with Dosch-Fleurot', Afterword, 105.

16 Marcosson, *Before I Forget*, 330, 340; see also ibid., Chapter 12, 'Trotsky and the Bolsheviks'.

17 Williams, *Shadow of Tyranny*, 318–19.

18 Syndicated to the *Topeka Capital* as 'Thompson Risks Life to Film Russian Revolution Scenes', 30 September 1917.

19 'Woman Saw Revolution Begin', *Boston Sunday Globe*, 30 June 1918.

20 See Rogers's account in Rogers, 3:10, 251–61.

21 Interview with Rogers's great-niece, Charlotte Roe, 2005, for the Association for Diplomatic Studies and Training Foreign Affairs Oral History Project, 12–13, http://www.adst.org/OH%20TOCs/Roe,%20Charlotte.toc.pdf

22 'Missouri Negro in Russia is "Jes a Honin' for Home"', *Wabash Daily Plain Dealer*, 29 September 1916.

Bibliography

ARCHIVES

Leeds University
LUL = *Leeds University Library; LRA = Leeds Russian Archive at Leeds University Library*
Bennet, Marguerite: letters written during the 1917 Revolution, LRA/MS 799/20–22.
Bosanquet, Vivian, 'Life in a Turbulent Empire – The Experiences of Vivian and Dorothy Bosanquet in Russia 1897–1918, LRA/MS 1456/362.
Buchanan, Lady Georgina: letters from Petrograd 1916, 1917, Glenesk-Bathurst Papers, Special Collections LUL/MS Dep. 1990/1/2843–2866
Christie, Ethel Mary, 'Experiences in Russia', LRA/MS 800/16.
Clare, Joseph, 'Eye Witness of the Revolution', LRA/MS 1094/8.
Coates Family Papers, Special Collections LRA/MS 1134.
Jones, James Stinton, 'The Czar Looked Over My Shoulder', LRA/MS 1167.
Lindley, Francis Oswald: Petrograd diary, November 1917, LRA/MS 1372/1 and untitled memoirs from July 1915 to 1919, MS 1372/2.
Lombard, Rev. Bousfield Swan: untitled typescript memoirs, LRA/MS 1099.

Marshall, Lilla, 'Memories of St Petersburg 1917', LRA/MS 1113.

Metcalf, Kenneth letter 3 (16) March 1917 from Petrograd, Metcalf Collection, LRA/MS 1224/1–2.

Pearse, Mrs May, 'Den-za-den' diary for 1917, Edmund James Pearse Papers, LRA/MS 1231/32.

Ransome, Arthur: telegram despatches to the *Daily News* December 1916–December 1917, and letters from Petrograd for 1917. Arthur Ransome Archive, Special Collections, LUL/MS BC 20c/Box 13: 38–184.

Seaborn, Annie, 'My Memories of the Russian Revolution', LRA/MS 950.

Springfield, Colonel Osborn, 'To Helen', handwritten memoir of Russia, 1917–19, Special Collections LUL, Liddle Collection, RUS 44.

Thornton, Nellie, 'An Englishwoman's Experiences during the Russian Revolution', Thornton Collection, LRA/MS 1072/24.

Other UK archives

Bowerman, Elsie: letters from Petrograd 1917, Elsie Bowerman Papers, Women's Library, GB 06 7ELB, at London School of Economics.

Bury, Sir George: 'Report Regarding the Russian Revolution prepared at the request of the British War Cabinet, 5 April 1917', Lord Davies of Llandinam Papers, C3/23, National Library of Wales.

Jefferson, Geoffrey: letters from Petrograd 1916–17, Geoffrey Jefferson Papers, GB 133 JEF/1/4/1–15; 2/1–5, Manchester University.

Kenney, Jessie: Russian diary, 1917, KP/JK/4/1; TS of Russian diary, KP/JK/4/1/1; 'The Price of Liberty' TS, KP/JK/4/1/6, Jessie Kenney Archive, University of East Anglia.

Kerby, Edith: Edith Bangham, 'The Bubbling Brook' [memoirs of Russia]; private archive.

Lindley, Sir Francis Oswald: report from Petrograd, FO 371/2998, The National Archives (TNA).

Locker Lampson, 'Report on the Russian Revolution, April 1917', FO 371/81396, TNA.

Pocock, Lyndall Crossthwaite: MS diary with photographs of service at Anglo-Russian Hospital 1915–1918, Documents.3648, Imperial War Museum.

Seymour, Dorothy: photocopy of MS diary 1914–17 and photocopy of letters from Petrograd 1917, Documents.3210, Imperial War Museum.

American archives

Armour, Norman, 'Recollections of Norman Armour of the Russian Revolution', TS, Box 2 Folder 32, Seeley G. Mudd Library, Princeton University Library.

Dearing, Fred Morris: unpublished MS memoirs (based on his diary), Fred Morris Dearing Papers, C2926, Historical Society of Missouri.

Fuller, John Louis Hilton, 'The Journal of John L. H. Fuller While in Russia', ed. Samuel A. Fuller, Indiana Historical Society, TS 1999, MO112.

—— 'Letters and Diaries of John L. H. Fuller 1917–1920, TS edited by Samuel Ashby Fuller, Indiana Historical Society.

Northrup Harper, Samuel: Petrograd diary 1917, Box 27 Folder F; letters from Petrograd Box 4, Folders 9, 10, 11, Northrup Harper Papers, University of Chicago Library.

Patouillet, Madame [Louise]: TS diary, October 1916–August 1918, 2 vols, Madame Patouillet Collection, Hoover Institution Archives.

Robins, Raymond: letters to his wife Margaret, Wisconsin Historical Society.

—— letters to his sister Elizabeth, Falers Library NY, Box 3, Folder 19, RR and MDR to ER, 1917.

Rogers, Leighton, 'An Account of the March Revolution, 1917', Leighton W. Rogers Collection, Hoover Institution Archives.

—— Rogers, Leighton: 1912–82, Box 3, unpublished TS of 'Czar, Revolution, Bolsheviks'; letters from Petrograd; Leighton W. Rogers Papers, Library of Congress.

Swinnerton, C[hester] T., 'Letter from Petrograd, March 27(NS) 1917', C.T. Swinnerton Collection, Hoover Institution Archives.

Urquhart May, Leslie: 1917 letter, from Petrograd Hoover Institution Archives.

Whipple, George Chandler: Petrograd diary, 7 August–11 September, vol. I: 77–167, George Chandler Whipple Papers, Harvard University Archives, HUG 1876.3035.

DISSERTATIONS & PAPERS

Gatewood, James Dewey, 'American Observers in the Soviet Union 1917–1933', University of Wisconsin, thesis 1968.

Ginzburg, Lyubov, 'Confronting the Cold War Legacy: The Forgotten History of the American Colony in St Petersburg. A Case Study of Reconciliation', University of Kansas, 2010; http://kuscholarworks.ku.edu/handle/1808/6427

Hawkins, Kenneth, 'Through War to Revolution with Dosch-Fleurot: A Personal History of an American Newspaper Correspondent in Europe and Russia 1914–1918', University of Rochester, NY, 1986.

Mould, Dr David H. (Ohio University), 'The Russian Revolution: A Conspiracy Thesis and a Lost Film', paper presented at FAST REWIND-II, Rochester, NY, 13–16 June 1991.

Orlov, Ilya, 'Beskrovnaya revolyutsiya?' Traur i prazdnik v revolyutsionnoi politike; http://net.abimperio.net/files/february.pdf

Vinogradov, Yuri, 'Lazarety Petrograda'; http://www.proza.ru/2010/01/30/984

DIGITAL SOURCES

Cordasco, Ella (née Woodhouse), 'Recollections of the Russian Revolution: https://web.archive.org/web/20120213165523/http://www.zimdocs.btinternet.co.uk/fh/ella2.html

Cotton, Dorothy: letter 4 March 1917 from Petrograd, Library & Archives of Canada: http://www.bac-lac.gc.ca/eng/discover/military-heritage/first-world-war/canada-nursing-sisters/Pages/dorothy-cotton.aspx

PRIMARY SOURCES

Books

Abraham, Richard, 'Mariia L. Bochkareva and the Russian Amazons of 1917', in Linda Edmondson, ed., *Women and Society in Russia and the Soviet Union*, Cambridge: Cambridge University Press, 2008, 124–41.

Allison, William Thomas, *Witness to Revolution: The Russian Revolution Diary and Letters of J. Butler Wright*, Westport Connecticut: Praeger, 2002.

Alston, Charlotte, *Russia's Greatest Enemy: Harold Williams and the Russian Revolutions*, London: Tauris, 2007.

Anet, Claude [Jean Schopfer], *Through the Russian Revolution: Notes of an Eyewitness, from 12th March–30th May*, London: Hutchinson, 1917.

Arbenina, Stella [Baroness Meyendorff], *Through Terror to Freedom*, London: Hutchinson, 1930.

Barnes, Harper, *Standing on a Volcano: The Life and Times of David R. Francis*, Missouri: Missouri Historical Society Press, 2001.

Beatty, Bessie, *The Red Heart of Russia*, New York: The Century Co., 1918.

Blunt, Wilfred, *Lady Muriel: Lady Muriel Paget, Her Husband, and Her Philanthropic Work in Central and Eastern Europe*, London: Methuen, 1962.

Botchkareva, Maria, *Yashka: My Life as Peasant, Officer and Exile*, New York: Frederick A. Stokes Co., 1919. Bruce, Henry James, *Silken Dalliance*, London: Constable, 1947.

Brun, Captain Alf Harold, *Troublous Times: Experiences in Bolshevik Russia and Turkestan*, London: Constable, 1931.

Bryant, Louise, *Six Red Months in Russia*, London: Journeyman Press, reprinted 1982 [1918].

Buchanan, Sir George, *My Mission to Russia and Other Diplomatic Memories*, vol. 2, Boston: Little, Brown & Co., 1923.

Buchanan, Meriel, *Petrograd, The City of Trouble 1914–1918*, London: W. Collins, 1919.

—— *Dissolution of an Empire*, London: John Murray, 1932.

—— *Ambassador's Daughter*, London: Cassell, 1958.

Cahill, Audrey, *Between the Lines: Letters and Diaries from Elsie Inglis's Russian Unit*, Durham: Pentland Press, 1999.

Cantacuzène-Speransky, Julia, *Revolutionary Days, Including Passages from* My Life Here and There, *1876–1917*, Chicago: Lakeside Press, 1999.

Chambrun, Charles de, *Lettres à Marie, Pétersbourg-Pétrograde 1914–18*, Paris: Librairie Plon, 1941.

Cockfield, Jamie H., *Dollars and Diplomacy: Ambassador David Rowland Francis and the Fall of Tsarism, 1916–17*, Durham, NC: Duke University Press, 1981.

Crosley, Pauline Stewart, *Intimate Letters from Petrograd 1917–1920*, New York: E. P. Dutton, 1920.

Cross, Anthony, 'A Corner of a Foreign Field: The British Embassy in St Petersburg, 1863–1918', in *Personality and Place in Russian Culture: Essays in Memory of Lindsey Hughes*, London: MHRA, 2010, 328–58.

Destrée, Jules, *Les Fondeurs de neige: Notes sur la révolution bolchévique à Petrograd pendant l'hiver 1917–1918*, Brussels: G. Van Oest, 1920.

Dorr, Rheta Childe, *Inside the Russian Revolution*, New York: Macmillan, 1917.

—— *A Woman of Fifty*, New York: Funk & Wagnalls, 1924.

Dosch-Fleurot, Arno, *Through War to Revolution*, London: John Lane, 1931.

Doty, Madeleine Zabriskie, *Behind the Battle Line*, New York: Macmillan, 1918.

Farson, Negley, *The Way of a Transgressor*, Feltham: Zenith Books, 1983.

Fitzroy, Yvonne, *With the Scottish Nurses in Roumania*, London: John Murray, 1918.

Francis, David R., *Russia from the American Embassy, April 1916–November 1918*, Charles Scribner's, 1921.

Gibson, William J., *Wild Career: My Crowded Years of Adventure in Russia and the Near East*, London: George G. Harrap, 1935.

Golder, Frank, *War, Revolution and Peace in Russia: The Passages of Frank Golder, 1914–1927*, Stanford: Hoover Institution Press, 1992.

Hall, Bert, *One Man's War: The Story of the Lafayette Escadrille*, London: Hamish Hamilton, 1929.

Harper, Florence MacLeod, *Runaway Russia*, New York: Century, 1918.

Harper, Samuel, *The Russia I Believe In: Memoirs 1902–1941*, Chicago: University of Chicago Press, 1945.

Hart-Davis, Rupert, *Hugh Walpole, A Biography*, London: Macmillan, 1952.

Hastings, Selina, *The Secret Lives of Somerset Maugham*, London: John Murray, 2010.

Heald, Edward Thornton, *Witness to Revolution: Letters from Russia*, Kent, OH: Kent State University Press, 1972.

Houghteling, James Lawrence, *Diary of the Russian Revolution*, New York: Dodd Mead, 1918.

Jefferson, Geoffrey, *So That Was Life*, London: Royal Society of Medicine Press, 1997.

Jones, James Stinton, *Russia in Revolution*, London: Herbert Jenkins, 1917.

Keeling, Henry V., *Bolshevism: Mr Keeling's Five Years in Russia*, London: Hodder & Stoughton, 1919.

Knox, Major-General Sir Alfred, *With the Russian Army 1914–1917*, vol. 2, London: Hutchinson, 1921.

Lockhart, Robert Bruce, *Memoirs of a British Agent*, London: Putnam, 1932.

Long, Robert Edward Crozier, *Russian Revolution Aspects*, New York: E. P. Dutton, 1919.

MacNaughton, Sarah, *My War Experiences in Two Continents*, London: John Murray, 1919.

Marcosson, Isaac, *The Rebirth of Russia*, New York: John Lane Co., 1917.

Markovitch, Marylie [Amélie de Néry], *La Révolution russe par une française*, Paris: Librairie Académique, 1918.

Maugham, Somerset, *A Writer's Notebook*, London: Heinemann, 1951.

Nostitz, Countess Lili, *Romance and Revolutions*, London: Hutchinson, 1937.

Noulens, Joseph, *Mon ambassade en Russie Soviétique 1917–1919*, 2 vols, Paris: Librairie Plon, 1933.

Oudendijk, William [Willem Jacob Oudendijk], *Ways and By-Ways in Diplomacy*, London: Peter Davies, 1939.

Paléologue, Maurice, *An Ambassador's Memoirs 1914–1917: Last French Ambassador to the Russian Court*, London: Hutchinson, 1973.

Pares, Bernard, *My Russian Memoirs*, New York: AMS Press, 1969 [1931].

Pascal, Pierre, *Mon journal de Russie ...* , vol. 1: *1916–1918*, Lausanne: L'Age d'Homme, 1975.

Patin, Louise, *Journal d'une institutrice française en Russie pendant la Révolution 1917–1919*, Pontoise: Edijac, 1987.

Pax, Paulette, *Journal d'une comédienne française sous la terreur bolchévique*, Paris: L'Édition, 1919.

Pitcher, Harvey, *Witnesses of the Russian Revolution*, London: John Murray, 1994.

Poole, Ernest, *The Dark People: Russia's Crisis*, London: Macmillan, 1919.

—— *The Bridge: My Own Story*, London: Macmillan, 1940.

Price, Morgan Philips, *My Reminiscences of the Russian Revolution 1917–21*, London: Allen & Unwin, 1921.

—— *Dispatches from the Revolution: Russia 1916–1918*, Durham, NC: Duke University Press, 1997.

Ransome, Arthur, *The Autobiography of Arthur Ransome*, London: Jonathan Cape, 1976.

Reed, John, *Ten Days that Shook the World*, Harmondsworth: Penguin, 1977.

Robien, Louis de, *The Diary of a Diplomat in Russia 1917–18*, London: 1969.

Rogers, Leighton, *Wine of Fury*, New York: Alfred A. Knopf, 1924.

Russell, Charles Edward, *Unchained Russia*, New York, D. Appleton, 1918.

Salzman, Neil V., *Reform and Revolution: The Life and Times of Raymond Robins*, Kent, Ohio: Kent State University Press, 1991.

—— ed., *Russia in War and Revolution: General William V. Judson's Accounts from Petrograd, 1917–1918*, Kent, Ohio: Kent State University Press, 1998.

Stebbing, E[dward] P[ercy], *From Czar to Bolshevik*, London: John Lane, 1918.

Stopford, Albert, *The Russian Diary of an Englishman: Petrograd, 1915–1917*, London: William Heinemann, 1919.

Thompson, Captain Donald C., *Blood-Stained Russia*, New York: Leslie-Judge Co., 1918.

—— *Donald Thompson in Russia*, New York: The Century Co., 1918.

Vandervelde, Emile, *Three Aspects of the Russian Revolution*, New York: Charles Scribner's, 1918.

Vecchi, Joseph, *The Tavern is My Drum: My Autobiography*, London: Odhams Press, 1948.

Verstraete, Maurice, *Mes cahiers russes: l'ancien régime – le gouvernement provisoire – le pouvoir des soviets*, Paris: G. Crès et cie., 1920.

Walpole, 'Official Account of the First Russian Revolution', Appendix B, in Rupert Hart-Davis, *Hugh Walpole*.

Weeks, Charles J., *An American Naval Diplomat in Revolutionary Russia: The Life and Times of Vice Admiral Newton A. McCully*, Annapolis: Naval Institute Press, 1993.

Wightman, Orrin Sage, *Diary of an American Physician in the Russian Revolution 1917*, New York: Brooklyn Daily Eagle, 1928.

Williams, Albert Rhys, *Through the Russian Revolution*, Moscow: Progress Publishers, 1967.

—— *Journey into Revolution: Petrograd 1917–18*, Chicago: Quadrangle Books, 1969.

Williams, Harold, *The Shadow of Tyranny: Dispatches from Russia 1917–1920,* privately printed by J. M. Gallanar, 2011.

Wilton, Robert, *Russia's Agony*, London: Edward Arnold, 1919.

Newspaper & magazine articles
'Anon.', 'Petrograd during the Seven Days', *New Republic*, 23 June 1917, 212–17.

Bliss, Mrs Clinton A., 'Philip Jordan's Letters from Russia, 1917–19. The Russian Revolution as Seen by the American Ambassador's Valet', *Bulletin of the Missouri Historical Society*, 14, 1958, 139–66.

Buchanan, Lady Georgina, 'From the Petrograd Embassy', *Historian*, 3, Summer 1984, 19–21.

Cockfield, Jamie H., 'Philip Jordan and the October Revolution', *History Today*, 28:4, 1978, 220–7.

Cotton, Dorothy, 'A Word Picture of the Anglo-Russian Hospital', *Canadian Nurse*, 22, 9 September 1926, 486–8.

Dorr, Rheta Childe, 'Marie Botchkareva, Leader of Soldiers Tells her Vivid Story of Russia', *La Crosse Tribune and Leader-Press*, 9 June 1918.

Dosch-Fleurot, Arno, 'In Petrograd during the Seven Days', *World's Work*, July 1917, 255–63.

'D. R. Francis Valet Dies in California', obituary for Philip Jordan, in *St Louis Post Dispatch*, 22 May 1941.

Farson, Daniel, 'Aux pieds de l'impératrice', *Wheeler's Review*, 27:3, Autumn 1983.

Farson, Negley, 'Petrograd, May 1917', *New English Review*, 13, 1946, 393–6.

Foglesong, David S., 'A Missouri Democrat in Revolutionary Russia: Ambassador David R. Francis and the American Confrontation with Russian Radicalism, 1917', *Gateway Heritage*, Winter 1992, 22–42.

Grey, Lady Sybil, 'Sidelights on the Russian Revolution', *Overland Monthly*, 70, July 1917, 362–8.

Harper, Florence, 'Thompson Risks Life to Film Russian Revolution Scenes: Graphic story of the Topeka war photographer at work told by woman correspondent of the London Daily Mail', *Topeka Capital*, 30 September 1917.

Hegan, Edith, 'The Russian Revolution from a Window', *Harper's Monthly*, 135:808, September 1917, 555–60.

McDermid, Jane, 'A Very Polite and Considerate Revolution: The Scottish Women's Hospitals and the Russian Revolution, 1916–1917', *Revolutionary Russia*, 21 (2), 135–51.

Marcosson, Isaac, 'The Seven Days', *Everybody's Magazine*, 37, July 1917, 25–40.

Mould, David, 'Donald Thompson: Photographer at War', *Kansas History*, Autumn 1982, 154–67.

Pares, Bernard, 'Sir George Buchanan: Eloquent Tribute from Professor Pares', *Observer*, 6 January 1918.

Pollock, John, 'The Russian Revolution: A Review by an Onlooker', *Nineteenth Century*, 81, 1917, 1068–82.

Recouly, Raymond, 'Russia in Revolution', *Scribner's Magazine*, 62:1, 1917, 29–38.

Reinke, A. E., 'My Experiences in the Russian Revolution', Part 1, *Western Electric News*, 6, February 1918, 8–12.

—— 'Getting On Without the Czar', Part 2, *Western Electric News*, 7, March 1918, 8–15.

—— 'Trying to Understand Revolutionary Russia', Part 3, *Western Electric News*, 7, May 1918, 6–11.

Russell, Charles Edward, 'Russia's Women Warriors', *Good Housekeeping*, October 1917, 22–3, 166–7, 169–70, 173.

Shepherd, William G., 'The Road to Red Russia', *Everybody's Magazine*, 37, July 1917, 1–11.

—— 'The Soul that Stirs in "Battalions of Death"', *Delineator*, 92:3, March 1918, 5–7, 56.

—— 'Ivan in Wonderland', *Everybody's Magazine*, 38, November 1918, 32–6.

—— 'Mad Kronstadt', *Everybody's Magazine*, 38, December 1918, 39–42.

Simons, George A., 'Russia's Resurrection', *Christian Advocate*, 92:66, 12 July 1917.

Simpson, James Young, 'The Great Days of the Revolution. Impressions from a recent visit to Russia, *Nineteenth Century and After*, 82, 1917, 136–48.

Somerville, Emily Warner, 'A Kappa in Russia', *The Key*, 35:2, 1918, 121–30.

Steffens, Lincoln, 'What Free Russia Asks of Her Allies', *Everybody's Magazine*, 37, August 1917, 129–41.

Thomas, Albert, 'Journal de Albert Thomas, 22 Avril–19 Juin 1917', *Cahiers du monde russe et soviétique*, 14:1–2, 1973, 86–204.

Walpole, Hugh, 'Dennis Garstin and the Russian Revolution', *Slavonic and East European Review*, 17, 1938–9, 587–605.

Washburn, Stanley, 'Russia from Within', *National Geographic Magazine*, 32:2, August 1917, 91–120.

Wharton, Paul [pseudonym of Philip H. Chadbourn], 'The Russian Ides of March: A Personal Narrative', *Atlantic Monthly*, 120, July 1917, 21–30.

Whipple, George Chandler, 'Chance for Young Americans in the Development of Russia', *Literary Digest*, 26 January 1918, 47–51.

Wood, Joyce, 'The Revolution outside Her Window: New Light shed on the March 1917 Russian Revolution from the papers of VAD nurse Dorothy N. Seymour', *Proceedings of the South Carolina Historical Association*, 2005, 71–86.

SECONDARY SOURCES

Books

Aitken, Tom, *Blood and Fire: Tsar and Commissar: The Salvation Army in Russia, 1907–1923*, Milton Keynes: Paternoster, 2007.

Allison, W., *American Diplomats in Russia: Case Studies in Orphan Diplomacy 1916–1919*, Westport: Greenwood, 1997.

Almedingen, E. M., *Tomorrow Will Come*, London: John Lane, 1946.

—— *I Remember St Petersburg*, London: Longmans Young, 1969.

Babey, Anna Mary, *Americans in Russia 1776–1917: A Study of the American Travellers in Russia from the American Revolution to the Russian Revolution*, New York: Comet Press, 1938.

Basily, Lascelle Meserve de, *Memoirs of a Lost World*, Stanford, CA: Hoover Institution Press, 1975.

Bolshevik Propaganda. Hearings Before a Subcommittee of the Committee on the Judiciary, United States Senate, 65th Congress 3rd Session … Feb 11 to March 10 1919, US Government Printing Office, 1919.

Brennan, Hugh G., *Sidelights on Russia*, London: D. Nutt, 1918.

Brogan, Hugh, *The Life of Arthur Ransome*, London: Hamish Hamilton, 1985.

Brown, Douglas, *Doomsday 1917: The Destruction of Russia's Ruling Class*, Newton Abbott: Reader's Union, 1976.

Chambers, Roland, *The Last Englishman: The Double Life of Arthur Ransome*, London: Faber & Faber, 2009.

Chessin, Serge de, *Au Pays de la démence rouge: La Révolution russe (1917–1918)*, Paris: Librairie Plon, 1919.

Child, Richard Washburn, *Potential Russia*, New York: E. P. Dutton, 1916.

Clarke, William, *Hidden Treasures of the Romanovs: Saving the Royal Jewels*, Edinburgh: National Museum of Scotland, 2009.

Coates, Tim, *The Russian Revolution, 1917*, London: HM Stationery Office, 2000.

Cross, Anthony, *In the Lands of the Romanovs: An Annotated Bibliography of First-hand English-language Accounts of the Russian Empire (1613–1917)*, Open Book Publishers.com, 2014.

Dearborn, Mary V., *Queen of Bohemia: A Life of Louise Bryant*, New York: Houghton Mifflin, 1996.

Desmond, Robert W., *Windows on the World: The Information Press in a Changing Society 1900–1920*, Iowa City: University of Iowa Press, 1980.

Fell, Alison S. and Sharp, Ingrid, *The Women's Movement in Wartime: International Perspectives 1914–1919*, London: Palgrave Macmillan, 2007.

Ferguson, Harry, *Operation Kronstadt*, London: Hutchinson, 2008.

Figes, Orlando, *A People's Tragedy: The Russian Revolution 1891–1924*, London: Jonathan Cape, 1996.

Filene, Peter G., *American Views of Soviet Russia 1917–65*, Homewood, IL: Dorsey Press, 1968.

Foglesong, David, *America's Secret War against Bolshevism: US Intervention in the Russian Civil War 1917–1920*, Chapel Hill: University of North Carolina Press, 1996.

Frame, Murray, *The Russian Revolution 1905–1921: A Bibliographic Guide to Works in English*, Westport, CT: Greenwood Press, 1995.

Gerhardie, William, *Memoirs of a Polyglot*, London: Duckworth, 1931.

Gordon, Alban, *Russian Year: A Calendar of the Revolution*, London: Cassell & Co., 1935.

Hagedorn, Hermann, *The Magnate William Boyce Thompson and His Times*, New York: Reytnal & Hitchcock, 1935.

Harmer, Michael, *The Forgotten Hospital*, Chichester: Springwood Books, 1982.

Hartley, Janet M., *Guide to Documents and Manuscripts in the United Kingdom Relating to Russia and the Soviet Union*, London: Mansell Publications, 1987.

Hasegawa, Tsuyoshi, *The February Revolution, Petrograd, 1917*, Washington: University of Washington Press, 1981.

—— 'Crime, Police, and Mob Justice in Petrograd during the Russian Revolutions of 1917', in Rex A. Wade, ed., *Revolutionary Russia: New Approaches*, London: Routledge, 2004.

Heresch, *Blood on the Snow: Eyewitness Accounts of the Russian Revolution*, New York: Paragon House, 1990.

Herval, René, *Huit mois de révolution russe (Juin 1917–Janvier 1918)*, Paris: Librairie Hachette, 1919.

Homberger, Eric, *John Reed. Lives of the Left*, Manchester: Manchester University Press, 1990.

Howe, Sonia Elisabeth, *Real Russians*, London: S. Low, Marston, 1918.

Hughes, Michael, *Inside the Enigma: British Officials in Russia 1900–1939*, London: Hambledon Press, 1997.

Kehler, Henning, *The Red Garden: Experiences in Russia*, London: Gyldendal, 1922.

Kennan, George, *Russia Leaves the War: Soviet–American Relations 1917–1920*, vol. 1, Princeton, NJ: Princeton University Press, 1989.

Kettle, Michael, *The Allies and the Russian collapse March 1917–March 1918*; London: André Deutsch, 1981.

Lange, Christian Louis, *Russia and the Revolution and the War: An Account of a Visit to Petrograd and Helsingfors in March 1917*, New York: Carnegie Endowment for International Peace, 1917.

Lehman, Daniel, *John Reed and the Writing of Revolution*, Athens, OH: Ohio University Press, 1997.

Lincoln, Bruce, *In War's Dark Shadow: The Russians before the Great War*, New York: Dial Press, 1983.

—— *Passage Through Armageddon: The Russians in War and Revolution 1914–18*, New York: Simon & Schuster, 1986.

Lockhart, Robert Bruce, *The Two Revolutions: An Eye Witness Study of Russia 1917*, London: Bodley Head, 1967.

Mackenzie, Midge, *Shoulder to Shoulder, A Documentary*, New York: Alfred A. Knopf, 1975.

Marcosson, Isaac Frederick, *Adventures in Interviewing*, New York: John Lane, 1919.

—— *Turbulent Years*, New York: Dodd Mead & Co., 1938.

Marye, George R., *Russia Observed: Nearing the End in Imperial Russia*, Philadelphia: Dorranee & Co., 1929.

Maugham, Somerset, *Ashenden*, London: Vintage Classics, 2000.

Merry, Rev. W. Mansell, *Two Months in Russia July–September 1914*, Oxford: Basil Blackwell, 1916.

Metcalf, H. E., *On Britains Business*, London Rich & Cowan, 1943.

Mitchell, David J., *Women on the Warpath: The Story of Women in the First World War*, London: Jonathan Cape, 1966.

Mohrenschildt, D. von, *The Russian Revolution of 1917: Contemporary Accounts*, New York: Oxford University Press, 1971.

Moorhead, Caroline, *Dunant's Dream: War, Switzerland and the History of the Red Cross*, London: HarperCollins, 1998.

Morgan, Ted, *Somerset Maugham*, London: Jonathan Cape, 1980.

Nadeau, Ludovic, *Le Dessous du chaos Russe*, Paris: Hachette, 1920.

Paget, Stephen, *A Short Account of the Anglo-Russian Hospital in Petrograd*, London, n.p., 1917.

Pearlstein, Edward W., *Revolution in Russia as Reported in the NY Tribune and NY Herald 1894–1921*, New York: Viking Press, 1967.

Pethybridge, Roger, *Witnesses to the Russian Revolution*, New York: Citadel Press, 1967.

Pipes, Richard, *The Russian Revolution 1899–1919*, London: Fontana Press, 1992.

Pitcher, Harvey, *When Miss Emmie Was in Russia: English Governesses Before, During and After the October Revolution*, Cromer: Swallow House Books, 1978.

Pollock, Sir John, *War and Revolution in Russia*, London: Constable & Co., 1918.

Poole, DeWitt Clinton, *An American Diplomat in Bolshevik Russia*, Wisconsin: University of Wisconsin Press, 2014.

Poutiatine, Olga, *War and Revolution: Extracts from the Letters and Diaries of the Countess Olga Poutiatine*, Tallahassee, FL: Diplomatic Press, 1971.

Powell, Anne, *Women in the War Zone: Hospital Service in the Great War*, Stroud: The History Press, 2009.

Purvis, June, *Emmeline Pankhurst, A Biography*, London: Routledge, 2003.

—— 'Mrs Pankhurst and the Great War', in Fell and Sharp, *The Women's Movement in Wartime*.

Rappaport, Helen, *Conspirator: Lenin in Exile 1900–1917*, London: Hutchinson, 2009.

Rivet, Charles, *The Last of the Romanofs*, London: Constable & Co., 1918.

Rosenstone, Robert A., *Romantic Revolutionary: A Biography of John Reed*, Harmondsworth: Penguin, 1975.

Sadoul, Captain Jacques, *Notes sur la révolution bolchévique, October 1917–Janvier 1919*, Paris: Éditions de la Sirène, 1919.

Salisbury, Harrison E., *Black Night, White Snow: Russia's Revolutions 1905–1917*, London: Cassell, 1978.

Sanders, Jonathan, *Russia 1917: The Unpublished Revolution*, New York: Abbeville Press, 1989.

Saul, Norman E., *Life and Times of Charles Richard Crane 1858–1939*, Lanham, MD: Lexington Books, 2013.

Seeger, Murray, *Discovering Russia: 200 Years of American Journalism*, Bloomington, IN: AuthorHouse, 2005.

Service, Robert, *Spies and Commissars: Bolshevik Russia and the West*, London: Macmillan, 2012.

Shelley, Gerald, *Speckled Domes*, London: Duckworth, 1925.

Sisson, Edgar Grant, *One Hundred Red Days: A Personal Chronicle of the Bolshevik Revolution*, New Haven, CT: Yale University Press, 1931.

Smele, Jonathan D., *The Russian Revolution and Civil War 1917–1921: An Annotated Bibliography*, London: Continuum, 2003.

Steffens, Lincoln, *Autobiography of Lincoln Steffens*, vol. 2: *Muckraking. Revolution, Seeing America at Last*, New York: Harcourt, Brace & World, 1958.

Steveni, William Barnes, *Petrograd Past and Present*, London: Grant Richards, 1915.

Stites, Richard, *Women's Liberation Movement in Russia: Feminism, Nihilism and Bolshevism, 1860–1930*, Princeton, NJ: Princeton University Press, 1978.

Swann, Herbert, *Home on the Neva: A Life of a British Family in Tsarist St Petersburg, and After the Revolution*, London: Gollancz, 1968.

Thurstan, Violetta, *Field Hospital and Flying Column, Being the Journal of an English Nursing Sister in Belgium and Russia*, London: G. P. Putnam's Sons, 1915.

—— *The People Who Run, Being the Tragedy of the Refugees in Russia*, London: G. P. Putnam's Sons, 1916.

Tyrkova-Williams, Ariadna, *From Liberty to Brest-Litovsk*, London: Macmillan & Co., 1919.

—— *Cheerful Giver: The Life of Harold Williams*, London: P. Davies, 1935.

Walpole, Hugh, *The Secret City*, Stroud: Sutton Publishing, 1997 [1919].

Wilcox, E. H., *Russia's Ruin*, New York: Scribner's, 1919.

Williams, Harold, *Russia of the Russians*, London: Isaac Pitman & Sons, 1920.

Windt, Harry de, *Russia as I Know It*, London: Chapman & Hall, 1917.

Winter, Ella and Hicks, Granville, *Letters of Lincoln Steffens*, vol. I: *1889–1919*, New York: Harcourt, Brace and Company, 1938.

Newspaper & magazine articles

'The Anglo-Russian Hospital', *British Journal of Nursing*, 9 October 1915, 293–4.

Barnes, Harper, 'Russian Rhapsody: A Small City North of Moscow Opens a Museum to Honor a Former St Louis Mayor', *St Louis Post-Dispatch*, 24 August 1997.

Birkmyre, Robert, 'The Anglo-Russian Bureau in Petrograd', *Review of Reviews*, 55, 1917, 262–3.

'Bolsheviki at Russia's Throat', *Literary Digest*, 55, October–December 1917, 9–11.

Britannia [formerly *The Suffragette*], June–November 1917,

Bullard, Arthur, 'The Russian Revolution in a Police Station', *Harper's Magazine*, CXXXVI, 1918, 335–40.

Chatterjee, Choi, 'Odds and Ends of the Russian Revolution, 1917–1920', *Journal of Women's History* 20:4, Winter 2008, 10–33.

Colton, Ethan, 'With the YMCA in Revolutionary Russia', *Russian Review*, 2: XXIV, April 1955, 128–39.

Corse, Frederick, 'An American's Escape from Russia. Parleying with the Reds and the Whites', *The World's Work*, 36:5, 1918, 553–60.

Cross, Antony, 'Forgotten British Places in Petrograd', *Europa Orientalis*, 5:1, 2004, 135–47.

Feist, Joe Michael, 'Railways and Politics: The Russian Diary of George Gibbs 1917', *Wisconsin Magazine of History*, 62:3, Spring 1979, 178–99.

Hunter, T. Murray, 'Sir George Bury and the Russian Revolution', *Rapports annuels de la Société historique du Canada*, 44:1, 1965, 58–70.

Jansen, Marc, 'L.H. Grondijs and Russia: The acts and opinions of a Dutch White Guard', *Revolutionary Russia*, 7:1, 1994, 20–33.

Jones, R. Jeffreys, 'W. Somerset Maugham, Anglo-American Agent in Revolutionary Russia', *American Quarterly*, 28:1, 1976, 90–106.

Karpovich, M., 'The Russian Revolution of 1917', *Journal of Modern History*, 2:2, 1930, 258–80.

'Lady Georgina Buchanan', obituary, *The Times*, 26 April 1922.

McGlashan, Z. B., 'Women Witness the Russian Revolution: Analysing Ways of Seeing', *Journalism History*, 12:2, 1995, 54–61.

Mason, Gregory, 'Russia's Refugees', *Outlook*, 112, 19 January 1916, 141–4.

Mohrenschildt, Dimitri von, 'The Early American Observers of the Russian Revolution', *Russian Review* 3(1), Autumn 1943, 64–74.

Mohrenschildt is also author of 'Lincoln Steffens and the Russian Bolshevik Revolution', *Russian Review*, 5:1, 1945, 31–41.

Neilson, K., '"Joy Rides?" British Intelligence and Propaganda in Russia 1914–1917', *Historical Journal*, 24:4, 1981, 885–906.

Sokoloff, Jean, 'The Dissolution of Petrograd', *Atlantic Monthly*, 128, 1921, 843–50.

Urquhart, Leslie, 'Some Russian Realities', *Littell's Living Age*, 296, 1918, 137–44.

Varley, Martin, 'The Thornton Woollen Mill, St Petersburg', *History Today*, 44:12, December 1994, 62.

Walpole, Hugh, 'Pen Portrait of Somerset Maugham', *Vanity Fair*, 13:4, 1920, 47–9.

Williams, Harold, 'Petrograd', *Slavonic Review*, 2:4, June 1923, 14–35.

Wynn, Marion, 'Romanov connections with the Anglo-Russian Hospital in Petrograd', *Royalty Digest*, 139, January 2003, 214–19.

Index